Acts of Desire

*Women and Sex on Stage,
1800–1930*

SOS ELTIS

OXFORD
UNIVERSITY PRESS

OXFORD
UNIVERSITY PRESS

Great Clarendon Street, Oxford, OX2 6DP,
United Kingdom

Oxford University Press is a department of the University of Oxford.
It furthers the University's objective of excellence in research, scholarship,
and education by publishing worldwide. Oxford is a registered trade mark of
Oxford University Press in the UK and in certain other countries

First Edition published in 2013

Impression: 1

British Library Cataloguing in Publication Data
Data available

ISBN 978–0–19–969135–7

Printed by the MPG Printgroup, UK

To Mark, with all my love and thanks

Acknowledgements

I owe a huge debt to innumerable friends, colleagues, and students, not only for great conversations, advice, tips, leads, and corrections, but also for their interest and enthusiasm over the years which have helped to make the work not only possible but a pleasure. There are so many people to whom I owe thanks that I am bound to have missed some names off the list—for which apologies in advance. My thanks to Jacqueline Baker at OUP for taking on the book and for guiding it through composition and publication, and to the two anonymous OUP readers for invaluable encouragement and advice. I also owe thanks to Anna Farkas, who did wonderful work as a research assistant, digging out reviews with great efficiency and ingenuity, and to Sophie Duncan for help with securing permissions. I have benefited from the expertise and helpfulness of librarians and archivists at the Bodleian Library and the English Faculty Library, Oxford, the British Library, the Ellen Terry Museum, National Trust Smallhythe Place, the V & A Theatre Archive, the National Archives at Kew, and the Houghton Library at Harvard University. I would like to thank the editor of *English Literature in Transition*, Professor Robert Langenfeld, for permission to reproduce some material in Chapter 5 which was previously printed in my article, 'Suffrage, Sex and the Single Girl: the fallen woman in Edwardian Feminist Drama', *ELT*, 50:1 (2007). My thanks to the Bodleian Libraries, the University of Oxford, the Tate Gallery, London, and the Fitzwilliam Museum, the University of Cambridge for permission to reproduce images.

Conversations with colleagues both inside and outside Oxford have supported, encouraged and guided me at every step of the way, and I am forever grateful for their generosity and wisdom. I would especially like to thank Mindy Chen-Wishart, Jim Davis, Tracy Davis, Ignacio Ramos Gay, Viv Gardner, Mara Keire, Laura Korobkin, Hermione Lee, Mary Luckhurst, Laurie Maguire, Kate Newey, David Mayer, Jane Moody, Simon Palfrey, Beth Palmer, Kerry Powell, Caroline Radcliffe, Tiff Stern, and Peter Yeandle. To Joel Kaplan and Sheila Stowell I owe a particularly large debt of gratitude, both for a model of scholarship to which I continue to aspire and for their extraordinary generosity in donating books and papers from which generations of Oxford scholars will benefit.

Alongside the kindness and support of colleagues, two other factors have been vital to the writing of this book. Firstly, my students, both graduate and undergraduate, with so many of whom I have spent hours discussing the texts, ideas, and performances which underpin this book. Their insights and ideas have inevitably challenged and informed my thinking, and I am eternally grateful to them not only for their enthusiasm and acuity, but also for their support. Secondly I would like to thank Brasenose College and the English Faculty at the University of Oxford for allowing me go to part-time, thereby enabling me to combine the pleasures of parenthood with the joys of teaching and scholarship while occasionally sleeping more than six hours a night.

I am grateful as always to my family, and in particular to my sister Clare for her unfailing enthusiasm and her ability always to ask the right difficult questions, and to Alfie and Zack for taking me away from my work and making life immeasurably more fun. Sarah Caro has been a wonderful friend and a source of vital support, energy, and encouragement, from helping to shape my initial book proposal through innumerable inspiring conversations over coffee and wine. Faith Binckes has been a fantastic support and an astute reader of various chapters, and Kirsten Shepherd-Barr has given invaluable advice throughout the composition of this book, right through to final drafts—no-one could hope for better friends and colleagues. Debbie Pinfold has, as always, gone far beyond the call of duty, and I am eternally grateful to her for innumerable helpful comments and suggestions, and for valiantly reading the whole final draft. My greatest debt, as always, is to Mark, for his generosity, patience, humour, kindness, love, and infuriatingly exacting editing—I'm not a good enough writer to put it into words, but thank you!

Contents

Abbreviations

Add MS	Additional manuscript
BL	British Library
Dicks'	Dicks' Standard Plays
LC Corr	Lord Chamberlain's Correspondence
LCD	Lord Chamberlain's Daybook
LCP	Lord Chamberlain's Plays Collection

List of Illustrations

Introduction

Reviewing the first English production of American playwright Eugene O'Neill's *Anna Christie*, in which a prostitute seeks refuge with the father who abandoned her years before, only be to confronted by his anger and reproaches when he learns how she survived for years on her own, the English critic James Agate was quick to note the long theatrical history which lay behind the play's central premise:

> The theme of *Anna Christie* is an inversion of that old French thing, the repentant courtesan. Every modern playwright since Augier and Dumas *fils* has had his whack at it, so that it comes into twentieth-century drama like a tin can kicked down the street by a parcel of vigorous schoolboys, and bearing the dints made by individual boots.[1]

The courtesan, repentant or defiant, was indeed a familiar figure on the British stage for well over a hundred years, from early in the nineteenth century until well beyond 1923, when Pauline Lord's mixture of childlikeness and *canaillerie* as Anna Christie brought to Agate's mind accounts of Eleonora Duse playing Dumas's famous courtesan, Marguerite Gautier.[2] Prostitutes, whether high-class courtesans or impoverished streetwalkers, were only one amongst many theatrical manifestations of fallen womanhood. Bigamous or adulterous wives, seduced maidens, and unmarried mothers were similarly common theatrical types. Indeed, these various incarnations of errant female sexuality were closely related and intertwined; seduction and betrayal were widely accepted as a first step on a woman's downward trajectory to the streets, while the unintentionally bigamous wife was the virtuous double to the knowing adulteress. Playwrights from the very beginning of the nineteenth century through to the 1920s and beyond took their turn at portraying the sexually errant woman, variously reproducing, challenging, adapting, revising, or reinforcing the conventions surrounding her theatrical depiction. Consciously or unconsciously in conversation with their predecessors, generation upon generation of playwrights left their own particular dents in the tin can.

By tracing the continuities, evolutions and interruptions in dramatic treatments of illicit female sexuality, I hope to render legible once more some of the dramatic gestures, interconnections, references, and meanings available in various forms to their contemporary audiences. A study of the history and practices of these plays reveals the conventions, tropes, allusions, and revisions with which playgoers and

---

[1] Review of *Anna Christie*, Strand Theatre, London, 21 April 1923, reprinted in James Agate, *Red Letter Nights* (Benjamin Blom: New York, 1944; reissued 1969), 347.
[2] Ibid, 349–50.

critics were once familiar; these plays can therefore be seen as constituting a repertoire according to Tracy Davis's recent definition of repertoire as a body of plays and
performances within which not only are meanings made intelligible to their audiences through 'processes of iteration, revision, citation and incorporation' of familiar material and techniques, but also a network of intertheatrical connections and
associations within which innovations and inventions could be interpreted and
understood.[3] Cutting across dramatic genres, the tropes and conventions common
to theatrical depictions of sexually errant women are detectable in melodramas,
farces, tragedies, problem plays, society dramas, musical comedies, and propagandist sketches, stretching across an impressively long period of theatrical history.
Common to 'high' and 'low' forms of theatrical entertainment, the continuities and
conversations between dramas played across geographic and historical divides.

This book is therefore an attempt to trace a history of theatrical depictions of
illicit female sexuality, a history not only of texts but of what Jacky Bratton has
named 'intertheatricality', the 'web of mutual understanding between potential
audiences and their players, a sense of the knowledge, or better the knowingness,
about playing that spans a lifetime or more, and that is activated for all participants
during the performance event'.[4] By looking at the evolution and development of
one strain of theatrical interest, a conglomeration and accumulation of plays whose
interconnections and inheritances can be observed, this study is an exercise in
'intertheatrical reading', which Bratton so rightly advocates as one which 'posits that
all entertainments, including dramas, that are performed within a single theatrical
tradition are more or less interdependent. They are uttered in a language, shared by
successive generations, which includes not only speech and the systems of the
stage—scenery, costumes, lighting and so forth—but also genres, conventions and,
very importantly, memory.'[5] Each audience and each audience member necessarily
possesses and draws on a different set of associations. It is therefore impossible and
inappropriate to attempt a definitive, single, or fixed reading of any play. The analyses offered here retrieve and render legible some intertheatrical meanings within
individual plays, but make no claim to be a single, dominant, or absolute reading.
Retrieving historical contexts and resonances does not mean fixing a text in time;
every play can be relocated in a new theatrical repertoire, rediscovered or revived, or
it can be an initiation, an audience member's first theatrical experience.

The enduring popularity of plays about seduced maidens, adulterous wives, and
repentant courtesans most obviously relates to their function as a warning to
potentially errant women and those tasked with guarding and preserving their
sexual virtue. From pitiful tales of country maidens tricked and abandoned by
untrustworthy aristocrats to *fin-de-siècle* society plays about 'women with a past'

---

[3] Tracy C. Davis, 'Nineteenth-Century Repertoire', *Nineteenth Century Theatre and Film*, 36:2
(December 2009), 7.
[4] Jacky Bratton, *New Readings in Theatre History* (Cambridge University Press: Cambridge, 2003),
37.
[5] Ibid, 37–8.

who must be unmasked and sent into exile, innumerable dramas were overtly concerned with demonstrating and enforcing the wages of sexual sin. As Agate noted of *Anna Christie* and the courtesan tradition in which it was placed,

> the earliest form of this type of play has been likened to a watering-can with which that good husbandman, the dramatist, douses those Colorado beetles, the adventuresses, pours upon them the caustic solution of morality, 'and so keeps them away from the crops'. Augier and Dumas pointed out that if beetles would insist upon being beetles, they must learn what to expect; their most lenient punishment was to be allowed to crawl on to a Louis Seize sofa and curl up in a romantic atmosphere of repentance and consumption. Two or more generations have played the gardener, diluting the solution now with comprehension and now with pity.[6]

Yet such plays were not just concerned with the oversight and policing of female sexuality. Whether centring on a daughter determined to marry without her father's blessing, or a wife questioning the different standards by which her infidelities and those of her husband were to be judged, these dramas inescapably engaged with and reflected contemporary debates about woman's place in the family. They were not only about women's sexual choices, they were also about gendered notions of deference, duty, and ownership; about women's civil, legal, political, and employment rights; about education, emancipation, the future of the nation, and the health of the race.

In the course of the nineteenth century human sexuality took an increasingly vital role in debates about the structure and future of society. The health of the individual and the health of the social body were seen to be inextricably intertwined. From Malthus's theories on the dangers of uncontrolled procreation leading to overpopulation, to Darwin's emphasis on sexual selection and its central role in human evolution, sexuality became a public as much as a private matter. The increasing popularity of eugenics towards the end of the nineteenth century sharpened concerns about contraception, hereditary disease, and selective breeding as a means to foster the strength and future of nation and empire. The unruly forces of individual desire posed a threat to the social body in its widest sense. As the social implications of sexual activity were debated, so too was the issue of who owned or exercised jurisdiction over women's bodies: fathers, families, husbands, the police and judiciary, the medical establishment, parliament, the nation, the empire, or the individual women themselves.

The prostitute and the 'fallen woman' have long been viewed by critics as potentially symbolic figures, weighted with significance as emblems of women's sexual and economic subjection, of social marginalization and exploitation, of the demonizing and pathologizing of female desire. Depictions of the prostitute can reveal much about the societies from which they emerge. The constraints of stage censorship required that plays at least paid lip-service to social and moral orthodoxies in order to secure a licence for public performance. Under the Licensing Act of 1737, every play intended for public performance had to be submitted first to the Lord Chamberlain's Office in the form of a play script. If the play were deemed acceptable and granted a licence, it could then be publicly performed—though the licence offered no legal

[6] Agate, *Red Letter Nights*, 347–8.

protection against prosecution for indecency, sedition, or any other public offence. Any theatre found guilty of performing an unlicensed play could have its performance licence revoked and be closed down. These laws remained essentially unchanged until the Theatres Act of 1968, innumerable campaigns and protests throughout the intervening years having secured only minor adjustments to the system. The Lord Chamberlain was head of the King's Household, appointed by the monarch, a post whose numerous duties rendered it impossible for him to undertake the reading of all manuscript plays submitted for licence, a job which was therefore devolved upon the Examiner of Plays, a member of staff whose appointment lay in the hands of the Lord Chamberlain. In cases of particular complexity or potential controversy, the Examiner was expected to consult the Lord Chamberlain before either granting or refusing a licence. The risks of prosecution and loss of livelihood for theatre managers were clear, while playwrights faced the frustration and expense of writing a play only to have it refused a licence. The power of the censorship system to ban the performance of any play deemed offensive to public decency and morality thus provided an inbuilt incentive for writers and managers to conform to orthodox standards.[7]

Despite the frequency with which suffering, shame, social ostracism, and death were visited upon a theatrical heroine who had sex outside of marriage, condemnation and punishment were not the universal rule. Notwithstanding the power of the censorship system, apparently conventional treatments of female weakness and woe might contain more challenging fault-lines, ambiguities, and undercurrents. Licences were secured on the basis of the written script alone, and many playwrights and performers were adept at deploying extra-textual references, subtexts, intertheatrical resonances, and all the possibilities of unscripted tones, gestures, and expressions in order to deliver meanings and implications not made manifest in the play's submitted text. In exceptional cases licences could be revoked or adjustments demanded after a further inspection of the play in performance, but such occurrences were rare; Lord Chamberlains tended to dislike such reversals as weakening the authority of the institution by implying naivety or a lack of information in the original judgements. The dynamics of performance thus allowed scope for more subversive and less orthodox implications. Studies of theatre censorship have necessarily and inevitably concentrated primarily on the records of what was banned— the plays which were refused a licence, cut, or revised in response to instructions from the Lord Chamberlain's Office, as detailed in the Lord Chamberlain's correspondence and the Lord Chamberlain's Daybooks, a series of ledgers in which decisions and excisions were recorded on all submitted plays from 1824 to 1903. As James Stottlar wrote in relation to his study of the theory and practice of William Bodham Donne, who was Examiner of Plays from 1857 to 1874, it was neither

---

[7] For a full account of stage censorship see Richard Findlater, *Banned! A Review of Theatrical Censorship in Britain* (MacGibbon & Kee: London, 1967); John Russell Stephens, *The Censorship of English Drama, 1824–1901* (Cambridge University Press: Cambridge, 1980); Dominic Shellard and Steve Nicholson, with Miriam Handley, *The Lord Chamberlain Regrets . . : A History of British Theatre Censorship* (British Library: London, 2004); David Thomas, David Carlton and Anne Etienne, *Theatre Censorship: From Walpole to Wilson* (Oxford University Press: Oxford, 2007); Steve Nicholson, *The Censorship of British Drama, 1900–1968*, 3 vols (University of Exeter Press: Exeter 2003–).

feasible nor tempting to read the five to six thousand unpublished play scripts which passed through Donne's hands; instead, Stottlar comments, the most straightforward scholarly method is to study the 'light side of the moon'—what was banned—and extrapolate the 'dark side of the moon' from that evidence, on the assumption that 'we can be reasonably sure that a systematic investigation of the other side of Donne's record would not produce any substantial surprises'.[8] By looking at licensed plays which depicted women's illicit desires, as well as those which were banned, this study reveals the Victorian censorship system to be leakier and more porous than it has often been taken to be. Many playwrights became adept at evading the censor's eye. While many plays centred on the concept of a woman's sexual 'fall'—the experience of illicit sexuality which inflicted irreparable damage on her moral fibre and started her on an inexorable downward path to ruin and despair—others contained hints, suggestions, and performative possibilities which questioned or undermined the underlying assumptions of women's sexual vulnerability and the disastrous consequences of extramarital sexual experience.

Much critical attention has been paid to Victorian sexual attitudes and gender ideology in the past few decades, from foundational studies by scholars such as Eric Trudgill, Nina Auerbach, and Mary Poovey, to more recent work by Judith Walkowitz, Jeffrey Weeks, Michael Mason, and Deborah Nord.[9] Particular attention has been paid to prostitution in the nineteenth century and the history and debates surrounding its regulation, and a number of scholars have further analysed the treatment of female sexuality, the 'fallen' woman and the prostitute in literature and the visual arts.[10] But the theatre is a barely detectable presence

---

[8] James F. Stottlar, 'A Victorian Stage Censor: The Theory and Practice of William Bodham Donne', *Victorian Studies* 13:3 (March 1970), 262.

[9] Eric Trudgill, *Madonnas and Magdalens: The Origins and Development of Victorian Sexual Attitudes* (Heinemann: London,1976); Nina Auerbach, *Woman and the Demon: The Life of a Victorian Myth* (Harvard University Press: Cambridge, MA,1982); Mary Poovey, *Uneven Developments: The Ideological Work of Gender in Mid-Victorian England* (University of Chicago Press: Chicago, IL, 1988); Judith Walkowitz, *City of Dreadful Delight: Narratives of Sexual Danger in Late-Victorian London* (Virago: London,1992); Jeffrey Weeks, *Sex, Politics and Society: The Regulation of Sexuality since 1800* (Longman: London, 1981); Michael Mason, *The Making of Victorian Sexual Attitudes* (Oxford University Press: Oxford, 1994) and *The Making of Victorian Sexuality* (Oxford University Press: Oxford, 1994); Deborah Epstein Nord, *Walking the Victorian Streets: Women, Representation, and the City* (Cornell University Press: Ithaca NY, 1995); Amanda Andersen, *Tainted Souls and Painted Faces: The Rhetoric of Fallenness in Victorian Culture* (Cornell University Press: Ithaca, NY, 1993). For extension of this forward into the Edwardian period and beyond, see e.g. Susan Kingsley Kent, *Sex and Suffrage in Britain, 1860–1914* (Routledge: London, 1990) and *Making Peace: The Reconstruction of Gender in Interwar Britain* (Princeton University Press: Princeton, NJ, 1993); Lucy Bland, *Banishing the Beast: Feminism, Sex and Morality* (Tauris Parke: London, 2002).

[10] See, for example, Edward. J. Bristow, *Vice and Vigilance: Purity Movements in Britain since 1700* (Gill and Macmillan: Dublin, 1977); Judith Walkowitz, *Prostitution and Victorian Society: Women, Class and the State* (Cambridge University Press: Cambridge, 1980); Trevor Fisher, *Prostitution and the Victorians* (Sutton: Stroud, 1997); Paula Bartley, *Prostitution: Prevention and Reform in England, 1860–1914* (Routledge: London, 2000); Nina Attwood, *The Prostitute's Body: Rewriting Prostitution in Victorian Britain* (Pickering & Chatto: London, 2011); Deborah Anna Logan, *Fallenness in Victorian Women's Writing: Marry, Stitch, Die or Do Worse* (University of Missouri Press: Columbia, MO, 1998); Linda Nead, *Myths of Sexuality: Representations of Women in Victorian Britain* (Blackwell: Oxford, 1990); George Watt, *The Fallen Woman in the Nineteenth-Century English Novel* (Croom Helm: London, 1984); Tom Winnifrith, *Fallen Women in the Nineteenth-Century Novel* (St Martin's Press: Basingstoke, 1994).

in such studies; the fictional narratives of Elizabeth Gaskell's Ruth Hilton, Dickens's Little Em'ly, Elizabeth Barrett Browning's Aurora Leigh, George Eliot's Hetty Sorrel, and Hardy's Tess D'Urbeyfield have been repeatedly scrutinized, analysed, and memorialized in criticism, while the names of once equally well-known heroines, whose sexual adventures were depicted on stage rather than in poetry or prose, such as Watts Phillips's Nelly Armroyd or Dion Boucicault's Formosa, have fallen into obscurity. Binary divisions which have long fascinated critics of Victorian sexual attitudes—between angels and demons, madonnas and magdalens, virtuous and fallen—soon break down when so many dramas centred on women whose sexual experiences place them liminally between the two categories; popular theatrical types such as the seduced maiden, tricked by a false promise of marriage, and the unintentionally bigamous wife, who believed her union to be entirely legitimate, have the potential to confound and confuse moral judgements, rendering problematic the very differentiation between licit and illicit love.

The marginalizing and neglect of the drama is particularly striking given theatre's popularity in the nineteenth century. In 1843 there were almost thirty-five theatres and houses in London specializing in some kind of theatrical entertainment; by 1866 a further twenty-five theatres had been licensed. According to the 1866 *Report from the Select Committee on Theatrical Licences and Regulations*, the capacity of six East End theatres amounted to 17,600 places nightly or 34.3 per cent of the total audience capacity of London theatres excluding Covent Garden and Her Majesty's, which were opera houses—putting the number of places available nightly for theatrical entertainment in West and East End at over 51,000.[11] By 1893 a further twenty-three theatres had opened. Between them, these venues drew audiences from every social class, and theatregoers were ready to defend their right to cheap and accessible seats, as the 1809 Old Price Riots at Covent Garden attested.[12] Nineteenth-century theatre had a cross-class and cross-gender appeal, and a consonant influence. As Elaine Hadley has demonstrated, for example, in her *Melodramatic Tactics: Theatricalized Dissent in the English Marketplace, 1800–1885* (1995), the tropes, language, and character types of melodrama were not confined to the stage, but were regularly deployed to polemical ends in a range of literary, social, and political contexts.[13] The remarkable consonance between early nineteenth-century sociological and evangelical writings on prostitution and melodramatic depictions of seduced and abandoned maidens demonstrates the close interaction between contemporary debates on and stage treatments of female sexuality. This symbiotic relationship was often more complex, however, than simple

[11] Michael R. Booth, *Theatre in the Victorian Age* (Cambridge University Press: Cambridge, 1991), 4–5.
[12] For further details on audience make-up see Jim Davis and Victor Emeljanow, *Reflecting the Audience: London Theatregoing, 1840–1880* (University of Iowa Press: Iowa City, IA, 2001); Booth, *Theatre in the Victorian Age*, ch. 1; Joseph Donohue (ed), *The Cambridge History of British Theatre*, vol. 2, *1660–1895* (Cambridge University Press: Cambridge, 2004), Part II.
[13] Elaine Hadley, *Melodramatic Tactics: Theatricalized Dissent in the English Marketplace, 1800–1885* (Stanford University Press: Stanford, CA, 1995).

mutual reinforcement. The unpredictability and uncontrollability of theatrical performance could serve to destabilize or complicate established notions, and the immediacy and potential power of theatrical performance drew an increasing number of writers to the stage as a forum for questioning, challenging, and debating moral orthodoxies. The very fact that theatrical productions were subject to a state control from which other literary and cultural media were free is testimony to contemporary perceptions of the disruptive potential of theatrical performance.

This study is roughly chronological, but it does not purport to be a history of sexual attitudes through the nineteenth and early twentieth centuries. Dramatists frequently responded to contemporary debates on sexual morality, and audiences' and reviewers' responses to individual plays can offer evidence of prevailing attitudes and standards. But such evidence must be treated warily; there is a significant difference between public utterance and private views, between the voice of the newspaper reviewer and of the private individual, and in particular between private practices and beliefs and socially approved orthodoxies. Theatre's immediacy and the public nature of performance make it a particularly sensitive and charged forum for engaging with sexual issues, and one where identifying individual views is especially problematic. Nonetheless, theatrical representations of seduction, adultery, bigamy, and prostitution offer an alternative, particular, and significant perspective on the shifting sexual attitudes of their times.

By cutting a slice through theatre history, taking an area of concern and tracing it through more than a hundred years of dramatic practice and production, surprising continuities are brought into focus. That nineteenth-century theatre was a web of recurring stock types, plot devices, and situations has long been recognized as a necessary result of an industry working to provide 'new' entertainments for nightly audiences. As Jacky Bratton has demonstrated, the mixed bill provided an opportunity for conversations between diverse theatrical entertainments and dramatic genres.[14] Cross-reference between plays, the interplay between alternative treatments of central situations, theatrical conventions and expectations, these were the essential stuff of theatre-going and theatrical production in the nineteenth century. Dramatic reviews littered with allusions and comparisons to other plays within the genre and playwrights deliberately reworking familiar plots further attest to intertheatricality as a central mode of composition and consumption. Martin Meisel's masterly study *Shaw and the Nineteenth-Century Theater* (1963) led the way in demonstrating how a playwright could challenge the ideological assumptions underlying theatrical conventions by writing plays which simultaneously drew upon and confounded generic expectations. Such a practice depends on audiences' familiarity with a wide theatrical repertoire, and hence regular theatre-going—an assumption which no sane playwright would operate on nowadays, and to which the closest analogy is the web of references and generic in-jokes in a television show like *The Simpsons*, whose appreciation is predicated on familiarity with a wide range of films and other television programmes. Victorian playwrights

[14] Bratton, *New Readings in Theatre History*, ch. 3.

habitually assumed a similar cultural knowledge and ability to cross-reference and connect. By looking at dramatic treatments of female sexuality across the decades, the extraordinary endurance of certain plots and devices is brought into focus, often revealing a greater complexity of meaning and implication for audiences versed in the traditions of the genre and its theatrical antecedents.

Theatrical productions were also in close conversation with other artistic media, exchanging plots, situations, character-types, techniques, and expertise with dance, opera, fine art, music, poetry, and the novel. The connections and resonances are potentially limitless. I touch on relations between melodramatic tableaux and Victorian narrative art in Chapter One, and on the relation between sensation drama and the sensation novel in Chapter Two, but this is only a beginning. Theatre's omission or passing mention in so many areas of Victorian academic research leaves a rich area of investigation, in which some excellent work has been done and much remains to do.[15]

This study is not and could never aspire to be comprehensive or inclusive. Taking on 130 years of theatrical history inevitably means being selective if any degree of depth is to be achieved. Many tens of thousands of plays were written and produced in this period, rendering it impossible to do more than scratch the surface. Furthermore, the focus of this study is predominantly the London stage, an area most thoroughly covered by contemporary reviewers, where the jurisdiction of the Lord Chamberlain's Office was strongest, and where records are most concentrated and accessible. But though this study is necessarily selective—and writing it has constantly involved difficult decisions about what to leave out and what to put in—I trust it is nonetheless significant. The plays selected for study here offer a mix of little-known, forgotten, and unpublished works and ones which are relatively well-known, or indeed canonical within what now constitutes the loose and ever-growing body of Victorian and Edwardian plays available in print or which have received critical attention. The close affinity between London and provincial repertoires, the activities of touring companies, and the practice of constantly reviving past successes, meant that plays' lives could stretch across considerable geographical and historical distances. Many of the early plays selected for discussion were deemed sufficiently popular and significant to be published in either Lacy's or Dicks' editions of plays later in the nineteenth century—only a tiny fraction of the plays produced during the nineteenth century were ever published, so this in itself renders them noteworthy. Furthermore, a number of these dramas remained central elements of the provincial theatre repertoire in later decades.

The beginning and ending dates of this study are necessarily arbitrary to a degree; 1800 does not mark the first dramatic treatment of the seduced maiden any more than 1930 marks the end of the tropes and traditions traced through this book. There is, nonetheless, a rationale for the opening date of this study. Katherine

---

[15] See, for example, Martin Meisel, *Realizations: Narrative, Pictorial and Theatrical Arts in Nineteenth-Century England* (Princeton University Press: Princeton, PA, 1983); Anselm Heinrich, Katherine Newey and Jeffrey Richards (eds), *Ruskin, the Theatre, and Victorian Visual Culture* (Palgrave Macmillan: Basingstoke, 2009); Juliet John, *Dickens and Mass Culture* (Oxford University Press: Oxford, 2010).

nal event with its characters, message, and language clearly accessible and legible for literate and illiterate spectators alike. Melodrama's power, according to Brooks, lay in uncovering the essential moral universe in a post-sacred era where good and evil could only be seen in personal terms, strongly characterized as hero and villain.[17]

In a less radical rupture than that posited by Brooks, these early nineteenth-century seduction melodramas can be seen to enact a transition and reconciliation between the traditional sacred institutions of Church and Monarchy in a society based on deferential hierarchy, and a rapidly emerging capitalist society in which 'family' is understood less as aristocratic lineage than as a private social unit of domestic virtue and affection. The erring daughter is an offence to the values of both systems, choosing her lover without her father's sanction and in disobedience to her role as a unit of social exchange within a kinship system, letting her sexual desires draw her from her proper place at the family hearth. The offended father, the most perfect image of God on earth in the words of Pixérécourt's Edouard, simultaneously represents sacred values of piety and religious precept—especially when as in *Love's Frailties* and J. T. Haines's *The Life of a Woman: or, The Curate's Daughter* (Surrey, 1840) he is also a clergyman. Social and familial duties override individual (especially female) desires. The father's blessing of his repentant daughter and son-in-law-to-be thus represents the sinners' reabsorption within a larger system of social responsibility. The popularity of seduction narratives in the eighteenth century has been explained as a response to the increased emotional and social independence of women and the threat that that posed to the patriarchal family. As Susan Staves explains,

> In the sentimental novels we have not ruined castles, emblems of a ruined aristocracy, or ruined monasteries or churches, emblems of the waning power of religion, but ruined daughters and ruined families. The novels at once acknowledge the ruin and its irreversibility and lament the loss of an idealized older family undisturbed by the free exercise of wills of its inferior members.[18]

By the end of the eighteenth century the notion of a father's 'ownership' was sufficiently weakened to render unfashionable the practice of fathers suing seducers for financial compensation for the loss of a daughter's services; but on stage the tableau of reconciliation and paternal blessing nonetheless reinstated paternal, religious, and familial authority, resisting the corrosive forces of individualism.

The relation between seduction and social irresponsibility is further reflected in the remarkable frequency with which gambling is linked to sexual immorality; in A. C. Campbell's *The London Banker; or, The Profligate* (1844), the delinquent son of the subtitle abandons his ruined lover and child and is blackmailed over gambling debts he cannot pay.[19] The aspiration to wealth without industry is akin to

[17] *Melodramatic Imagination*, 15–17.
[18] Susan Staves, 'British Seduced Maidens', *Eighteenth-Century Studies*, 14:2 (Winter 1980–1), 122.
[19] A. C. Campbell, *The London Banker; or, The Profligate*. First produced Grecian Theatre, 17 January 1844. Dicks' No. 723. See also, e.g. William Bayle Bernard, *The Farmer's Story* (Lyceum, 1836), *Victorine, Lost in London*, and *London by Night*.

the desire for sex without responsibility. The father's blessing of the repentant seducer includes in its iconography the young man's acceptance of his role in a social system of contract, exchange, and accountability. The final tableau of forgiving father can thus be read as resolution in both sacred and secular terms, letting the family stand as both private domestic unit and as part of a wider network of social interconnection.

In *Melodramatic Tactics* (1995), Elaine Hadley has interpreted dramas of women falling, repenting, and seeking male forgiveness as affirming the family as a last bastion of deferential community, where men could continue to regulate their relationships with women according to natural law, while relationships outside the home were increasingly dominated by commercial relationships of contract and exchange.[20] Dramas such as *The London Banker* where gambling and seduction are equated, and where both seducer and his victim must seek paternal forgiveness, however, imply an essential tension not between deferential and commercial structures, but rather a tension between a socially responsible acceptance of contract and exchange and an individualistic (often aristocratic) flouting of its rules. While such melodramas reflect the shifting values and relationship structures of nineteenth-century society, seduction and its ills are, in line with the moral dynamics of melodrama, to be blamed on the character of the individual, not on wider social forces.

In seduction melodramas the maiden's imminent fall is first signalled by moral flaws, which distinguish her clearly from her enduringly chaste counterparts. Buckstone's Henriette confirms that she is destined for a sexual fall when she throws aside her rustic admirer's simple nosegay to rifle through a basket of fine clothes.[21] Victorine's fate is similarly presaged by her delight in male admiration, fine clothes and carriages, and her preference for romantic fiction and indolence over honest labour.[22] Notably, the payment for lost virtue is always made in silks and jewels, never in hard cash; tempted into sin by vanity and frivolity, rather than financial hardship, fallen women are paid in finery and luxury goods. The exchange of sexual services for rent or food lies outside the melodramatic framework. It took a particularly dastardly villain even to hint at the direct sale of sex for money, as in this unusually frank discussion between felon and accomplice in Campbell's *The London Banker*:

RECKLESS: Progressing towards our rendezvous, I encountered the brilliancy of a pair
of as beautiful black eyes as ever fixed their captivating glance upon an admirer of the
sex. Judge of my surprise when I heard a voice proceeding from the mouth beneath
them, asking for charity, in hollow, supplicating tones.
SPADE: You relieved her?
RECKLESS: I should have done so, but she objected to the terms.

---

[20] Elaine Hadley, *Melodramatic Tactics: Theatricalized Dissent in the English Marketplace, 1800–1885* (Stanford University Press: Stanford, 1995), ch. 4.
[21] J. B. Buckstone, *Henriette the Forsaken*. First performed Theatre Royal, Adelphi, 5 November 1832. Dicks' No. 821.
[22] Buckstone, *Victorine*, Act I.

SPADE: I guess them.

RECKLESS: Precisely. Her eye flashed fire, and she turned upon me a look of ineffable and most decided contempt. [23]

Such a blunt equation of economic and sexual vulnerability was rare. Poverty and necessity did not drive heroines to sell their virtue. Indeed, melodramatic virtue is impregnable to the most adverse of social and economic circumstances. Abandoned on the streets at the age of eight, with prison her only refuge from hunger and cold, the lost heroine of Charles Dillon's *The Mysteries of Paris* (1844) is still chaste at sixteen, thanks to 'an expression so pure, so virginal, that e'en the robbers—the assassins among whom she lived, pitied and protected her'.[24] True female virtue is unassailable. In Dion Boucicault's *The Poor of New York* (first performed in New York in 1857, and subsequently retitled for performance in Dublin, Liverpool, London or any other suitable location), both the heroine and her mother, starving and unable to find work, attempt suicide in order to relieve their family of their upkeep. The villain's spoilt daughter, by contrast, deprived of her father's ill-gotten wealth, ridicules the idea of working honestly for her bread, preferring the primrose path to ruin: 'I am fit for the same fate as yours—infamy', she declares to her father, who is generously spared a jail sentence so that he may follow her on to the streets and save her from a fate apparently worse than death.[25]

The city and its streets were commonly figured as a site of sexual danger and temptation, in contrast to the safety and seclusion of the heroine's (often rural) home. In Haines's *The Life of a Woman; or, The Curate's Daughter* the rustic maiden learns too late that leaving the domestic sphere for the dangers of the metropolis invariably spells disaster; foreseeing her doom, Fanny asks, '[S]hall I perish in the streets of this very London, which, in the lightness of my heart, I longed so to behold—die, a starving outcast and degraded wretch in the very place I, in my folly, deemed a heaven of happiness?'[26] Watts Phillips's *Lost in London* is a classic of the genre, in which Nelly Armroyd, the young wife of a miner, having been seduced away from her moorland cottage, mourns her lost virtue in the resplendent surroundings of her lover's London residence. She is found by her faithful friend Giddy Dragglethorpe, who attributes Nelly's unhappiness to her transplantation from her native soil, for 'where the tree was first planted theer th' roots mun be'.[27] The tag of

[23] Campbell, *London Banker,* I, i, 3. This is in marked contrast to earlier eighteenth-century seduction narratives, where a heroine's fall into prostitution was generally motivated by extreme financial hardship; see Katherine Binhammer, *The Seduction Narrative in Britain, 1747–1800* (Cambridge University Press: Cambridge, 2009), 40–8.

[24] Charles Dillon, *The Mysteries of Paris. A Romance of the Rich and Poor*. First performed Royal Marylebone Theatre, 2 September 1844. Dicks' No. 980, II, v, 15.

[25] Dion Boucicault, *The Poor of New York*. First performed Wallack's Theatre, New York, December 1857. Dicks' No. 381, V, iii, 21.

[26] J. T. Haines, *The Life of a Woman; or, The Curate's Daughter*. First performed Surrey Theatre, 20 April 1840. Dicks' No. 468, III, ii, 17.

[27] Watts Phillips, *Lost in London*. First performed Theatre Royal Adelphi, 1867. LCP, BL Add MS 53057G, II, i, 22. For further discussion of melodramatic depictions of the city see Katherine Newey, 'Attic Windows and Street Scenes: Victorian Images of the City on the Stage', *Victorian Literature and Culture* (1997), 253–62.

the title is stated so often that 'lost' and 'London' begin to sound like synonyms. They close the play when Job finally pronounces them over the freshly expired corpse of his adulterous wife:

JOB: She ha' left us. But not for ever. Not for ever! Though lost in London. I shall find her there (*points upwards with a bright hopeful look*)

Tableau.[28]

The unwelcoming streets of the capital thus stand in antithesis to the kinder refuge of heaven. The appeal of such narratives to London theatre audiences may have been dual: scenes of rural tranquillity and the innocent pleasures of dancing on the village green could feed the nostalgia of city audiences, of which a considerable proportion would have recently moved from the country; while the trials and confusions of country innocents naively attempting to negotiate a hostile urban landscape offered metropolitan audiences both humorous entertainment and a comparative sense of sophisticated savviness.[29]

Initiative and resourcefulness were the very last attributes allowed to the seduced heroine, who was called upon to display an extraordinary degree of passivity. Her vulnerability and helplessness frequently bordered on the semi-conscious. The crisis in which *Lost in London*'s Nelly Armroyd leaves her domestic hearth provides a model of such behaviour. Cursing her own vanity and resolving to reject her tempter, the accidental entry of her lover Gilbert rather than her husband determines Nelly's fate:

NELLY: Leave him! leave him for *ever*! I cannot! No—I cannot do it! (*Footsteps heard— latch moved*) It is Job! he has returned! Job! Job! my husband! (*Rushes up stage but recoils with a cry of terror as Gilbert Featherstone appears*) Gilbert Featherstone!
GILBERT: Nelly! (*He advances—she retreats*)
NELLY: No! No! Not a step further! I implore! I entreat! (*She staggers—is about to swoon—Gilbert springs forward and catches her in his arms*)
GILBERT: Nelly! Dear Nelly! (*He places her in chair. Scene closes.*)[30]

Next discovered on dreary moorland, wrapped in a shawl, Nelly wishes to return home but Gilbert declares it too late, picks her up and forces her off to a waiting chaise, just as her friend Giddy Dragglethorpe rushes breathlessly into view.

Nelly's physical helplessness and the repeated failure of a last-minute rescue combine not only to blur the lines between abduction and seduction, but also imply that the responsibility for safeguarding a tempted woman lies outside her own inadequate hands. Agnes learns this lesson explicitly in *The Lear of Private Life*. Crushing her doubts about attending a moonlit assignation with her lover,

---

[28]   *Lost in London*, III, 45.
[29]   The 1851 census was the first in which urban population outnumbered rural. Increasing migration from country to city increased rapidly, with the proportion of urban to rural population reaching 5 to 4 by 1861, and by 1881 more than two-thirds of Great Britain's inhabitants were living in towns and cities. See Norman McCord, *British History, 1815–1906* (Oxford University Press: Oxford, 1991), 315.
[30]   *Lost in London*, I, i, 9.

she asks herself, 'Am I then so weak in resolution, that I fear to trust myself?'[31] To which the answer is a resounding affirmative, as she yields to her lover's persuasion and begs in advance for divine clemency: 'Great heaven, that gave me all a woman's weakness, if I have erred, oh, judge me as a woman, nor blame me for the absence of that strength which thou hast not bestowed upon me.'[32] Whereupon she faints into the wicked squire's arms and is borne away to London.

The fallen maiden plays out an exemplary progress to abject ruin, propelled by an ineluctable logic from first fall to degradation and poverty on the hostile streets of the metropolis. Bereft of inner resources, she expends her remaining energy on repentance and self-hatred; the urge to self-destruction is the ultimate proof that the fallen heroine retains a sense of moral value and is therefore worthy of the audience's sympathies. The knowledge of guilt is often enough to kill a woman: either suddenly, like Buckstone's Agnes de Vere, who poisons her husband for attempted adultery and then expires herself with purely melodramatic logic: 'I am dying of a broken heart'; or more slowly like Nelly Armroyd, who ends her days in an ill-furnished attic, 'waiting and praying for death', which duly arrives.[33] The moral lesson is often explicit: Elinor, in William Travers's *A Poor Girl's Temptations* (1858), who has left her honest home for the luxurious life of a kept woman, is thrown out onto the streets, where, destitute and degraded, she takes poison and begs anyone listening to: 'Shun I implore you the guilty draught of sinful pleasures, though the cup be crowned with glittering gems. Lest you find too late, as I have done, it is the path to ruin, misery and death.'[34]

Melodrama's representation of the fallen woman—vain and frivolous, seduced, abandoned, and dying horribly, while her aged parents grieve—had a life well beyond the confines of the stage. A product of prevalent conceptions of female sexuality and offering a neat way of avoiding more complex questions of social causation and responsibility, the theatrical magdalen was a widely accepted, universally recognizable figure. The women who thronged the porticoes and galleries of London theatres, clustered in the Strand and Regent Street, and made the capital an international byword for public indecency, were depicted by journalists, moralists, and social analysts as living embodiments of melodrama's imagined maidens.

In *Prostitution in London* (1839), Dr Michael Ryan estimated that there were at least 80,000 prostitutes in the capital, a figure quickly challenged by Ralph Wardlaw in his *Lectures on Female Prostitution: its Nature, Extent, Guilt Causes and Remedy* given in 1842, in which he pointed out that such a number would mean that one in five women aged between fifteen and thirty were involved in the profession.[35] Ryan's was among the highest estimated numbers, but that such a figure could be posited is

---

[31] *The Lear of Private Life*, Dicks' No. 924, I, iii, 6.

[32] Ibid, 7.

[33] J. B. Buckstone, *Agnes de Vere; or, The Wife's Revenge*. First performed Theatre Royal, Adelphi, 10 November 1834. Dicks' No. 805, III, 15; *Lost in London*, III, i, 32.

[34] W. Travers, *A Poor Girl's Temptations; or, A Voice from the Streets* (City of London Theatre, 1858), LCP, BL Add MS 52972 H, III, iv, 24.

[35] Quoted in Trevor Fisher, *Prostitution and the Victorians* (Sutton: Stroud, 1997), 14.

a sign of the degree of anxiety surrounding prostitution. A wide range of publications on the subject appeared in the 1840s, from clergymen, doctors, and laymen, declaring the reluctant necessity of investigating such a distasteful but socially urgent issue. Whether written in the rousing rhetoric of religious evangelism, demanding an end to male debauchery and appealing for generous subscriptions to rescue funds, or offering tables of statistics and recommending government regulation, sanitary inspections, and legalized brothels, these publications replicated the theatrical tropes of fallen womanhood with a remarkable degree of consistency. The irresponsibility, vanity, and aversion to mundane industry which mark the theatrical heroine out for imminent seduction are faithfully listed by the evangelical physician William Tait in his *Magdalenism: An Inquiry into the Extent, Causes and Consequences of Prostitution in Edinburgh* (1840) under the heading of 'Natural Causes', which 'may be arranged in the following order:—Licentious Inclination—Irritability of Temper—Pride and Love of Dress—Dishonesty and Desire of Property—Indolence.'[36] William Acton, surgeon to a venereal hospital and a leading advocate of government regulation, offered a remarkably similar list as the causes of female vice:

> Natural desire.
> Natural sinfulness.
> The preferment of indolent ease to labour.
> Vicious inclinations …
> Necessity, imbued by
>   The inability to obtain a living by honest means consequent on a fall from virtue.
>   Extreme poverty.
> ….love of drink, love of dress, love of amusement.[37]

Acton's emphasis remains on individual character as the primary determinant of a prostitute's career, though extreme poverty is allowed a place on the list, just after that fateful first fall. Tait similarly placed 'Seduction' at the head of his list of 'Accidental Causes'.[38] As on stage, expensive clothes play as vital a role in these texts, both as instigators of woman's fall and markers of her corruption. So Tait declares:

> The love of finery may be said to be the besetting sin of woman, and with these persons the passion is extremely conspicuous. Satins and silks, with the most superb trimmings and ribands, are all their desire; and they would sacrifice everything for the love of fashion.[39]

Acton similarly describes prostitutes' immoral earnings as 'recklessly squandered on the adornment of their bodies', though his proposals for controlling the ills of

---

[36] William Tait, *Magdalenism: An Inquiry into the Extent, Causes and Consequences of Prostitution in Edinburgh* (P. Rickard: Edinburgh, 1840), 83.

[37] William Acton, *Prostitution, Considered in its Moral, Social and Sanitary Aspects in London and other Large Cities and Garrison Towns. With Proposals for the Control and Prevention of Attendant Evils* (2nd edition. John Churchill and Sons: London, 1870), 165.

[38] *Magdalenism*, 81.

[39] Ibid, 58. For how an assumption of vanity as a motive influenced analysts' questioning of prostitutes, see Mariana Valverde, 'The Love of Finery: Fashion and the Fallen Woman in Nineteenth-Century Social Discourse', *Victorian Studies,* 32: 2 (Winter, 1989), 168–88.

prostitution focus on state regulation and sanitary inspections—in contrast to Tait's emphasis on moral education—and the suppression of female vanity.[40]

The appeal of this melodramatic model of causation is obvious: it locates responsibility in the individual, in the strength of character which either resists or succumbs to temptation, while marginalizing environmental and economic factors. William Logan's *The Great Social Evil* (1871) provides a graphic demonstration of such logic taken to an extreme. He recommends extending the moral education of the lower classes, on the basis that very few middle-class daughters are employed in prostitution, from which he happily concludes that this 'speaks volumes for the excellence of the educational and moral discipline to which they are subjected'.[41] On the one occasion that Logan does postulate a woman driven to prostitution by absolute financial necessity, it is a seamstress whom he depicts, unable to support her hungry child or ailing mother on the pittance she can earn, forced to 'rush upon the streets, there to seek the hire which her lawful calling has cruelly denied her'.[42] Logan does not locate the seamstress in an economic framework of class exploitation or the ruthless mechanism of a competitive capitalist economy; rather, her plight is framed by a disquisition on the evils consequent on women's love of finery. Paid starvation wages by avaricious female employers to make gowns for callous female clients, the seamstress's fate provides further evidence of the moral frailty of women.

Evangelical writers on prostitution most clearly reproduce and evoke the melodramatic model of prostitution and fallenness. Society's setting of moral standards and the inculcation of moral habits in the young and the lower classes are given great weight in their analysis of both causes and remedies for the ills of prostitution. But the crucial emphasis is on individual moral fibre and self-control, with social structures playing a primarily instructive role. Melodrama's tales of weak-willed women, tempted by riches then tortured by conscience, following their inevitable path to a miserable death, offered a convenient and powerful means of appealing to their readers' sympathies. Pathetic scenes straight from the stage are played out between tables of statistics. William Tait, for example, devotes several pages to a vivid picture of aged parents tortured by their daughter's fall, the mother's tears and the father's silent gaze at the breakfast table, the village gossip scattering their few remaining hopes, the news of death bringing no relief for their 'bleeding wounds'.[43] His treatise is methodically categorized, listing classes of prostitutes, their manners and habits, the causes and consequences, in the form of a scientific sociological study, but the scenes and rhetoric of both pulpit and popular stage are threaded through his text, as when he offers the familiar formula of silks and misery:

> Although some prostitutes may live amidst a profusion of riches, and be decked in the most splendid attire, and partake of the most expensive luxuries which the world can

[40] *Prostitution*, 73; *Magdalenism*, 87.

[41] William Logan, *The Great Social Evil. Its Causes, Extent, Results, and Remedies* (Hodder and Stoughton: London, 1871), 182.

[42] Ibid, 226.

[43] *Magdalenism*, 172–5.

'larger dependence on the maintenance of her moral instinct'.[54] Once damaged, tragic consequences follow upon her first taste of sexual knowledge:

> Coleridge, somewhere in his Table Talk, remarks that man's morality is more depend-ent on strength of thought, and woman's on force of feeling and pure instincts. From this it appears to result, that more men than women fall, but that more fallen men recover themselves than fallen women;—that more men than women are reclaimed from vice. Whatever influence, then, threatens to trample down that fine network of moral instinct, that very appreciable kind of divinity which peculiarly hedges woman round, ought above all things to be the object of her dread, abhorrence and prompt and indignant scorn; for when that safeguard is gone, well-nigh all is gone, and the ruin is as frightful as the precipitation is swift.[55]

As Tait similarly concludes, a 'man may by industry, perseverance, and determina-tion' raise himself to a higher rank, whereas the 'general law' in regard to women 'appears to be, like that of gravitation, always pressing downwards'.[56] Greg simi-larly asserts that women's sexual desire is 'dormant, if not non-existent' until awoken by undue familiarities or sexual intercourse with a man.[57] Unable to envis-age the possibility of women possessing the power of self-restraint, conscious choice, or active will power, he concludes that 'If the passions of women were ready, strong, and spontaneous in a degree even remotely approaching the form they assume in the coarser sex, there can be little doubt that sexual irregularities would reach a height, of which, at present, we have happily no conception.'[58] This is the logic that connects the seduced maiden to the tearful courtesan and the sui-cidal streetwalker; having once taken that first fatal step, the sinful woman lacks the moral agency and active force to recover herself, relying instead on the inter-vention and commanding force of man.

The intimate relation between melodramatic treatments of the fallen woman and serious analyses of prostitution is graphically illustrated by a review of William Travers's *A Poor Girl's Temptations* in the *Morning Chronicle*. Describing the play as 'founded on the dark, knotty, sad, painful, and perplexing problem, known as the "Social Evil"', the unnamed reviewer congratulates Travers for his 'simple, faithful, uncoloured, but too severely true picture' of a condition that so many statesmen have shrunk from confronting.[59] Travers's drama of a country girl seduced by a devious aristocrat, kept in repentant but silken splendour, and then thrust out to perish by her own hand on the street when her lover's desires are transferred to another, is applauded as 'no romantic or over-coloured picture'.[60] Moreover, the reviewer's description of how and why Elinor succumbs reads as a remarkably

---

[54] *Great Social Evil*, 152.

[55] Ibid, 152–3.

[56] *Magdalenism*, 34. For further discussion of modesty and Victorian concepts of female virtue, see also Peter T. Cominos, 'Innocent Femina Sensualis in Unconscious Conflict', in Martha Vicinus (ed.), *Suffer and Be Still: Women in the Victorian Age* (Methuen: London, 1980), 155–72.

[57] Greg, 'Prostitution', 457.

[58] Ibid.

[59] *Morning Chronicle*, 2 March 1858, 5.

[60] Ibid.

faithful reproduction of Greg's analysis of such women's motivations. Setting the two passages side by side, one a response to a theatrical production, the other serious sociological analysis, there is an extraordinary consonance of tone, imagery, and underlying assumptions. So the critic writes that Travers's Elinor

> falls from a mere exaggeration and perversion of one of the best qualities of woman's heart, a weak generosity, which cannot refuse anything to the passionate entreaties of the man she loves, the strange, sublime unselfishness of the warm, fond, heart of a woman, a positive love of self-sacrifice; and she proves her devotion to the idol she has enshrined by casting down before his altar her richest and most cherished treasure.[61]

A few years earlier Greg's *Westminster Review* article analysed the dynamics of seduction in almost identical terms:

> They yield to desires in which they do not share, from a weak generosity which cannot refuse anything to the passionate entreaties of the man they love. There is in the warm fond heart of a woman a strange and sublime unselfishness, which men too commonly discover only to profit by,—a positive love of self-sacrifice,—an active, so to speak, an *aggressive* desire to show their affection, by giving up to those who have won it something they hold very dear.[62]

The melodramatic formulations marry seamlessly the writings of theatre critic and social analyst.

In this context the testaments of prostitutes themselves can sound a startlingly different note. W. R. Greg was emphatic in declaring that 'poverty is the chief determining cause which drives women into prostitution', and he quotes at length Henry Mayhew's letters to the *Morning Chronicle*, in which Mayhew gives verbatim reports of his interviews with women who lived on sub-starvation wages, working fourteen hours a day for three or four shillings a week, and forced to resort to the streets to feed or clothe themselves or their children. One woman tells how, despite her starving baby's legs being frozen to her side by the cold, she was turned away from the workhouse because she did not have an order for admittance, leaving her to return to prostitution as her sole means of survival.[63] Her pitiful plight mirrors the fallen Agnes of *The Lear of Private Life*, but the causational frames that surround each narrative are in stark contrast. Notably, Greg carefully chose the testaments of women who expressed shame and disgust at the measures to which they were forced to resort, thus maintaining a familiar moral and sentimental narrative, alongside the stark details of economic exploitation and social neglect.

Other first-person narratives of women selling sexual services, collected by Bracebridge Hemyng and Henry Mayhew and published in Mayhew's *London Labour and the London Poor* in 1861, contrast starkly with the traditional melodramatic narrative of moral weakness, fall, and passive decline. A flower girl and a sixteen-year-old streetwalker, for example, both talk of committing minor criminal acts in order to secure food and lodging in prison, as the only available alternative

---

[61] Ibid.
[62] Greg, 'Prostitution', 459.
[63] Ibid, 466.

to selling their bodies, while the flower girl's parents, far from weeping over her tragic fall, sent her out on her trade and lived off her meagre earnings.[64] However abject their circumstances, these women were still making choices, fighting for survival and negotiating their limited opportunities—yet Mayhew locates them in Volume IV alongside procuresses, bullies and brothel-keepers, thieves and beggars under the heading 'Those That Will Not Work'. A letter to the *Times* in 1858 from 'Another Unfortunate' offers an even starker contrast. Detailing an abused and deprived childhood, the writer challenges the very notion of a fall: living without privacy in close physical intimacy with boys and men, and entirely outside the strictures of religious doctrine, 'I lost—what? not my virtue, for I never had any.'[65] She tells how she gained education and accomplishments courtesy of one client, and now, as a self-supporting sex worker who patronizes local businesses, she asks by what right she should be condemned or her liberties infringed, especially by representatives of the middle classes whose income depends on the sweated labour of those beneath them, selling their bodies to supplement inadequate wages.

This counter-narrative of wider social responsibility, economic and environmental causation, and a pragmatic struggle for survival in an indifferent society runs entirely counter to the predominant melodramatic narrative. Yet the routine suffering not only of the fallen heroine but also of stubbornly virtuous characters on the streets of the metropolis was a standard ingredient of melodrama. So, for example, the trials of the destitute in Dion Boucicault's *The Poor of New York* vividly represent the desperate situation of the unemployed and the underpaid. Boucicault's starving women may choose death before dishonour, and be rewarded with the restoration of their stolen fortune, but the play ends not only by acknowledging the artifice that secured the audience's sentimental pity, but also with a plea to respond in similar fashion to the real poor outside the theatre's walls, as the hero turns directly to the audience in the play's closing moments:

PAUL: (*To the public*) Have the sufferings we have depicted in this mimic scene, touched your hearts, and caused a tear of sympathy to fill your eyes? If so, extend to us your hands.

MRS FAIRWEATHER: No, not to us—but when you leave this place, as you return to your homes, should you see some poor creatures, extend your hands to them, and the blessings that will follow you on your way will be the most grateful tribute you can pay to the POOR OF NEW YORK.[66]

For all the coincidences and climaxes of the plot, one of the central attractions of such urban-based melodramas was the accuracy and detailed physical realism of their reproduction of the city landscape, inhabitants, and customs. The protagonists' struggle for survival could thus double as a tear-jerking spectacle and a naturalistic reminder of the actual conditions of life for millions of the poorest in society.

---

[64] Mayhew, *London Labour and the London Poor*, Vol. IV. First published 1861. Reprinted in Fisher, *Prostitution and the Victorians*, 30–3.
[65] Letter to the *Times* (24 February 1858), quoted in Fisher, 41.
[66] *Poor of New York*, V, iii, 21.

Boucicault shows New York in the grip of financial speculation, its economic depression the result of widespread gambling on prospects in a society where money alone buys status. In the context of such a profit-driven society, the sufferings of the poor and the sexual vulnerability of the heroine can be read as the consequences of a widespread failure of social responsibility. Many seduction melodramas linked gambling to seduction, as twinned desires for gratification without liability or industry. By painting a society addicted to speculation, Boucicault unusually does not depict the seducer's moral weakness as a flaw that divides him from a wider network of economic responsibility and contract; rather, the pursuit of profit without obligation appears as a natural extension of capitalist enterprise. Boucicault thus provocatively links the sexual vulnerability of the poor to society's pursuit of wealth. Though far from the systematic underpayment identified by Greg as the primary cause of prostitution, the relation between the fracturing of social responsibility in the industrialized city and the plight of the heroine is brought suggestively into play.

The seduced heroine may perish on the hostile streets or throw herself from Waterloo Bridge, but her passivity and despair are not the only female responses to the challenge of urban survival on the melodramatic stage. Haines's *The Life of a Woman* pairs its tragically helpless heroine with a resilient and resourceful sidekick. Dorcas Downey enters '*showily dressed in red cloak and plenteous display of ribbons*' but her misplaced vanity and social ambitions do not mark her out for doom. Streetwise without ever having left the country, she intends to use her looks for profit but only on her own terms; as she sings with sexually suggestive knowingness:

> *Sure every belle must have a beau*
> *To make this world wag well,*
> *But lest he'd have my clapper go,*
> *My beau must ring his belle.*[67]

While Fanny is tricked into the hands of a procuress, raped, sold on, drugged, and imprisoned, finally dying of shame and despair, Dorcas negotiates the capital with exemplary skill. She not only rescues and protects Fanny, but also tricks two procurers of country innocents into the hands of the law to teach them 'not to try and outwit a Yorkshire lass again' (III, i, 16). Where Fanny declares herself 'indeed punished for my helpless degradation', Dorcas can honestly boast that 'if I hadn't known a bit how to take care of myself, I should ha' been as wretched and as helpless as she be now' (II, iii, 13; II, ii, 11). Far from being in need of a man's protection, Dorcas is easily the most quick-witted and energetic character in the play, remaining intelligently wary of the double-edged offer of male help and attention. In *Lost in London*, Nelly Armroyd is similarly paired with Giddy Dragglethorpe, '*a strapping redcheeked angular specimen of the Lancashire breed*' who sports '*a wildly grotesque*' bonnet in imitation of London fashion.[68] Giddy tracks her fallen friend

---

[67] *Life of a Woman*, I, i, 3.
[68] *Lost in London*, I, i, 6.

to London, supporting Nelly on her deathbed by taking work as a laundress. Negotiating the city with ease, Giddy slaps the villain's footman for cheeking her and is rewarded with a proposal of marriage, as he expresses the hope that their children would inherit her strong hand (II, ii).

While the heroine's tragic suffering pays the wages of sin, the fate of more minor characters may be determined by mundane pragmatics rather than a punitive poetic justice. In Thomas Egerton Wilks's *Woman's Love; or, Kate Wynsley, the Cottage Girl* (1841), the eponymous Kate has left the village suspiciously fat and returned thin, and is accused of being no better than she ought. The audience is soon informed that Kate is secretly married to a visiting aristocrat, and her pregnancy blessed by marriage. Meanwhile the village girls discuss her disgrace in tones of outraged morality, condemning her as 'a forward slut' and demanding her expulsion from the community.[69] Their asides, however, make it clear that they too have walked in Lover's Grove, passed the bounds of accepted behaviour and even secretly given birth. They are well aware of each other's sexual practices but their consciences remain untroubled—as does their uneventful course in the background of the play. It is Kate, rendered sensitive by an education which has 'expanded my mind and refined my perception', who is pained even by the suspicion of sexual irregularity, unlike her laxer peers (I, ii, 4–5). The village chorus provides a seam of mundane realism running through the melodramatic main plot: based on a study of parish registers, Michael Mason has calculated that, before the more widespread use of contraception in the 1860s, between a third and a half of English brides were pregnant, suggesting that the sexual habits of Wilks's gossips were common practice.[70]

In seduction dramas where the fallen heroine finally marries her seducer, the main plot itself has a problematic relation to the melodramatic conventions of poetic justice. The disgraced maiden's final betrothal is at best an adulterated enactment of virtue rewarded: no matter how persecuted, the heroine's wayward passions significantly reduce her moral standing, while her lover's lightning transformation from betrayer to betrothed could make him appear a dubious prize. Class operates as a crucial mitigating factor in this equation. The ardent aristocrats of *Love's Frailties* and *Clari* are torn between their desire for the lower-class heroine and the social unsuitability of the match. The final offer of marriage is thus presented not only as recompense for their unscrupulous dealings, but also as a virtuous overcoming of class barriers. Indeed, a large degree of villainy seems to be required for marriage to the lustful aristocrat to be figured as anything but a happy ending. In J. B. Buckstone's *The Duchess de la Vaubaliere* (Adelphi, 1837) the wicked Duke is forced by the king to marry Julie, an innocent country girl he has abducted. Once married, however, the Duke loses interest in Julie and plots her murder. The depth of his

---

[69] T. E. Wilks, *Woman's Love; or, Kate Wynsley, the Cottage Girl*. First performed Royal Victoria Theatre, 12 April 1841. Dicks' No. 414, I, ii, 5.

[70] Michael Mason, *The Making of Victorian Sexuality* (Oxford University Press: Oxford, 1994), 67.

dastardliness is explained when he is revealed to be the illegitimate offspring of a bigamous second marriage, and his brother, the rightful heir, appears in the nick of time to rescue Julie and send his bastard sibling to the Bastille. In *Henriette the Forsaken*, Buckstone's hero is another upper-class bounder, who not only seduces the humble Henriette but allows her father to be executed for a murder he himself committed. Considerable space is given to Ferdinand's agonized musings on the duties he owes to his class, and his horror at the idea of cross-class marriage is shared by the despoiled heroine and her father. The play ends with Ferdinand mortally wounded in a duel, expiring in the arms of Henriette, in a tableau that represents both the expiation of his sin and her inseparable connection to him.[71] For all the class conflict implied in such plots, their social conservatism is evident.

The Cinderella-like rise of these seduced maidens further complicates the moral message of the seduction melodrama. The heroine's lack of moral discipline and disregard for her father's authority may be punished with humiliation, shame, and even temporary insanity, but in terms of class mobility her final reward is considerable. In order to attract the eye of the local noble the seduced maiden is conventionally endowed with a superior degree of dignity, intelligence, and charm. So Giddy Dragglethorpe admiringly describes her fallen friend as so full of grace and beauty that she seems 'a kind o' queen'.[72] *Love's Frailties*, *Henriette the Forsaken*, and *Lost in London* all offset the heroine's superior dress sense, refined speech and romantic sensibilities with rustic sidekicks, whose awkwardness and comically coarse manners mark them as suited to remain in their humble station. The dangers of social aspiration are emphasized: a village dame comments of Susan in *Love's Frailties*, 'Take my word for it, that young girl will come to no good. This comes of *edication*. They no sooner learn to read and write, but they must fall in love with the richest man they meet' (I, i, 4). The comic nature of this warning only serves to emphasize the ambiguity of the melodrama's overall message: the heroine's social ambitions are fulfilled, despite a temporary delay, and the gap between the refined and beautiful heroine and her clumsy rustic companions forestalls any real nostalgia for a state of lower-class rural contentment, however morally superior.

The offsetting of the high-class heroics and pathetic appeals of the leads by the comic shenanigans of lower-ranked characters is standard melodramatic practice. In James L. Smith's opinion these counter-voices ultimately serve to reinforce the central moral for the average 'Joe' in the audience:

> While the hero lives on love alone, the funny man orders up hot meat and vegetables and gravy. His function, apart from being funny, is to voice Joe's latent scepticism of the heroic code within the confines of the play itself; this siphons off Joe's disbelief, and strengthens his committed sympathy for noble but impracticable virtue.[73]

Conversely, Jacky Bratton has argued that melodrama is, in Bakhtin's terms, heteroglot, 'a *system* of languages that mutually and ideologically interanimate each

---

[71] J. B. Buckstone, *Henriette the Forsaken*. First performed Theatre Royal, Adelphi, 5 November 1831. Dicks' No. 821, III, iii, 18.
[72] *Lost in London*, III, i, 32.
[73] Introduction, *Victorian Melodramas*, xiii.

other', and that 'the contradictions highlighted by examining their different voices are read as deliberate mediations, the means whereby a consensus is tacitly negotiated, and ideological and hegemonic work is done'.[74] Dorcas and Giddy's ingenuity and determination interact with the central narrative of the heroine's fall, with its attendant implications of female vulnerability and the need for seclusion and male authority and protection; their combination of ambition and resourcefulness suggests, however, that, with the necessary pragmatism and worldly wisdom, women are well able to fend for themselves. Further, as Bratton has observed, alternative systems of moral value are brought into play by the range of voices within the drama. Bratton notes of the moment in Buckstone's version of *Victorine* when the fallen heroine learns that her keeper is rejecting her and she exclaims 'Ruined! Ruined!':

> The moment is charged with the ambiguity of the whole play: it is by the pragmatic morality of the comic world that she is 'ruined' at this point, by the loss of her financial support; in the native world of the heroine, she was ruined long since.[75]

The downward spiral of a sexually fallen woman may thus be read less as a product of ineluctable natural forces than as the incidental result of one woman's ineptitude and over-developed conscience. One strand of the play can imply the need for greater male protection and constraint for frail and vulnerable women, while another strand suggests the value of worldly wisdom and sexual awareness for women, who are well capable of fending for themselves. The more pragmatic, cynical or worldly voices heard in a melodrama interact with the tortured conscience and high moral tone of the suffering heroine's central story; if read as a Bakhtinian dialogue, these plays do not present explicit and simple moral lessons, but instead offer a more open-ended debate on causation, social responsibility, and sexual morality.

The multivocality and the interplay of competing moral systems within seduction melodrama can be seen most clearly within the often complex role of tableau in these plays. J. T. Haines's *The Life of a Woman; or, The Curate's Daughter* offers a particularly intriguing example of such multifaceted operation. When the newly re-furbished Surrey Theatre reopened on 20 April 1840, it competed with the rival attractions of Greenwich Fair by announcing Haines's *The Life of a Woman*, described on the playbill as 'an entirely New Original Pictorial Drama of Interest, forming a VILLAGE TRAGEDY!...Presenting a living embodiment & moving amplification of the conception of the immortal HOGARTH'S Celebrated Series of Pictures, denominated The HARLOT'S PROGRESS.'[76] Following the Victo-

[74] Jacky Bratton, 'The Contending Discourses of Melodrama', in Jacky Bratton, Jim Cook, and Christine Gledhill (eds), *Melodrama: Stage, Picture, Screen* (BFI Publishing: London, 1994), 39. Bratton quotes M. Bakhtin, *The Dialogic Imagination*, ed. Michael Holquist, trans. Caryl Emerson and Michael Holquist (University of Texas Press: Austin, TX, 1981), 47.

[75] Bratton, 'Contending Discourses of Melodrama', 44.

[76] Playbill, quoted in Martin Meisel, *Realizations: Narrative, Pictorial, and Theatrical Arts in Nineteenth-Century England* (Princeton University Press: Princeton, NJ, 1983), 119.

Fig. 1. William Hogarth, *A Harlot's Progress* (1732), Plate I, © Victoria and Albert Museum, London.

rian theatrical practice of pictorial 'realization', Haines's melodrama freeze-frames the play's action at set moments in tableaux which reproduce Hogarth's prints on stage, carefully mimicking costumes, poses and settings.[77] Yet Haines's play was far from being a faithful dramatization of Hogarth's work. Though moments in his play reproduce scenes from Hogarth's prints, the dramatic narrative into which they are woven differs significantly from its eighteenth-century source, as Haines revised and sanitized the harlot's tale to suit the theatrical tastes of his own century. Removing the satirical and political implications of the original, Haines produced a sentimental tragedy of seduced innocence and wicked villainy, which reproduces all the standard tropes of Victorian melodramatic treatments of fallen womanhood.

Hogarth's celebrated series of prints *The Harlot's Progress* (1732) opens with a country girl being accosted in the street by a procuress, under the leering gaze of a prospective client (*Fig. 1*). Subsequent prints chart her progress through the hands of a rich keeper; then as a highwayman's moll, surrounded by prophylactics and treatments for venereal disease, with an arresting officer at the door; imprisoned and beating hemp; then dying of the pox, her child crouching beside her; and

---

[77] For an authoritative account of this practice see Meisel, *Realizations*.

Fig. 2. William Hogarth, *A Harlot's Progress* (1732), Plate II, © Victoria and Albert Museum, London.

finally dead and coffined at a raucous wake, complete with drunken prostitutes and lascivious clergymen (*Figs. 2–6*). Hogarth's series offers a warning narrative of decline and death: the pretty country girl enmeshed in prostitution and crime, and declining to a dreadful syphilitic death. Beyond this, however, the specific and recognizable identities of characters in the prints delivered a pointed satire on wealth, corruption, and the double standards of eighteenth-century justice. The leering onlooker in Hogarth's opening print was a portrait of the notorious aristocratic rapist Colonel Chartres, accompanied by his servant John Gourlay, and serviced by Mother Needham, an infamous procuress who was known to have supplied the colonel. The arresting magistrate in Plate III was Justice Gonson, renowned for his enthusiastic pursuit of prostitutes, whose arrest he seemed to regard as a competitive sport. The lower-class characters have equally specific referents: the prostitute Hackabout (the name is legible on her coffin in Plate VI) was arrested by Gonson in 1730 for disorderly conduct in the same year that her brother Francis Hackabout and James Dalton (the name on the hat-box over the harlot's bed in Print III) were hanged as highwaymen. Colonel Chartres was convicted in 1730 of the rape of Anne Bond, a country girl employed as a maidservant in his

Fig. 3. William Hogarth, *A Harlot's Progress* (1732), Plate III, © Victoria and Albert Museum, London.

house, and removed to Newgate prison, but his rich and influential friends, among whom Sir Robert Walpole was numbered, secured his discharge and a king's pardon on the same day that Dalton was sentenced to death.[78] Hogarth's prostitute and her procuress cater to the appetites of their social superiors, only to be crushed by a punitive justice system which smiles indulgently on the crimes of the rich. The church, meanwhile, neglects its duties: a parson is too busy scanning a letter of preferment to his bishop to rescue the girl from Needham's clutches, and clergy-men grope the drunken prostitutes at her funeral. As Ronald Paulson has com-mented, the progress of Hogarth's Hackabout reflects Bernard de Mandeville's brutal summary of the value of prostitution in his *Modest Defence of Publick Stews* (1724), in which he likens society to a butcher who in order to save his meat from flies will 'very Judiciously cut off a fragment already blown, which serves to hang up for a cure; and thus, by sacrificing a Small Part, already Tainted, and not worth Keeping, he wisely secures the Safety of the rest'.[79]

---

[78] For full details on the genesis and context of *The Harlot's Progress* see Ronald Paulson, *Hogarth*, 3 vols (1991–3), vol. 1, *The 'Modern Moral Subject', 1697–1732* (Lutterworth Press: Cambridge, 1992), chs 8 and 9.

[79] Quoted in ibid, 254.

Fig. 4. William Hogarth, *A Harlot's Progress* (1732), Plate IV, © Victoria and Albert Museum, London.

The specific individuals depicted in Hogarth's prints appear as named characters in Haines's play: Colonel Chartres, John Gourlay, Justice Gonson, and Jem Dalton all feature in *The Life of a Woman* and are advertised on the playbill. The only character specifically renamed is the harlot herself, who becomes the vicar's daughter, Fanny—an intriguing choice of name for those audience members versant with eighteenth-century literature, whose most famous country maiden turned prostitute was Fanny Hill, the heroine of John Cleland's *Memoirs of a Woman of Pleasure* (1748), a gleefully pornographic narrative of her erotic adventures. Yet Haines's Fanny is an anguished and passive victim. She is tricked into visiting London by the promise of employment to save her family from penury, whereupon she is raped by Chartres and handed on by him to a rich moneylender, who soon grows tired of her tears and repentance and throws her out. Drugged and carried unconscious to a highwayman's crib, she is unjustly arrested and, once released, dies of no apparent physical cause beyond misery and shame. Hogarth's social satire is carefully excised. The clergyman, in the form of Fanny's father, is a model of piety and probity; grief-stricken at his daughter's fall, his tragic suffering and death take centre stage, pushing his daughter's demise to the sidelines. The

Fig. 5. William Hogarth, *A Harlot's Progress* (1732), Plate V, © Victoria and Albert Museum, London.

justice system as embodied by Sir John Gonson becomes rigorous and even-handed. Gonson tracks down Chartres and Gourlay with the help of Fanny's resourceful maid Dorcas, and the curtain falls on Gonson as moral arbiter, forcing the '*horror struck*' Chartres to view the victims of his crimes (III, v, 21). Haines's Fanny is not, like Hogarth's harlot, a socially aspirant product of a venal society, but a pathetic maiden, whose vanity and frivolity make her vulnerable to the dastardly plot hatched by a collection of villains. The sexual energy of Hackabout is erased; Fanny is a repentant victim of her own shame, too aware of her ignominy to face her father, while innocent of taking lovers on the side, plying her trade, or acting as a highwayman's moll. Fitting the same punishment to a far lesser crime, Haines gleefully acknowledges the harshness of his moral in a verse epigraph to the prison scene:

> *Misfortune* oft, *crime's* punishment may bear,
> But search will prove *some* seed of error there,
> To thinking minds this lesson this makes plain,
> The *slightest* step from virtue brings its pain.

(III, i, 15)

Fig. 6. William Hogarth, *A Harlot's Progress* (1732), Plate VI, © Victoria and Albert Museum, London.

Hogarth's complex web of social, economic, and sexual exploitation and opportunism is replaced with the moral binaries of melodrama, wherein crimes result from individual villainy and if virtue is not always triumphant it is always clearly recognizable.

The playbills that advertised *The Life of a Woman* as 'a living embodiment' of Hogarth's harlot and her progress were designed to provoke audience curiosity as to how explicitly and faithfully the details of the prints were to be realized in performance. The practice of realization and the advertising of plays on its attractions only make sense if a significant proportion of the audience would recognize the original images—as Meisel has pointed out, playgoers could be familiar with images from print shop windows and reproductions in penny magazines.[80] The second print in Hogarth's series is a particularly interesting case in point: Hogarth's scene shows Hackabout clearly enjoying the fruits of

---

[80] Meisel, *Realizations*, 93. For the popularity of realizations at the East End Britannia Theatre, catering to a predominantly working-class and lower-middle-class audience in the mid-nineteenth century, see Janice Norwood, 'The Britannia Theatre: Visual Culture and the Repertoire of a Popular Theatre', in Anselm Heinrich, Katherine Newey and Jeffrey Richards (eds), *Ruskin, the Theatre and Victorian Visual Culture* (Palgrave Macmillan: Basingstoke, 2009).

her fall; she is kicking over the tea-table to cover the exit of a new lover under the nose of her rich keeper, one breast escaping provocatively from her expensive dress, either as a result of her lover's caresses or in a further effort to distract attention. Haines's play radically rewrites the context for this picture: Fanny is bewailing her fate, miserably tearful for all the wealth that surrounds her, when she is tricked into receiving the highwayman Jem Dalton, who pretends to offer her reconciliation with her father. Hogarth's print is realized when Dorcas hurries Dalton out the door, and the tableau is succeeded by the entry of Fanny's one-time sweetheart Adam, whom she greets with horror, screaming, 'No, no, come not near me—touch me not—I am as an accursed pestilence' (II, iii, 13). Where Hogarth's print celebrates the harlot's sexual energy and resourcefulness, as well as depicting the unscrupulous dealings that lose her a luxurious lifestyle, Haines transforms the picture into one about the impossibility of obtaining pleasure at the cost of sexual purity. The accuracy of the play's realization of the print is unlikely to have extended to a display of the heroine's naked breast, such a spectacle risking the revocation of the theatre's licence and a prosecution for indecency, yet familiarity with Hogarth's original not only provided a prurient draw but also a competing narrative to interact with Haines's sanitized version. Notably, the Dicks' edition of the play uses precisely this scene to advertise the script (*Fig. 7*). The prints are thus reproduced within a framework which seeks to rewrite their meanings, while simultaneously referencing the original series.

Notably, contemporary reviewers disagreed over the moral nature of Haines's play. The reviewer for the *Morning Chronicle* praised Haines's drama of sexual ruin, remorse and death as 'in its language and general tone…better than the majority of such productions generally are'.[81] The reviewer hoped that the tears wrung by Fanny's death might strengthen the moral fibre of its spectators, and counterbalance the influence of the alternative entertainments at the nearby fair: 'It evidently produced a very strong effect upon a very miscellaneous audience, and may possibly have averted, in some cases, those evils which Greenwich Fair has from time immemorial been noted for inducing.'[82] The critic for the *Odd Fellow* was considerably more cynical, both about the moral influence of such dramas and their intent. Noting the presence of a Jack Sheppard-like highwayman in Haines's melodrama—he plays a minor role, enamoured of Fanny and unsuccessfully attempting to free her from her abductors— the reviewer expresses disgust that the manager should 'pander to the beastly appetite that in such filth as "Nix my dolly, pals," could find agreeable food'.[83] He then expresses a similar distaste for Haines's main plot:

> The Easter novelty at Mr. Dividge's theatre is a drama in which the series of Hogarth's pictures called 'The Harlot's Progress' is sought to be embodied. Could these kind of things be turned to anything like a moral use, we should be the very first to hail them,

[81] 'The Theatres', *Morning Chronicle* (21 April 1840).
[82] Ibid.
[83] *Odd Fellow* (25 April 1840), 66. 'Nix my dolly, pals' is a quote from W. Harrison Ainsworth's popular ballad, composed for his Dick Turpin novel *Rookwood* (1834).

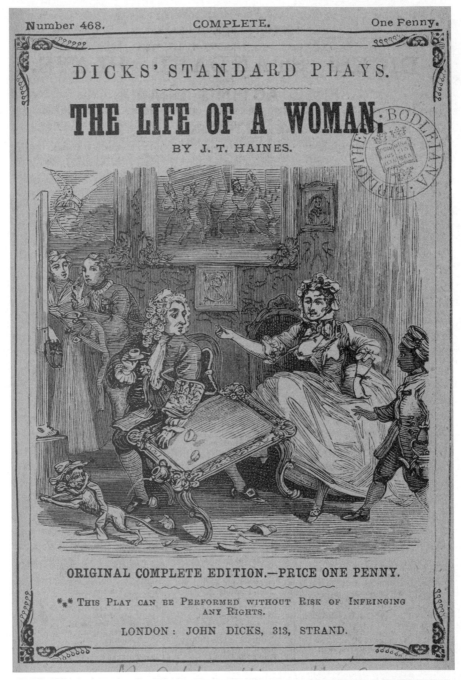

but knowing, as we unquestionably do, that their effect is to enlist the sympathies of the young and thoughtless upon the side of depravity, we cannot look upon their performance with any feeling other than sorrow. The bill which the lessee of the Surrey Theatre has thought fit to put forth is a choice specimen of minor theatre blackguardism—'The Curate's Daughter,' 'The Boudoir,' 'The Seduction.' Alas! how long will these things be tolerated?[84]

The bill's appeal, he implies, is to prurient and possibly vitiated tastes, drawn by the titillating spectacle of illicit sexuality. Indeed, the pairing of Haines's melodrama with a farcical interlude entitled *The Wet Nurse* seems to reinforce the validity of such suspicions.[85] That audiences and performers shared a humorous consciousness of the potentially salacious appeal of seduction dramas is also suggested by Mrs Yates's much-lauded performance as Buckstone's Victorine, in which, 'Some laugh was raised when she began, at the end of the first act, to undress in order to go to bed, as if she was seriously going through the preparatory operation.'[86] Such details confirm Peter Thomson's suspicions about the lubricious attractions of the genre:

> Melodrama was at once family entertainment and soft pornography. It was not the pious protestations of the heroine that interested the audience, but the threat to her virtue. The smothered libido of the nineteenth century escaped into melodrama.[87]

The prospect of frail female flesh under threat was an inviting one.

Haines's realization of Hogarth's prints thus served as a potentially salacious draw for audiences, while his relocation and re-inscribing of the pictures within an alternative story arc produced a complex relation between the melodrama's action and the import and implication of the original prints. This implies a more complex and multiple role for theatrical tableaux and their relation to narrative art than has yet been critically recognized. The very term 'tableau', the French word for picture, reveals the close relation between melodramatic dramaturgy and the techniques of narrative art, as Peter Brooks sums it up:

> [T]here tends throughout melodramas, and most especially at the end of scenes and acts, to be a resolution of meaning in *tableau*, where the characters' attitudes and gestures, compositionally arranged and frozen for a moment, give, like an illustrative painting, a visual summary of the emotional situation.[88]

Seduction melodramas were inevitably filled with tableaux of women fainting at the crucial moment of abduction, crying in tears and silks, and kneeling in shame to pray for forgiveness. The familiar story arcs of seduced women, filled with regret and self-hatred, mourning their lost homes and rapidly declining unless rescued by protective male relatives, provided a rich source for emotionally laden pictures, both on stage and on the painter's canvas. Repetition and reproduction of central tropes

---

[84] Ibid.
[85] Review in *Times* (21 April 1840), 5.
[86] 'Adelphi Theatre', *Times* (19 October 1831), 4.
[87] Peter Thomson, Introduction to *Plays by Dion Boucicault* (Cambridge University Press: Cambridge, 1984), 6.
[88] *Melodramatic Imagination*, 48.

reinforced the power of these plots, making them so familiar as to be accepted as self-evident truths—such that social commentators and campaigners could assert their existence without producing evidence or statistics to support them. The familiarity of the plot trajectory made it possible for one frozen moment to convey a whole tale. The fallen woman thus became a staple subject of narrative painting by the mid-century. Works such as Richard Redgrave's *The Outcast* (1851), Frederick Stanhope's *Thoughts of the Past* (1852), Frederick Walker's *The Lost Path* (1863), Dante Gabriel Rossetti's *Found* (1863), and Alfred Elmore's *On the Brink* (1865) (*Fig. 8*), all give snapshots of the fallen woman's progress, from Elmore's runaway,

Fig. 8. Alfred Elmore, *On the Brink* (1865), © Fitzwilliam Museum, Cambridge.

dressed and ready for flight, to Rossetti's bedizened prostitute held in the forceful grip of a sturdy rustic determined to drag her from the corruption of the city. These narrative paintings do not refer to any specific literary work or myth, but purport to realism in the contemporaneous dress and anonymity of their figures.

To contain a whole story in one moment, the painter must be able to draw on an established iconography and set story arcs, as Martin Meisel explains:

> The problem for the narrative painter...is to represent a subject of *finite* duration, whose phases are necessarily not all present at once. His subject, then, is not representable in a single frame except with the help of such modifying agents as a convention that permits the 'simultaneity' of stimulus and response; as symbolism does the work of literary fore-shadowing and retrospection; as a shared knowledge of specific stories and story formulas which permits the spectator to supply the broken pattern with sequential meaning.[89]

The readable language of stage gestures and the familiar plot formulae of the melo-dramatic stage helped to supply this communal symbolism, making it possible to project the story forwards and backwards.

The dramatist's success, however, depended on an ability to create tension, sus-pense and surprise. While dramatic plots could provide the stories for narrative paintings and famous pictures be realized in dramatic tableaux, the artistic impera-tives of the different media could result in alternate implications drawn from the same material. So, for example, the melodramatic fallen woman's traditional choice of a watery grave inspired Thomas Hood's 1844 poem *The Bridge of Sighs* and a plethora of paintings from George Cruikshank's *The Drunkard* series, to E. Fitzpatrick's *The Unfortunate* (1858), and G. F. Watts's *Found Drowned* (1867). The drowned woman's body could be read symbolically as a suffering penitent, simultaneously purged and destroyed by the river.[90] But the laws of dramatic suspense meant that the theatrical heroine's fate remained crucially uncertain: last-minute rescue is always an option; in Milner's version Victorine is declared dead at the scene, whereas Buckstone has her seized by the hair and dragged to safety.[91]

Holman Hunt's *The Awakening Conscience* (1853–4) (*Fig. 9*) could similarly be read as a tableau from a seduction drama: the young woman, surrounded by the shiny furniture and trashy trappings for which she has exchanged her virtue, sud-denly overcome by a sense of sin which lifts her in horror from her lover's lap. Symbolic details, such as the cat eying the corpse of a dead bird, further clarify their past relation. John Ruskin commended the painting for its readability, find-ing in it not only a tale of the woman's past but also her future: 'the very hem of the poor girl's dress, at which the painter has laboured so closely, thread by thread,

[89] Meisel, *Realizations*, 20.

[90] For further discussion of the artistic representation of the drowned woman see Meisel, *Realiza-tions*, 133–40; Lynda Nead, *Myths of Sexuality: Representations of Women in Victorian Britain* (Blackwell: Oxford, 1990), ch. 6; L. J. Nicoletti, 'Downward Mobility: Victorian Women, Suicide, and London's "Bridge of Sighs"', *Literary London* (March 2004), online at http://www.literarylondon.org/london-journal/march2004/nicoletti.html.

[91] See, e.g., *Love's Frailties* and *London by Night*; W. T. Moncrieff, *The Scamps of London* (1843); Edward Stirling, *The Bohemians; or, The Rogues of Paris* (1843); George Cruikshank, *The Drunkard's Children* (1848); Milner, *Victorine*, IV, i, 14; Buckstone, *Victorine*, III, iv, 20.

Fig. 9. William Holman Hunt, *The Awakening Conscience* (1853–4), © Tate Gallery, London.

has story in it, if we think how soon its pure whiteness may be soiled with dust and rain, her outcast feet failing in the street'.[92] As Kate Flint has noted, Ruskin misidentifies some details in the picture, including wrongly naming Frank Stone's engraving *Cross Purposes* as a woman taken in adultery, but it is Ruskin's conviction that the scene must be a stage in the inevitable decline of the fallen woman that is striking.[93] Ruskin's doom-laden prediction fits ill with Hunt's pairing of the painting

---

[92] John Ruskin, Letter to the *Times* (25 May 1854), *The Complete Works of John Ruskin*, ed. E. T. Cook and Alexander Wedderburn, 39 vols (George Allen: London, 1903–12), vol. XII, 334.
[93] Kate Flint, *The Victorians and the Visual Imagination* (Cambridge University Press: Cambridge, 2000), 216.

with his *The Light of the World*, in which Jesus knocks on a door, symbolic lantern in hand. As Martin Meisel has pointed out, Ruskin's description of the lost girl's face, 'rent from its beauty into sudden horror; the lips half open, indistinct in their purple quivering; the teeth set hard; the eyes filled with the fearful light of futurity' is actually that of an earlier version of the painting, which Hunt subsequently painted over with the rapt, eager expression of the finished work.[94] Consistently referring to the painting as *The Awakened Conscience*, Hunt thus moved his fallen woman another stage towards a vision of salvation, suggesting redemptive action would follow his tableau. Ruskin's mistaken certainty thus speaks volumes both about the prevalence of set story arcs, but also their multiplicity, and the significance and power of performance, where a woman's change of expression could suggest an entirely different set of consequences.

As Meisel has noted, Watts Phillips incorporated a realization of *The Awakening Conscience* in his *Lost in London*. When Nelly Armroyd listens to her seducer Featherstone sing lightly of betrayed love, her '*face has appeared to struggle with contending emotions during the singing*'.[95] But Phillips is faithful neither to Hunt's nor Ruskin's version of the story behind the picture; Nelly's conscience is not awakened, for it has never slept, giving her no peace at all throughout the entire course of the play, nor does her sense of shame spur her to action—her rescue must wait for the intervention of her friend Giddy and faithful husband Job. Suspense is crucial; if an audience knows what will follow the tension is inevitably lost.

The notion of the readability of the tableau or narrative painting and the predictability of the fallen woman's fate is thus disrupted by the need for an element of dramatic tension and surprise, and by the degree to which any individual viewer subscribed to the belief in a sinful woman's inevitable demise. Tableaux have been interpreted as moments of weighted significance, summarizing and crystallizing the preceding action and expressing the play's moral meanings in significant form. As Peter Brooks declares, 'In the tableau more than in any other single device of dramaturgy, we grasp melodrama's primordial concern to make its signs clear, unambiguous, and impressive.'[96] However, as Caroline Radcliffe has noted, by introducing stasis into the play's flow and referencing an exterior medium, the effect of the tableau contains a paradox: 'Time is frozen, breaking the usual prescriptive "here and now" of theatre, both lessening and heightening reality.' The stage picture could be described, she argues, as a transition between 'transparency'—an awareness of the artifice and mechanism of theatre—and 'hypermediation'—the coming together of theatre's appeal to all the senses.[97]

Tableau's operation is thus inherently contradictory and multiple. In matters of sexual judgement the supposed clarity and readability of tableau in fact provides a means of representing the more complex and multi-voiced dialogue running through the play. This tension within a tableau is as old as melodrama itself. Several

[94] Meisel, *Realizations*, 365–8.
[95] *Lost in London*, II, i, 19.
[96] *Melodramatic Imagination*, 48.
[97] Caroline Radcliffe, 'Remediation and Immediacy in the Theatre of Sensation', *Nineteenth Century Theatre and Film* 36:2 (2009), 50.

scholars have noted the influence on the early formation of melodrama of the German writer August von Kotzebue's sentimental dramas, most notably *Menschenhass und Reue* (1790), in which an adulterous wife is reunited with her estranged husband after years of repentance and charity on her part and reclusive despair on his. The play appeared in four different English translations at the end of the eighteenth century, one of which, *The Stranger* by Benjamin Thomson, remained immensely popular throughout the nineteenth century, performed regularly every year until 1842.[98] The play ends with the estranged couple about to part, when their children rush forward to embrace them; husband and wife '*gaze at each other—spread their arms, and rush into an embrace. The CHILDREN run, and cling round their Parents. The curtain falls.*'[99] The family reunited as the curtain descends is the archetypal resolution of melodrama, expressing the sacredness and importance of familial ties. But the inclusion of a sexually guilty woman in this formation raises disruptive issues of judgement and consequence. In her preface to the1806 edition, Elizabeth Inchbald defended the play's morality by emphasizing the considerable suffering which precedes this reconciliation. She then pointed out the ambiguity of the play's ending; as the curtain falls on the final embrace, audience members can project the action forward according to their own particular moral strictures:

> Notwithstanding all these distressful and repentant testimonies, preparatory to the reunion of this husband and wife, a delicate spectator feels a certain shudder when the catastrophe takes place,—but there is another spectator more delicate still, who never conceives, that from an agonizing though affectionate embrace, (the only proof of reconciliation given, for the play ends here), any further endearments will ensue, than those of participated sadness, mutual care of their joint offspring, and to smooth the other's passage to the grave.[100]

Silence may speak volumes but it is also conveniently ambiguous.

The development of melodrama from the sentimental and romantic dramas of the eighteenth century involved the simplification of character, moving from the psychological complexity of tragic and romantic heroes in conflict with themselves to an externalized conflict between good and evil embodied in hero and villain. In Peter Brooks's formulation, melodrama is driven by the desire to express all: 'Nothing is spared because nothing is left unsaid; the characters stand on stage and utter the unspeakable, give voice to their deepest feelings, dramatize through their heightened and polarized words and gestures the whole lesson of their relationship.'[101] Far from being ambiguous, Brooks argues, these gestures reach towards

---

[98] See Lothar Fietz, 'On the Origins of the English Melodrama in the Tradition of Bourgeois Tragedy and Sentimental Drama: Lillo, Schröder, Kotzebue, Sheridan, Thomson, Jerrold', in Michael Hays and Anastasia Nikolopoulou (eds), *Melodrama: The Cultural Emergence of a Genre* (St Martin's Press: New York, 1996).

[99] *The Stranger*, as performed at the Theatre Royal, Drury Lane. Translated from the German of Kotzebue by Benjamin Thomson. Printed, under the authority of the Managers, from the Prompt Book. With remarks by Mrs Inchbald. (Longman, Hurst, Rees and Orme; London, 1806), V, ii, 72.

[100] 'Remarks', ibid, 5.

[101] *Melodramatic Imagination*, 4.

meanings that cannot be articulated by mere language. The melodramatic body can express the ineffable, communicate the presence of innocence and purity as an evident truth, unarguable in its silence: 'it is the fullness, the pregnancy of the blank that is significant: meaning-full though unspeakable'.[102]

The climax of Edward Fitzball's *Mary Melvyn; or, A Marriage of Interest* (1843) serves as a perfect example of such significant gestures. Suspected by her rich and aged husband of an adulterous love for her cousin and former sweetheart, Mary Melvyn is persecuted through three acts, culminating in a stormy midnight trek across the Isle of Wight to prevent her husband committing murder. Shot by his own hired assassin, her husband finally accepts her innocence thanks to the revealed truth of melodramatic gesture:

MARY: Melvyn, I am not guilty –
MELVYN: Not guilty, Mary?
MARY: No, on my soul!
(Appealing to Heaven.)
MELVYN: That fervent aspiration! I believe thee—God forgive me—one bitter pang is spared me!—I fall victim to my own device.' 'Twas jealousy urged me to the deed—too late I see my error—[103]

But this moment's revelation stands in stark contrast to the ambiguities and uncertainties of the rest of the play. Believing her cousin Frank dead, Mary allowed her greedy guardian to bully her into marrying Melvyn, but Frank's unexpected return drives her husband into increasingly uncontrolled fits of jealousy. Mary is persuaded to take part in amateur theatricals, leaving Melvyn further disturbed by the idea that she is skilled in '*assuming a character*' (I, iv, 6). Playing Louis XIV's mistress, the significance of Mary's appearance and gestures are uncertain:

(Tableau of Mary, as La Valière clinging to the convent pillar; the king near her. Applause.)
MELVYN: My wife! Can it be?

(I, iv, 7)

A troubled wife plays a guilty mistress trying to resist temptation, under the suspicious eyes of a husband who reads excessive significance into her skills of expression. Moreover, if the tableau being enacted is intended as a specific reference to those in Edward Bulwer Lytton's scandalous 1837 play, *The Duchess de La Valliere*, it becomes doubly ambiguous; Lytton's play contains two scenes in which the Duchess seeks shelter in a convent from Louis's unlawful desires: in one scene she succumbs and becomes his mistress, in the second she rejects his blandishments and enters a convent.[104] Depending on which of these scenes Mary Melyvn's tableau

---

[102] Ibid, 73 and ch. 3 'The Text of Muteness'.
[103] Edward Fitzball, *Mary Melvyn; or, A Marriage of Interest*. First performed Theatre Royal, Adelphi, 13 February 1843. Dicks' No. 622, III, iii, 15.
[104] Lord Lytton, *The Duchess de la Valliere*. First performed Theatre Royal, Covent Garden, 4 January 1837. Dicks' No. 847, II, iii, 12–13, and V, iv, 27–8.

is taken from, it may be a prelude to sin or to redemption. In Fitzball's play-within-a-play, gesture is thus expressive but its meanings are multiple and unfixed. Moreover, performing roles is the norm in *Mary Melvyn*: a flirt pretends affections to stir up her admirer's jealousy, and he in turn pretends indifference to provoke hers; even Melvyn performs decorous restraint in front of his servants. Deceit is not a villainous camouflage but a seamless part of the fabric of social interaction.

Mary's soliloquies leave the audience in no doubt of her enduring feelings for Frank, but whether *Mary Melvyn* is to be a drama of sin and repentance remains unpredictable almost until the final curtain. Tortured by her suppressed feelings for Frank and her husband's resentful suspicions, Mary kneels before a portrait of her dead mother. The portrait evokes two strong dramatic associations: the absence of a mother's care leaving the daughter vulnerable to temptation and error, and the memory of the dead mother reminding the daughter of her duties. As Mary addresses the painting—'Image of my sainted mother, whose tender cares were lost to me ere I knew how to value them'—Frank enters and urges Mary to leave her violently jealous husband (II, iii, 10). The symbolism of the setting signals clearly to the audience that Mary's virtue is in danger, but whether it will fall remains perilously in the balance.

Mary Melvyn's fidelity to her marriage vows ultimately wins out over manifold trials and temptations, but though her virtue is made manifest in the closing moments of the play, she herself protests against an invasive questioning of her inner feelings. Marriage, she implies, is dependent on a degree of emotional privacy. So she reproaches her husband:

> You wring the expression from me, you grasp my heart till the blood *will* gush forth. Why am I unceasingly to be chidden? Why suspected?—you have no cause to upbraid me—what I did with my affections ere I became your wife you have no right to inquire. (II, i, 8)

A woman's heart is not necessarily on her sleeve, and the precise reading of gesture and tableau is a more complex matter than might at first appear.

The multiple voices in melodrama, from passive victim to resourceful maid, could thus set up tensions between moral idealism and pragmatic realism. The familiar trajectories of seduction plots had a widespread hold on the cultural imagination, but the dramatist could exploit their very predictability to open up conflicting possibilities—a tableau could be located between alternative narratives, providing a tension-filled crossroad from which the drama could proceed in less predictable directions. A tableau could summon up more than one set of referents, introducing not a synchronicity but a tension between the play's action and the stage picture's potential meanings. 'Freeze-framing' a play's action has traditionally been read as an opportunity to make the drama's meanings manifest, to impress their moral truth upon the audience, but the pause could equally be one for thought, a moment to apprehend not the simple truths but the complex contradictions and possibilities of the drama's multiple implications. Seduction dramas could simultaneously parade their fearful moral lessons, stimulate prurient curiosity, and include alternate voices to disrupt any absolute statement. Gesture might evoke the ineffable, yet, as the collection of bigamy dramas examined in the next chapter will show, unspoken emotions could provide a dangerously unsettling undercurrent.

2

Bigamy and Sensation

However many errant maidens pre-empted the ceremony of marriage and suffered for their hastiness, once married the melodramatic law of female sexual continence was sacrosanct. Adultery was a rare occurrence on the melodramatic stage. Wives were faithful. If husbands succumbed to alcoholism, gambling, and criminality, or were tempted away by dangerous sirens, their loyal spouses suffered stoically, reminding audiences that the wages of sin were often paid by the sinner's dependants, not by the malefactor himself. The one popular exception to this rule of marital fidelity was accidental bigamy, wherein a previous spouse's unexpected return from the dead produced an inconvenient excess of lovers, rendering an apparently blessed union illegal and adulterous. By setting love against legality, accidental bigamy offered a loophole whereby sympathy could be maintained for spouses who found their passions at war with their marriage vows. Plots of respectable moral probity could thus enable the performance of illicit desire.

Accidental bigamy was not always a complicating factor for the traditional moral binaries of melodrama, as evidenced by Pixérécourt's *La Femme à deux maris* (1801), in which the revelation that they are not legally married merely provides the noble protagonists with further opportunity for demonstrating their faultless probity. As discussed in the previous chapter, *La Femme à deux maris* is essentially concerned with the heroine's youthful elopement with Fritz, an offence against her father's authority for which she has spent the rest of her life attempting to atone. The revelation that Fritz faked his own death, deliberately entrapping Eliza in a bigamous marriage so he can claim any money settled on her as his own, serves to fuel her father's anger, delaying his parental pardon until Fritz has been conveniently dispatched by the assassin he hired to shoot Eliza's new husband, Edouard. Bigamy does not pose a problem to the clear moral values of Pixérécourt's melodrama. When Eliza and Edouard discover that their blissful marriage has no legal standing, they act with perfect honour. Without a second's hesitation, the lovers agree that they must part, submitting to the cruel separation that delicacy and virtue require. Concerned only with each other's well-being, they both display selfless generosity: Eliza leaves Edouard their children to comfort him; Edouard makes ample financial provision for Eliza's future. When they embrace, it is not a moment of temptation but an acknowledgement of each other's extraordinary virtue:

Eliza, pénétrée d'admiration, cherche pendant un moment à lui exprimer sa reconnaissance; mais trop émue pour parler, elle se précipite dans ses bras. Cette scène muette demande à être bien sentie de part et d'autre.[1]

[Eliza, filled with admiration, tries for a moment to express her gratitude to him; but too overcome to speak, she throws herself into his arms. This mute scene must be deeply felt on both sides.]

This moment of ineffable emotion, the apotheosis of melodrama in Peter Brooks's theory, stands alongside the final tableau of paternal forgiveness as a high-water mark of the play. Actors and audience are called upon to feel inwardly the emotions that cannot be articulated, and to witness the unimpeachable honour of the lovers, who submit entirely to the rule of law.[2]

Where Pixérécourt's noble protagonists behave with perfect probity, displaying not a flicker of hesitation in fulfilling their moral duty, later playwrights exploited the potential tensions within the bigamy plot. While remaining outwardly obedient to the melodramatic mandate of moral rectitude in literal plot terms, a number of later bigamy dramas introduced the suggestion of illicit desires and torn loyalties through sub-plots, tableaux and hinted but unrealized plot trajectories. The most enduringly popular of these dramas was J. T. Haines's *My Poll and My Partner Joe*, which opened at the Royal Surrey Theatre in September 1835, with T. P. Cooke playing the hero Harry Hallyard—a role he was to play 269 times in the course of his career; Cooke was still impressing audiences with the extraordinary vigour of his 'double-rowing hornpipe' two decades later.[3] The 'Poll' of the title is Harry's sweetheart Mary, whom he is about to marry when he is snatched away by a pressgang at the villain's behest. An adventurous four years at sea ensue for Harry, during which he heroically boards an enemy ship, overpowers the villain's illegal slaving vessel, reunites enslaved lovers and successfully storms an enemy fort. Finally released from service a rich man, Harry returns to embrace his sweetheart, only to be bewildered by her greeting:

MARY: 'Tis he!—'Tis so, then; my dear Harry, you are alive, and—(*rushing into his arms but recollecting herself, and screaming*) No! (*shuddering back*) No! Don't come near me—don't touch me, Harry!—don't touch me, I say!—It is past—Oh, cruel deceit!—Don't touch me! I dare not—I—Oh! my brain is bursting!

HARRY: (*seizing her arm*) What does this mean?

MARY: Oh, for mercy's sake! unhand me! you must not come near me! I am—I cannot speak the word! Let me go—let go! (*struggling wildly*) I shall go mad! (*breaking from*

---

[1] R. C. Pixérécourt, *La Femme à deux maris* (Paris, 1802) III, ii, 57.

[2] Pixérécourt's request for genuine feeling on the actors' part for the proper playing of this scene is also an intervention in contemporary debates on acting. He implicitly aligns himself with Romantic theories of acting, such as those expressed in John Hill's *The Actor* (1750), which emphasized sensibility as the actor's most important quality. Diderot refuted this theory in his 'Paradoxe sur le comédien' (1773), arguing that gesture, like all the actor's other techniques, belonged to the realm of artifice and that the true art of the actor was precisely that he did not feel the emotions he portrayed but reproduced them by conscious imitation. For further discussion of this debate, see George Taylor, *Players and Performances in the Victorian Theatre* (Manchester University Press: Manchester, 1989).

[3] *Era* (11 October 1857), 11.

him) There—there! Oh, pity me! when you know all, pity me! (*rushes distractedly into the house*).[4]

Harry's understandable puzzlement is resolved when it is revealed that Mary, believing Harry dead, has married his former boating partner Joe. Harry berates Mary and Joe for betraying his trust, but his tirade is interrupted by the news that Joe has been mortally wounded while unloading a barge. Joe is carried in on a stretcher and uses his last moments on earth to exonerate Mary:

HARRY: Joe, I grieve to see you thus; but unless my mother's voice from the grave assured me of—

JOE: Hold; here—here—here's your mother's will, where she leaves the sticks in the cottage, and the wherry, and all to me, to marry Mary. You'll see how she urges it for your sake. Read, Harry, read!—That is her voice from the grave!

HARRY: (*looking at the will*) Poor old mother!
(*Kisses it and weeps*)

JOE: Do you forgive her—forgive Mary?

HARRY: (*dropping on his knee by his side*) I do.

MARY: And Joe?

HARRY: Yes, yes!

JOE: Then I'm happy.—I'm dying! Harry! Mary!
(*he pulls their hands together, joins them and dies across them*)

HARRY: He is dead!—Mary!

MARY: Harry! Harry!
(*they rush into each other's arms, recollect themselves, and kneel in prayer by the side of Joe.—the others take off their hats, and surround him, and the curtain slowly descends.*)

(III, iv, 50–1)

The final tableau places Harry, his Poll and his partner Joe in a triangle at its centre, framed by the wondering boatmen.

Though there is no actual bigamy in the play, Harry having been press-ganged before he could marry Mary, the emotional crux of the drama is the division of loyalties that results from Harry's unexpected return from the dead. Reviewers confidently located *My Poll* simultaneously in the categories of nautical and bigamy dramas, both likening it to Douglas Jerrold's *Black-Ey'd Susan* and calling it 'a sort of melo-dramatic parody of Southerne's tragedy of "The Fatal Marriage"'—a seventeenth-century play in which the renascent first husband and accidentally bigamous wife commit suicide in horrified reaction to their predicament.[5] Where Southerne's heroine looks with disgust on the still-warm

---

[4] John Thomas Haines, *My Poll and My Partner Joe* (Lacy's Acting Edition No.1058: London, 1866), III, iii, 46.

[5] *Caledonian Mercury* (11 February 1836); *Athenaeum*, No.156310 (October 1857), 1271.

sheets of her bigamous wedding bed, Haines's Mary is spared any actual sexual guilt.[6] Yet, Haines structures his melodrama in order to suggest ideas of sexual impropriety, while avoiding any technical sin.

When Mary responds with shame and confusion to her former sweetheart's return from the dead, the audience is left as perplexed by her response as Harry himself.

In the previous scene Joe worried about Mary's inability to throw off her melancholy at Harry's death, spending her time putting flowers on his mother's grave and dreaming that Harry is still alive. The revelation that Mary is now married to Joe is only delivered after Mary's conflicted reaction to Harry's return, when a friendly third party explains the situation to the bewildered sailor. Mary's distress thus first appears as the shame of a fallen woman, shrinking from the man of whom she is now unworthy. By ordering the scenes in this way, Haines both raises sensational possibilities and avoids dwelling on the complicated emotional and moral implications of Mary longing for a former sweetheart while married to his best friend. As in *La Femme à deux maris*, Harry demonstrates the selfless nobility of his love by urging Mary to accept his money, ensuring she will never be stranded on the shoals of adversity, while Joe's convenient demise removes any legal barrier to the lovers' union. The emotional complications of a marriage made for three, first glimpsed but not understood when Mary pines for her lost lover while married to his partner, are evaded by the rapid sequence of events. Yet the potentially comic hiccough of Mary and Harry's interrupted embrace over Joe's corpse embodies in physical form the emotional dilemma at the heart of the play. Alongside the nautical sensations of Harry's adventures at sea, these two moments provide the affecting climaxes of the play, and were marked out by reviewers as such. The *Caledonian Mercury* commended Mrs Fisher's performance of Mary's reunion with Harry, in particular 'the wild abandonment with which she flew into his arms, succeeded by her bewildered gaze, as the fatal truth dawned on her', but found the similarly rapid sequence in which the lovers 'rein in their ardour as they meet across the body of poor Joe' to be 'a little incongruous'.[7] Reviewing a revival at the Surrey Theatre three years later, a critic in the *Odd Fellow* expressed even greater disquiet at the interrupted embrace; marking it as 'something...which we would like to see omitted', the reviewer commented witheringly that 'This may be a "point" in melodrama, but, notwithstanding, is not what persons of the *calibre* of Mrs Honner [playing Mary] and Mr T. P. Cooke should resort to.'[8] Even Haines's accelerated glimpse of emotional impropriety had the power to offend.

---

[6] Thomas Southerne, *The Fatal Marriage; or, the Innocent Adultery* (1694), in *The Works of Thomas Southerne*, Vol. II, ed. Robert Jordan and Harold Love (Clarendon Press: Oxford, 1988), 4, iii, pp.66–7. Notably, when it was performed by David Garrick in 1784, the more explicit references to bigamous sex were carefully edited out; see *Isabella; or, the Fatal Marriage. A Tragedy*. Altered from Southerne by D. Garrick. Marked with the variations in the Manager's Book at the Theatre Royal in Drury Lane. (London: C. Bathurst, T. and W. Lowndes; W. Nicoll, and T. Wheildon, 1784), 38.

[7] *Caledonian Mercury* (11 February 1836).

[8] *Odd Fellow* (1 October 1842), 2.

So popular was this bigamy formula that Thomas Egerton Wilks had two bigamy plays running in the same year: *Halvei the Unknown; or, The Bride of Two Husbands* (its subtitle acknowledging his debt to Pixérécourt's original) opened at the Adelphi on 24 January 1841, and *Woman's Love; or, Kate Wynsley, the Cottage Girl* opened less than three months later at the Royal Victoria Theatre on Easter Monday (an appropriate date for a drama of unexpected return from death). In both of these plays, while the noble protagonists behave with perfect probity, a tantalizing suggestion of illicit desire is raised, if never realized, in the plays' subplots and false leads. Wilks's Halvei the Unknown is an unscrupulous criminal who gambled away his young wife's fortune, murdered a man for money, and was sentenced to the galleys. Seven years later he has escaped and is blackmailing his wife, Clara. Believing him dead, Clara has remarried and given birth to two daughters, whom she wishes to protect from the public disgrace of illegitimacy. Clara is soon suspected of adultery by her second husband, Lyonnet St Claire; but it is the family lawyer, Philip D'Arville, who is accused of being her lover, thanks to a series of clandestine meetings in which he acts as go-between for Halvei. In a fit of jealous rage, St Claire challenges the lawyer to a duel, but as Clara struggles to disarm her husband, one of the pistols goes off and wounds Halvei, who is hiding in the garden to evade arrest for yet another crime. Enlightenment follows:

ST CLAIRE: Halvei! her first husband living! I see it all.

D'ARVILLE: Yes, Halvei, the escaped convict—the galley slave! St Claire, this is the wretch to whom you owe all your misery—chance has avenged you on him, and proved the innocence of your poor wife.

HALVEI: (*Gasping, and supported C. by two soldiers*) Here—here's a wonder—a lawyer speaking truth! You're right, old fellow—but I shan't be strangled by the law—no hanging holiday for your rascally rabble.... (*His eye wandering round*) Aha! my rival—and Clara, too! All's over, wench—my, my—my last game's played, and he (*points down*)—he's waiting for the stakes. I—I dare not ask you to forgive me—yet—

CLARA: From my soul I do, unhappy man.

HALVEI: Then ble—bless you, I was about to say—but, no, no, no,—'twon't do—a blessing from my lips would prove more t'other. One favour, girl—the last—let me look on your face, and press your hand before I die—you'll not refuse me? No—(*To St Claire*)—that's well—that's well. Eh? But how dark it grows! yet though it's pleasant—through the chilling mists, to see this gentle face look kindly on me—and now farewell to earth—a long, a last good night to my bless-ed lit-tle wife! (*Music.— Falls dead.—Tableau, the moon shining strongly on the group.*)[9]

As the comic pathos of his death scene suggests, Halvei is a primary focus of the play. Energetically resourceful and unrepentantly self-knowing, he shares gleeful asides with the audience; helping himself to Clara's jewellery box, he declares, 'I am

[9] Thomas Egerton Wilks, *Halvei the Unknown; or, The Bride of Two Husbands*, Dicks' No. 690, II, iii, 16.

her lawful husband—what's her property is mine. What's the use of getting married if you can't do as you like with your own wife?' (III, ii, 14). His reasoning is that of Pixérécourt's villainous Fritz, but Halvei is more a Jack-Sheppard-style criminal hero than a villain. Clara's love is devoted exclusively to her second husband and her probity is never in question—Halvei's only hold over her is his threat to destroy her daughters' reputation—but Wilks excises the possibility of adulterous desire from the main plot, only to relocate elsewhere. By displacing suspicions of infidelity onto the family lawyer, Wilks is left free to indulge in a touching and extended farewell between first husband and wife without raising difficult questions of split allegiances and future affection, while keeping the idea of sexual impropriety hovering in the play's margins.

Wilks's second bigamy drama also steps carefully around the inherent potential for sexual impropriety, only to exploit its possibilities elsewhere in the play. At first seemingly destined to be the humbly-born protagonist of a seduction drama, Kate Wynsley, the persecuted heroine of *Woman's Love,* has to endure the suspicion of unmarried motherhood before her nobly born husband, Wilford Clitheroe, reveals their clandestine marriage.[10] Her joy is short-lived, however, as the second act opens six years later with the news that Kate has died at sea and Clitheroe is now remarried to the sharp-tongued Lady Adeline, whose jealousy of his low-born first wife leads her to persecute her stepdaughter Jessie. A new governess arrives, none other, of course, than Kate, who was separated from husband and child by a shipwreck and held prisoner by the French for six years while all believed her dead. Kate becomes her own daughter's governess, under the pseudonym of 'Mrs Graham', and slowly realizes she is in the house of her own husband—whose real name she never knew and whom she has hitherto been unable to trace. Selflessly noble, Kate determines to keep her identity secret if Clitheroe is indeed happily married. In answer to her tentative enquiries, Clitheroe declares his first wife is best off dead: Kate would suffer agonies to find him remarried, while his second wife would go mad if she found herself an adulteress. Kate and Clitheroe thus demonstrate their absolute honour, motivated only by concern for others despite their own suffering. Kate determines to withdraw unrecognized, renouncing all claim to her beloved husband and child. Kate bids a pathetic farewell to the daughter who never knew her, and her fervent embraces are only just awaking Clitheroe's suspicions, when the butler announces that someone has drowned on the lake, and a body is carried in:

CLITHEROE: I will know the horrid truth! (*Unveils the body*) My wife! *My wife—cold and lifeless!*

KATE: His wife! Then Clitheroe is free! Lord Castledale, would you be sad *now* to hear of Katherine's death?

---

[10] A further possible plot trajectory for this scenario of the humble maid secretly married to a noble in disguise is revealed by C. H. Hazlewood's *Jessy Vere; or, the Return of the Wanderer* (first performed Britannia Saloon, February 1856), in which Jessy's aristocratic husband not only allows his wife to be branded a fallen woman, but is further tempted to reject her, steal their child, and even envisage her murder.

CLITHEROE: No, no! He or she who could announce to me that Kate yet lives, would be like an angel of light appearing to me in the hour of the saddest visitation.

KATE: Then I am that angel of light! Clitheroe!

CLITHEROE: Ha!

KATE: (*Throws back veil.*) Clitheroe!

CLITHEROE: (*Offers to embrace her with frantic joy*) Kate! My own loved—my long lost—my lamented Kate!

KATE: Hold, hold, my husband! My own—my own love! In the presence of the early dead, let us for a time forget our own happiness, and reverently bend the knee in humble supplication for the departed!

[*Music slow and solemn.—They all kneel reverently and picturesquely—Kate teaching Jessie to kneel and raise her hands together.—Clitheroe at the bier.*

CURTAIN FALLS SLOWLY.[11]

More mindful of the proprieties than Haines's Mary, Kate arranges the appropriately decorous final tableau, forestalling a passionate embrace over her rival's corpse. By binding the unintentional bigamy plot of the second act to a drama of suspected seduction in the first act, Wilks again produced a play that raised the spectre of illicit sexuality only to excise it carefully from the action. The nobility of the leads is carefully established, and the convenient speed of Lady Adeline's death leaves no time to develop the dangerous implications of a beloved first wife living in the same house as a patently difficult second one. Yet the very speed with which Adeline is dispatched serves not only to avoid an overcrowded marriage but also to place the dead wife's corpse in the same frame as the reunited lovers. While the dialogue expresses nothing but modest decorum, Clitheroe's forestalled embrace over his dead wife's corpse speaks volumes for the disturbing power of gesture.

J. B. Buckstone's *Ellen Wareham*, which opened at the Haymarket Theatre in April 1833, exploited more fully the inherent emotional and moral tensions of the accidental bigamy plot. Buckstone's play was adapted from Arabella Sullivan's novel *Ellen Wareham*, published in the third volume of *Recollections of a Chaperone* (1833), edited by Lady Dacre. The play begins halfway through the novel's action, with Ellen happily married to her second husband Mr Hamilton, her first husband, Mr Cresford having been reported dead at Verdun several years previously, whilst imprisoned by Bonaparte. Hamilton and Ellen live in domestic bliss with their baby daughter and Ellen's two children by her first marriage. Their peace is shattered by Cresford's return from the dead; he had feigned his own death in order to escape from prison, but then been arrested and held in Germany for four years as a madman. On receiving the news, Ellen immediately parts from Hamilton, to greet her first husband, but the reunion is not a happy one. Angry and jealous at Ellen's remarriage, Cresford has her arrested for bigamy, and she is only saved from a prison sentence by last-minute confirmation that Cresford's letter,

---

[11] Thomas Egerton Wilks, *Woman's Love; or, Kate Wynsley, the Cottage Girl*, Dicks' No.414, II, iii, 16.

informing her of his plan to fake his own death, was never delivered, thus proving Ellen innocent of deliberate bigamy when she married Hamilton after a discreet two years of widowhood. Obedient to the code governing extraneous spouses, Cresford promptly dies, leaving the way clear for Ellen and Hamilton to legalize their union.

Eschewing the moral clarity of a villainous plot, *Ellen Wareham* hangs on the mundane misery of marriage to an obsessively jealous husband. As in the novel, Buckstone's Ellen enjoys domestic bliss with Hamilton, in contrast to the trials of her early marriage to the rich but constitutionally possessive Cresford, who would never return from a party without 'a cloud on his brow, or something restless and suspicious in his manner'.[12] No sooner has Cresford reclaimed his wife than he switches from rapturous kisses to accusations of falsehood: 'Ellen, you never loved me, or you could not have done what you *have* done' (II, i, 10). He forces from Ellen the admission that she pities but does not love him, and he responds by asserting his paternal rights, demanding custody of his children, 'by the law of the land', behaviour which draws reproof from Ellen's elderly father: 'Your right I do not deny, but surely this is not the manner in which an Englishman and a gentleman would enforce it' (II, i, 11). Pixérécourt's Fritz and Wilks's Halvei are villains, each wanting his wife's money not her love; and for each heroine the trials of her marital past remain buried and unexamined. Cresford, by contrast, tortured by Ellen's love for her second husband and ready to assert his legal rights, is guilty only of an obsessive desire for absolute ownership of his wife. His present conduct is a window into his former married life, and there is a clear continuity of behaviour. As Ellen comments sadly on entering their former home: 'His love! Poor Charles! That has ever been a source of woe to both of us' (III, iv, 16).

Ellen and Hamilton are cast as adulterers by a twist of fate; but where other dramatists are careful to excise any suspicion of illegal desire from the main plot, displacing it decorously into a subplot, Buckstone exploits the spectacle of a marriage suddenly declared adulterous. Ellen and Hamilton act with all the probity of Pixérécourt's noble models, but they are also torn between duty and feeling, tortured by desires which have been suddenly outlawed. Hamilton even plays the tempting lover, suggesting they fly the reach of British laws, to which Ellen replies with dignity, 'Live with you as your mistress? Never! Anything would be more tolerable to me than to have you cease to respect me' (I, i, 6). She determines instead to 'submit as patiently as human nature can submit, for the sake of my dear—my innocent children!' When Hamilton draws her gently towards him, she dashes his hand away and retreats, rejecting an embrace that is now criminalized. But she cannot help admitting that up until that moment she was 'the happiest woman in the world', to which Hamilton gratefully responds: 'Bless you for what you have just uttered—bless you, my own Ellen!' (I, i, 7).

These moments of temptation, where Ellen's and Hamilton's desires break through their strict self-control, are taken directly from the novel, but the novelist is careful to batten them down tightly in a narrative of studied decorum. In Arabella

---

[12] J. B. Buckstone, *Ellen Wareham*, Dicks' No. 837, I, i, 4.

Sullivan's novel, Ellen's 'spotless lofty purity' is repeatedly emphasized, and the only criticism levelled at her by anyone apart from her obsessive first husband is that 'her delicacy' is 'rather overstrained'.[13] Ellen is a paragon of propriety, and the novel's happy ending is the poetically just reward for her virtue; legally re-married to his beloved Ellen, Hamilton looks on her 'with an expression of holy love', and muses out loud that 'if she had not been as virtuous as she is beautiful, as pure as she is kind, as firm as she is affectionate, if she had listened to me, when I wished to fly to America, we should never have known this hour of unalloyed happiness'.[14] As a reviewer noted in the *Literary Examiner,* the novel's treatment of bigamy is 'so excellently...managed...that there is no room for the entrance of a coarse idea'.[15] The novel is careful to narrate Ellen's every thought, excising any possibility of adulterous desire and announcing her eventual happiness as a reward for unswerving virtue. Buckstone's adaptation, by contrast, exploits the gap left by unspoken thoughts, leaving actors and audience free to deduce the emotional currents running under the surface. Where the novel sets the temptations of unlawful desire in direct opposition to Ellen's unhesitating purity, the drama offers a more ambiguous spectacle in which accidental bigamy doubles as a sympathetic portrayal of adulterous desire.

Cresford's prosecution of Ellen for intentional bigamy is a vindictive act of jealous anger in both novel and play. But where the novel gives a detailed account of the trial, Buckstone's drama keeps the doors of the courtroom resolutely closed, omitting the specifics of the bigamy trial in favour of a stand-off between the two claimants to Ellen's love. No sooner is it announced that Ellen is free than Cresford rushes out of court and prevents Hamilton congratulating her: 'Stand back, sir— back! The law of the land has just pronounced this woman to be my wife, and *you* her paramour' (III, i, 14). Ellen tearfully asks Cresford to be kind to their children, and is led away by her friend Lady Coverdale, and the vengeful husband is left isolated in his anger:

CRESFORD: I have sought revenge; wished to be feared if I could not be loved; a wild, ungovernable impulse urged me on, and I have obeyed it. But what is the end? A lone home and a breaking heart; the hatred of all who are bound to me by the nearest and dearest ties. Hatred! Is there no love for me? No one to cherish, to look to me with eager eyes, to welcome me with smiles, with open arms? None, none, none! I was never loved. *He, he* had her first affections—her *whole* affections. But I must to London—to my children, who will shrink from me, and return my kisses with fear. Even there I cannot meet with love. Oh, I shall go mad! (III, i, 14)

In this staging, the unseen prosecution mirrors a trial for adultery, a jealous husband's accusation of another man's 'criminal conversation' with his wife. In the

<hr/>

[13] Arabella Jane Sullivan, *Ellen Wareham*, in *Recollections of a Chaperone*, Volume III, edited by Lady Dacre (London: Richard Bentley, 1833), 137, 60.

[14] Ibid, 317.

[15] *Literary Examiner* (27 January 1833), 52.

novel, Hamilton secures Ellen's acquittal by proving Cresford's letter went astray; in the play it is Lady Coverdale who takes on the role of saviour, becoming a legal authority who not only produces witnesses but also quotes relevant statutes to secure Ellen's acquittal, while Hamilton appears only as the passive object of her husband's covetous rage.

Where the novel grants Cresford an ultimately peaceful end, reconciled with his wife and begging her forgiveness, Buckstone emphasizes the jealous husband's agonies up to the very end; Cresford's deathbed scene is not one of emotional resolution but of enduring turmoil, haunted by delirious visions of his rival:

CRESFORD: Who is that? What face is that? It is Hamilton. Take him from my sight. I cannot look upon him. I madden when he is before me. Away, away! What place is this? Who binds my hands? My dungeon, have I returned to you again? Have I been home and found all false and faithless there, and have I turned to my dark cell as to a friend. Welcome, welcome! (*Ellen approaches him, he looks at her earnestly and kisses.*) My wife—my wife restored to me. Bless you—bless you, Ellen! May you yet be happy! Bless you, Ellen—bless you! (*He falls dead.*) (III, iv, 16)

Cresford dies still tortured by sexual jealousy. His claiming of Ellen as 'my wife restored to me' is not the familial reunion of conventional melodramatic closure, but a reiteration of the harsh possessiveness that characterizes Cresford's marital behaviour.[16] As the *Athenaeum*'s reviewer commented: 'The interest of the piece is of a painfully disagreeable kind, and it terminates most fittingly with an incident which leaves upon the minds of the audience an impression of joyful wretchedness and miserable delight.'[17]

The artist who illustrated the 1880s publication of the play in the Dicks' Standard Plays series chose to emphasize the issue of adultery implicit in the play. Declaring itself 'Now printed for the first time', the Dicks' edition is illustrated with a scene from the first act, where Ellen kneels before Hamilton, who sits numbly clutching Cresford's letter (*Fig. 10*). The illustrator chooses not to have Ellen kneel decorously before Hamilton, but places her across her husband's lap, legs apart, rear towards the viewer, and hands clutched together in the traditional pose of theatrical anguish.[18] The servility and awkwardness of this pose suggest

16 In W. E. Burton's adaptation of the novel, by contrast, the spectre of adultery is decorously minimized. Reproducing the clear moral binaries of Pixérécourt's *La Femme à deux maris*, in reference to which it is subtitled, Burton's drama repeatedly emphasizes the legal dilemma of bigamy, while presenting Cresford as dangerously deranged from the start, in contrast to the exemplary virtue of Ellen and Hamilton. So, for example, Cresford regrets prosecuting Ellen for deliberate bigamy in a court case which 'Enabled her to prove how innocently she contracted the second marriage—how exemplary her conduct—how conscientious his behaviour.' William Evans Burton, *Ellen Wareham; The Wife of Two Husbands* (Thomas Hailes Lacy: London, 1833), II, iv, 31.
17 *Athenaeum*, No. 288 (May 1833), 284.
18 Harry Neville instructs that hands 'clasped or wrung' denotes 'Affliction, despair' in *Voice, Speech and Gesture: A Practical Handbook for the Elocutionary Art*, by Hugh Campbell and Harry Neville (Charles William Deacon & Co; London, 1895), 133. *The Actor's Hand-Book, and Guide to the Stage for Amateurs,* by 'The Old Stager' (John Dicks: London, 1884), advises similarly that Despair demands a posture in which 'the arms are bent at the elbows, the fist clinched hard'. (21) It further notes in

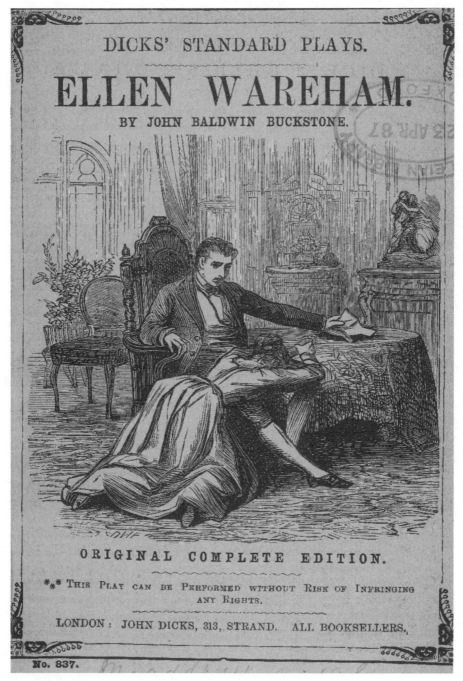

Fig. 10. Cover of J. B. Buckstone, *Ellen Wareham*, Dicks' Standard Plays edition. Shelfmark: M.adds. III e. 19e/837 (reproduced by permission of the Bodleian Libraries, University of Oxford).

Fig. 11. Augustus Egg, *Past and Present* (1858), © Tate Gallery, London.

abasement, as though Ellen were expressing shame and begging for mercy—whereas she is actually pleading to be woken from this awful dream, and seconds later she repels with dignity the suggestion that they flee British jurisdiction. More specifically, the positioning of both husband and wife unmistakeably mirrors Augustus Egg's famous *Past and Present* (1858) (*Figs. 11–13*), which depicts a woman caught out in adultery and the terrible consequences for her and her family. The central picture of Egg's triptych leaves little space for interpretive doubt. The husband clutches the incriminating letter, the wife lies prostrate, the door to their domestic sanctum stands open, a young daughter looks around in surprise, while the house of cards, unwisely built upon a volume of Balzac, collapses. Further symbols of sexual guilt determine the picture's meaning: an apple cut in half to expose its rotten core; on the walls hang a depiction of the Fall and one of a shipwreck, entitled *The Abandoned* by Clarkson Stanfield, exhibited at the Royal Academy in 1856. Egg's central scene was flanked by two further paintings: one showing the

reference to actors fainting in a jealous fit: 'As he must frequently fall upon the ground, he should previously raise both hands clasped together, in order to denote anguish, and which will at the same time prevent him from hurting himself' (22). The pose of Egg's prostrate adulteress may, therefore, reflect the influence of practical stagecraft on the iconography of despairing guilt.

Fig. 12. Augustus Egg, *Past and Present* (1858), © Tate Gallery, London.

two daughters, now grown up and left to fend for themselves in poverty; the second, their mother, sheltering under a bridge with her illegitimate child huddled in her shawl. Egg's triptych remained untitled in the catalogue of the 1858 Royal Academy exhibition in which it was displayed, but was identified instead by a fragment of narrative:

> August the 4ᵗʰ. Have just heard that B— has been dead more than a fortnight, so his poor children have just lost both their parents. I hear *she* was seen on Friday last near the Strand, evidently without a place to lay her head. What a fall hers has been![19]

The Dicks' frontispiece for *Ellen Wareham* carefully reproduced not only the letter clutched in the husband's hand, his haggard introspective look, the wife's clutched hands and billowing skirt, but even the shape of the cloth draped over the circular table. The illustration decodes the adultery implicit in the play, and, indeed, markets the play on that basis to any potential purchaser whose eye should be caught by the familiar image.

[19] Quoted in T. J. Edelstein, 'Augustus Egg's triptych: a narrative of Victorian adultery', *Burlington Magazine*, Vol. 125, No. 961 (April 1983), 202.

Fig. 13. Augustus Egg, *Past and Present* (1858), © Tate Gallery, London.

The psychological depth of *Ellen Wareham*, as compared to Wilks's *Halvei* and *Woman's Love*, gives clearer expression to the undercurrent of adulterous desire that runs through these dramas of unintentional bigamy. For all their sudden plot twists and rapid evasions, all these dramas still hinge on a conflict between duty and desire, sympathetically framing a spouse's love for someone to whom they are not legally married. The bigamy plot could thus give expression to anxieties about errant desire and the exclusive ownership of one spouse by another. When Black-stone's legal principle of 'feme covert', whereby the wife had no separate identity in law from her husband, was still the governing principle of legislation on marriage, the dramatizing of a wife's reclaiming by a previous spouse carried an unsettling emotional resonance, a disturbing reminder that a wife retains a separate emotional and sexual identity from her husband. The happy resolution of a bigamy plot requires that only the truly desired spouse live past the final curtain, but such a scenario demands at least a retrospective acknowledgement of unhappy marriage, and the implication that a wife's happiness is occasionally secured by a husband's demise—however decorously she kneels by the corpse in the final tableau.

It was in the 1860s and 1870s that bigamy became the literary *crime du jour*, shooting to prominence in the best-selling sensation novels of Mary Elizabeth

Braddon and Ellen Wood, and spawning a wealth of eager imitations.[20] Braddon herself referred to *Lady Audley's Secret* (1861–2) and *Aurora Floyd* (1862–3) as her 'pair of Bigamy novels', and she fully exploited the inherent opportunities in a form of guileless adultery.[21] As Margaret Oliphant remarked:

> She has brought in the reign of bigamy as an interesting and fashionable crime, which no doubt shows a deference to the British relish for law and order. It goes against the seventh commandment, no doubt, but does it in a legitimate sort of way, and is an invention which could only have been possible to an Englishwoman knowing the attraction of impropriety, and yet loving the shelter of the law. [22]

The plots of these novels are familiar: Aurora Floyd, like the hapless heroines of *La Femme à deux maris* and *Halvei the Unknown,* in a youthful fit of headstrong disobedience married an unscrupulous scoundrel, under whose yoke she suffered until relieved by his apparent death. The scoundrel (in Aurora's case a coarse but handsome groom) returns from the dead and attempts to blackmail the heroine who has unwittingly contracted a bigamous marriage, but his villainy is cut short by his unexpected demise. Lady Audley's 'secret' is her excess of spouses: having been left penniless to fend for herself when her husband George Talboys left to seek their fortune overseas, Helen Talboys changed her name to Lucy Graham and worked as a governess, until she unscrupulously accepted a proposal from the rich Sir Michael Audley, gaining a position she attempts murder to retain. Though Helen Talboys takes the surname 'Graham' when she becomes a governess (the same pseudonym as Wilks's Kate Wynsley adopts), it is the suffering heroine of Wood's *East Lynne* (1861) who mirrors Kate Wynsley's tearful trials, disguised as a governess to her own child but forbidden to reveal her true identity. Wood spares her hero, Archibald Carlyle, the technical guilt of bigamy—he divorced his erring first wife Isabel for adultery, and only remarried when he mistakenly believed her dead—but when he discovers that Isabel has been living in disguise in the same house as his new wife, his reaction echoes the title of Pixérécourt's *La Femme à deux maris*: 'The first clear thought that came thumping through his brain was, that he must be the husband of two wives.'[23]

The connection between these 'sensation novels' and the basic ingredients of melodrama has long been recognized: both comprise a mixture of shocking events, thrilling crimes, pathetic suffering, and devious villainy. But beyond such general outlines, critics have located the inspiration behind the sensation novel elsewhere: Margaret Oliphant traced the roots of sensation fiction back to the self-assertion of Charlotte Brontë's heroines, whereas modern critics, while noting the debt that the sensational novel's atmosphere and dramatic events owe

---

[20] For an account of the extraordinary popularity of the bigamy novel, see Jeanne Fahnestock, 'Bigamy: The Rise and Fall of a Convention', *Nineteenth-Century Fiction* 36 (June 1981), 47–71.

[21] Braddon, letter to Bulwer-Lytton, December 1862, quoted in Robert Lee Wolff, *Sensational Victorian: the Life and Fiction of Mary Elizabeth Braddon* (Garland Publishing: London and New York, 1979), 154.

[22] Margaret Oliphant, 'Novels', *Blackwood's Edinburgh Magazine*, 102 (September 1867), 263.

[23] Ellen Wood, *East Lynne* (Oxford World's Classics: Oxford, 2005), ch. LXI, 614.

to the melodramatic stage, have located the complications of bigamy and adultery more specifically in the debates surrounding the 1857 Matrimonial Causes Act and journalistic coverage of subsequent scandalous divorce trials.[24] Far from noting sensation fiction's appropriation not only of specific dramatic situations, but also of theatrical techniques to generate multiple possible plot trajectories and suggest more complex emotional currents running under an apparently decorous surface, critics have tended to set melodrama in direct contrast to the subversive moral ambiguities of Wood's and Braddon's novels. Jennifer Carnell is typical in contrasting the disruptive moral complexity of sensation fiction and melodrama's supposedly set moral binaries, the assumed audience sympathy with virtue and repulsion from vice, and the predictability of outcomes: 'In melodrama, part of the enjoyment of the audience stemmed from knowing what they would get. In sensation fiction the outcome is less certain.'[25] Yet there is an intimate connection between the sensation novel and the melodramatic stage, not just in terms of plot structures but also in terms of strategies and methods. Above all, bigamy dramas from earlier in the century had developed the central techniques which sensation novels subsequently deployed in order to pay outward homage to the imperatives of poetic justice, propriety, and social custom, while tantalizingly evoking emotions and attitudes excluded by the literal trajectory of the action and plot.

Lyn Pykett has noted the unfixed narrative perspective of sensation fiction as one of its most unsettling devices, allowing reader sympathy to move from major to minor characters, from upright judge to errant heroine.[26] The multiple competing voices of melodrama provide an obvious model for the sensation novel's interlaced narrative points of view. As Pykett observes, in Ellen Wood's *East Lynne* the anguished conscience and self-torturing regret of the adulterous Lady Isabel are juxtaposed with the amoral resilience of Afy Halijohn, a lower-class woman who has also lived in sin with the villainous Francis Levison but who wears her sexual past lightly, blithely manoeuvring to secure as rich a husband as possible. Afy's blithe pragmatism undermines any claims to universal applicability on the part of the suffering heroine, her agonies of conscience being located more specifically in relation to the particular morality and circumstances of her class and conscience. This juxtaposition between the suffering heroine's psychic pain and the pragmatic resilience of her comic counterparts thus mirrors the stock dynamics of melodrama, where the comic resourcefulness of Dorcas Downey in Haines's *The Life of*

---

[24] See, for example, Winifred Hughes, *The Maniac in the Cellar: Sensation Novels of the 1860s* (Princeton University Press: Princeton, NJ, 1980); Ann Cvetovich, *Mixed Feelings: Feminism, Mass Culture, and Victorian Sensationalism* (Rutgers University Press: New Brunswick, NJ, 1992); Barbara Leckie, *Culture and Adultery: The Novel, the Newspaper, and the Law, 1857–1914* (University of Pennsylvania Press: Philadelphia,PA, 1999).

[25] Jennifer Carnell, *The Literary Lives of Mary Elizabeth Braddon: A Study of her Life and Work* (Sensation Press: Hastings, 2000), 194. See also Winifred Hughes, *The Maniac in the Cellar*, ch. 1; Leckie, *Culture and Adultery*, 127–8; Rohan McWilliam, 'Melodrama', and Heidi J. Holder, 'Sensation Theatre' in *A Companion to Sensation Fiction*, ed. Pamela K. Gilbert (Wiley-Blackwell: Oxford, 2011).

[26] Lyn Pykett, *The Improper Feminine: The Women's Sensation Novel and the New Woman Writing* (Routledge: London, 1992), chs 11 and 13.

a Woman or the sexual opportunism of the village girls in Wilks's *Woman's Love* offer an alternative to the passive affect of the principal heroine.[27]

In *Women's Theatre Writing in Victorian Britain* (2005), Katherine Newey argues for the early 1860s as a watershed in Victorian theatrical history. Dramatizations of *Lady Audley's Secret* and *Aurora Floyd*, she explains, brought vast audiences to view heroines who mixed virtue and vice, active in the pursuit of their desires; the popularity of Braddon's bigamous heroines on stage was 'a marker of Victorian popular culture's shift into modernity through the representation of "women's stories" on the popular stage'. The most significant element in these productions, according to Newey, was 'the embodied representation of the feeling (sensational) woman (body)'.[28] Yet the vital ingredients of this perceived revolution had long been present in earlier bigamy and seduction dramas, whose plots had long centred on women's bodies and their sexual destiny and the 'patterns of masochistic female suffering and victimization' which Newey describes as the legacy passed on as template for generations of women's popular entertainment by sensation novels and their dramatic adaptations.[29] Quite apart from the frail female flesh placed centre stage in seduction dramas, the common formula of so many melodramas was the semi-pornographic thrill of an unscrupulous villain threatening sexual assault upon a virtuous heroine.

Above all, sensation fiction's emotional subtext mirrors the performed but unspoken desires of the bigamy drama. Just as earlier bigamy dramas summoned and suppressed the phantom of adulterous desire, exploiting the ambiguous possibilities of tableau and gesture, so Lyn Pykett has argued that women's sensation fiction deployed a similar gap between plot and performance. Pykett notes the inflated language, intense physicality and heightened imagery used by Braddon to describe her heroines at key moments: she terms this 'melodramatic excess' and notes that it is 'one of the hallmarks of Braddon's style, as it is of the sensation novel in general':

> It is an irruption into the narration of that feeling (particularly the erotic feeling) which is repressed in the narrative...It appears in its most highly wrought form in set-pieces and dramatic tableaux which stage the heroine/villainess as a spectacle; she may be presented as the object of a public gaze within the text, or the scene may be staged for the reader. In such scenes the female body becomes a sign (or system of signs) which is imperfectly read, or misread, by the characters within the text, but which is legible to the narrator, and hence to the reader—even if what is legible is finally the sign's elusiveness.[30]

Pykett here uses the term 'melodramatic' not to draw an analogy between the methodologies of the theatre and sensation fiction, but rather to reference the exaggerated emotion and fraught scenarios of melodramatic discourse and literary modes. As an example of this melodramatically excessive narration Pykett cites a

---

[27] See Cvetovich, *Mixed Feelings* for discussion of the 'Politics of Affect' and the role of the sensation novel in constructing the middle-class woman as a feeling (often as opposed to doing) subject.

[28] Katherine Newey, *Women's Theatre Writing in Victorian Britain* (Palgrave Macmillan: Basingstoke, 2005), 93, 94.

[29] Ibid, 95.

[30] Pykett, *Improper Feminine*, 97–8.

description of Aurora Floyd asleep, seen through the eyes of her doting husband John: though unaware that, as a schoolgirl, Aurora eloped with and married a handsome groom, whose continued existence renders her current marriage bigamous, John's vision of his wife is coloured by the sexual sin of which he is ignorant: 'her masses of ebon hair uncoiled and falling about her shoulders in serpentine tresses, that looked like shining blue-black snakes released from poor Medusa's head to make their escape amid the folds of her garments'.[31] Aurora is framed in a narrative tableau, described in freighted imagery of sexual allure and insidious if unconscious power and menace, though seen through the eyes of a husband who knows none of the facts of her sexual past. It was the unsettling power of such scenes that enabled the disruptive effects of sensation novels to resonate beyond their poetically just conclusions, just as the unspoken desires and interrupted gestures of earlier bigamy drama tableaux expressed the more disturbing subtext below the surface propriety of their plots. Indeed, Archibald Carlyle's farewell to his dying first wife in Wood's *East Lynne* replays the interrupted embraces of so many bigamy dramas: 'Lower and lower bent he his head, until his breath nearly mingled with hers. But, suddenly, his face grew red with a scarlet flush, and he lifted it again'—a familiar combination of death and unspoken desire staged in a broken gesture.[32]

The influence of theatrical sources and methods on Mary Elizabeth Braddon's writing was hardly surprising given that she worked as an actress from 1852 to early 1860 under the name Mary Seyton, touring a number of provincial towns and cities in England and Scotland, and appearing for a season at the Surrey Theatre in London. Her acting repertoire included Haines's *My Poll and My Partner Joe* in 1853 in Southampton, as well as such staples as *Clari, Victorine, Black-Ey'd Susan* and Bulwer Lytton's *The Lady of Lyons*.[33] After leaving the stage, she maintained a friendship with playwright J. B. Buckstone, who nicknamed his daughter 'Audley' after her most famous heroine.[34] In Braddon's novel *The Doctor's Wife* (1864), she draws an affectionate portrait of a jobbing writer for the penny dreadful serial fiction market, who envies the author of *La Femme à deux maris*: 'I think I should like to have been Guilbert de Pixérécourt, the father and prince of melodrama, the man whose dramas were acted thirty thousand times in France before he died (and how many times in England?).'[35] Together with a familiarity with popular dramatic plots, Braddon was also well aware of the multiple uses of tableau, not only, as one playwright's handbook put it, to provide the audience with a 'concentrated summing-up of the whole act', but also as a more ambiguous signposting of potential plot developments, a picture readable in more than one

---

[31] Mary Elizabeth Braddon, *Aurora Floyd* (Oxford University Press, World's Classics: Oxford, 1996), 271.
[32] Wood, *East Lynne*, ch. LXI, 616.
[33] Carnell, *Literary Lives*, Appendix One: Calendar of Mary Braddon's Theatrical Career.
[34] Wolff, *Sensational Victorian*, 73; letter from J. B. Buckstone to Braddon, 12 March 1866, quoted in Carnell, *Literary Lives*, 144.
[35] Mary Elizabeth Braddon, *The Doctor's Wife* (Oxford University Press: Oxford, 1998), 47.

way.[36] Having seen Alfred Elmore's painting of a young woman outside the window of a gaming room, listening intently to the shadowed man whispering in her ear (*Fig. 8*), Braddon wrote to the artist suggesting a range of possible titles which emphasized both the symbolic weight of the picture but also the uncertainty of its trajectory: ' "A Perilous Moment", "Trembling in the Balance", "On the Brink", "Lost? or Saved?", "A Dangerous Adonis", "A Woman's Peril".'[37] Elmore finally selected 'On the Brink', a title that draws on the link between gambling and seduction, while leaving forever undecided the fate of the young woman, listening to the young gamester's words but caught in a moment of thoughtful hesitation. Thoroughly versed in dramatic techniques of indirection, suggestion and implication, Braddon thus took the lead in deploying in the novel the bigamy play's potential for suggesting in the performance (narration) what was suppressed in the plot (narrative).

Sensation fiction brought to prominence elements which had always been inherent in melodrama, thinly but decorously veiled by the proprieties of poetic justice, but it also had a more specific influence in a dramatic genre which predated the first sensation novels while sharing their soubriquet: the sensation drama. To the thrills, last-minute rescues, breathtaking escapes, villains, and heroes of melodrama, the sensation drama added the crucial ingredients of a contemporary setting and a spectacular scene which exploited the very latest in dazzling stage effects. Dion Boucicault was the inventor and master of this formula, which he first brought to the stage in *The Poor of New York* (1857), featuring the collapse of a burning building during a snowstorm, complete with horse-drawn fire engine on stage. Boucicault set the play during a recent financial crisis, inspired by reading an illustrated newspaper with the thought that 'the stage might be employed in a similar manner to embody and illustrate the moving events of the period'.[38] His next play *Jessie Brown; or, the Relief of Lucknow* (1858) was so contemporaneous it staged the relief of Lucknow a month before the besieged town was actually relieved by Sir Colin Campbell. *The Octoroon; or Life in Louisiana* opened in the following year, featuring a slave auction, a blazing paddle-steamer, and a villain caught in the act on a photographic plate. *The Octoroon* also set the pattern for Boucicault's skilfully managed intervention in controversial subjects. Zoe, the heroine of the play, is one-eighth black and finds herself up for sale to the villain, finally committing suicide rather than submit to her fate. Zoe's tragic plight and the romance between her and the play's white hero were enough to make the play an inflammatory contribution to the controversy over abolition; but Boucicault was careful not to alienate any faction of his potential audience, portraying all the Southern slave-owners in his play as humane and kind-hearted while the villains are all Northerners. This

---

[36] 'A Dramatist', *Playwriting: A Handbook for Would-Be Dramatic Authors* (London, 1888), 18, quoted in Martin Meisel, *Realizations: Narrative, Pictorial, and Theatrical Arts in Nineteenth-Century England* (Princeton University Press: Princeton, NJ, 1983), 45.

[37] Braddon to Alfred Elmore, undated *c.*1865, quoted in Carnell, *Literary Lives*, 178.

[38] Dion Boucicault, 'Leaves from a Dramatist's Diary', *North American Review* 149 (July/December 1889), 230.

careful balancing act helped to deliver another commercial success, though a number of reviewers took angry issue with the author for attempting to 'elevate the Negro to the same level with the whites'.[39] Boucicault was a pragmatist; when *The Octoroon* failed to please audiences in London, he gave the play a happy ending, advertising it as 'A new Last Act of the Drama, composed by the Public, and edited by the Author.'[40] Yet, with Zoe denied any legal right to prevent the sale of her body to a man she detests, her sexual subjection made the play's slave auction scene a sensational staging of exactly what Boucicault saw as the worst evils of slavery, which were not in his eyes the savage beatings depicted in *Uncle Tom's Cabin* but rather 'features in slavery far more objectionable than any hitherto held up to human execration, by the side of which physical suffering appears as a vulgar detail'.[41] This political balancing act was one which Boucicault was to perfect in his later Irish plays, *Arrah-na-Pogue* (1864) and *The Shaughraun* (1874), in which crowd pleasing spectacle, humour, sentiment, and lashings of local colour made box-office gold out of dramas which celebrated Fenian heroism and Irish ingenuity in outwitting the impositions of English laws and military colonialism—but where the villains were not English officers, but Irish middlemen and informers.[42]

Katherine Newey is careful to use the broader term 'sensation drama' to describe the plays which brought about a vital change in material theatre practice in the 1860s, yet the only specific examples she gives are theatrical adaptations of female-authored sensation novels.[43] The first play in English theatre history to achieve a long run and to be widely dubbed a 'sensation play', however, was Dion Boucicault's *The Colleen Bawn; or, The Brides of Garryowen*, which opened in New York on 27 March 1860, and then at the Adelphi Theatre, London, on 10 September 1860 where it ran for 230 straight nights. The play's unprecedented box-office success empowered its author to license his own touring productions, mounted under his own supervision and reproducing the West End production, an innovation which brought him £500 a week. By retaining control of his play's production rights, and so raising both the financial and artistic status of the playwright, Boucicault, in his own words, 'contributed mainly to a fundamental change in theatrical affairs throughout the world'.[44] *The Colleen Bawn* was dubbed a 'sensation drama' before *Lady Audley's Secret* or *East Lynne* had even been published, let alone dramatized, and

---

[39] Review in *The Spirit of the Times*, quoted in Richard Fawkes, *Dion Boucicault: A Biography* (Quartet Books: London, 1979), 110.

[40] Playbill for *The Octoroon* at the Adelphi Theatre, London, November 1861, reproduced in Fawkes, *Dion Boucicault*, 129. Both versions of the final act are published in *Selected Plays of Dion Boucicault*, chosen and introduced by Andrew Parkin, Irish Drama Selections 4 (Colin Smythe: Gerrards Cross, 1987).

[41] Letter to the *Times*, quoted in Fawkes, *Dion Boucicault*, 109.

[42] For political re-readings of Boucicault's Irish plays see Nicholas Grene, *The Politics of Irish Drama: Plays in Context from Boucicault to Brecht* (Cambridge University Press: Cambridge, 1999); Elizabeth Cullingford, *Ireland's Others: Ethnicity and Gender in Irish Literature and Popular Culture* (Cork University Press in association with Field Day: Cork, 2001); Dawn Duncan, *Postcolonial Theory in Irish Drama from 1800–2000* (Mellen: New York, 2004); Jacky Bratton, Richard Allen Cave et al. (eds), *Acts of Supremacy: the British Empire and the Stage, 1790–1930* (Manchester University Press: Manchester, 1991).

[43] Newey, *Women's Theatre Writing*, 69.

[44] Boucicault, 'Leaves from a Dramatist's Diary', 232.

the play furthermore turned on attempted bigamy. *The Colleen Bawn* was inspired by Gerald Griffin's *The Collegians* (1829), a novel which in turn was based on an actual murder case in Limerick ten years earlier, in which a young peasant girl was murdered by the more nobly born man to whom she was secretly married. Bouci-cault's weak-willed Hardress Cregan is an Irish landowner who contemplates mar-riage to a rich heiress despite being already secretly married to the beautiful peasant girl of the title, Eily O'Connor. Mistakenly believing that Hardress has sanctioned his first wife's murder, his servant Danny throws Eily into an underground lake, but she is rescued by Myles-na-Coppaleen, a lovable rogue and smuggler, played by Boucicault himself, who spectacularly dived headfirst into the lake to bring Eily to safety. Reunited with Eily after her unexpected return from the dead, Hardress over-comes his family's snobbery and embraces his lowly born wife. Boucicault's genius was to marry this plot of attempted bigamy, villainy, and last-minute rescue with the music and scenery of Ireland to produce a drama which deployed the full resources of theatre technology and illusion in staging Eily's attempted murder and rescue from the lake, while celebrating the peasant heroine's Irish brogue and shaming the hero for his social snobbery and failure to embrace his native culture. *The Colleen Bawn* revolutionized Irish drama, giving birth to a new kind of stage Irishman, gifted with energy, resourcefulness, and an unshakeable sense of honour and cour-age; the play also transformed the economics of stage authorship and made sensa-tion the new theatrical fashion. Braddon herself humorously paid tribute to the impact of Boucicault's sensation drama and in particular his famous 'diving header' to save the Colleen Bawn, when in *Aurora Floyd* the narrator comments on the the-atrical tastes of previous decades that

> It was not the fashion in those days to make 'sensation' dramas of Shakespeare's plays. There was no 'Hamlet' with the celebrated water scene, and the Danish prince taking a 'header' to save poor weak-witted Ophelia.[45]

The close affinity between Boucicault's spectacular and provocative plays and the controversial fictions of Braddon and Wood was reflected in the terms in which both genres were condemned by morally outraged critics. Huge commercial suc-cess, cross-class appeal, contemporaneous setting, and thrilling incidents designed to appeal to and play on an audience's or reader's nerves provoked censure in remarkably similar critical terms. In his 1863 diatribe against sensation novels, D. H. Mansell noted the importance of contemporaneity in securing sensation fiction's shocking impact, as 'it is necessary to be near a mine to be blown up by its explosion'; he then proceeded to condemn such novels as 'poison' and 'morbid' fare, 'called into existence to supply the cravings of a diseased appetite, and con-tributing themselves to foster the disease, and to stimulate the want they supply'.[46] Henry Morley deployed a similar imagery of debased appetite in his reception of the Adelphi Theatre's stage version of *Aurora Floyd*, commenting that 'the players, who seek only to please the palate of the town, will cook the garbage that is in

---

[45] Braddon, *Aurora Floyd*, 11.
[46] D. H. Mansell, 'Sensation Novels', *Quarterly Review* 113: 226 (April 1863), 488, 486, 483.

demand. Omelets are accounted flavourless; a strong taste in the mouth is the one thing desired.'[47] Consistently disgusted by Boucicault's output, Morley dismissed the playwright's 'unlimited series' of phantoms and 'Octoroons', similarly drawing on images of appetite and addiction: 'The temptation is very great to meet debility by stimulants.'[48] Morley confidently declared, 'Nobody can feel less mercifully than I do towards some of the claptrap dramas of Mr Boucicault, and the corresponding school of fiction', pairing the two genres under the shadow of his disapproval.[49]

The exchange between the sensation novel and sensation drama was a reciprocal and mutually beneficial one; theatrical adaptations of *East Lynne*, *Lady Audley's Secret*, and *Aurora Floyd* all filled theatres and became long-standing favourites in both London and regional theatre repertoires. But, for all the critical opprobrium and box-office enthusiasm that greeted theatrical versions of women's sensation novels, the adaptations themselves tended to exercise discretion in their depiction of the illicit desires that had thrilled so many readers and provoked so many critics. In John Oxenford's adaptation of *East Lynne*, for example, Lady Isabel deserts her husband and children for the arms of her wicked cousin, outwardly motivated solely by misplaced jealousy, the adulterous desire with which she struggles in the novel having been carefully excised from the play-script. Similarly, once she takes up residence in disguise under the roof of her divorced and remarried husband, she endures the pains of an unrecognized mother while her awakened desire for her ex-husband, which tortures her in the novel, is never articulated.[50] It was not until T. A. Palmer's 1874 adaptation that Lady Isabel's illicit desires were given overt articulation in a play whose overly sensational passions won it little approval. Oxenford's remained the favoured version.[51]

Fittingly, it was Boucicault who exploited to the full both the sexual subtexts inherent in bigamy as a plot device, and the sensational technique of suggesting in the narration (or performance) what is suppressed in the narrative (or plot). Boucicault's *Hunted Down; or, The Two Lives of Mary Leigh*, a bigamy drama written in the wake of the huge success of the sensation novel, opened in Manchester in July 1866 as *Hunted Down*, and was revised and the subtitle added before it transferred to the St James's Theatre, London in November, incidentally providing Henry Irving with his West End debut in the role of the villainous

---

[47] Henry Morley, *The Journal of a London Playgoer from 1851 to 1866* (Routledge: London, 1866), entry 21 March 1863, 293.

[48] Ibid, 19 June 1852, 54; 13 April 1863, 295.

[49] Ibid, 25 March 1865, 367.

[50] John Oxenford, *East Lynne*. First performed Surrey Theatre, 5 February 1866. Reprinted in Michael Kilgariff (ed.), *The Golden Age of Melodrama: Twelve 19th Century Melodramas* (Wolfe Publishing: London, 1974), 278–307. Revived 1867 at the Lyceum, 1869 at Sadler's Wells, in 1875 at the Globe, and in 1878 at the Standard.

[51] T. A. Palmer, *East Lynne*. First performed in Nottingham, 19 November 1874. Reprinted in Adrienne Scullion (ed.), *Female Playwrights of the Nineteenth Century* (J. M. Dent: London, 1996), 295–346. Palmer did, however, win in the end, as the composer of the immortal line, 'Oh, Willie, my child, dead, dead, dead! and he never knew me, never called me mother!' (III, ii, 336). In Oxenford's and the Adelphi Theatre version (Dicks' No. 331) Lady Isabel is more mercifully treated and William calls her mother before he expires.

Rawdon Scudamore.[52] Boucicault later claimed the play was written to fulfil a wager that he could write three plays which would succeed in inverse relation to their merits: 'a society drama, relying mainly on its literary treatment', a domestic drama and a sensation drama.[53] The resulting plays, *Hunted Down*, *The Long Strike* (an adaptation of Elizabeth Gaskell's *Mary Barton*), and *The Flying Scud* (which ends with the hero's horse spectacularly winning the Grand National) fulfilled Boucicault's box-office predictions. Eschewing the marvellous stage effects of his sensation dramas for a 'society drama' relying on its 'literary treatment', *Hunted Down* had its roots in the earlier tradition of bigamy dramas while making full use of resonances and ambiguities of meaning in its carefully constructed dialogue.

The heroine of the title, Mary Leigh is happily married to a successful painter, John, with whom she has two children. A malicious busybody turns up some old letters, forcing Mary to confess to her sister-in-law, Lady Glencarrig, that when she wed John she was the widow of a notorious forger, Rawdon Scudamore. Mary had married Rawdon when just sixteen because the only way to pay off her father's gambling debts was through her marriage settlement. Rawdon left her at the altar and he drowned soon afterwards while seeking to evade arrest. John knows nothing of his wife's embarrassing first marriage, because her visible suffering at any mention of her past has led John tactfully to avoid any mention of it. But Rawdon, according to stage convention, returns inconveniently from the dead, having faked his drowning to escape arrest, and proceeds to blackmail money out of Mary. He prevents her revealing the truth to John by threatening to claim possession of her children—under English law children were assumed to be offspring of the mother's legal husband unless he should choose to contest parentage. Mary's trials are exacerbated when Rawdon falls in love with her, now that she has grown into a beautiful woman from the lanky schoolgirl he married. Rawdon's unwanted attentions lead Mary to be suspected of an adulterous affair with him by both her sister-in-law and by Rawdon's devoted but neglected lover, Clara. When John is finally informed of their suspicions, he springs to her support, just as she is about to abandon her home in tearful disgrace. Rawdon thereupon reveals himself as Mary's legal spouse and demands his right to her children, at which point Clara reveals the truth: he was already married to her when he wed Mary. Mary and Rawdon's marriage was thus invalid, and Mary has been legally married to John all along. Mary asks John to replace her wedding ring on her finger, and husband and wife joyfully embrace.

Boucicault constructed his plot with 'considerable care', as the *Daily Telegraph* approvingly commented, in order that 'the unpleasantness that would otherwise be

---

[52] The printed licensing copy in the Lord Chamberlain's Plays Collection (BL Add MS 53052H) is dated December 1865, and was licensed for the St James's in July 1866. The text contains inconsistencies in characters' names and scene numbers (Mary's surname fluctuates between 'Leigh' and 'Dayes', for example), suggesting an interrupted process of revision. It is difficult to establish whether it was the version performed in Manchester or London, but details of the play seem consistent with plot summaries provided in contemporary reviews of the London performance.

[53] Boucicault, 'Leaves from a Dramatist's Diary', 234.

suggested by a plot of this kind is altogether removed'.[54] But while ensuring that Mary's first marriage was not only invalid but also unconsummated, Boucicault introduced in plot, dialogue, and situation the constant presence of illicit sexuality. Before the bigamy plot is even introduced, the settled sorrow of Clara, who works as an artist's model for John, raises the suspicion that she is a fallen woman, a suspicion which seems confirmed when she describes herself as 'one beyond the reach of help'.[55] Mary similarly first appears to harbour past sexual guilt when she is confronted by her sister-in-law with letters 'full of such reproaches as left no doubt concerning the relations subsisting between the writer and her faithless correspondent' (I, 8). Mary at first denies all, but left alone she offers the audience the classic posture of despairing guilt: 'MARY *who has affected composure, now falls, with a groan, with her face on the table*' (I, 10). Suspicions of her fallenness only seem to be symbolically confirmed when it is revealed that Mary has recently modelled for her husband in his painting of 'The Death of Jane Shore', a mistress of Edward IV, whose tearful repentance was a theatrical staple.[56] No sooner is the shadow of sexual sin lifted by the revelation of her first marriage, than Mary is once again plunged into guilt by Rawdon's return from the dead. She determines at once to pursue the virtuous course taken by Pixérécourt's and Buckstone's wives with two husbands, and leave her bigamous marriage: 'Do you think I can share this man's home now, when every day becomes an imposture and every night a crime?' (I, 15). Forced to remain in the house where she believes her presence has been transformed from a 'blessing' into 'a curse', Mary suffers all the guilt of a woman wracked by adulterous passion, and at first seems to close up at her husband's approach 'like a sensitive plant' (I, 16; II, ii, 22). Her self-control finally cracks, however, and she begs John to run away with her like an adulterous lover:

MARY: Heaven forgive me. No, no: I—I cannot leave him (*she clings to him*) Forgive me for all I have made you suffer, will you not? There, do not speak; but listen to me. Can you consent to leave England with me—taking with us our children—and seek a refuge where no trace shall ever betray our seclusion? Can you, for my sake, sever yourself from every other tie on earth, desert your ambition, and give up your life?

(II, ii, 26)

Mary's travails provide the familiar spectacle of suffering virtue, though her love for John and their children is in conflict with social morality and legality. Boucicault sets love against law right through the final showdown, when John confronts Rawdon who seeks to claim mother and children:

RAWDON: She is my lawful wife—and these—
JOHN: Lay but a finger on them, or on her, and by the Heaven you insult I will make her your widow! (LADY GLENCARRIG *and the party hold* JOHN *back*.) This

---

[54] *Daily Telegraph* (6 November 1886), 6.
[55] Dion Boucicault, *The Two Lives of Mary Leigh*, LCP, BL Add MS 53052H, I, 7.
[56] Nicholas Rowe's *The Tragedy of Jane Shore* (1714) remained popular throughout the nineteenth century, joined in 1876 by a new version by W. G. Wills.

woman is mine!—was given into my hands by HIM who made her. These are my flesh and blood. The law cannot unmake them, and shall not tear them from me, while I have a life to stand before them and defend my own.

RAWDON: I know how to enforce my rights, and the opinion of society will bring you to your senses.

(III, ii, 32–3)

The opinion of society actually offers its sympathy and support to the beleaguered Mary, even before she is revealed to be John's legal spouse.

In addition to staging Mary's enduring attachment to John in the language of illicit desire, Boucicault doubles the ghostly presence of adultery in the play by having both Lady Glencarrig and Clara suspect Mary of a liaison with Rawdon. Clara finds a letter from Mary to Rawdon declaring that he has made her wretched, that she now turns with a sick heart from husband and children, and that if he comes near her she can bear her life no longer and will leave home. A scene follows in which Clara confronts Mary in the hearing of Lady Glencarrig, each woman suspecting the other of sexual guilt: Mary believes herself guilty of bigamy and that Clara is Rawdon's rejected mistress; Clara and Lady Glencarrig believe Mary to be Rawdon's mistress. Begging Mary not to take Rawdon from her, Clara sets off a sequence of declarations that ambiguously sound like confessions of guilt:

MARY: Oh—woman—why do you torture me? would that I could break the bonds that unite us! Has he not brought desolation to my breast—dishonour to my home?
CLARA: You had prepared to leave it—to desert Mr Dayes and your children.
MARY: Oh! would that I could take with me the shame that they must share!
CLARA: I know what it is to love—and from my heart I pity you.
MARY: She—she pities me; yes—her fault is less than mine, and low as she is, she can look down on me.
CLARA: Promise me, if he comes here, you will refuse to see him.
LADY GLENCARRIG: You may rest assured of that. (MARY *utters a suppressed cry and recoils*. LADY G. *advances*.) Mrs Dayes will resign herself to respect her position, however she may be unworthy to occupy it.

(II, iii, 27)[57]

Adultery is everywhere and nowhere. Excised from the plot it is nonetheless repeatedly performed; in Pykett's terms, it is the irruption in the narration of what is suppressed in the narrative. The play's construction invites audience sympathy for women who find their passions at war with society's laws, women who enact multiple forms of sexual temptation, guilt, and remorse, but who are finally revealed to be technically guiltless of a single misdemeanour.

Boucicault's play had exploited bigamy drama's old sleight-of-hand to the full, and critics approved of *Hunted Down*'s skilful negotiation of such murky waters, com-

[57] The name 'Dayes' instead of 'Leigh' here is an indication of incomplete revision, as is the misnumbering of this as scene ii in the script.

mending Boucicault on the 'consummate' and 'delicate' skill of the writing in his 'elegantly constructed' play, in which the 'human element' and 'psychological development' were declared to be the dominant concern.[58] Boucicault's subtext of illicit desire is only covertly alluded to, the heroines' passions being summed up as an 'obvious state of distress and emotion' for which the delicacy of the writing in some measure 'compensate[s]'.[59] Only Miss Herbert's performance of Mary's agonized farewell to her children was given specific description and commendation. Like Ellen Wareham and *East Lynne's* Lady Isabel before her, Mary Leigh's enactment of imminent maternal separation drew audiences' tears and applause, making it hardly surprising that by 1872 *Hunted Down* and *East Lynne* were touring in repertory together.[60]

While sensation drama set new standards for theatrical representations of women's desires, events outside the theatre made women's bodies and passions an increasingly prominent focus for public discussion. The publication in 1857 of Flaubert's famous novel of rural adultery *Madame Bovary*, and the *succès de scandale* in the following year of Alexandre Dumas *fils's La Dame aux Camélias,* about a tragically doomed courtesan (on which much more will be said in the next chapter) made French literature and its supposedly degrading influence on English morals a constant theme in the British press. The 1857 Matrimonial Causes Act, which brought in its wake journalism of the divorce court and detailed reporting of adulterous liaisons, has long been acknowledged as pushing the boundaries of what could be discussed in print, as well as introducing lurid tales of sexual adventures within the supposedly sacred domestic sphere to a scandalized and fascinated public. Society was further shocked by the appearance in London of a phenomenon previously dismissed as exclusively French: the *demi-monde*. Alexandre Dumas *fils* first popularized the term in his 1855 play, *Le Demi-Monde*, in which a fallen woman struggled to re-enter polite society by tricking a respectable young man into marriage, only to be foiled by one of her previous lovers—a man who gains the title of 'honnête homme' [honest man] by opening the young man's eyes to a sexual past to which he himself has contributed.[61] Dumas defined the term to mean the *déclassés*, those who had fallen in status, including divorcees, merry widows, and those abandoned by husband or lover, who lived somewhere between respectable high society and the low life of the common prostitute. By the 1860s the meaning had expanded to include high-class courtesans, the mistresses and companions of the rich. In the 1850s the London areas of Brompton, St John's Wood, Portland Road, and Regent's Park were infamous as the location of the villas of rich men's mistresses, but such women reached a new level of visibility with the opening of Hyde Park to the *demi-monde*, strictly on horseback; Rotten Row became the gathering place for ambitious horse-riders, so-called 'horsebreakers', who by a mutually beneficial arrangement with livery stables would ride their best

    58 *Times* (7 November 1866), 6; *Athenaeum*, 2037 (10 November 1866), 615.
    59 *Athenaeum* (10 November 1866), 615.
    60 See review for Prince of Wales's Theatre, Liverpool, *Era* (15 September 1872), 12.
    61 Alexandre Dumas, *fils, Le Demi-Monde, Théâtre Complet*, II (Calmann Lévy: Paris, 1890), V, v. First performed Théâtre du Gymnase-Dramatique, 20 March 1855.

horses in Hyde Park in order to attract rich clients for both the stables and themselves. Two scandals attracted particular attention in 1861, making the *demi-monde* the talk of the town: one was the legal battle by General Windham to have his nephew certified insane after he married Agnes Willoughby, the rich mistress of a brothel-keeper; the other was the rise to prominence of Catherine Walters and her fellow horsebreakers.[62] In 1861 Sir Edwin Landseer's *The Taming of the Shrew* was acclaimed as picture of the year at the Royal Academy Exhibition, and the young lady subduing a fiery steed was generally agreed to be an unmistakeable likeness of Catherine Walters, best known as the pretty horsebreaker 'Skittles'—soon even more famous as the mistress of Lord Hartington, the most eligible bachelor in London. The matter became sufficiently public knowledge for the *Times* to publish in June 1861 a letter signed by 'Seven Belgravian Mothers' (but almost certainly penned by prankster James Matthew Higgins) decrying the difficulty of securing husbands for their respectable daughters when the horsebreakers absorbed men's money and attention.[63] Editorials in the *Daily Telegraph* discussed the dangerous lure of these 'Circes', and predicted their imminent fall from St John's Wood to 'the gin shop and the kennel'.[64] In July 1862 the *Times* even published a letter requesting 'Anonyma' to adopt an alternative route as the crowds turning out to view her notorious beauty were making it very difficult to access the Exhibition.[65]

Prostitution in a more mundane form also came to increasing public notice in the final years of the 1860s, as arguments raged over whether to extend further or repeal new legislation, known as the Contagious Diseases Acts. The Acts, passed in 1864 and extended in 1868 and 1869, were introduced in response to phenomenally high levels of venereal disease in the armed forces. The CD Acts, as they became known, provided for the compulsory genital examination of suspected prostitutes in garrison towns and ports, and the incarceration of infected women in 'lock hospitals' until they were cured. The designers of the Acts and many of their supporters saw them as a first step towards regulating and containing prostitution, advocating a full system of state-licensed brothels and regular medical inspections along the lines of the system already operating in Paris and a number of other European capitals.

In the 1870 edition of *Prostitution, Considered in its Moral, Social and Sanitary Aspects,* William Acton used the scandal of the 'pretty horsebreakers' to reinforce his dire warnings about the ubiquitous threat of unregulated and avaricious prostitutes. Acton confidently stated that the *demi-monde* was no longer confined to Paris, and its 'yellow chignoned denizens' and 'dashing *equestriennes*' were scandalously ubiquitous and openly acknowledged in the Park.[66] Seeking to awake society to the urgent need to control the literally infectious infiltration of the prostitute

---

[62] See Henry Blyth, *Skittles: The Last Victorian Courtesan. The Life and Times of Catherine Walters* (Rupert Hart-Davis: London, 1970).

[63] *Times* (27 June 1861).

[64] *Daily Telegraph* (13 December 1861, 28 June 1861).

[65] *Times,* (3 July 1862).

[66] William Acton, *Prostitution, Considered in its Moral, Social and Sanitary Aspects in London and other large cities and garrison towns. With proposals for the control and prevention of its attendant evils.* (Second edition. John Churchill & Sons: London, 1870), 300.

into polite society, he warned urgently against the folly of men choosing to marry prostitutes, while calmly stating that, 'it may be relied on that the story of the much-abused *Dame aux Camélias* is, I might almost say, an every-day one'.[67] According to Acton, everywhere the 'woman of pleasure' deployed 'the terrible sword of jealousy...beside all the smaller weapons of the female arsenal' in order to exploit men's passions and so 'gain a rapid victory over every consideration of reason and expediency'.[68] This new incarnation of the fallen woman, active, resourceful, ambitious, and successful, was clearly a force to be reckoned with.

While a seemingly endless stream of plays about women of the *demi-monde* dominated the Paris stage, the office of the Lord Chamberlain and hosts of English adapters and theatre managers carefully edited the French originals to produce heavily bowdlerized and sanitized versions of the sexual exchanges and relations being dramatized: such goings on were peculiarly Gallic and simply did not happen in happy English homes or among the higher echelons of society. It was not until 1869, therefore, that the first home-grown modern English courtesan was given theatrical life, by none other than Dion Boucicault. *Formosa; or, the Railroad to Ruin* opened on 5 August, filling the vast auditorium of the Theatre Royal, Drury Lane, for 117 nights and making more than £12,000 for Boucicault and the theatre's manager, Frederick Chatterton. Cashing in on the success of his previous sensation drama, *The Flying Scud* (1866), which climaxed with a magnificent staging of the Grand National, this new sensation play offered the Oxford and Cambridge boat race rowed across the stage. The titular heroine of *Formosa* is Jenny, the daughter of a respectable prize-fighter turned publican, whose virtuous parents believe her to be a lady's companion, not realizing that she lives a double life as Formosa, 'The most celebrated of those tawny sirens of Hyde Park! The High Priestess of Ruin!'[69] Jenny is in love with Tom, an aristocratic Oxford student and stroke of the university boat. Tom's villainous cousin Compton Kerr recognizes Jenny as Formosa, and threatens to reveal her shameful identity unless she helps lure Tom to ruin, thereby spiking Oxford's chances of winning the boat race and enabling Kerr to make a fortune by backing Cambridge. Jenny complies and Tom is finally arrested for debt, having been cheated out of a fortune by Kerr and his associates at Formosa's luxurious Fulham villa. But Jenny's parents arrive at the villa by accident, and their sorrow and her shame prompt the courtesan to throw off her ill-gotten riches, using them instead to buy Tom out of debtors' prison. Two sensational scenes bring the play to a climax: the Cambridge crew demonstrate their sporting honour by springing Tom from gaol; and Oxford rows across the stage to victory.

The play appeared conventionally moral, and was granted a performance licence by the Lord Chamberlain's Office without demur. Formosa's wicked influence can be discerned even when she is disguised as an innocent maiden; before he knows Jenny's true identity, Tom senses the difference between his attraction to her and his love for Nelly, the pure adopted daughter of his Oxford tutor: 'Nelly is an angel—and as such

---

[67] Ibid, 46.
[68] Ibid, 47.
[69] Dion Boucicault, *Formosa; or, The Railroad to Ruin*, LCP, BL Add MS 53078Q, I, i, 7.

I love her—but I love Jenny like the devil' (I, I, 7). In her dramatic repentance scene Formosa throws her jewels to the ground and humbly begs her parents: 'I can never be to you what I was; but don't leave me to become what I shall be' (III, ii, 52). The play's initial critical reception was patronizingly dismissive. The *Times* described it as 'inoffensive' and declared a reluctance to 'deny plebeians the luxury of seeing a penitent courtesan flee from a career of glittering vice', commenting ironically on the 'gallons of sentiment' needed for the gullible public to believe that latent virtue could exist in either Formosa or her prize-fighting father.[70] Other papers were similarly indulgent (though many column inches were expended on the real rigours of boat race training and the absurdities of Boucicault's publican-cum-pugilist being employed as a coach), until a storm broke a week later in a series of letters and reviews inveighing against the dubious morals of a play which allowed delicate feelings to a woman the effect of whose profession would in truth 'deaden every worthy feeling'.[71] The *Illustrated London News* denounced the play as 'grossly indelicate and inconsiderately immoral', 'simply an elegant excuse for fashionable vice', and took particular exception to the suggestion that Formosa 'with all her treachery and meretricious habits, is good at bottom'.[72]

The critic and playwright John Heraud sent the Lord Chamberlain's Office a copy of his vituperative response to the play in advance of its publication in the *Illustrated London News* on 28 August, demanding that the play's licence be rescinded on the grounds that it could only encourage vice by rewarding its harlot's progress not 'in the manner of Hogarth, by the punishment and ruin of the vicious', but with her marriage to 'a gentleman of fortune and high breeding, who had been "spoony" on her for some time'.[73] The Examiner of Plays, William Bodham Donne, was forced to defend the licensing of *Formosa* to his outraged superior, arguing that vice and virtue were clearly distinguished in the play, that it offered 'none of the immoral casuistry that disfigures so many French comedies' and that in Formosa 'the spirit of a Magdalen is never dead'.[74] Donne was, however, forced to admit that

> The marriage of Formosa to which objections were raised was either an addition after the copy was sent me, or is so obscurely hinted in it, that when I read of it in the newspapers it extremely amazed me. I should certainly have struck it out, had I been aware of it. It is a compensation quite inconsistent with the general texture of the plot.[75]

Donne was a scrupulous reader, giving careful attention to both dialogue and stage directions, but Boucicault had outwitted him. Lord Spooner is a good-hearted but foolish admirer of Formosa, whose offers of expensive gifts are rejected by the courtesan, who declares that 'I wish to preserve one love I have inspired—pure and

[70] *Times* (7 August 1869) 12.
[71] *Athenaeum* (14 August 1869), 217.
[72] *Illustrated London News* (14 August 1869), 167.
[73] John Heraud to Spenser Ponsonby, 25 August 1869, Lord Chamberlain's Correspondence Files, Public Records, National Archive, Kew, LC Corr 1/221.
[74] W. B. Donne to Viscount Sydney, 2 September 1869, LC Corr 1/221.
[75] Ibid.

unsullied' (II, i, 26). She scrupulously declines his repeated proposals of marriage until Spooner joins her in attempting to buy Tom out of debtors' gaol. Formosa finds her jewels insufficient to secure Tom's release, and Spooner offers the title-deeds and mortgage to his estate, winning her admiring gratitude:

JENNY: I wish my worthless life could repay you for this night's work.
SPOONER: (*Dropping the parchments, and seizing her hand.*) Oh, Jenny!—don't—don't say that if you don't really mean it.
JENNY: I do mean it!

(IV, i, 54–5)

This snatch of dialogue is the only clue to their engagement, until a stage direction at the end of the play. The final scene is at Barnes Bridge, crowds gathered to cheer on the boat race, when '*Enter* DOREMUS, NELLY, EDITH, MRS BOKER, JERRY, *and* SPOONER, MRS DUDLEY, DUDLEY' (IV, iv, 59). All the named characters in the play are listed here, apart from the villains who have just been arrested. But no character named 'JERRY' exists—the name must be a typo for 'JENNY'. The mistake seems tantalizingly deliberate, a way of smuggling past the censor's watchful eye a stage direction which allowed the heroine to stand significantly beside her admirer. Whether the coded confirmation of their impending marriage was further enhanced by a prominently displayed ring on Jenny's finger or suggestively bridal garb remains uncertain.[76] Boucicault's sleight of hand secured the play a licence, enabling him to argue that his courtesan's marriage had been officially sanctioned.

Boucicault's skill in negotiating the censor was matched by the play's subtle critique of social mores. No explanation is offered as to how Formosa became a courtesan—there is no narrative of temptation, fall or economic necessity—but Formosa's story is paralleled with that of the good girl, Nelly, whose ex-convict father claims her from her foster-parents and pulls her down into poverty. Nelly endures hunger and long hours of labour (ironically making silk slippers for Formosa) rather than surrender her virtue. Boucicault makes it clear that society offers higher economic rewards for vice than for virtue: Bob hopes that his long-lost daughter will prove a good earner, and questions her guardian:

BOB: Is she good-looking?
DOREMUS: She is an angel.
BOB: That ain't much of a line o' business.

(I, iii, 21)

At which Bob resolves to try her chances in the music halls.

Boucicault's treatment of his heroine's profession differs markedly from stage convention. Her jewels, dresses, and riverside villa are signs not of what has been

---

[76] Reviewers consistently deduce Formosa's marriage, but none are more explicit than *Little's Living Age* in attributing this to 'a hint in the fourth act' (18 September 1869), 756.

done to her but of what she has done: she has agency and power, unlike the passively tearful heroines of seduction drama, and, like sensation heroines before her, is an unconventional mixture of resourcefulness, generosity, pragmatism, and genuine feeling. Not only does Formosa escape the watery fate of so many wicked women, but it is a man who takes her place: Nelly's wicked father throws himself into the Thames in a fit of shame. Formosa is intelligently aware of the dynamics of male vanity and social display on which her status depends; she remarks with wry discernment that Tom is only devoted to her

> Because I am the fashion. He wears me as he wears a cravat, because I become him. He despised the love of the modest country girl: he was ashamed of a weakness for poor Jenny. But when he met the too-well-known Formosa in the Park, surrounded by his betters, contending for her smile, when he saw the eyes of ladies of rank follow her equipage with more envy than contempt, his vanity brought him to my feet.

(II, i, 25)

Formosa is part of a whole system and milieu, surrounded by card sharps and women who have used their sexual charms to win themselves rich husbands and escorts. For all the extravagant hokum of the boat race and debtors' prison, it was the perceived verisimilitude of Boucicault's treatment that raised critical hackles. The *Illustrated London News* declared that 'while aiming at realism and eschewing poetry, he substitutes the vulgarest literalism', and the *Times* quoted Macaulay in support of its theory that '"a hundred little touches are employed to make the fictitious world appear like the actual world", and his objection applies with the fullest force to plays like *Formosa*, in which "realism" is the writer's main object'.[77] The *Athenaeum* similarly took the play as a serious reflection of contemporary life, while objecting strenuously to Formosa's 'ingenuousness' and 'purity'; in the language of William Acton and his fellow campaigners, the reviewer thundered that such women were a form of pollution:

> Nor is it unduly to limit the province of the dramatist to prohibit him from presenting upon the stage and investing with sentimental associations what is the foulest blot upon our social system and the greatest obstacle to our physical well-being.[78]

It was not the depiction of prostitution on stage which provoked moral outrage— no such furore had greeted Travers's *A Poor Girl's Temptation* (1858) or Haines's *The Life of a Woman* (1840). Indeed, the Victoria Theatre tried to cash in on the success of *Formosa* by staging *The Life of a Woman* under the title of *The Harlot's Progress, the Real Road to Ruin*, attempting to bag both the moral high ground and some invaluable publicity.[79]

In his diatribe in the *Illustrated London News*, John Heraud objected to *Formosa* precisely because it did not subscribe to the tropes and assumptions of earlier seduction dramas, all of which he reproduced with unshakeable confidence in their validity. Instead of being content with 'plain and homely' garments or at best 'the tawdry finery that bedecks the country barmaid', Formosa

---

[77] *Illustrated London News* (14 August 1869), 167; Editorial, *Times* (26 August 1869), 8.
[78] *Athenaeum* (14 August 1869), 217.
[79] *Era* (10 October 1869), 10.

'flaunts it in magnificent apparel', a corrupting vision when we 'reflect on the seduction which dress is to women generally, and how frequently they are tempted by it to the commission of sin'.[80] She should never have aspired above her station and mixed with 'the very elite of the educated youth of England', but have been content to marry 'her parent's potboy, or, at most, the neighbouring cheesemonger's apprentice' as would have happened had she properly 'remained in her primitive condition'.[81] Heraud's concern about the effect of Boucicault's 'flagitious drama' on 'the humble daughters of the land' is shot through with assumptions of paternalistic authority, not only over stupidly impressionable working-class girls but over the lower classes as a whole, who ought to be ashamed of themselves: 'Our playwrights and actors, indeed, perform before a degraded public, incapable of appreciating poetry, and undisciplined to moral action.' The Lord Chamberlain must ban the play to protect the rabble from itself.

Heraud's language was a response to the class dynamics of Boucicault's play. Melo-dramatic squires had long been given to seducing lowly maidens, but said maidens suffered appropriately for aspiring above their social station, and the aristocrats gener-ally returned to a proper sense of social and sexual responsibility. Boucicault presents a more insidiously pervasive dynamic of class exploitation. The *demi-monde* and the aristocracy are closely entwined with a very fine line separating criminality from high living. Card sharps and countesses rub shoulders at Formosa's villa: a swell reproaches his wife, just returned from her opera box: 'What's the use of dressing you like a lady, if you open your mouth and let Newington Butts out of the bag?' (II, i, 24, 28). Crimi-nality is the stylish norm; when Kerr's accomplice is arrested, he begs not to be taken to Bow Street: 'It sounds so low! Marlborough Street is the fashion!' (IV, iii, 59). A narrow margin separates the hero and villain of *Formosa*: Tom and Compton Kerr are aristocratic cousins, both enmeshed in vast debts from living and gambling beyond their considerable means. Tom treats lower-class women like disposable toys, playing with Jenny's affections when he thinks her a humble innkeeper's daughter, then pursu-ing her for social kudos when he learns she's a notorious horsebreaker. Drawn down into a vulnerable underclass, Nelly is treated by Tom as sexual prey:

> She implored me to have mercy on her, and not to add shame to her misfortune, but I saw she would yield to my importunity. So I persevered. She feared her love might overcome her—for she fled—and next day she disappeared.

> (II, i, 30)[82]

The only upright aristocrats in this cynical collection are the comical Spooner and the Earl of Eden, the diminutive cox of the Oxford boat, played in the first produc-tion by a Miss M. Brennan.

---

[80] *Illustrated London News* (28 August 1869), 215. Subsequent quotations are from same article.
[81] Heraud's curious choice of profession here may have been inspired by *East Lynne's* Afy Halijohn, who, after having an affair with aristocratic Francis Levison, finally settles for marriage with a cheesemonger.
[82] The issue of class exploitation was a significant factor in the campaign for repeal of the CD Acts. Josephine Butler, for example, quotes two letters from working men protesting against the sacrifice of their daughters to supply upper-class sexual appetites in the name of preserving the virtue of upper-class women: see Josephine E. Butler, *Social Purity* (Morgan and Scott: London, 1879), 23–7.

Taken aback by the critical ire that greeted the play, W. B. Donne surmised that protests against the play could be traced back to Barracks and the Clubs, because in *Formosa* 'certain social arrangements are struck at which, if not peculiar nor confined to persons of rank and wealth, are yet, from obvious causes, more prevalent where wealth and leisure abound.... I suspect one cause of the exclamations against *Formosa* is that it lifts a corner of the veil that hides a good many Anonymas.'[83] A review of the London production in the *New York Times* supports Donne's analysis of the class antagonisms underlying responses to the play. Noting the ubiquity of 'golden-haired Anonymas' in Hyde Park and in private boxes at theatres, the reviewer recorded that 'a solitary hiss from a private box' greeted the line about Newington Butts, and then,

> A little further on, the virtuous mother of the poor syren, overwhelmed with grief at the discovery of her daughter's position, makes some uncomplimentary allusion to aristocratic vices, and the house is pierced unpleasantly with four or five possibly aristocratic hisses. And then the whole house, thoroughly warmed up by and wound up in the action of the piece, and adopting the offending sentiments as their own, burst into one of those whirlwinds of applause that, in a great crowded theatre, become sublime.[84]

Courting the publicity that comes with such controversy, Boucicault and his theatre manager deliberately fuelled the class fire. A letter to the Editor of the *Times*, signed by Chatterton, but bearing the mark of Boucicault's style, explained that Drury Lane Theatre, the traditional home of British drama, had been facing financial ruin thanks to the refusal of high-born audiences to patronize literary drama: 'Shakespeare spelt ruin and Byron bankruptcy.' So Chatterton called Boucicault to the rescue, because 'he wrote for the middle classes and the working classes, who alone could be relied upon to support any intellectual entertainments; and that where they led their betters would follow'.[85] The audience, and in particular its female members, are offered as more reliable arbiters of taste than the *Times*'s critic: 'If he sees indecency where they do not, am I not permitted to suspect that he brings the excitement of an unchaste mind to the subject?'[86] A letter signed by Boucicault himself followed two days later to cement the argument. Accused, as he put it, of committing 'an indecent assault' upon the 'chastity' of the English stage, Boucicault declared *Formosa* to be a deliberate challenge to the limitations imposed on the popular theatre. First challenging 'obscurantism', whereby girls' innocence is supposedly protected by an ignorance of the world, he refused to shut the convent doors, because 'The proprieties and delicate sentiments which form the bases of society are engendered by a knowledge of wrong as much as by a sense of right.'[87] Boucicault then compared the constraints imposed on the popular stage to the considerable licence allowed to French and Italian opera, an entertainment

---

[83] Donne to Lord Chamberlain, 2 September 1869, LC Corr 1/ 221.
[84] *New York Times* (1 September 1869).
[85] Letter to the Editor, *Times* (24 August 1869), 10.
[86] Ibid.
[87] Letter to the Editor, *Times* (26 August 1869).

primarily aimed at the educated elite. Claiming a democratic mandate, Boucicault described *Formosa* as 'a revolution of the English stage', locating it simultaneously as a blow for women's education, free speech, and the right of the theatre to treat serious sexual subjects: 'I have broken down a barrier which prejudice had established. I have proclaimed a literary thoroughfare, and with the full approbation of the public. And I mean to keep it open.'[88] Whatever Boucicault's intentions, the genie was out of the box and the best efforts of critics and the Lord Chamberlain's Office would prove powerless to put it back.

[88] Ibid.

3

English Decency and French Immorality

Outraged by Boucicault's depiction of the *demi-monde* gathered at Formosa's luxurious villa at Fulham, 'An Amateur Critic' wrote to the *Times* in August 1869, describing the play as 'a long farewell, to that regard for decency which the national drama has so far been able to set off against its many minor follies and faults'.[1] French theatre has long been characterized by such indecent displays, the writer declared, adding acerbically that,

> At one or two of the Parisian theatres a performance would scarcely be considered complete without it. But I have never before seen or heard of anything like this open introduction of harlotry on the stage in an English play, and I have hitherto always fondly believed that this was one of the best recognised and not least important distinctions between the dramas of the two nations, that, however necessary it may be to exercise caution in Paris, one can in London always take one's unmarried sister or country cousins to a theatre without risk of prostitution, in all the glory of paint, powder, costly jewelry [*sic*], and superb dresses, being flaunted before them.[2]

This characterization of French theatre as mired in immorality, as opposed to the chastity and purity of the English stage, was a critical cliché by the 1860s, its terms of national difference deeply imbedded in contemporary critical discourse. In Augustus Egg's triptych *Past and Present* (1858) (*Figs. 11–13*), for example, French influences are shown to have played a role in the wife's adultery and the consequent destruction of the family: the children's collapsing house of cards is built on a volume of Balzac, and the mother, painted destitute under the arches of the Adelphi bridge, clutching her illegitimate child and gazing hopelessly over the moonlit waters, has her predicament ironically juxtaposed with a poster advertising 'Pleasure Excursions to Paris'. The threat presented by French indecency, the role of censorship in policing these matters, and the problem of how to read moral meaning were heated topics of debate through the 1850s and into subsequent decades.

Adaptations and translations of French plays had long been familiar fare on the English stage, and the repeal of the patent theatre monopoly in London in 1843 produced a huge increase in demand for Parisian imports. A massive expansion of theatrical activity and an accelerating demand for plays, together with an absence of effective international copyright agreements, meant that English theatre managers eagerly snapped up plays that had already proved their mettle in France. A disgruntled Dion Boucicault later described it as a 'deluge of French plays that

---

[1] Letter to the Editor from 'An Amateur Critic', *Times* (19 August 1869), 7.
[2] Ibid.

set in with 1842 and swamped the English drama of that period'.[3] Boucicault's self-interest in the matter was clear; his complaint about foreign invasion was in the context of sharply reduced fees for his own original compositions when theatre managers could rely on translations at a fraction of the cost. For good or ill, the development of the English theatre through the remainder of the nineteenth century was integrally tied to events on the Parisian stage.

Adaptations and translations made commercial sense, and the new international copyright laws of 1851 proved unenforceable, since it was impossible to discriminate clearly, as the Act required, between permissible 'fair imitations' and illegal 'piratical translations'.[4] Furthermore, playwrights were far from scrupulous in acknowledging their sources, and critics regularly complained that plays were advertised as 'new' or 'original' when in fact they were barely altered translations of a French work. This lack of transparency led critics to play a constant game of source spotting to the detriment, as some complained, of honestly creative playwrights who fell under the universal suspicion of borrowing from Parisian models.[5] The influx of French plays was also seen as a threat to the moral health of the English stage. Henry Morley in a prologue to his *Journal of a London Playgoer* (1866) called for a national drama 'with a clean tongue and a steady pulse' which could be held 'in wide honour as one of the strongest of all secular aids toward the intellectual refinement of the people'.[6] Despairing of the inherent immorality of so many French plays, Morley urged adapters to turn to the old English dramatic stock of the Renaissance instead of the putrid products of Paris: 'It would be easier as well as wholesomer to pare the sound old English apple than to scoop and cook and sugar these rotten French windfalls to the English taste.'[7] As John Bishop has noted of mid-century theatrical criticism: 'The notion of "French" drama helped critics define an "English" dramatic domain and police its borders, highlighting at once the virtues and deficiencies of domestic genius.'[8] Bishop argues that anti-French sentiment was a means of shaping English identity in an era of increased geographic mobility and communication, resulting in a particular distaste for the hybrid Anglo-French nature of adaptations.[9] Home-grown products, no matter what their subject matter, were superior to those tainted by Gallic influences. Boucicault even drew praise in the *Examiner* for *Formosa*'s pathetic scenes and epigrammatic dialogue but especially because '*Formosa*, let us add, as another recommendation, is *not* adapted from the French.'[10]

---

[3] Dion Boucicault, 'The Decline of the Drama', *North American Review*, 125:2 (September 1877), 243.

[4] See John Russell Stephens, *The Profession of the Playwright: British Theatre 1800–1900* (Cambridge University Press: Cambridge, 1992), 102.

[5] See, eg, Henry Morley, *The Journal of a London Playgoer from 1851 to 1866* (Routledge: London, 1866), 26, 259; William Archer, *The Old Drama and the New: An Essay in Re-valuation* (Dodd, Mead and Co.: New York, 1929), 32–3. See also, Frank Rahill, *The World of Melodrama* (Pennsylvania State University Press: University Park, PA, 1967), chap. XXIII, 'The Fine Art of Plagiarism'.

[6] Morley, Prologue, *Journal of a London Playgoer*, 11.

[7] Ibid, 28.

[8] John Bishop '"They manage things better in France": French Plays and English Critics, 1850–1855', *Nineteenth Century Theatre*, 22:1 (Summer 1994), 5.

[9] Ibid, *passim*, esp. 22–9.

[10] *Examiner* (14 August 1869), 520.

When William Bodham Donne was promoted in 1854 to Examiner of Plays from his previous role of deputy, he was in no doubts as to the primary challenge that faced him, declaring that 'The theatre indeed, at the present moment, is in more danger from the social and sentimental corruptions of the French stage than from exhibitions of open ruffianism or the coarser species of vice and crime.'[11] His diagnosis of the primary threat to the English stage characterized the mid-century shift in the focus of stage censorship from political issues to the protection of 'public morals'. The 'deluge' of French plays whose arrival Boucicault deplored in the 1840s only increased in number through subsequent decades. Regular seasons of visiting French companies at the St James's Theatre under John Mitchell's management from 1842 onwards only compounded the censor's problems.[12]

In a pamphlet written in 1853, enumerating the failures of the international copyright act, the actor and manager Charles Mathews expatiated on the immorality of French drama, characterizing its subject matter as, 'Milliners' girls and lawyers' clerks living together in the most unceremonious manner; actresses talking openly and unblushingly of their numerous lovers; ballet-girls, with accidental children by unknown fathers...', a characterization which a reviewer in the *Westminster Gazette* noted was not in the slightest degree exaggerated.[13] Looking back in 1907 on the development of French theatre through the nineteenth century, the critic A. B. Walkley offered a far more sympathetic view of its concerns, explaining that French playwrights were concerned above all with 'ideas about society', and more specifically 'ideas about private ethics, the relations of men and women, fathers and children, the disparity between the Civil Code and the moral law'.[14] These issues were brought to the fore in France by the instability of laws and penalties relating to matters of sexual morality.

In England, the debates over marriage laws, custody rights, and laws governing married women's property which preceded and succeeded new legislation such as the Infants and Child Custody Bill of 1839, the Matrimonial Causes Act of 1857, and the Women's Property Act of 1870 all served to focus journalistic and public attention on the role and rights of mothers and wives. But for all that such legislation chipped away at the principle of 'feme covert' whereby, in Sir William Blackstone's words, 'the husband and wife are one person in law', in comparison with the upheaval and reversals of French law in the aftermath of the French Revolution the legal status of English women remained remarkably stable.[15] Though the 1857 Act made divorces available through civil law courts, rather than through the slow

[11] William Bodham Donne, *Essays on the Drama and on Popular Amusements* (Tinsley Brothers: London, 1863), 130–1. Quoted in Dominic Shellard and Steve Nicholson, with Miriam Handley, *The Lord Chamberlain Regrets...: A History of British Theatre Censorship* (British Library: London, 2004), 54.

[12] For further details of the French seasons at the St James's Theatre, see W. Macqueen-Pope, *St James's: Theatre of Distinction* (W. H. Allen: London, 1958), and John Stokes, *The French Actress and Her English Audience* (Cambridge University Press: Cambridge, 2005).

[13] *Lettre de Charles Mathews aux Auteurs Dramatiques de la France. With a Translation according to the terms of the International Convention,* quoted in 'The English Stage', *Westminster Gazette* (January 1853) vol. 59, 95.

[14] A. B. Walkley, *Drama and Life* (Methuen: London, 1907), 25.

[15] Sir William Blackstone, *Commentaries on the Laws of England* (1765–9), quoted in Joan Perkin, *Women and Marriage in Nineteenth-Century England* (Routledge: London, 1989), 1–2.

and expensive business of a private Act of Parliament, wives were only able to separate from their husbands by proving not only adultery but also bigamy, cruelty, incest, or desertion, whereas husbands had only to prove their wives adulterous. Lord Chancellor Cranworth argued in 1857 in the House of Lords that such unequal treatment was both inevitable and natural given that, 'A wife might, without any loss of caste... condone an act of adultery on the part of the husband', but a husband could not possibly do so because 'among other reasons... the adultery of the wife might be the means of palming spurious offspring upon the husband'.[16] The safeguarding of inheritance and property rights remained paramount, and English wives were not granted divorce on the same grounds as their husbands until 1923.

In France, constant revisions and reversals of laws governing adultery, divorce, property rights, and inheritance both reflected and fuelled heated debates on sexual morality. The French obsession with adultery was ascribed by Alexandre Dumas *père,* in his mid-century memoirs, to the changes to marriage law brought in by the Napoleonic Code in 1804. Outlawing primogeniture, the new laws decreed that all children within a marriage, including daughters, must inherit equally. From this moment, Dumas explained,

> [A father] cared very much whether these children were really his, because the child who is not at all his, but shares his fortune with those who are, is, plainly speaking, a thief.
>
> And that is why adultery is a crime in the nineteenth century and why cuckoldry was a joke in the seventeenth century.[17]

Numerous changes to matrimonial and familial law followed the French Revolution and the introduction of what became known as the Civil Code, many of which were subsequently overturned with the return of the Bourbon monarchy in 1814. Most notably, divorce was authorized in 1792, considerably restricted in 1803 and then outlawed altogether from 1814 until the Naquet Law of 1884. Alongside changes in divorce and inheritance law, punishments for male and female adultery were frequently revised, though the relative inconsequentiality of the former as compared to the heinousness of the latter was repeatedly enshrined in unequal legal penalties. As a result of this legal instability, debates raged over the morality of marriage, and the notion of the transparently 'natural' was lost, as Patricia Mainardi has observed:

> When laws change repeatedly within a lifetime, reversing themselves several times, the result is often widespread insecurity and cynicism: once the guise of 'normalcy' has fallen away and all theoretical positions must be argued, ideology is revealed in all its nakedness.[18]

---

[16] Hansard, vol.145, 496; quoted in Perkin, *Women and Marriage*, 24.

[17] Alexandre Dumas, 'Le cocuage, l'adultère et le code civil', *Mes Mémoires* (1852–5), quoted in Patricia Mainardi, *Husbands, Wives, and Lovers: Marriage and its Discontents in Nineteenth-Century France* (Yale University Press: New Haven, CT, 2003), 2.

[18] Mainardi, ibid, 3.

Adultery became a literary and artistic obsession in nineteenth-century France, inspiring a plethora of paintings, cartoons, novels, and plays depicting cuckolded husbands and wives caught *in flagrante*.

Alongside and underlying these changes in legislation, a wider social debate had been taking place in France since the mid-eighteenth century over the relative merits of companionate marriage, based on love—the *mariage d'inclination*—and the *mariage d'intérêt* or *mariage de raison*, arranged by the older generation and viewed as a union of family interests. A faint reflection of this debate can be traced in early nineteenth-century English melodramas of cross-class seduction and marriage. When foolish maidens disregard parental authority and fall victim to aristocratic wiles, their consequent suffering and remorse imply that parentally sanctioned marriage within their own class would have been the wiser choice. But the frequent reformation of melodrama's aristocratic seducers, seeking their future father-in-law's forgiveness and blessing on their cross-class match, conversely implies that true love can conquer all. What starts as a cautionary tale recommending a *mariage de raison*, submission to parental authority, and the necessary suppression of personal desires, thus ends with the romantic triumph of the *mariage d'inclination*.

Eugène Scribe's hugely successful play *Le Mariage de Raison* (1826) argued the superior merits of class, property, and reason over passion and romance as a basis for matrimony.[19] The virtuous and pretty orphan Suzette, daughter of a chambermaid, has been brought up in the aristocratic household of General de Bremont and is now being courted by his son Edouard. The General warns against the inevitable unhappiness of cross-class misalliances, confessing the misery and intellectual frustration that followed from his own unhappy first marriage to a woman below his station. Determined that his own son should make a financially advantageous match, the General marries Suzette off to his aged and one-legged retainer Bertrand. Undeterred, his wayward son Edouard tries to tempt Suzette into an adulterous elopement, only to be thwarted by Bertrand's timely arrival. The revelation that Edouard is a serial philanderer and that Bertrand had generously settled money on her long before their marriage finally reconciles Suzette to her *mariage de raison*.

An English adaptation of Scribe's play by Edward Fitzball opened at the Adelphi Theatre on 3 November 1828, tailored to the more sentimental tastes of an English audience.[20] In Fitzball's comedy, Ellen is the object of aristocratic young Alfred's unscrupulous attentions, but adultery is never in question—Alfred's father has no power to marry her off, and, even when free and single, she responds with virtuous outrage to Alfred's suggested elopement. Alfred is duly unmasked as a fickle and unscrupulous libertine, and the wisdom of his father's opposition is confirmed—disinterested wisdom in this case, as no wealthier match is in prospect for his son. Romance is also given its due. The one-legged Bernard is transformed by Fitzball into Linstock, a retired solder who is deeply but silently in love with Ellen, and

---

[19] First performed Théâtre Gymnase, Paris, 10 October 1826. It was reprinted four times in its first year.
[20] Edward Fitzball, *A Libertine's Lesson*, Dicks' No. 598.

whose romantic suitability is revealed not just in his financial generosity but in his heroism—Ellen's love for Linstock is confirmed when she learns that he lost his arm fighting a dangerous duel to rescue Alfred from the consequences of his serial philandering. Fitzball thus treated his audience to a happy marriage of both love and reason, neatly evading the conflicts at the heart of Scribe's original. By removing even the possibility of adultery and sidestepping the serious debates on which the play hinged, Fitzball demonstrated the principles of theatrical adaptation that were to dominate the English theatre for decades to come.

Given the significant and enduring influence of French theatre in England, it is necessary to trace the development of theatre in France through the second half of the nineteenth century in order to understand its impact on the representation of sexual issues on the English stage. By the mid-century adultery had become a cliché on the Parisian stage, a predictable vaudeville plot. An 1846 cartoon by Gavarni showed a complacent husband, happily absorbed in the play before him, while beside him his wife and friend exchange sly looks: 'Au Théâtre Français. Le Cent-et-unième Représentation de *Le Mari, La Femme et L'Amant*' [At the Théâtre Français: the hundred-and-first performance of *The Husband, The Wife and the Lover*].[21] At the beginning of the 1850s the Comédie Française was dominated by the mechanical 'well-made' plays of Scribe and his imitators, in which precisely engineered plot construction was of primary importance. The early verse dramas of Émile Augier started to move the topic of adultery from the province of comic frivolity to that of sentimental morality, emphasizing the need to protect society and the home from the incursions of prostitution and adultery. But social realism established itself on the Parisian stage in the form of Alexandre Dumas *fils*'s *La Dame aux Camélias*, which premiered at the Théâtre de Vaudeville on 2 February 1852, influencing theatrical depictions of the fallen woman for decades to come in both England and France. The play was a huge and instant success, from the opening act through to the final curtain, when, according to Théophile Gautier, the author was showered with bouquets which spectators 'tore from their bosoms, drenched with tears'.[22]

Adapted by Dumas from his 1848 novel of the same name, *La Dame aux Camélias* stages the love and self-sacrifice of a consumptive courtesan, Marguerite Gautier, who falls in love with a respectable young man, Armand Duval. Abandoning the luxuries and excesses of Paris, Marguerite retires for the summer to a secluded rural retreat with Armand, recovering her health but ruining her finances, as she sells off jewels, carriages and cashmeres to finance their idyll. Concerned for his son's honour and property, M. Duval confronts Marguerite. He appeals to the courtesan's newly revealed moral conscience, asking her to abandon Armand for the sake of his sister, a pure girl whose marriage to a noble young man has been prevented by her brother's scandalous affair. Marguerite accepts as bitter truth

[21] *Affiches Illustrées: Annonces, réclames, enseignes*, in *Le Charivari*, 28 May 1846, reproduced in Mainardi, 223.

[22] Quoted in Marvin Carlson, *The French Stage in the Nineteenth Century* (Scarecrow Press: Metuchen, NJ, 1972), 121.

M. Duval's assertion that Armand's love will turn to contempt as her aging face destroys the illusion that holds him. Begging a chaste fatherly kiss as blessing from M. Duval, she breaks off her relationship with Armand, telling him that she is returning to Paris as the mistress of another man. Her sacrifice is rewarded by declining health and public humiliation, when Armand denounces her supposed greed, contemptuously flinging money at her as she faints. The final act sees Marguerite dying of consumption, isolated and debt-ridden, longing for a last glimpse of Armand. A letter from M. Duval announces he has taken pity on her plight and has told his son the truth. Armand duly arrives to beg her forgiveness, make plans for their happy future, and witness her death.

Gautier congratulated the young playwright on having staged 'des scènes de la vie moderne comme elles se passent dans la réalité' [scenes of modern life as they really happen], noting in particular Dumas's courage in avoiding the standard subterfuge of explaining Marguerite's position on the outskirts of society by making her a dancer or an actress.[23] The play set a radical new standard in detailing the economics and conditions of a high-class prostitute's life. Marguerite Gautier was openly modelled on a real courtesan with whom Dumas had a year-long affair, Marie Duplessis, who lived luxuriously at a rate of 3,000 francs a month and died of consumption at twenty-three, leaving behind personal effects worth 89,000 francs and debts amounting to 50,000 francs.[24] Dumas broke with theatrical precedent by setting his play in present-day Paris—thereby cementing the relationship between Marguerite Gautier and Marie Duplessis for those familiar with her fate—previous treatments of the courtesan like Victor Hugo's *Marion de Lorme* (1831) and Augier's *L'Aventurière* (1848) having been more safely located in the morality and costumes of the distant past. *La Dame aux Camélias* also broke with centuries of euphemistic tradition by making unavoidably explicit the fact that Marguerite exchanges sex not just for silks and jewels but for hard cash. The play is punctuated by precise sums of money: Marguerite asks her protector, the Comte de Giray, to pay off debts amounting to 15,000 francs; when Armand contemptuously throws his gambling winnings at Marguerite the audience knows that they amount to precisely 800 louis; cheque books and creditors' bills are essential stage properties. The rich trappings of Marguerite's life are both her carefully accumulated savings and the necessary tools of her trade—she must advertise herself as a luxury commodity in order to attract more purchasers.[25] The play's

[23] Théophile Gautier, quoted in Roger Clark, introduction to Alexandre Dumas *fils*, *La Dame aux Camélias*, ed. R. Clark (Bristol Classical Press: London, 1994), 29.

[24] Dumas's novel was published in 1848 and had become a best-seller within a year of Duplessis's death. Dumas cashed in quickly on its success, writing the dramatized version in a week in the summer of 1849.

[25] An entry under 'courtisane' in Larousse's *Grand dictionnaire universel* (1867) explains that, 'The *courtisane* knows that she needs a *mise-en-scène* that will bring her close to the man who pays her. In other words she is a gambler who constantly doubles her stake. She receives one thousand francs per month from an entreteneur; by spending those thousand francs on entertainment and clothing expenses, she rarely fails to catch the eye of a spendthrift, who hastens to offer her three or four thousand, assuming that such a woman could not cost any less.' Quoted in Charles Bernheimer, *Figures of Ill Repute: Representing Prostitution in Nineteenth-Century France* (Harvard University Press: Cambridge, MA, 1989), 97.

courtesans are skilled operators in this market, and their acquired wealth is their only provision for old age in a profession which has a narrow window of opportunity—as the hardened Prudence warns Marguerite, selling off her jewels, cashmeres, and carriages to support her romantic idyll with Armand will lose her livelihood, income, and savings.

Contemporary French reviewers were struck by the accuracy and forthrightness of Dumas's portrait of the world of high-class prostitution. Marguerite is surrounded by women who live by the sale of their own or others' bodies, and the negotiations and exchanges of their profession are taken matter-of-factly for granted. Each category of kept woman, as recorded by Parent-Duchâtelet, the dedicated chronicler of Paris's sex trade, is included: from the faithful *grisette* Nichette, who lives in unmarried harmony with her lover Gustave and works honestly as a laundress to support herself, and whose life becomes an ideal to imitate for the reformed Marguerite; to the mercenary Olympe who complains that Saint-Gaudens has given her a coupé for her birthday but not the horses to go with it, and laughs openly at his request to be loved for himself alone; and Prudence, whose body has grown too old and fat to be saleable and who lives on the earnings of her younger colleagues, acting as procuress and go-between. Their clients are equally pragmatic: Saint-Gaudens, for example, feels too old for the undignified position of *amant de coeur,* hiding in cupboards and waiting in doorways while his lover entertains wealthier men, and he now accepts the need to pay more lavishly for his *amours*, acknowledging with humorous resignation the infidelity of his mistresses. While Marguerite falls in love and dies tragically, she is surrounded by women who negotiate their own financial terms, who live openly according to their own moral code, and whose lives continue mundanely into the future after the curtain has fallen.

For all the detailed verisimilitude of Marguerite's milieu, the play was still firmly rooted in the traditions of Dumas's predecessors; as A. B. Walkley observed: '*la Dame* is not the beginning of Realism as we know it; rather it is an end—one among many—of Romanticism.'[26] Marguerite's redemption through love, her shame and self-sacrifice make her, as Walkley notes, 'a true sister of Marion Delorme' and legions of other repentant and self-immolating magdalens.[27] She is no rebel against society's values, but humbly accepts her own position as an outcast; however open and unashamed she may appear in the first two acts, when M. Duval declares that her looks will soon fade and Armand's eyes will be opened to the disgrace and degradation of their relationship, Marguerite exclaims 'Oh! la réalité!...je me le suis dit bien des fois avec terreur.' [Oh! reality!...I've said it to myself in terror so many times] (III, iv, 153–4). She is as staunch a believer in bourgeois values as M. Duval himself, and accepts his arguments as self-evident truths.

Dumas also considerably revised the facts of Marie Duplessis's life and his own affair with her in order to bring them in line with romantic conventions. Born

[26] A. B. Walkley, 'Dumas Fils', *Playhouse Impressions* (T. Fisher Unwin: London, 1892), 75.
[27] Ibid.

Alphonsine Plessis, Marie Duplessis was almost certainly sexually abused by her father and pandered out to an elderly man, before she started an independent career as a kept woman at the age of fifteen. She graduated quickly from the bourgeois Monsieur Nollet to the Duc de Guiche, who gave her an education in music, dancing, deportment, and elocution, in addition to introducing her to literature and the arts. Rewriting Marie's history into the traditional narrative of repentance and lost innocence, Dumas erased the brutality of her early life and her rapid acquisition of wealth, education and independence courtesy of her success as a courtesan. The career of a prostitute must necessarily be constituted as a fall not a rise, so Marguerite longs for the purity of her country childhood: 'je me suis souvenue de mon enfance,—on a toujours eu une enfance, quoi que l'on soit devenue' [I remembered my childhood—one has always had a childhood, whatever one has become] (II, xiii, 132). This expression of nostalgia is prompted by her distaste for the emptiness of her luxurious existence, delivered in a speech which combines a conventional moral message about money not meaning happiness, alongside Marguerite's clear-sighted understanding of the motives which bring lovers to her side: 'En effet, nous avons des amants qui se ruinent, non pas pour nous, commes ils le disent, mais pour leur vanité; nous sommes les premières dans leur amour-propre, les dernières dans leur estime.' [In effect, we have lovers who ruin themselves, not for us, as they claim, but for their vanity; we are the first in their self-importance, the last in their esteem.] (II, xiii, 131–2). The duc de Mauriac, the rich and fatherly protector of the play, who finds in Marguerite the image of his own daughter, tragically killed by consumption, is the most marked revision of the facts: Dumas was careful to erase the real reputation of Duplessis's keeper, the octogenarian Count Gustav Ernst von Stakelberg, who met her at the spa town of Bagnères, and whose taste for young girls led him to be known as an 'executioner of virgins'.[28]

The play's hero, Armand Duval, constitutes the play's most palpable romanticizing of both the real-life events and the original novel version of *La Dame aux Camélias*. To create his fiction, Dumas merged his own affair with Duplessis with that of Edouard de Perrégaux, who married her in 1846 at a register office in London, but who afterwards seems to have broken off all contact until he attended her funeral a year later, finally ordering her body to be exhumed from its unmarked grave and reburied in a permanent plot.[29] Looking back on the play in 1867, Dumas remarked that Duplessis only ever played the first two acts of his drama, over and over again, never sacrificing herself for love because none of her lovers

---

[28] Virginia Rounding, *Grandes Horizontales: the Lives and Legends of Marie Duplessis, Cora Pearl, La Païva and La Présidente* (Bloomsbury: London, 2003), 46.

[29] Dumas included verbatim in the novel a letter he sent to Duplessis, declaring that 'Je ne suis ni assez riche pour vous aimer comme je le voudrais, ni assez pauvre pour vous aimer comme vous le voudriez.' [I am neither rich enough to love you as I would like, nor poor enough to love you as you would like.] Dumas *fils*, *La Dame aux Camélias*, preface d'André Maurois, édition établie et annotée par Bernard Raffali (Gallimard: Paris, 1974), 161. Dumas presented the original letter to Sarah Bernhardt, one of the most famous impersonators of Marguerite Gautier, in 1884. See F. A. Taylor, *The Theatre of Alexandre Dumas Fils* (Clarendon Press: Oxford, 1937), 10. Dumas claimed the identity of Armand for himself in a letter to Bernhardt on 28 January 1884, accompanying a copy of the play into which he had pasted his 1845 letter.

ever wanted it.[30] In the play, for all his jealousy and impulsiveness, Armand is driven by love. The lovers' final reconciliation never takes place in the novel, where Marguerite is repeatedly persecuted and humiliated by an enraged Armand, who tortures her by lavishing caresses on his new mistress Olympe, finally winning his way back to Marguerite's bed, only to insult her with proffered payment and further rejection. In the novel, Armand is motivated by pride right from the start; humiliated by Marguerite's teasing, Armand remembers fondly his bourgeois mistress, whose melancholy letters have previously drawn his mockery. He is determined to possess Marguerite in order to reassert his mastery and self-esteem, aroused by the challenge of attaining a universally desired luxury object. Her expense is part of her eroticism; it is the difficulty of obtaining her which constitutes her charm: 'il est bien heureux que l'imagination laisse cette poésie aux sens, et que les desires du corps fassent cette concession aux rêves de l'âme' [it is fortunate that the imagination leaves this poetry to the senses, and that the desires of the body make this concession to the dreams of the soul].[31] In the play Armand becomes the only one compassionately concerned with Marguerite's illness amidst all the careless gaiety of her circle, and their relationship blossoms into true love, the thwarting of which forms the tragic centre of the drama.

It was this particular mixture of romance and realism which secured the play's success, and which constituted its radical departure from theatrical and moral convention. Marguerite is both self-supporting and calculating courtesan and self-sacrificing and genuinely loving woman. The play's tear-inducing tragedy hinges not on her fall from innocence, but on the doomed course of her relationship with a respectable young man, an unlawful love which even Marguerite never dreams of cementing in matrimony. The play was sufficiently controversial for its first performance to be delayed for three years after its composition in 1849; it was banned by the French censors as an offence to public morality, and did not reach the Paris stage until February 1852, when a change of regime put the Ministry of the Interior under the control of the comte de Morny, half-brother to Napoleon III and an enthusiastic supporter of the play.

The commercial success of Dumas's play helped to set new standards in the theatrical depiction of illicit sexuality, while sparking off considerable critical debate. A great wave of plays on prostitution, adultery, and illegitimacy followed, and the fallen woman in all her various incarnations became a central figure on the Parisian stage. Émile Augier, Henri Meilhac, Ludovic Halévy, Victorien Sardou, Lambert Thiboust, Octave Feuillet, Alfred Hennequin, Henri Becque and countless other playwrights tackled issues of female sexual morality in the following decades. In his study on *The 'Courtisane' in the French Theatre from Hugo to Becque (1831–1885)*, Sidney Braun lists some seventy plays on prostitution, adultery, and the fallen woman between 1852 and 1885.[32] Outraged by what they saw as Dumas's

---

[30] Alexandre Dumas *fils*, 'A Propos de *La Dame aux Camélias*', *Théâtre Complet*, I (Calmann Lévy: Paris, 1896), 10.

[31] *La Dame aux Camélias*, 78.

[32] Sidney D. Braun, *The 'Courtisane' in the French Theatre from Hugo to Becque (1831–1885)* (John Hopkins Press: Baltimore, MD, 1947).

immoral sentimentalizing of a woman who sold sex for money, a number of play-wrights constructed plays as a direct riposte to Marguerite Gautier. In Théodore Barrière and Lambert Thiboust's *Les Filles de Marbre* (1853), for example, a young artist, Raphaël, falls in love with a courtesan, Marco, and they retire together to the solitude of a villa in the Bois de Boulogne.[33] But Marco takes none of Marguerite's pleasure in the purity of rural seclusion; growing restless and bored, she is drawn ineluctably back to the company of other courtesans, humiliating Raphaël before them and mocking his love. His eyes opened, Raphaël denounces Marco and dies painfully of a broken heart despite his mother's care. *Le Mariage d'Olympe* (1855) by Émile Augier was another overt counter to the romance of Marguerite. A young man of good family marries Pauline Morrin, formerly known as the famous courte-san Olympe Taverny, believing her to be inherently good and genuinely repentant. Olympe, however, rapidly tires of virtuous married life and is drawn back to her old ways, engaging in affairs and taking expensive gifts. As she threatens to destroy the family's honour, her father-in-law, the Marquis de Puygiron, shoots her.

A conversation in the very first scene of *Le Mariage d'Olympe* establishes the context for Augier's vituperative assertion of the irreparably corrupted nature of the courtesan. The Marquis is shocked to hear of the changes which have taken place in French society in the twenty-two years he has been abroad: courtesans not only disport themselves openly the Bois de Boulogne and in the best boxes in the theatre, but are actually represented on stage. As his friend Montrichard explains, they even marry into good families, courtesy of the latest absurd doctrine:

> ...c'est la réhabilitation de la femme perdue...déchue, comme on dit; nos poètes, nos romanciers, nos dramaturges remplissent les jeunes têtes d'idées fiévreuses de rédemption par l'amour, de virginité de l'âme, et autres paradoxes de philosophie transcendante...que ces demoiselles exploitent habilement pour devenir dames, et grandes dames.
>
> [...it's the rehabilitation of the lost woman... fallen, as they say; our poets, our novel-ists, our playwrights are filling young heads with feverish ideas of redemption through love, of virginity of the soul, and other paradoxes of transcendent philosophy...which these women skilfully exploit to become ladies, and great ladies at that.][34]

Olympe's irredeemable corruption can thus be taken as a refutation of *La Dame aux Camélias* and other similar treatments of the fallen woman: rehabilitation is a delusional myth. Dumas had been careful to end his novel by declaring that Mar-guerite was an exception, and that the very value of her story lay in its rarity.[35] Augier's anti-heroine shares her name with Dumas's mercenary and disloyal Olympe who delights in torturing Marguerite to secure financial rewards from a vengeful Armand. The circle that surrounds Marguerite includes fallen women of various shades of greed and pragmatism. The fact that Augier felt the need to create a dramatic antithesis to the self-sacrificing Marguerite demonstrates his disgust even at Dumas's single exception to a general rule: noble prostitutes are an impos-sibility, *nostalgie de la boue* is the only truth.

---

[33] First performed Théâtre du Vaudeville, 17 May 1853.
[34] Émile Augier, *Le Mariage d'Olympe, Théâtre Complet*, III (Paris, 1897), I, i, 434–5.
[35] *La Dame aux Camélias*, 310.

The fallen women whom Augier's Montrichard sees everywhere in upper-class society were not purely a figment of his fictional imagination; in Second Empire Paris the life of the *demi-monde* on stage reflected reality off stage. The duc de Morny, with whose help *La Dame aux Camélias* finally reached the stage in 1852, later became lover and financer of Cora Pearl, one of the most notorious courtesans of Paris. 'Les grandes horizontales' gained positions close to the richest and most powerful men in European society: Cora Pearl, born in Plymouth as Emma Crouch, daughter of a bigamous musician, was mistress in turn to the duke of Rivoli, to William, Prince of Orange, and to Prince Napoleon Joseph, cousin of the Emperor himself; Apollonie Sabatier, known as 'La Présidente', the illegitimate daughter of a viscount and a laundress, was kept by Richard Wallace, illegitimate son of the Marquess of Hertford, on whose death Wallace settled a huge fortune upon her; La Païva, born Esther Lachman and married at seventeen to a tailor, became mistress and then wife of Count Guido Henckel von Donnersmarck, who built in her honour the breathtakingly expensive Hotel Païva in Paris.[36] So ubiquitous and powerful was their presence that, when France was humiliatingly defeated in the Franco-Prussian war, the country's failure was blamed by many on the debilitating influence of courtesans like Cora Pearl and La Païva, who found it politic to exile themselves temporarily from France.

In 1867, disgusted by what he saw as his society's moral degeneration, Dumas wrote a new preface to his most famous play, 'A Propos de *La Dame aux Camélias*', in which he declared that fifteen years ago Marguerite was a possibility, now she could only be a legend in a society where courtesans and high-born women alike sold their bodies for money. Mercenary marriages and the inevitable concomitant adultery were reducing France to universal prostitution, the national blood muddied by the offspring of courtesans whose wealth bought them membership of a money-obsessed society.[37] Dumas dedicated his dramatic career to analysing, judging and inveighing against 'La Bête', the monster of female sexual incontinence, which manifested itself in the twin forms of prostitution and adultery. The Victorian critic A. B. Walkley summed up Dumas's dramatic theme as

> The revolt of the polygamous (or the polyandrous) instinct against the official monogamy of the West....To examine his theatre is an exercise in permutations and combinations. You have so many fixed elements: husband, husband's mistress, wife, wife's lover; you combine these elements in all possible ways, and to each way corresponds a play of Dumas *fils*. [38]

In Dumas's *Diane de Lys* (1853) a husband shoots his wife's lover; in *La Princesse Georges* (1871) a husband returns cowed to his wife in fear of being shot by his mistress's husband; in *L'Ami des femmes* (1864) a betrayed wife narrowly avoids committing adultery

---

[36] For details of all these women, see Rounding, *Les Grandes Horizontales*. Far from suffering the early death common among theatrical courtesans, these women lived long and generally comfortable lives. In the case of La Païva her longevity and wealth were such as to be celebrated in the rumour that her widowed husband preserved her body in formaldehyde, where it remained as though still animated, dancing in embalming fluid to the horror of his next wife.
[37] Dumas *fils*, 'A Propos de *La Dame aux Camélias*', 20–42.
[38] Walkley, 'Dumas Fils', *Playhouse Impressions*, 75–6.

thanks to the intervention of the titular friend, who knows women's frailty better than they do themselves; in *L'Étrangère* (1876) a woman hovers on the brink of adultery until her brutish and unfaithful husband is shot by a concerned witness. Pardon may be granted the fallen woman in circumstances of exceptional suffering and repentance—as in *Denise* (1885) and *Les Idées de Madame Aubray* (1867)—but any woman seeking to justify her own extramarital sex by invoking male sexual incontinence and the notion of an equal sexual morality must be taught the error of her ways—as in *Le Demi-monde* (1855) and *Francillon* (1887). Dumas invented the '*pièce à thèse*' or thesis play, its wisdom often communicated by a *raisonneur* who sees clear-sightedly through others' confusion to deliver a verdict which is further expounded in a lengthy preface. Dumas's *La Femme de Claude* (1873), for example, was prefaced by a long analysis of the perilous state of French morality under the influence of 'La Bête' and offered the simple advice of 'Tue-la!' [Kill her!], an instruction that was duly followed by the play's hero, who shoots his wife Césarine when he finds her guilty not only of persistent adultery but of attempting to sell a super-weapon to France's enemies.[39] Aberrant female sexuality had become the most pressing topic of theatrical debate, an issue on which hung the health of French morality, French society, and even the French military.

Given the extraordinary popularity among French dramatists of plays centring on questions of female sexual morality, and the heavy dependence of the burgeoning English stage on French translations and adaptations, it was hardly surprising that William Bodham Donne was bracing himself in 1854 to tackle an onslaught of imported theatrical immorality. It was not, however, the Examiner of Plays alone who faced a challenge; French adaptations might be cheaper and already road-tested, but managers and playwrights still faced the tricky task of how, in Henry Morley's words, to 'scoop and cook and sugar' them to suit English tastes.[40] As the popularity of seduction and bigamy dramas earlier in the century testifies, fallen women were reasonably familiar figures; it was crucially a question of the manner and style of their theatrical treatment. Notably, English plays picked out for critical approval often had sexually frail heroines. In 1852 Henry Morley singled out Tom Taylor and Charles Reade's *Masks and Faces* for particular commendation as 'a very manly and right-minded little comedy'.[41] The play's heroine, Peg Woffington, is an actress with a notorious sexual reputation, who takes pity on the wife of one of her lovers and sends him back chastened to the family hearth, while she herself ends the play as irrepressibly joyful as she began it. Morley expressed himself delighted that the authors 'do not suppress the sins of Mrs Woffington, in the act of exhibiting what virtues as well as sorrows neighboured them; and, while they represent her with a touching sense of her own degradation, they have yet the courage to show her accepted for her virtues by the innocent and pure'.[42] Morley commended

[39] Alexandre Dumas *fils*, 'A M. Cuvillier-Fleury', prefatory letter to *La Femme de Claude*, *Théâtre Complet*, V (Calmann Lévy : Paris, 1890), 171, 219. See also, Alexandre Dumas *fils*, *Le Dossier 'Tue-La!', constitué, étudié et plaidé par André Lebris* (Édouard Aubanel: Avignon).
[40] Morley, Prologue, *Journal of a London Playgoer*, 28.
[41] Ibid, 27 November 1852, 58.   [42] Ibid.

the play in explicit contrast to French plays on a similar theme (of which he gave no specific examples), in which nicely bred women were despised and an 'ale-house Polly' esteemed and respected. In literal terms of plot and dramatic balance, *Masks and Faces* would seem an unusual choice to exemplify healthy moral tone—after all, Reade felt obliged to conclude his novelized version of the play with Peg's reform, conversion and penitent death.[43]

Echoing Morley's emphasis on the English taste for purity, the critic Dutton Cook decreed that 'a heroine possessed of a clean bill of moral health is almost indispensable to dramatic prosperity'.[44] Yet the theatrical performance that drew his highest praise was Ellen Terry's as the betrayed heroine of *Olivia*, W. G. Wills's 1878 adaptation of *The Vicar of Wakefield*. The moment he singled out for particular praise was when Olivia, having eloped with the local squire, learns that their marriage is fake and expresses her indignation and remorse 'with a vehemence of emotion and tragic passion such as the modern theatre has seldom exhibited. Only an artist of distinct genius could have ventured upon the impulsive abrupt movements by means of which she thrusts from her the villain who has betrayed her.'[45] Joseph Knight commented of the same gesture that 'it touched absolute greatness'.[46] Terry's performance combined charm and frailty, and the impulse that appealed so strongly to English critical tastes was a perfect physical expression of a woman's natural sense of virtue outraged, her moral instincts overriding her other passions in spite of her former weakness. However frail or faulty their heroines, both plays offered a clear delineation of right and wrong; virtue and vice are instantly recognizable and the plots focus on event, not any form of moral or social debate. Moreover, sentiment and morality run side by side: the audience's sympathies are called upon exactly in line with conventional moral judgements.

This, in the view of A. B. Walkley, was the crucial difference between French and English tastes, between a theatre primarily concerned with ideas about society, its structures, strictures, and morality, and one where such 'criticism of life' was to be carefully excluded in order to keep itself 'pure' and avoid French immorality.[47] It was all, as William Archer observed, a matter of how you defined morality: 'Our stage, if it is not immoral, is certainly not moral, whereas the French stage is moral in its very immorality. Our dramas have no relevance to the moral facts and problems of English life, as the dramas of Augier, Dumas, Feuillet, and Sardou have to those of French life.'[48] For a 'handsome salary' the Lord Chamberlain or his deputy, the Examiner of Plays, are given 'unlimited powers to ensure that our stage shall on no account be moral', thus ruthlessly suppressing the heresy that a 'serious play...may conceivably affect human thought and action outside the theatre'.[49] English tastes

[43] Charles Reade, *Peg Woffington* (Richard Bentley: London, 1853).

[44] Dutton Cook, review of *Ninon*, Adelphi Theatre, February 1880, *Nights at the Play: A View of the English Stage*, II (Chatto and Windus: London, 1883), 244.

[45] 'Olivia', Court Theatre, April 1878, ibid, 182.

[46] Joseph Knight, *Theatrical Notes* (Lawrence & Bullen: London, 1893), 218.

[47] A. B. Walkley, *Drama and Life* (Methuen: London, 1907), 25–6.

[48] William Archer, *English Dramatists of To-Day* (Sampson Low, Marston, Searle and Rivington: London, 1882), 7–8.

[49] Ibid, 203.

did not favour plays that hinged on debates or moral problems. As W. B. Donne observed, faced with another bundle of French plays proposed for M. Félix's season in London, 'It is not that any of the plays now before me are positively indecent, coarse, or *au fond* immoral.... But in them are discussed certain moral questions—a kind of philosophy that is neither understood nor relished in this country.'[50]

The process of adapting French plays on provocative issues of sexual morality to suit English theatrical tastes was often less a case of adaptation than evisceration. Tom Robertson was the master of English sentimental comedy, acutely attuned to his audiences' sensibilities, and widely credited with bringing about the renaissance of English theatre in the 1860s. Robertson's adaptation of Augier's early courtesan drama *L'Aventurière* (1848) for the Haymarket Theatre in 1869 serves as a perfect example of the radical surgery necessary to avoid scandalizing or bewildering an Anglo-Saxon audience with a Gallic play.

Augier's *L'Aventurière* hinges on whether Clorinde, a woman with a dubious sexual past, should be permitted to marry Monteprade, a rich widower more than twice her age. The opinion of Monteprade's prodigal son Fabrice is absolutely not; despite having a rich sexual past of his own, Fabrice is determined to prevent Clorinde becoming stepmother to his innocent sister Célie. Fabrice unmasks Clorinde as 'La Cléopâtre', a notorious actress, but her enduring dignity and self-possession enable her to retain her hold on Montprade.[51] Fabrice thereupon pretends to be a rich German prince in disguise, and tricks Clorinde into transferring her affections to this more splendid prize. Finally rejected by Monteprade, Clorinde spurns any form of financial compensation, tears up Fabrice's proffered cheque and retires to a convent. Though the fallen woman is declared unfit to be a wife or stepmother, exactly how harshly she is to be judged remains open to debate. Confronting a disdainful Célie, Clorinde asks by what right the young woman condemns her, having never known the temptations of poverty and hunger, or how one renounces honour for a morsel of bread. Célie replies with remorseless certainty that circumstances make no difference to morality: Clorinde can only prove her repentance by excluding herself from society; this is God's law, the only one possible for 'les honnêtes gens' [honest people] (III, 237–9). The fallen woman's self-justification is passionate and forceful, but the virgin is given the last word.

The climactic confrontation of the play is between Clorinde and Fabrice. When she dares to suggest she could have made a good wife and stepmother, filling his dead mother's place, Fabrice denounces her as a viper to be crushed beneath his heel:

---

[50] Letter from W. B. Donne to the Lord Chamberlain, 24 March 1871, Lord Chamberlain's Correspondence, National Archive, Kew, LC Corr 1: 246. The plays in question were: George Sand, *L'Autre*; *Le Bâtard;* Victor Hugo, *Lucrezia Borgia*; *Seraphine*; Victorien Sardou, *Fernande*; Augier, *Le Mariage d'Olympe*.

[51] Émile Augier, *L'Aventurière*, First performed Comédie Française, 23 March 1848. *Théâtre Complet*, I (Calmann Lévy: Paris, 1897). Characters variously refer to Clorinde as an 'aventurière' [adventuress], 'saltimbanque' [acrobat] and a 'courtisane' [courtesan] (III, 213, 215; IV, 257). That she is not a pure woman is unequivocal, but the precise nature of her past remains indeterminate. For a superb analysis of the particular poise and self-control that Madame Plessy brought to the role of Clorinde, see John Stokes, *The French Actress and Her English Audience* (Cambridge University Press: Cambridge, 2005), chap. 3, 'Memories of Plessy'.

Vous, une femme? Un lâche est-il un homme? Non...
Eh bien! je vous le dis: on doit le même outrage
Aux femmes sans pudeur qu'aux hommes sans courage,
Car le droit au respect, la première grandeur,
Pour nous c'est le courage, et pour vous la pudeur.
Une femme, vous!—Tiens, va-t'en! (IV, 257)

[You, a woman? Is a coward a man? No...So, I tell you, the same contempt is due
to women without modesty as to men without courage, because the right to respect,
the greatest virtue, for us is courage, and for you is modesty. A woman, you! Hah!
clear off!]

This speech is a turning point in the play, one which finally masters Clorinde, who
has always longed to meet a man stronger than herself. Rejecting Fabrice's money,
she exits with dignity, inspired by the desire to win his respect. Fabrice thus freely
expresses his disdain for a woman with a sexual past no murkier than his own,
inviting attention to the double standard while allowing it to dictate the play's conclusion—though Fabrice ends the play a lonely and aging bachelor like his father.

In his adaptation *Home*, which opened at the Haymarket Theatre on 14 January
1869, Tom Robertson carefully extracts the uneasy questions about rehabilitation,
judgement, and the role of circumstances and environment in shaping a woman's
sexual choices that lie at the heart of Augier's play. Robertson's *Home* is in modern
prose, but the English dramatist's characteristic mixture of a measured dose of
domestic realism, humorous sentiment, and some arch theatrical self-consciousness
creates a reassuringly cosy atmosphere. Clorinde becomes the widowed Mrs Pinchbeck, who has fooled old Mr Dorrison into an engagement, but is outwitted by his
son Alfred. Crucially, it is only after Mrs Pinchbeck has been thoroughly routed,
having transferred her attentions to a supposedly richer man, that she is allowed
even a modicum of sympathy; where the action of Augier's play centres on debates
over sexual judgement, in Robertson's play the action is over before any question is
raised, so the pity finally allowed to the disappointed widow never raises a critical
dilemma. Clorinde's self-justification is cut, along with her impoverished past, her
dignity and her self-control; Mrs Pinchbeck is just a passive victim of bad men,
married off by her brother to unscrupulous husbands: as she wistfully puts it, 'I am
but a woman, and I had been schooled in the belief that all the world was bad.'[52]

Inspired by the good example of the innocent young girls in the play (who are
allowed no understanding of what is happening around them), Mrs Pinchbeck
tears up the proffered pay-off and ends the play a reformed woman (though she
was clearly not guilty of anything more than serial marriage and a mercenary eye
for a new husband). She determines to live honestly by her musical talents, and
Alfred watches her departure with comfortable superiority, declaring her to be 'a
real woman, who can't help being right-minded even when she's wrong' (III, 273).
Fabrice's devastating condemnation of the woman without modesty is reduced to
Alfred's refusal to be angered by Mrs Pinchbeck, 'Because you're a woman, and

---

[52] Thomas William Robertson, *Home* (Samuel French: London, 1869), Act III, 272.

I acknowledge the superiority of your sex over yourself' (III, 269). Alfred's sexual history is also erased—his only error is to have been a hot-headed youth who ran away to join the army. He ends the play happily united with the virtuous maiden, declaring his intention to pass their honeymoon at 'Home!', which concluding word he utters as he gazes contentedly at the portrait of his dead mother on the wall while his fiancée plays 'Home, sweet Home' on the piano (III, 274). Domestic bliss reigns, having never seriously been threatened.

Despite Robertson's careful dilution of Augier's play, even his sanitized version raised complaints. A reviewer in the *Pall Mall Gazette* objected that, 'There is some danger...of the adventuress attaching to herself more public sympathy than is strictly her due.'[53] While agreeing on the poetic justice of the widow's expulsion and the undoubted success of the piece, all the critics commended the play's 'fresh and natural' atmosphere, though the *Athenaeum* still found it necessary to emphasize the extent to which it was still premised on lax French behaviour, for 'Englishmen do not often open their houses in the fashion indicated in the play to people of whom they know nothing'.[54]

Robertson's excision of unsettling debates, toning down of sexual guilt, sheltering of young innocence, and injection of sentiment are mirrored in other playwrights' treatment of French sources. When James Albery rewrote Augier's *Les Fourchambault* (1878) as *The Crisis* in 1878, for example, he reduced 'Augier's ethics to palatable proportions', as the *Daily Telegraph* put it, in order not to shock the mythical 'young lady of fifteen' of whom the modern theatre manager lived in fear.[55] In *Les Fourchambault* an unmarried mother has brought up her illegitimate son alone, using her financial acumen to help him accumulate a significant fortune. On witnessing the imminent bankruptcy of the father who abandoned them, she persuades her son to use his wealth to rescue his father's business. Albery's adaptation erases the mother's past sexual guilt—an obscure glitch in the law rendered her marriage invalid. Albery also minimizes her business skills, removing her self-sufficiency and self-command, and instead inserting a conventional tableau in which she buries her head in her hands in shame when telling her son of his illegitimacy.[56] The delinquent father and recipient of her generosity is facing ruin thanks to his wife's extravagance. Considerably sillier than in Augier's original, this woman refuses to use her own money to bail out her husband's business, stubbornly declaring she has seen her lawyer 'and he says no one can touch a penny of my money' (III, 334). In an implied attack on the new rights granted by the 1870 Married Women's Property Act, she clings greedily to her settlement, deaf to her children's pleas and the loss of family honour, until it is demonstrated to her that she has spent three times more of her husband's earnings than she ever brought to the marriage in the first place. The illegitimate son opens her eyes

---

[53] *Pall Mall Gazette* (19 January 1869), 9.

[54] *Athenaeum*, No.2152 (23 January 1869), 137.

[55] *Daily Telegraph* (23 February 1885), in *The Dramatic Works of James Albery, Together with a Sketch of his Career, Correspondence bearing thereon, Press Notices, Casts, etc.* ed. Wyndham Albery, in 2 vols. Vol II (Peter Davies: London, 1939), 292.

[56] James Albery, *The Crisis*, in ibid, Act II, 330. First performed Haymarket Theatre, 2 December 1878.

to her parasitic position, forcefully overriding her objections, and leaving her humiliated but admiring of his unwonted male mastery: 'He is the kind of husband I
should have had', she gasps (III, 345). Like Robertson before him, so Albery excises
any real sexual guilt, injects an exaggerated degree of shame, and advocates female
passivity. Thus can French fare be made acceptable.

Preparing French plays for the English stage was not, of course, simply a matter of
catering to audiences' tastes but also, crucially, a question of what would be licensed
by the Lord Chamberlain's Office. As Examiner of Plays, William Bodham Donne
carefully read stage directions in French, German, and Italian as well as English, and
policed innuendo as well as overt statements. Donne did not impose a blanket ban on
errant sexuality; as his response to the furore over Boucicault's *Formosa* demonstrated,
implications and context were crucial. He claimed a careful discrimination between
'immoral' and merely 'painful' plays; he gave *Phèdre* as an example of the latter, in
which illicit desires are presented with a clear frame of moral judgement, repentance,
and punishment, and are thus unlikely to corrupt public morals—especially when
performed in a foreign language and so only accessible to an educated (and therefore
presumably more morally robust) elite.[57] But a consistent rationale behind the cuts he
demanded in the name of public morals was not always apparent.

It was predictable enough that the stage direction in *Un Frère Terrible*, '*à la fin
du pas ils prennent une attitude voluptueuse*' [at the end of the step they adopt a
voluptuous attitude], should be marked for omission, but less obvious why a man's
reverence for flannel petticoats drying on a washing line in *Howard Hawk* should
be censored.[58] Only reading the farce *John Wapps or some Information Received* can
supply a clue to why the statement '*She* knows, *she* knows, Tom, that I never
neglected it, and yet now she—oh!' should be marked by Donne for omission 'as
taken with the context they are positively indecent'.[59] As Miriam Handley has
pointed out, censoring lewdness resulted in a prohibition on on-stage finger-
squeezing in *Bibb and Tucker Comedy* (1873) but, in *Mathilde and the Mulatto*
(1861), the audience was permitted to delight in the spectacle of Mathilde, drugged
and growing languid, while her would-be rapist gloats that 'before ten minutes you
will be entirely at my mercy!'—the implied judgement being that no inappropriate
on-stage touching, no matter how trivial, could be permitted but entertainment
could quite fairly be derived from the threat of sexual violence, an entertainment
which, after all, had a long tradition in the endangered virtue of the melodramatic
heroine.[60] As a censor Donne was a literalist and scrupulously thorough. All references to God, for example, were excised, including the deletion of Little Jo the
crossing sweeper learning the Lord's Prayer on his deathbed in a stage adaptation

---

[57] Letter to the Lord Chamberlain, 2 September 1869, LC Corr 1/221.
[58] Entries for *Un Frère Terrible,* St James's, 31 May 1852, and *Howard Hawk*, Surrey, 13 September
1858, in Lord Chamberlain's Daybook (LCD), BL Add MS 53703, pp.90, 127.
[59] Entry for *John Wapps*, Surrey, 13 October 1860, in ibid, 195.
[60] Entries for *Bibb and Tucker Comedy*, LCD, BL Add MSS 53705, p.6 and 53703, p.190, quoted
in Shellard and Nicholson with Handley, *The Lord Chamberlain Regrets*, 46.

of *Bleak House* in 1854.[61] But in matters of sexual morality such blanket bans were neither feasible nor, certainly from a commercial point of view, desirable. The task of policing French imports was clearly one which taxed Donne's patience and tolerance, as he responded in 1871 to M. Félix's request to have a ban lifted from *La Vie Parisienne*: 'In my opinion the less that is said or shown of its *Vie* the better. Nay, it appears to me that the wish for a reversion of the sentence is as signal an instance of bad taste and absence of feeling in a Frenchman as can be imagined.'[62]

In her 1875 novel, *Hostages to Fortune*, Mary Elizabeth Braddon drew on her years as an actress to give an inside view of a theatre manager's negotiation of the censor. The usual method, her manager declares, is to 'make our plots more improbable than the wildest fairy tale', resulting in a 'purely English style of construction in which probability is sacrificed to propriety'.[63] Donne was well aware of this technique, whereby the original sexual motive was removed and a patently inadequate one put in its place, leaving a logical disconnect inviting audiences to deduce what had been excised. Faced with Sardou's *Fernande*, in which a cast-off mistress tricks her ex-lover into marrying the fallen woman of the title, Donne commented of a bowdlerized version: '*Fernande* has no blemish on her character: yet her remorse is retained, and so the play is absurd. The *raison d'être* for repentance not existing. I think the accommodation was a very thin veil for the real state of the case.'[64] Confronted with nothing more than a logical gap, however, Donne granted it a licence. Braddon's fictional theatre manager goes further, however, determining to smuggle past the censor an infamous Parisian drama *L'Ange Déchu*, re-titled *The Fallen Angel*. She fancies 'the immorality is too refined to appear in a hasty perusal' and, sure enough, 'By one of those accidents which make theatrical adventure the most hazardous of speculations, the piece passes the censorship unchallenged.'[65]

Where Braddon showed indecency sneaking surreptitiously past the censor, William Archer went further, declaring that the censorship system repressed '[a]dvanced ideals' and 'the mere handling of any problem of delicacy and importance', while concurrently fostering '[v]ulgar sensualism' and 'coarse frivolity'.[66] Certainly the popularity of farcical treatments of marital infidelity supported Archer's assertion: the more comical a depiction of adultery, the more likely it would be treated with indulgence. Dion Boucicault's *Forbidden Fruit* (1880) was a case in point. The plot revolves around the hapless attempts of a lawyer to enjoy an evening's holiday from marital fidelity in the company of a beautiful circus performer, who is eager to be cited in a divorce case in order to gain valuable publicity.[67] G. A. Sala reviewing the play in the *Illustrated London News* noted the inaccurate reproduction of English

---

[61] Entry for *Bleak House*, Strand, 29 May 1854, LCD, BL Add MS 43703, p. 20.

[62] Letter to the Lord Chamberlain, 26 May 1871, LC Corr 1/246.

[63] Mary Elizabeth Braddon, *Hostages to Fortune*, 3 vols (John Maxwell: London, 1875), III, 281.

[64] Letter to Lord Chamberlain, 24 March 1871, LC Corr 1/246.

[65] Braddon, *Hostages to Fortune*, III, 281, 282.

[66] William Archer, 'The Censorship of the Stage', *About the Theatre: Essays and Studies* (T. Fisher Unwin: London, 1886), 164.

[67] First London performance, Adelphi, 3 July 1880.

life resulting from translating details such as a '*cabinet particulier*' and the working practices of lawyers straight from its French source, only to conclude that these 'absurd anomalies' were its saving grace, because 'Were it a realistic piece, the fundamental frivolity of the piece would make it not funny but objectionable.'[68]

Critics frequently cited James Albery's *Pink Dominos* (1877), an adaptation of *Les Dominos Roses* by Alfred Hennequin and Alfred Delacour, as an example of the freedom allowed to farcical treatments of marital infidelity but forbidden to serious considerations of sexual morality. Hugely popular, it ran for an astonishing 555 consecutive performances. The pink dominos of the title are cloaks worn by two wives who, suspecting their husbands of infidelity, invite them anonymously to an illicit rendezvous in the Cremorne Gardens. Unknown to one of the wives, her maid Rebecca has borrowed her mistress's old pink cloak as a disguise for her own adventures in the same pleasure gardens. Endless confusing partner swapping ensues in the secluded private dining rooms, during which the wives react with virtuous indignation to the heated advances of each other's spouses. Rebecca, however, is more compliant, leading to suspicions of illicit sexual activity when her sexual readiness is ascribed to the two wives. All is smoothed over once Rebecca's role has been clarified, and the husbands exonerate themselves by pretending they knew all along that the women with whom they arranged their assignations were their own wives. The *Daily Telegraph* complained of these shenanigans that the usual 'deodorising process' involved in adapting the 'muddy sources' of French drama had been neglected in this case, unconvinced by its claim to be a harmless farce.[69] Critics in the *Sunday Times* and the *Illustrated Sporting News* were, however, satisfied that the farcical nature of the play rendered harmless its 'somewhat questionable frolics' because they in no way aspired to social commentary or realism.[70] Whereas the *Illustrated Sporting News* claimed that the search for 'evil' by prurient playgoers would be fruitless, the *Sunday Times*'s critic hinted at the presence of coded meanings: 'There are many things in it which the seeker after innuendo will find to his taste, but there is nothing that may not be seen without a shock to that kind of innocence which is allowed to see any play at all.'[71] This coded indecency is most suggestively present in Rebecca's domino, a pink cloak that sustains a different injury in each sexual encounter: stained by one man spilling his coffee on it; a hole burnt in it by another's cigarette; torn by the eager advances of a third, who compounds his injury by piercing Rebecca with his pin in an attempt to repair it.[72] Stained, pierced and torn by a series of men, the sexually available woman's cloak may stand as a symbol for her body for those in the know, while nothing more than millinery damage is sustained in the eyes of the pure. So William Archer complained of Charles Wyndham's management at the Criterion Theatre that it was

---

[68] *Illustrated London News* (10 July 1880), 31. Sala, like a number of other reviewers suggests *Le Procès Veauradieux* as a likely model. See also *Times* (8 July 1880), 5, and *Daily Telegraph* (5 July 1880), 3.
[69] *Daily Telegraph* (5 April 1877), reproduced in Albery, *Dramatic Works*, Vol. II, 205.
[70] *Illustrated Sporting and Dramatic News* (21 April 1877), ibid, 208.
[71] *Sunday Times*, 8 April 1877, ibid, 206.
[72] *Pink Dominos*, in Albery, *Dramatic Works*, vol. II, Act II, 253, 257, 258.

financed by 'pieces which perpetually hover on the border-line of impropriety', generally French plays, rearranged to pass the Lord Chamberlain, 'and then leaving the audience to read between the lines, which it does with the utmost alacrity and penetration.'[73]

The permeability of the censorship system and the subtle ways in which meanings could be conveyed to those in the know are perhaps best exemplified by the performance history of *La Dame aux Camélias* on the London stage. Marguerite Gautier was the most famous theatrical courtesan of the nineteenth century, and her influence and impact can be traced through the succeeding century. The notoriety and reputation of Dumas's play posed a particular problem for theatrical censorship, its complex textual and theatrical history providing adapters and performers with resonances and references which proved impossible for the authorities to control. In order to understand this web of intertheatrical and intertextual meanings, it is necessary first to look back at Dumas's original novel from which he adapted his play, and at the particular associations and medical aetiology of consumption, the disease from which Marguerite dies.

As a disease, consumption—or tuberculosis as it is now known—perfectly combined the realism and romanticism of Dumas's play. According to nineteenth-century medical opinion, Marguerite's affliction could be directly traced back to her sexual promiscuity; a medical textbook warned its readers in 1852 that 'Of all vices, however, none are so apt to lead on to consumption as the unnatural or unrestrained indulgence of the sensual passions.'[74] The intrusion of such medical 'reality' into the text also fits with old Duval's assumption that Marguerite and Armand's relationship will have 'ni la religion pour appui, ni la famille pour résultat' [neither religion as a support, nor family as a result] (III, iv, 153), based presumably on the widely-held belief that female sterility was an inevitable concomitant of prostitution.[75] But Marguerite's death from consumption can be read both as a realistic (and poetically just) result of a life of sin, and, conversely, as a reflection of the spirituality and purity of her love. As Clark Lawlor has noted in his study, *Consumption and Literature* (2006), there was a strong Romantic tradition that read consumption as a sign of passion and genius, a tradition which would allow Marguerite to take her place alongside numerous fictional heroines whose tragic death by consumption is traceable to heartbreak and unrequited love.[76]

Nineteenth-century accounts of death by consumption, both fictional and historical, tended towards two contrasting extremes: either the easeful death, a painless

---

[73] Archer, *English Dramatists of To-Day*, 211.

[74] Richard Payne Cotton, *The Nature, Symptoms and Treatment of Consumption* (John Churchill: London, 1852), 70, quoted in Linda Hutcheon and Michael Hutcheon, *Opera: Desire, Disease, Death* (University of Nebraska Press: Lincoln, NE, 1996), 38. Dr Ryan similarly warned in his *Prostitution in London* (London, 1839) that 'this direful and I believe incurable disease … is often accelerated by venereal excesses'. 312. Quoted in Rounding, *Grandes Horizontales*, 56.

[75] See for example William Acton's assertion specifically in reference to prostitutes marrying that such unions are 'frequently barren', *Prostitution, Considered in its Moral, Social and Sanitary Aspects* (John Churchill and Sons: London, 1870), 40.

[76] Clark Lawlor, *Consumption and Literature: The Making of the Romantic Disease* (Palgrave Macmillan: Basingstoke, 2006), see esp. chs 1, 6.

and peaceful fading away as the subject grew ever more emaciated, the extreme pallor of their skin rendered deceptively healthy by the flushed cheeks and bright eyes of fever; or a racked and agonized death, accompanied by rasping breath, bulging eyeballs, emaciation, and swollen joints. In the novel of *La Dame aux Camélias*, Marguerite's death is long drawn-out and agonized, narrated through journal entries and letters by Marguerite herself and then her loyal prostitute friend Julie. Stretching over more than two months, these entries detail Marguerite's slow decay, tortured by pain, coughing blood, covered in burning plasters, unable to speak or move. Her excruciating physical decay is frequently juxtaposed with her former luxury: Julie describes her as dying 'au milieu de quelle misère dorée' [in the midst of such gilded misery] and Marguerite reflects on the irony of her wasted body, 'le corps couvert d'emplâtres qui me brûlent. Va donc offrir ce corps qu'on payait si cher autrefois, et vois ce que l'on t'en donnera aujourd'hui!' [my body covered in burning plasters. Go and offer this body for which they used to pay so much, and see what they'll give for it now!] (302, 297). This is the death prefigured in the novel's opening: Marguerite first enters the novel as a corpse, disinterred from its unmarked grave, her eye sockets empty, her lips eaten away, her cheeks two greening cavities. The body of the prostitute is reduced to its true essential nature: disease and decay. Marguerite's decomposing flesh only confirms the common view of prostitutes as, in the words of Parent-Duchâtelet, 'les matières putrides' [putrid matter]; their surface beauty being only a deceptive and temporary disguise for the rot beneath, the fallen woman being, in William Logan's words, 'a living and breathing sepulchre'.[77] The exhumation of Marguerite's grotesque corpse is also the direct antithesis of the common trope in narratives of the lives of holy martyrs, whose long-dead bodies are found to be miraculously preserved, the purity of the soul reflected in the incorruptibility of the flesh.[78]

But where the novel's opening implicitly contrasts Marguerite's corrupted flesh and corrupt life with the miraculous purity of a holy martyr, the novel's ending radically undermines that very dichotomy. The final chapters chart in painfully drawn-out detail the progress of Marguerite's disease, her tortured body, writhing in its gilded bedchamber. Dumas thus offers a poetically just reward for the courtesan's former vice, but he also hints more subversively at a transcendent purgation of the flesh. Julie, the prostitute tending to her dying friend, likens Marguerite's agonies to those of a saint: 'Jamais martyre n'a souffert pareilles tortures' [no martyr ever suffered such tortures], she comments, describing Marguerite's room as 'cette chambre à coucher qui avait retenti autrefois de tant de mots étranges, et qui n'était plus à cette heure qu'un tabernacle saint' [this bedroom in which once rang with so many strange words, and which is now no more than a holy tabernacle] (305).

---

[77] Parent-Duchâtelet, quoted in W. R. Greg, 'Prostitution', *Westminster and Foreign Quarterly Review*, 53: 2 (July 1850), 482; William Logan, *The Great Social Evil* (Hodder and Stoughton: London, 1871), 153. William Acton similarly asserted that prostitutes together deteriorate as 'a heap of rubbish will ferment', each one 'like a disease', 'corrupt and dependent on corruption'. *Prostitution*, 11–12, 166.

[78] See Alan Thacker, 'The Making of a Local Saint' in Alan Thacker and Richard Sharpe (eds), *Local Saints and Local Churches in the Early Medieval West* (Oxford University Press: Oxford, 2002).

Unwilling to burden Armand with the guilt of her suicide, Marguerite explains her final frenetic passing from one man to another: 'Je passai à l'état de corps sans âme, de chose sans pensée' [I passed into the state of a body without soul, a thing without thought] (293). Body is divided from soul: the prostitute's degraded body is scourged by intense suffering and reduced to decaying matter; the loving woman's soul rises free, purged and transcendent.

On dramatizing his novel, Dumas romanticized and sanitized Marguerite's death, moving it far closer to the easeful death tradition associated with heartbreak, and erasing both the graphic detail of her decline and the potentially blasphemous imagery surrounding it. Bedridden in the play's final act, Marguerite's hope and strength is momentarily revived by a last-minute reunion with a remorseful Armand—a reunion that never takes place in the novel. Her last words are an ironic revival of hope: 'Mais je vais vivre?...Ah! que je me sens bien!' [But am I going to live?...Ah! I feel so well!], upon which she peacefully breathes her last (V, ix, 210). This cruel delusion adds a poignant dramatic irony to the play's tragic finale, while incidentally fitting into the medically recorded phenomenon of 'spes phthisica' wherein the consumptive patient is filled with delusional hope and a deceptive sense of well-being.[79] The death that wrung so many tears from Paris audiences thus hovers ambiguously between the agonizing consequences of sexual promiscuity and the poetic fading of romantic disappointment.

Having taken the Paris stage by storm, it was inevitable that London theatre managers would be eager to cash in on the sensational and sentimental spectacle of Marguerite's doomed love, and it was equally predictable that the censor would jib at it. In 1853 a translation of Dumas's play, entitled *Camille*, was submitted for a performance licence at Drury Lane, but, on W. B. Donne's recommendation, it was refused. In 1854, however, Donne happily granted a licence to an adaptation of Barrière and Thiboust's *Les Filles de Marbre*, a dramatic riposte to Dumas's romantic courtesan, in which a prostitute ridicules, betrays, and ruins her besotted lover. *The Marble Heart* was duly performed at the Adelphi Theatre without raising any of the public clamour and debate that had greeted its appearance in Paris.[80] As George Henry Lewes observed, not having been treated to the 'poesy of corruption' of which *La Dame aux Camélias* was the most popular example, its English audience found it unnecessarily platitudinous to stage the 'moral truism...that courtesans are venal'.[81]

Donne was at this point only deputy to the often absent official Examiner of Plays, John Mitchell Kemble, who returned in 1856 from one of his many archaeological studies abroad to resume his duties and grant a licence to *La Traviata*, an operatic version of *La Dame aux Camélias* by Giuseppe Verdi with a libretto by Francesco Maria Piave. To assuage sensibilities the opera was set in 1700, placing the courtesan's tale in the more acceptable theatrical tradition of historically distanced mistresses and

---

[79] See Hutcheon and Hutcheon, *Opera*, 44.
[80] *The Marble Heart*, adapted by Charles Selby, produced at the Adelphi, 22 May 1854.
[81] 'The Theatres', *Dramatic Essays by John Forster and George Henry Lewes. Reprinted from the 'Examiner' and the 'Leader'*, with notes and introduction by William Archer and Robert W. Lowe (Walter Scott: London, 1896), 276, 277.

magdalens—a device made even more transparent by the fashionably crinoline-like dresses worn by Signora Piccolomini, as the heroine Violetta, in contrast to the archaic stockings and ruffles of her male counterparts.[82] Considerably pared and toned down from the original play, *La Traviata*'s libretto was an uneasy hybrid of Romantic language and new naturalism, mixing archaic expressions with precise sums in modern currency ('Venti luigi' [Twenty louis]), medical terms ('La tisi non le accorda che poch' ore' [The tuberculosis will not allow her more than a few hours]), and actual bills and receipts on stage, as handed by Violetta in evidence to her lover's disapproving father.[83] The father's role was considerably extended, so he is present at the public insulting of Violetta and her deathbed reconciliation with his son, Alfredo. The effect of these changes was to personalize the central conflict; where Dumas's play brings Marguerite up against the moral laws of society, as articulated by M. Duval, Verdi's opera offers a clash of individuals with differing concepts of love and virtue.

Promoted to chief Examiner in 1857, Donne was asked to account for the inconsistencies that allowed his predecessor's licensing of *La Traviata*, which he justified on the basis that 'the words are then subsidiary to the music'.[84] The secondary role and the linguistic inaccessibility of the Italian libretto's precise meaning to all but a well-educated few were vital in securing its licence, on the assumption that Violetta's profession could remain euphemistically vague for the majority of the opera's audience. But the music itself also played a significant role, not only shifting focus from the libretto, but also predicting and framing Violetta's death. The plaintive, mournful, and delicate music of the overture predicts the courtesan's death, like the novel effectively introducing her corpse before her living body makes its entrance. The melody of the overture is repeated as the curtain rises on Act III to reveal the dying bedridden heroine, bringing to fruition the musical themes introduced in the overture, so that their conjunction at the climax of her death creates a satisfying and inevitable sense of artistic structure and completion. Susan McClary has summed up the musical impetus: 'it is precisely the overpowering necessity of diatonic closure that causes audiences to *desire her death*: the tonal cards are stacked against her from the outset. Indeed, nineteenth-century opera's demand for blood sacrifice, which marks it as different from most drama or literature of the day, is grounded in "purely" musical, tonal procedures.'[85] Violetta's last

---

[82] Such inconsistencies became a convention, as Bernard Shaw in 1890 commented on a production 'with Violetta in the latest Parisian confections and Alfredo in full Louis XIV fig, that is familiar to every opera-goer', G. B. Shaw, *Music in London* (London, 1932), I, 97; quoted in Julian Budden, *The Operas of Verdi*, vol. 2 *From Il Trovatore to La Forza del Destino* (Oxford University Press: New York, 1984), 165.

[83] For analysis of the libretto, see Fabrizio della Seta, 'New Currents in the Libretto', *The Cambridge Companion to Verdi*, ed. Scott L. Balthazar (Cambridge University Press: Cambridge, 2004). For details of suppressions in the English translation of the score submitted for licence at the Surrey Theatre in 1857, see Roberta Montemorra Marvin, 'The Censorship of Verdi's Operas in Victorian London', *Music and Letters*, 82:4 (November 2011), 582–610.

[84] 1866 *Report*, 2284, quoted in John Russell Stephens, *The Censorship of English Drama 1824–1901* (Cambridge University Press: Cambridge, 1980), 83.

[85] Susan McClary, 'Foreword. The Undoing of Opera: Toward a Feminist Criticism of Music', Catherine Clément, *Opera, or the Undoing of Women*, translated by Betsy Wing (Virago: London, 1989), xiv.

words are the ecstatic exclamation 'Oh gioia!' on a high B flat, as she celebrates her newfound sense of life and dies on a powerful, almost orgasmic climax.[86]

The opera was a popular and commercial success, but the realism of Maria Piccolomini's performance in the death scene became a focus for critical unease. The *Times* commended the actress on the 'minute details of the final victory of death', recounting how as she endeavoured with tottering steps to reach a chair, the audience sat with bated breath and 'audibly rejoiced when she was fairly seated'.[87] The *Athenaeum*, however, judged the 'slow pulmonary death of the Lady of Pleasure' to be even more repulsive when accompanied by an orchestra than in its original Paris production.[88] By August a critic in the *Times*, possibly in the face of the opera's continuing popularity, expressed clear discomfort at the graphic suffering of Piccolomini's performance, condemning the opera as 'repulsive from the physical and phthisical nature of the woes which it illustrated'.[89] In the same issue of the *Times* an article headed 'Theatrical Moralities' was reprinted from the *Spectator*, suggesting darkly that the 'ladies of the aristocracy' filling the theatre's boxes would find their moral 'instinct' becoming 'dulled' from such 'familiarity with evil', and calling for a rejection of French art's 'hankering after prurient sentiment and melodramatic situation'.[90] Spurred to defend his theatre's fare, the manager Mr Lumley declared that retaining Violetta's profession and her painful death were essential to the moral message of the opera: 'As it stands, the melancholy catastrophe illustrates the Nemesis that attends on vice, and that cannot be entirely averted even by the most touching and devoted repentance. Strike out from the character the evil which had blighted it, and the last scene would have offended against the dramatic canon—that suffering should only be exhibited for the purpose of teaching a moral lesson.'[91] Lumley further declared that, 'I know nothing in it which it can be supposed to offend, unless it is in being too exquisitely true to nature.' Lumley's simultaneous appeal to realism and poetic justice reveals precisely the grounds for critical offence: if the courtesan's death was an inevitable and naturalistic result of her wicked life, then its roots were to be found in the medical history of consumption which encompassed venereal disease. The graphic detail of Piccolomini's performance thus gave disturbing physical reality to the prostitute's body, reminding the audience of her previous sexual history. Moreover, the painful naturalism of her demise introduced a troubling actuality to the theoretical concept of poetic justice. Where the death of the sexually sinful woman was a given of so many texts and dramas, critics responded with discomfort to the spectacle of such a fate played out in realistic detail as entertainment. As the *Times* commented with cold irony, 'she coughed herself to death before their eyes, and nothing was so fascinating as the last agony'.[92]

---

[86] For detailed analysis of the musical structure of *La Traviata*, see Budden, 156–63.
[87] *Times* (26 May 1856), 12.
[88] *Athenaeum* (31 May 1856), No. 1492, 688.
[89] *Times* (4 August 1856), 5.
[90] Ibid.
[91] B. Lumley, letter to the Editor, *Times* (11 August 1856), 7.
[92] *Times* (4 August 1856), 5.

The youth and grace of Maria Piccolomini, who looked barely twenty, further complicated critics' responses, winning their admiration while prompting many to distinguish carefully between performer and role. The *Times*, for example, insisted that such delicacy and pathos could not possibly be found among Parisian *lorettes*, concluding caustically that the enthusiastic audience found at least some of the 'charm' of the spectacle in 'the contrast of the actress and the part she was called on to sustain—just the sort of attraction which the fine gentlemen of the Caroline era felt in hearing the broadest indecencies put into the mouths of young and pretty women'.[93] Henry Morley similarly, having condemned the 'bad music' and 'detestable libretto', celebrated Piccolomini's transcendent performance: 'Out of impurity she produces something exquisitely pure, and out of absurdity a pathos irresistible.'[94] After a scathing moral commentary on the libretto, including the assumption that Violetta's death had venereal causes as 'the consequence of young imprudences', Morley rapturously praised the very different heroine created by Piccolomini's performance, lifted up by a 'pure and deep love…out of all sin, and developing all that is noblest in woman', 'dying at last true to the high nature which had been once developed in her'.[95] By 9 August Morley had sufficiently recovered from his rapture to express delight at the strong moral objections now being lodged against the opera.[96] The radical inconsistencies in Morley's response suggest a conflict between head and heart, intellectual condemnation and emotional sympathy. This was exactly the response feared by George Henry Lewes when, having seen the first production of the play in Paris, he condemned it as 'this hideous parody of passion…this idealisation of corruption', 'a subject not only unfit to be brought before our sisters and our wives, but unfit to be brought before *ourselves*', warning that, 'The very skill with which young Dumas has treated it, makes his crime the greater, because it tends to confuse the moral sense, by exciting the sympathy of the audience.'[97] This was the crux of the controversy: the courtesan was both sexually promiscuous woman and romantic heroine, her heart-wringing death both the tragic end of a sincere and self-sacrificing love and potentially the consequence of a venereally contracted disease.

Lumley, the manager of Her Majesty's Theatre, declared of *La Traviata* that 'No one who sees or reads the opera without a previous acquaintance with the French tale will find in it the slightest matter of offence', effectively underlining the difficulty of controlling extra- and inter-textual resonance.[98] Donne appears to have been well aware of this in his sustained opposition to *La Traviata*, which he decried to his friend Fanny Kemble as 'now performing…in the full bloom of her original horrors!'[99] In the wake of the opera's licensing, however, Donne felt obliged to allow English and burlesque versions for the Surrey theatre for the sake of consistency, a

---

[93] Ibid.
[94] Morley, *Journal of a London Playgoer*, 27 May 1854, 135.
[95] Ibid, 136–7.
[96] Ibid, 9 August 1856, 149–50.
[97] 'La Dame aux Camélias', *Dramatic Essays*, 241–2.
[98] Letter to the Editor, *Times* (11 August 1856), 7.
[99] W. B. Donne to Mrs Fanny Kemble, 28 May 1856, *William Bodham Donne and his Friends*, ed. Catherine B. Johnson (Methuen: London, 1905), 197.

decision which he later regretted, requesting the support of the Lord Chamberlain in refusing a licence to the original French version in 1859. Though obliged to defer to his superior's decision, Donne declared his opposition to 'this odious piece' in no uncertain terms: 'I retain all my repugnance to the story: it is a glorification of harlotry: in its last act it profanes the sanctity of death.'[100] Even the potential stage realism of Marguerite's death does not explain Donne's curious phraseology—as though the fallen woman is too unworthy even to die. Instead Donne's reference seems to be to the imagery which fills the final chapters of Dumas's novel, where Marguerite is likened to a Christian martyr or a saint; Donne's description thus recognized the inerasable connection between the original and its various stage versions. The Lord Chamberlain agreed with Donne, and in June 1860 a licence was again refused to the play in the form of Matilda Heron's euphemistically titled *Camille: or, the Fate of a Coquette*, though Donne admitted that English versions could by then be seen everywhere in the provinces.[101] In 1862 Donne found himself further embroiled in inconsistency and compromise when he allowed Sadler's Wells Theatre to complete a week's run of its unlicensed *Lady of the Camellias* on the grounds that interrupting the run would be financially crippling and that the manager could be forgiven for thinking the play allowable because 'this is an old play, which though never licensed has been performed all over the Kingdom'.[102]

An English adaptation of *La Dame aux Camélias* was finally granted a licence in 1875, the intervening years having seen the murders, bigamous marriages, and assorted scandalous goings on in sensation dramas of all descriptions, and more specifically the licensing of Boucicault's *Formosa* in 1869.[103] James Mortimer's heavily bowdlerized adaptation, entitled *Heartsease*, opened at the Princess's Theatre, London on 5 June 1875, starring the Polish-born actress Helena Modjeska, without raising a single voice of moral outrage. So thoroughly had Mortimer sanitized Dumas's play that the *Daily Telegraph* likened his process of adaptation to a patented stain remover, which attained its purpose 'by sacrificing the colour and texture of all material subjected to the treatment'.[104] While retaining the structure and the most of the dialogue of the original, *Heartsease* goes to great pains to render its heroine—renamed Constance Hawthorne in a combination of purity and rural simplicity—guiltless of any error except that of being an actress, her theatrical profession being the sole reason for her social exclusion and M. Duval's objection to her marriage to his son. Constance spares Armand the scandal of marrying an actress, and instead engages herself to Varville (whose family is presumably less finicky in such matters). Armand accuses her of making a mercenary marriage but he learns the truth of her self-sacrifice in time to beg forgiveness, and Constance dies with no guilt to purge. The 'constant agitation' of her life is nothing more than the thrill as she stands before the footlights, such professional excitements being set against the more peaceful pleasures of domesticity; Nichette, transformed from

[100] Letter from W.B. Donne to Spencer Ponsonby, 26 March 1859, LC Corr 1/70.
[101] See W. B. Donne, letter to Spenser Ponsonby, 11 June 1860. LC Corr 1/83.
[102] W. B. Donne to Spencer Ponsonby, 4 August 1862, LC Corr 1/113.
[103] Donne had also retired as Examiner of Plays in August 1874, to be replaced by E. F. S. Pigott.
[104] *Daily Telegraph* (7 June 1875), 10.

a *grisette* into a virtuously engaged maiden, nonetheless deplores Constance's un-
feminine occupation and longs for her to find someone 'who would win her from
the feverish life she leads & teach her contentment in one more tranquil & enduring'.[105] Even the heroine's extravagance is excised: where Marguerite has spent
enough on bouquets to feed an honest family for a year, Constance merely recalls
having flowers thrown at her in one night 'so costly that their value would have
kept a poor family a whole year' (III, 60).

Press responses to Helena Modjeska's performance as Constance in 1875 and
when the play was revived in 1880 displayed a relief at the Polish actress's avoid-
ance of any explicit enactment of the heroine's consumptive death and the associated risk of disturbing reference to the physical and sexual realities of Dumas's
original work. Critics writing in the *Daily Telegraph* and the *Athenaeum* complimented in relieved tones the 'moderation of the means' the actress employed in her
death scene, a restraint that eschewed modern 'ultra realism'.[106] Unlike the painful
detail of Piccolomini's death, which served as a graphic reminder of the disease
wracking the courtesan's body, the beauty of Modjeska's death smile made her end
'a poem', a fittingly peaceful ending for a woman apparently dying of nothing
more disreputable than heartbreak.[107] Mortimer's version thus avoided the confusion of the moral sense which so concerned George Henry Lewes, but the very
propriety and decorum of *Heartsease* was so marked as to complicate the play's
meanings and frame of reference. Mortimer's 'stain removing' process did indeed
extract all colour and texture, leaving a sentimental and tearful romance, which
offered audiences no sufficient rationale for the social ostracizing of the play's heroine. Excision can thus produce a palpable absence, a logical space which is in itself
a notable presence. The very feebleness of class and a theatrical profession as substitute for Dumas's exposition of the courtesan's life left a perceptible gap not only
for those familiar with the original, but even for the more protected members of
the audience who were merely aware of the aura of scandal which had kept Dumas's
play off the English stage for over two decades. As journalist, newspaper editor,
author of over thirty plays, and for five years American attaché in Paris, Mortimer
was presumably well aware of the techniques employed by adapters seeking to
evade the control of the Lord Chamberlain's censorship. The particular excisions
and extra-textual resonances in *Heartsease* suggest a skilful deployment of the play's
origins in order to reintroduce the very meanings it decorously removes.

The title of Mortimer's *Heartsease* was borrowed from a deathbed speech from
the dying heroine of an earlier adaptation of Dumas's play, *Camille; or, The Fate of
a Coquette*, by Matilda Heron, which had been refused a licence by Donne in
1860. Heron's Camille is a woman whose guilt remains vague and unspecified,
amounting to nothing more than having dared under the 'sacred' support of the
Duke de Meuriac to enter high society, from which she was summarily rejected

[105] James Mortimer, *Heartsease*, LCP, BL Add MS 53149A, III, 56.
[106] *Athenaeum*, No.2741 (8 May 1880), 611.
[107] *Daily Telegraph* (3 May 1880), 2.

when her humble class origins were discovered.[108] Heron's Camille offers Armand wildflowers as she lies dying:

> Armand, the day I met your father, I wore upon my breast these little flowers, the same you gave me in the morning. When I left you that evening and came to Paris, I took the flowers and kissed them; but they were withered, bloomless, faded—and with them every little hope that blossomed on my heart! I have kept them ever since. (*Takes flowers from casket*.) See how pale and blighted they have grown. They are called 'heart's-ease'—a pretty name!
>
> (V, 20)

A consonance is thus established between heroine and flower: both are natural, delicate and doomed. Heron's Camille gives Armand a camellia, bidding him return when it is faded, but the flower is deliberately re-coded as a symbol of her purity and vulnerability:

> It is a strange flower, Armand—pale, scentless, cold; but sensitive as purity itself. Cherish it, and its beauty will excel the loveliest flower that grows; but wound it with a single touch, you can never recall its bloom, or wipe away the stain. Take it, and remember me.
>
> (I, 7)

Mortimer adopted and further sanitized Heron's imagery; in *Heartsease* Constance gives Armand a heartsease when they first meet and tells him to come back 'in a few short hours' when its bloom has gone (I, 30). The fragility of both Constance's life and Armand's love are linked to the flower. He gives her wild flowers at the beginning of Act III, in their rural retreat, and she breaks off with him by writing with reference to the fragile fading blooms he picked that morning that 'my love like them will be dead' (III, 71). Just before she dies, Constance draws out the withered flower he gave her in the country: 'I have treasured it as you see & we have faded together' (V, 122). The heroine thus dies stainless and much maligned, a delicate wildflower unable to withstand the rough treatment of the world.

For those who were familiar with the novel, the flower imagery that ran through *Heartsease* offered a particularly self-advertising revision. The framing narrator of Dumas's novel explains Marguerite's soubriquet of 'la Dame aux Camélias' by the fact that those are the only flowers she ever wears, white camellias for twenty-five days of the month, red camellias for the remaining five days—though the narrator does not venture further to explain their relation to Marguerite's menstrual cycle and sexual availability (27). When Armand first asks to visit Marguerite's bed, she gives him a red camellia and explains that you can't always carry through an agreement on the same day you sign it, asking him to return when the flower has changed colour (119). In a parliamentary debate on censorship and obscenity on 9 July 1857, Lord Campbell opened with a commentary on French fiction; holding up

---

[108] Matilda Heron, *Camille; or, the Fate of a Coquette*, Dicks' No.614, II, 8. First produced at the National Theatre, Cincinnati, 14 January 1856. Heron played Camille herself with considerable success, and was later to enhance her scandalous theatrical repertoire by starring as Braddon's Lady Audley.

a copy of Dumas's novel, he explained that it 'gave a description of the white and the red camellia, in a manner that trenched upon modesty, and which he could not state'. Campbell declined to 'shock their Lordships by going any further', but the cryptic nature of his reference suggests that he expected his audience to be able to fill in the blank.[109] In his dramatized version, Dumas has Marguerite offer Armand a camellia (colour unspecified), telling him to return when it is faded (I, xii, 97). Dumas insisted that he invented the association between the courtesan and the flower, but receipts show that Marie Duplessis had certainly purchased them her-self.[110] In both Dumas's novel and his play, the camellia acts as a site of numerous interacting systems of signification. In realistic medical terms, it is the only flower which Marguerite will wear because it does not produce a scent to irritate her tu-bercular cough. It advertises the timetable of her sexual availability, but it is also a tool in her self-construction as a luxury commodity: worn in and out of season, the flowers are an ostentatious expense.[111] That Matilda Heron and James Mortimer should choose flowers, the most scandalous detail of the work and the one that most graphically represented the physical reality of the prostitute's body and pro-fession, as the site for their most extravagant romanticizing suggests a dual process of excision and emphasis. A sanitized text emerges to placate the censor and main-tain a respectable front before an uninformed audience, while, for those familiar with the original, an ironic reminder is offered of what has been omitted, reintro-ducing the physical realities which have been romanticized and announcing the process of censorship itself.

Reviewing Mortimer's *Heartsease* in 1875, the critic for the *Athenaeum* was alert to this textual palimpsest, the intrusive ghostly presence of previous incarnations, declaring, 'Far better in all respects is the original in its integrity than all these ver-sions, in which the blanks suggest the employment of words worse than those which have been really omitted.'[112] For all the delicacy and restraint of Modjeska's performance as Constance, the play remained irretrievably corrupt; the playwright's very attempts to purify the polluted sewer of the original had only served to heighten its sexual indecency and suggestiveness, in the critic's words:

> So skittish and erratic is the Muse of French comedy, that it is better to leave her in the clothes she herself affects. If you drape her in seemly attire, her mincing walk and uncon-

---

[109] *Hansard's Parliamentary Debates*, vol. 146, 1152 (356 Vols, 3rd series, 1857–8), quoted in Bar-bara Leckie, *Culture and Adultery: the Novel, the Newspaper, and the Law, 1857–1914* (University of Pennsylvania Press: Philadelphia, PA, 1999), 42.

[110] Rounding, *Grandes Horizontales*, 62.

[111] A further possible layer of meaning is added by the Victorian language of flowers, according to which the white camellia could symbolize 'Excellence in Woman' (see Edmund Evans, *The Floral Birthday Book: Flowers and Their Emblems* (Routledge: London, 1878), 121). Further complicating this symbolism, Rounding states that in the wake of *La Dame aux Camélias* 'prostitutes capable of falling in love [were] henceforth known as *camélias*' (*Grandes Horizontales*, 62–3). Intriguingly, Josephine Butler surrounded the body of a prostitute she had nursed on her deathbed with camellias, though whether a precise meaning was to be read into the choice of flowers remains uncertain (see Millicent G. Fawcett and E. M. Turner, *Josephine Butler: Her Work and Principles, and their Meaning for the Twentieth Century* (Association for Moral and Social Hygiene: London, 1927), 151–2).

[112] *Athenaeum*, No.2485 (12 June 1875), 798.

ventional gestures appear the more shocking. You can never be sure that she will not lift or rend her decent skirts, and bring discredit upon the virtue whose garb she wears.[113]

For those in the know, *Heartsease* skilfully exploited this heightened impact of illicit sexuality when presented under an outward show of modesty and decorum.

Perhaps the most remarkable example of such self-advertising censorship was Mrs Kennion's *Nina; or, the Story of a Heart*, which was first licensed for performance at the Theatre Royal, Wigan. The play borrowed extensively from Mortimer's *Heartsease*, staging the love and consumptive demise of a much maligned but entirely virtuous actress and taking its sentimental title from yet another deathbed scene where the heroine points to the wildflowers at her breast:

> See they are withered, scentless, faded and with them every little hope that blossomed on my heart. Look how pale and blighted they have grown, they are called heartease (*sic*) a pretty name. You will keep them, they will remind you of the story of my heart.[114]

As the *Era* reported when the play first opened, it was originally entitled '*Nana*', but the single letter alteration was made at the Lord Chamberlain's insistence.[115] The *Era* merely noted that 'this "new" play is made up of very old materials', but the drama's originality lay in merging Mortimer's *Heartsease* with an even more bowdlerized adaptation of Zola's *Nana* (1880). Nina/Nana is Mortimer's Constance, surrounded by a full cast of characters from Zola's novel: Bordenave the theatre director, Rose Mignon the jealous rival, and Zoe the faithful maid are all present; Fontan becomes an evil Svengali, trying to draw Nina/Nana back from true love to resume her successful theatrical career; George Hugon is the schoolboy whose passionate ardour Nina decorously rejects, earning her the grateful support of his aristocratic mother; and to this cast-list is added Philippe Duval, the true love for whom she sacrifices career and then life itself. Zola's sensual actress, whose only asset is her body and who picks up, bleeds dry, and discards lovers with unthinking good humour—'une force de la nature, un ferment de destruction, sans le vouloir elle-même, corrompant et désorganisant Paris entre ses cuisses de neige' [a force of nature, a ferment of destruction, without any intention on her part, corrupting and throwing Paris into chaos between her snowy thighs]—is merged with Dumas's famous courtesan to produce a heroine of impeccable virtue and purity.[116] The transformation of two of the sexually most scandalous texts of the nineteenth century into a sentimental tearjerker of immaculate propriety was so astonishing that it is hard to believe that Mrs Kennion was not performing a public feat of *hutzpah*, a tongue-in-cheek demonstration for those in the know of quite

---

[113] Ibid.

[114] Mrs Kennion, *Nina; or, the Story of a Heart*, LCP, BL Add MS 53336 L. IV, 111–12. Previously (II, 35) these flowers were named as violets which the heroine promises 'shall take the place of Camillas' (*sic*), an inconsistency which incorporated a further possible reference to *La Traviata*'s renamed heroine Violetta.

[115] *Era* (15 April 1885), 15. The heroine's name is altered to 'Nina' on the title page of the licensing copy and the two subsequent pages, and then left as Nana throughout.

[116] Émile Zola, *Nana* (Gallimard: Paris, 2002), 224.

how much English censorship demanded and quite how far the process of white-washing could go.[117]

For two years Mrs Kennion 'captivated all hearts by a most ladylike impersona-tion' of Nina in what was advertised, without naming the specific texts in question, as an adaptation 'from the works of Alexandre Dumas and Emile Zola'.[118] When the play finally secured a London premiere at the Strand Theatre on 13 July 1887, after over 300 performances across the provinces, any pretence at keeping the play's origins decorously unnamed was finally abandoned. Mrs Kennion announced in an opening speech that the play was an adaptation of *La Dame aux Camélias* inter-mixed with scenes from Zola's *Nana*, and the *Era's* critic abandoned some of his previous circumspection, noting that the incorporation of one lady 'of such a ques-tionable character' with another lady 'of still more questionable character' to pro-duce 'this two-headed creature... chaste as ice and purer than snow' simply stretched credulity too far. The reviewer refrained from informing the *Era's* more innocent readers as to the nature of the sins and errors of Nina's original incarna-tions—that knowledge was to be left to those familiar with indecencies of French literature—he simply enumerated Nina's extraordinary acts of virtue, concluding that 'we smile and confess that we are cynical'.[119] *Nina* is simultaneously a chastely sentimental tear-jerker and an ironic demonstration of the demands of English theatrical decorum.

Resigned perhaps to the impossibility of controlling the intertheatrical and extra-textual resonances of any version of Dumas's tale, in 1881, a year after Mor-timer's *Heartsease* appeared on the English stage, Dumas's *La Dame aux Camélias* was finally licensed in its full and original form for a French-language performance by the Gymnase Company at the Gaiety Theatre, London—its indecencies thus being theoretically only comprehensible to an educated elite, for whom bowdler-izing was already an elaborate and ineffective game. The Gaiety performance starred Sarah Bernhardt; famous already for her nervous power and lithe presence, she was greeted as the ideal embodiment of Dumas's courtesan. In her 'absolute interpretation', Bernhardt at last confronted London audiences with the courte-san's body, desired and desiring, consumed not only with tuberculosis and heart-ache but also with passion.[120] The *Pall Mall Gazette* described Bernhardt 'dwelling with insatiable hunger' upon her lover's lips and face, for in her portrayal of love 'The surrender is absolute, and... coyness or timidity does not for a moment inter-fere with or check it.'[121] Where Dumas's novel separated body and soul, mortifying and purging the courtesan's sinful flesh in order to free her spirit, Bernhardt's phys-ically expressive performance used the body as a means of expressing the soul. She performed the moment of death as a sudden and rigid fall, stripped of anything

---

[117] It is worth noting that audience members could have been familiar with details of either novel via reviews or comments in the popular press, rather than necessarily by virtue of having read the origi-nal French.

[118] *Era* (19 September 1885), 5; (12 December 1885), 16.

[119] *Era* (16 July 1887), 8.

[120] *Pall Mall Gazette* (13 June 1881), 11.

[121] Ibid.

but empty finality, while the focus of the scene was not on Marguerite's suffering but on the intensity of her yearning for Armand and her rapture at their reunion. The transcendent quality which critics responded to was thus not in contradistinction to her physicality, but an expression of the courtesan's passion. As the critic in the *Times* wrote, the intensity of her passion recalled the religious transcendence of the novel:

> in the fifth act we see the martyr whom M. Dumas asks the world to canonize. Marguerite is dying of consumption, with but one hope and desire, that of seeing Armand. Mddle. Bernhardt plays this scene with an angelic sweetness which gives it almost the character of a transfiguration. We can almost fancy the halo of a saint, upon her forehead. [122]

Yet where the novel suggests a separation of soul and body, the sexually sinful flesh punished and decaying while the spirit is freed, in Bernhardt's performance soul and body are necessarily one. Far from the fragile wildflowers of bowdlerized versions, Bernhardt's Marguerite was sensual, insistent, and hungry for her lover's embrace, her passion both physical and spiritual.

Whereas the novel's readers were distanced by the framing narrator of the novel, doubly removed witnesses to Armand's desires, the theatre audience gazed directly upon the desired body of the courtesan in the form of Sarah Bernhardt, who by 1881 had already established an international reputation as a celebrity performer, a focus of intense public interest and desire. Bernhardt was also adept at negotiating the commercial marketplace; she traded deliberately on her sexuality, creating an air of exoticism, fascination, and danger through her choice of roles on stage and carefully managed publicity off-stage, and earned considerable sums through advertising endorsements.[123] The spectacle of the courtesan coughing herself to death in the supposedly inevitable mechanism of poetic justice was thus combined with the spectacle of the openly sexual actress, healthy, successful, and returning night after night—a contrast which only became more marked as Sarah Bernhardt made the role one of the most famous in her repertoire, reviving it repeatedly in subsequent decades. Yet one thing was clear as Bernhardt played Marguerite Gautier to fascinated and rapturous London audiences, including the Prince of Wales and his wife: the desired and desiring woman was a troubling, unruly, but potentially highly lucrative spectacle.

[122] *Times* (13 June 1881), 13.
[123] See e.g. Sarah Bernhardt, *My Double Life: The Memoirs of Sarah Bernhardt* (State of New York Press: Albany, NY, 1999); Susan A. Glenn, *Female Spectacle: The Theatrical Roots of Modern Feminism* (Harvard University Press: Cambridge, MA, 2000).

4

Sex Problems and Nature's Law

Where for decades playwrights had been driven to employ all their ingenuity and stagecraft in order to smuggle the spectacle of the sexually transgressive and actively desiring woman onto the stage, by the 1890s the 'woman with a past' had become a theatrical obsession, her sexual history openly acknowledged and her place in society endlessly discussed. The *fin-de-siècle* English stage was dominated by a succession of plays on adulterous wives, unmarried mothers, conniving adventuresses, and repentant sinners seeking redemption. The 'fallen' woman, in all her various manifestations, was a central figure in an extraordinary number of plays by the leading playwrights of the day: Arthur Wing Pinero and Henry Arthur Jones alone produced some seventeen plays on the subject between them, and Oscar Wilde, Sydney Grundy, Bernard Shaw, and R. C. Carton all offered their own dramatic variations on the theme. By 1895 keen playgoer Kate Terry Gielgud complained that 'The public has been satiated with social and physiological problem-plays; it begins to tire of the eternal sex question.'[1] Nonetheless, plays centring on sexual questions and judgements remained ubiquitous well into the twentieth century, a trend gently mocked in J. M. Barrie's 1905 comedy *Alice Sit-by-the-Fire*, in which the inevitable effect of theatregoing on a young girl's imagination is to convince her that her mother must be having an affair.

It is never possible definitively to trace the causes of a literary phenomenon, but the coming together of century-long melodramatic traditions, the influence of the French theatre, and the impact of Ibsen, alongside heated debates about women's rights, marriage, and sexual morality at the *fin de siècle* provided the perfect conditions for the 'fallen woman' play to flourish. Whether repenting their sins and retiring to a convent, like the delinquent mother in Pierre Leclerq's *Illusion* (Strand Theatre, 1890), living a life tortured by guilt over the illegitimacy of her child, like the grieving heroine of Ernest Genet's *The Reckoning* (Town Hall, Chelsea, 1891), or eschewing repentance, and subsequently dying of no diagnosable cause other than dancing on a Sunday, like the Quaker turned seductress of Henry Arthur Jones's *The Dancing Girl* (Haymarket Theatre, 1891), women with a past were to monopolize the English stage for over a decade.

It is worth tracing in detail the particular social and theatrical circumstances which helped to produce such an extraordinary proliferation of plays dealing with illicit female sexuality, its policing and punishment. The wide range of plays concerned with sexually transgressive women, loosely grouped together and labelled

---

[1] Kate Terry Gielgud, *A Victorian Playgoer*, ed. Muriel St Clare Byrne (Heinemann: London, 1980), 24.

'sex-problem plays', evolved both from the long history of seduction, bigamy, and courtesan dramas of the previous decades, and from new influences from abroad. An exploration of those roots helps to explain the generic hybridity of the resultant drama, a complex mixture which was perhaps the secret of its wide appeal, while often raising difficult issues of interpretation both for contemporary audiences and for later critics.

One of the clearest causative factors for the extraordinary ubiquity of the 'fallen woman' play at the *fin de siècle* was the multifaceted campaign for increased rights and opportunities for women in legal, political, social, industrial, and commercial spheres. Just as the earlier nineteenth-century French artistic obsession with adulterous wives and courtesans could be traced to the debates surrounding frequent changes in divorce and inheritance laws, so the unprecedented popularity of English 'fallen woman' plays can be set in a context of late-Victorian changes in marriage and property laws. The 1870s and 1880s saw a steady erosion of the principle of 'feme covert'. The 1873 Custody of Infants Act and the 1878 amendment to the Matrimonial Causes Act, for example, extended mothers' custody rights over their children in the event of divorce or separation, and the 1884 Married Women's Property Act crucially gave wives the right to own property in their own names and to keep their own earnings, thus giving them a recognized independent legal identity separate from their husbands. The extent of popular social debate over the function and nature of marriage is evident in the response to Mona Caird's polemical article 'Marriage', published in the *Westminster Review* in 1888. Positioning marriage as part of a long history of man's destruction of ancient matriarchy, Caird argued that marriage and the concept of woman's 'virtue' being marital fidelity were the result of 'man's monopolizing jealousy, through the fact that he desired to "have and to hold" one woman as his exclusive property'.[2] An astonishing 27,000 letters were sent to the editor of the *Daily Telegraph* in response to the paper's consequent debate, 'Is Marriage a Failure?'.[3]

With the introduction and extension of the Contagious Diseases Acts in the 1860s, and the campaign for their repeal in the 1870s and '80s, sexual morality and its relation to gender roles, state law, and religious precept were increasingly hotly contested. The Acts' defence of male sexual privilege, enforcing medical inspection and incarceration for the infected on any woman identified by police as a prostitute (with no requirements or definitions set as to how that identification should be made, leaving it as an entirely arbitrary power in officers' hands), unmatched by any restriction upon similarly infected men, became the focus for the first organized women's political protests. The repeal campaigners' attack was effectively two-pronged. Firstly, Josephine Butler and her co-workers challenged the denial of civil rights to women liable to inspection and detention, arguing that all working women were vulnerable to these extended police powers. Furthermore,

---

[2] Mona Caird, 'Marriage', *Westminster Review*, 130:2 (July 1888), 193.
[3] Harry Quilter, 'Preface',in Harry Quilter (ed.), *Is Marriage a Failure?* (Swan Sonnenschein: London, 1888).

they argued for a continuity of fellowship between so-called 'fallen' and 'good' women. Challenging the language and treatment which dismissed prostitutes as human detritus, many repeal campaigners argued for compassion and an acknowledgement of common womanhood; no woman should be subjected to such degrading treatment, or reduced by legislation to a state-regulated and controlled supply for male appetite.[4] The second aspect was an attack on male licence: sexual continence and chastity were ideals for men as well as women, campaigners argued, and profligacy was morally as well as physically damaging for men. So, for example, Josephine Butler, refuted the 'pernicious belief' that men's promiscuity left no mark on them, and warned that marriage does not 'transform a man's nature, nor uproot habits that have grown with his years: the licentious imagination continues its secret blight', and the 'poison in his soul' may be transmitted to his children.[5] In the wake of the Acts' repeal in 1886, debate continued on these central issues of how male and female sexual activity was to be judged or controlled, though tensions became increasingly apparent between those primarily concerned with civil rights and those ready to sacrifice (women's) liberties in the name of morality and 'social purity'.[6]

The debates over sexual morality, the state's role in regulating prostitution, the sexual double standard, and marriage and divorce laws only grew more heated towards the end of the century, intensified by the wider struggle for improved legal, professional, and employment rights for women. There was a wide divergence of views on female sexuality, marriage, and morality held by those involved in the various campaigns for women's rights. They covered the full spectrum from social purity feminists like Sarah Grand, whose best-selling novel *The Heavenly Twins* (1893) warned of the dangers to women's health from venereally diseased husbands, to 'free union' advocates writing for *The Adult*, a journal dedicated to arguing for freedom in sexual relationships and equal rights for children born out of wedlock. Suffrage leader Millicent Fawcett was characteristic of many feminist campaigners, when she labelled the self-styled emancipator of women Grant Allen 'not a friend but an enemy' of women's enfranchisement for having written *The Woman Who Did* (1895), another best-selling novel, in which Allen's heroine scorns to accept the degrading laws of marriage as they stand and instead enters a free union in order to fulfil her biological destiny. As Fawcett commented in a scathing review, the cause of female suffrage could only be set back by his endeavours to 'link together the claim of women to citizenship and social and industrial independence, with attacks upon marriage and the family'.[7] The press furore which

---

[4] See, e.g. Josephine Butler, *Personal Reminiscences of a Great Crusade* (Horace Marshall & Son: London, 1896) and Josephine Butler, *On the Moral Reclaimability of Prostitutes* (London: 1870).

[5] Josephine Butler, *Social Purity* (Morgan and Scott: London), Address given to Cambridge undergraduates in May 1879, 9–10.

[6] Perhaps the most egregious example of this was the 1880 Industrial School Act, empowering the removal of children of prostitutes and consigning them to Industrial Schools, condemned strongly by the National Vigilance Association as kidnapping and imprisonment. See Sheila Jeffreys, *The Spinster and Her Enemies: Feminism and Sexuality, 1880–1930* (Pandora: London, 1985), ch. 1.

[7] Millicent Fawcett, '*The Woman Who Did*', *Contemporary Review*, 67 (January–June 1895), 630. See also, e.g. Grant Allen, 'Plain Words on the Woman Question', *Fortnightly Review*, 52 (October 1889).

greeted sensational and outspoken works such as *The Heavenly Twins* and *The Woman Who Did*, alongside other works which acknowledged women's active desires and challenged sexual orthodoxy, such as novels and stories by 'New Woman' writers George Egerton, Mona Caird, and Olive Schreiner, attested to the critical unease surrounding such issues. Just as sensation fiction in the 1860s had been condemned as a dangerously debased and potentially corrupting form of literary entertainment, so 'New Woman' fiction was similarly surrounded by cultural anxieties about women's reading and the power of literature to mislead the vulnerable; in Marie Corelli's *The Sorrows of Satan* (1895), Lady Sybil proposes an adulterous affair to her husband's best friend, having been morally degraded by the consumption of too many New Woman novels—the friend rejects her advances in outraged disgust, a rebuff all the more striking for the fact that he is the devil in disguise. If such matters were regarded as too dangerously controversial and sensitive for treatment in prose fiction, how much more shocking and explosive could they be when discussed in the public forum of the theatre?

Censorship put severe constraints upon the theatre's capacity for openly engaging with such contemporary debates, but melodrama had a long history of tackling difficult subjects, not through direct discussion but via implication and association. Far from losing its popularity in the later decades of the nineteenth century, melodrama proved adept at reflecting cultural anxieties and debates. So, for example, the 1880s saw the rise of a new breed of remorseless villainesses, sexually fallen and tireless in their attacks on more virtuous women. These dangerous harpies can be seen as a theatrical embodiment of the fears expressed by proponents of the Contagious Diseases Acts, who justified the arrest, inspection, and forcible detention of venereally infected women by painting in vivid colours the threat posed to society by unrestrained and contagious women. William Acton, a keen proponent of the Acts, began his book *Prostitution* (1870) by advocating examination and regulation on the grounds of a compassionate and sympathetic understanding of the prostitute's lot. Women could pass through the travails of the profession with as little moral and physical damage as possible, he declared, if forcibly treated for any venereal infection. But in a remarkable passage in the middle of the book, compassion was replaced with vituperation, as he described the prostitute as less than human, not just diseased but herself pollution incarnate:

> She is a woman with half the woman gone, and that half containing all that elevates her nature, leaving her a mere instrument of impurity; degraded and fallen she extracts from the sin of others the means of living, corrupt and dependent on corruption, and therefore interested directly in the increase of immorality—a social pest, carrying contamination and foulness to every quarter to which she has access.... Such women, ministers of evil passions, not only gratify desire, but also arouse it. Compelled by necessity to seek for customers, they throng our streets and public places, and suggest evil thoughts and desires which might otherwise remain undeveloped.[8]

---

[8] William Acton, *Prostitution, Considered in its Moral, Social and Sanitary Aspects in London and other Large Cities and Garrison Towns* (2nd edn. John Churchill and Sons: London, 1870), 166.

Likening the prostitute's tempting powers to a match on dry gunpowder, Acton portrays the man as a helpless and hapless victim of a 'mercenary human tigress'.

This dehumanized force of malevolence, appetite, and pollution took theatrical shape as the remorselessly vengeful discarded mistress of late-Victorian melodrama. The scorned fallen woman turned avenger had been a familiar figure in earlier melodramas, from *The Miller and His Men* to *The Inchcape Bell*, but she rarely reached the end of the play without repenting and attempting to make amends. The villainess of Augustus Harris's spectacular *fin-de-siècle* melodramas was of another breed entirely. In *Human Nature* (1885), co-written by Harris and Henry Pettitt, Cora, the cast-off mistress of Captain Temple, frames Mrs Temple for adultery and gives false evidence in court so that she loses custody of her young son, whom she sees delivered to almost certain death at the hands of an evil baby-farmer. No pleas for mercy will soften Cora's vindictive hatred for her persecuted rival. Not even the knowledge that her passion for Temple will never be reciprocated can stop her; she swears to poison his future by sending his old love-letters at intervals to his wife. Cora's implacable cry of 'I'll be revenged—revenged!' is, however, interrupted by the unexpected return of her long-lost husband, who expresses his own unreciprocated passion by murdering her.[9] Harris's *Youth* (1881), co-written with Paul Merritt, contains not one but two demonic seductresses. The notorious courtesan Mrs Walsingham begins the play seeking to reform herself, but having been summarily ejected from the parish as a personal embarrassment by Reverend Darlington, who in his wilder youth had impregnated and abandoned her, Mrs Walsingham rapidly abandons her plans for 'Bitter Repentance' and embraces 'Sweet Revenge'.[10] She lures the vicar's son, Frank, into the clutches of her *demi-mondaine* niece, Eve de Malvoisie, and (her name being insufficient warning of her dangerous nature) he foolishly marries her. Eve proceeds to wreak vengeance, squandering the family's money, and then framing Frank for a crime committed by her own adulterous lover.

Both these plays adhered unswervingly to the sexual double standard. Having found Cora living in the bosom of his family as an old school-friend of his wife's, Captain Temple coldly commands his ex-mistress to leave as her presence is 'an insult' to Mrs Temple (I, 11). Having engaged in some spectacular feats of military prowess and bravery in foreign lands, while his faultless wife is harried and persecuted, the errant captain is finally reunited with his all-forgiving spouse. Similarly, Reverend Walsingham plays the concerned and wounded father to his son, Frank, who in turn redeems his sexual frailties with Eve by fighting heroically for queen and empire against overwhelming odds. Frank's heroism is rewarded by the news that, in time-honoured style, Eve was already married when she married him, thus leaving him free to return to the all-forgiving arms of his childhood sweetheart. Cora, Eve, and Mrs Walsingham are agents of destruction, wreaking havoc on

⁹ Augustus Harris and Henry Pettitt, *Human Nature*, LCP, BL Add MS 53342H, V, ii, 78. First performed Drury Lane, 12 September 1885.

¹⁰ Augustus Harris and Paul Merrit, *Youth*, LCP, BL Add MS 53256K, I, 17. First performed Drury Lane, 6 August 1881.

honest families whose happiness they resent, and as such must be expelled. The men who shared in their sexual pleasures have learnt the error of their foolish ways, and are to be welcomed back as brave and wiser men.

This stark divide was nothing new to melodrama—the repentant betrayer had, after all, always been considered a good catch as a husband—but it provoked a wide range of responses from reviewers, indicating a clear lack of consensus when it came to sexual morality. The stunning hypocrisy of *Youth's* Reverend Darlington was accepted by the *Illustrated London News*, for example, as 'the way of the world', the reviewer only expressing his regret that the 'fiendish Mrs Walsingham' and 'demoniacal Eve' are not run in by the country constabulary.[11] The *Pall Mall Gazette*, by contrast, condemned Darlington as 'a clergyman who for downright heartlessness and immorality has no equal in fiction', a view with which the *Athenaeum* heartily concurred.[12] Opinions fractured similarly over *Human Nature*. The *Athenaeum* commended Temple for his 'blunt bravery and honesty', and the *Illustrated London News* called him a 'manly English hero', but the *Daily Telegraph*, by contrast, found 'something repulsive' in Temple's pluming himself on his domestic virtue to the woman he abandoned, and denied the need for Temple to 'shake her off as if she were a pollution. She whom he, brave man, had polluted!'[13] A similar distancing from the play's assumed moral norms was perceptible in audience responses: as the *Athenaeum* noted of one performance of *Youth*, the Reverend Darlington's avowal to his son that 'so soon as he found a woman he had seduced was likely to prove an incubus to him he got rid of her, afforded the public one of the heartiest bursts of laughter it has known for some time.'[14]

Michael Booth detects symptoms of melodrama's decline in such inappropriate audience laughter in response to performances in the 1880s.[15] But Drury Lane melodramas continued to draw large and enthusiastic audiences right to the end of the century, demonstrating their ability to adapt to a changing moral climate. Just as the spectacular military scenes could be updated to fit with contemporary campaigns—the first production of *Youth* set its battles in Afghanistan; a revival two years later relocated them to a recent Egyptian campaign—so the sensational plots and confrontations could be refigured to appeal to changing sexual attitudes.[16] Augustus Harris and Henry Pettitt's *A Life of Pleasure* (Drury Lane, September 1893), for example, perfectly demonstrates how the age-old tale of seduction and abandonment could be so reworked. The play's heroine, Norah, is the familiar cottage girl, educated above her station and victim of the false promises of Captain Chandos, who abandons her in favour of the rich heiress, Lady Mary. But when Chandos attempts to hand Norah on to his debauched friend, Sir John, she is saved from the fatal lure of 'a life of pleasure' by a music-hall artiste who persuades

---

[11] *Illustrated London News* (13 August 1881), 147.

[12] *Pall Mall Gazette* (9 August 1881), 11–12; *Athenaeum*, No. 3021 (19 September 1885), 379.

[13] *Athenaeum*, No. 3021 (19 September 1885), 379; *ILN* (19 September 1885), 291; *Daily Telegraph* (14 September 1885), 3.

[14] *Athenaeum* (13 August 1881), 220.

[15] Michael Booth, *Melodrama* (Herbert Jenkins: London, 1965), 178.

[16] *Times* (10 August 1881), 4; *Times* (30 April 1883), 9.

Norah of the superior merits of hard work.[17] Converted to self-respect by a female performer whose professional status indicates not sexual availability but economic independence, Norah confronts her seducer and denounces him as 'Heartless, cruel and cowardly—a betrayer of women, a traitor to me—this is how I drink to him! (*Takes up glass of wine and dashes it in his face*)' (III, iii, 35). While critics were uneasy about the realistic recreation of the notorious Empire promenade in which this scene was set, complete with 'demi-reps' and 'dudes', they applauded the 'stately figure' of Mrs Bernard Beere as Norah, whose defiance was seen as a neat reversal of the public humiliation of Marguerite Gautier.[18] Norah's moment of triumph retained its appeal, drawing cheers from audiences when revived in 1895 and 1898.[19] The play's ending offered a further twist on the old formula, when the seducer not the seduced dies by taking poison: having failed in his attempt to murder Norah, Chandos swallows the fatal dose as the arresting officers arrive, and is declared dead as the curtain descends.[20] Revisions to the licensing copy of *A Life of Pleasure*, however, show the limit to the authors' challenges to conventional melodramatic morality. Early on in the play's action, Lord Avondale pays off Chandos's debts in the belief that the captain will then make an honest woman of poor Norah, but Avondale then pauses to question the wisdom of securing such a match: 'God knows if I am doing right in insisting that you should give her your name— that she should give herself for life to such a man as you have proved yourself to be' (III, i, 2). This passage is struck out, however—not by the censor's hand but by the play's pragmatic authors, who clearly knew precisely how to tread the line between novelty and familiarity.

A Life of Pleasure revised the moral structure underpinning the century-old traditions of seduction melodrama, but its challenge was tacit and implicit, embedded in plot and action rather than directly articulated. As bigamy drama had demonstrated, the unspoken implications of performance could offer more radical interventions than were permitted explicit articulation in the text. *A Life of Pleasure*'s most unconventional and unsettling intervention in contemporary sexual debates was a scene which offered a graphic demonstration of the validity of the notion of marital rape. Contrary to melodramatic convention, the play's hero fails to arrive in the nick of time in order to prevent Lady Mary's marriage to Captain Chandos. Learning of her husband's perfidy only once he has acquired full legal rights over her wealth and person, Lady Mary locks herself in her boudoir. Chandos then breaks in, disables the electric bell, and proceeds to threaten his new bride with sexual violence in the language of the marriage service:

---

[17] Augustus Harris and Henry Pettitt, *A Life of Pleasure*, LCP, BL Add MS 53533H. III, iii, 33.

[18] *Athenaeum* (30 September 1893), 462; *Era* (23 September 1893), 9. A year later, in 1894, the National Vigilance Association was to campaign for the removal of the Empire Theatre's licence on the grounds that the promenade was a nightly resort of prostitutes.

[19] *Era* (18 May 1895), 9; *Era* (1 October 1898), 10.

[20] Interestingly, either the *Leeds Mercury*'s critic's conventional expectations overpowered his observation or he left before the play ended and wrongly predicted the conclusion, as, contrary to all the other critics' accounts, the paper reported that Norah finally commits suicide (22 September 1893), 5.

CHANDOS: I should be sorry to behave other than as a loving and tender husband, but—
LADY M: You shall answer for this.
CHANDOS: Answer to whom? The law says you are my wife—and to-day of your own free will you solemnly swore to love—to honour and obey me.
LADY M: Love, honour and obey you—who tricked me into this marriage—there can be nothing in common between us—you come here like a thief in the night to a defenceless woman, who is heart-broken, it is cowardly of you, for you must see how I am suffering.
CHANDOS: If you are ill, it is all the more my duty to be with you now, for did I not promise on my part that in sickness or in health I would love you and cherish you.

(V, v, 32)

The time-honoured scene in which the villain threatens the virtue of the heroine is thus laid over a husband claiming his conjugal rights. Lady Mary is estranged from her husband within minutes of speaking her wedding vows, but the scene nonetheless enacts a wife's revulsion and fear at a husband's violent assertion of his legal rights—this at a time when the issue of marital rape when the rights of husband over his wife's body were being hotly contested in the courts.[21]

From mid-century onwards, French boulevard drama continued to anatomize and analyse the morality of marriage and female sexuality. The meticulously constructed Scribean *pièce bien faite* and the Dumasian *pièce à thèse* asked audiences to consider whether adulterous wives should be banished, forgiven, or shot, whether seduced maidens should be married or sent to nunneries. Disabled of their central sexual mainspring and point of debate by the Lord Chamberlain, such plays reached the English stage as mechanical and sentimental dramas of little social or intellectual relevance. But in the 1870s, the first tentative efforts were made by British playwrights to compose plays which attempted a direct 'criticism of life' in the French style. W. S. Gilbert's *Charity* (1874) is an example of such an early 'problem' play, engaging with issues of sexual morality but doing so via a familiarly English sentimental drama, complete with a convoluted plot of contested wills and hidden identities, far from the Dumasian *pièce à thèse*. Gilbert's involved plot centres on Mrs Van Brugh, a generous philanthropist and pillar of the local community, who is revealed to be an unmarried mother, having failed to legalize her relationship with her daughter's now-deceased father—the reasons for which remain vague and opaque. All shrink from her as one 'whose very existence is an unholy stain on God's earth', but her daughter soon relents and declares her feelings unchanged towards a mother who is still 'the type of gentle charity, tender

---

[21] In 1888 in *Regina v. Clarence* it was pronounced that a husband could not be found guilty of raping his wife, even if she refused sex because he had venereal disease. See George Robb, 'Marriage and Reproduction', in H. G. Cocks and Matt Houlbrook (eds), *Palgrave Advances in the Modern History of Sexuality* (Palgrave Macmillan: Basingstoke, 2006), 91. In 1891 *Regina v. Jackson* ruled that a man could no longer imprison his wife in his home in order to enforce restitution of conjugal rights. In response to the ruling, the *Times* lamented that 'one fine morning last month marriage in England was suddenly abolished'. Quoted in Jane Lewis, *Women in England, 1870–1950: Sexual Divisions and Social Change* (Indiana University Press: Bloomington IN, 1984), 120.

helpfulness, brave, large-hearted womanly sympathy'.[22] As part of her atonement, Mrs Van Brugh has devoted herself to rescuing streetwalkers, one of whom, Ruth, has become a faithful servant in her household. Departing from decades of melo-dramatic tradition, Ruth's history is explicitly one of economic deprivation, exploi-tation, and exclusion, closely echoing the first-person accounts which had only recently been collected and published by sociologists such as Henry Mayhew. Ruth's story moves a sympathetic clergyman to tears, and he finds himself unable to condemn her for a life which 'has been—has been what God knows it couldn't well have helped being under the circumstances' (I, 13). The play's emphasis on the economic roots of prostitution and its challenge to any clear divide between 'good' women and 'bad' fitted closely with arguments being propounded by opponents of the CD Acts. As Mary Hume-Rothery wrote in her open letter to Gladstone, argu-ing against the state regulation of prostitution, 'there is not one of the mothers, wives, sisters, or daughters whom you cherish... who dare safely assert that, had she been born into the same unprotected, unfenced position, in the very jaws of poverty and vice... might not have slipped, like them, into that awful gulf from which society at large has too long done its best to make escape hopeless'.[23] Gilbert also takes aim at the sexual double standard, as smugly propounded by the play's villain, a hypocritical evangelist named Smailey, who denounces both Mrs Van Brugh and Ruth as social pariahs but, when he is revealed as Ruth's original seducer, pleads his own 'extreme youth and—and inexperience'—having been a mere forty, while Ruth was a comparatively mature sixteen (II, 20). Finally convicted of for-gery and deception, Smailey is hauled off to prison, while Mrs Van Brugh and her daughter end the play seeking happiness in the New World—the favourite com-promised destiny for reformed sinners, offering an ambiguous conflation of crimi-nal transportation and utopian escape. The play was not a success with audiences, a fact which William Archer blamed on a combination of involved and improbable plot and its 'unpleasant' subject.[24]

Wilkie Collins's *The New Magdalen* (1873) was the most radically provocative play to argue for the forgiveness and rehabilitation of a repentant prostitute, but it did so within a 'sensation drama' whose convolutions helped to undermine and confuse its moral message, demonstrating the difficulties inherent in attempting to give a popular audience the excitement and sentimental thrills it expects while simultaneously engaging overtly in contemporary social debates. The play's hero-ine is Mercy Merrick, a former street-walker turned hospital nurse whose attempts at social reintegration have repeatedly been thwarted whenever her past history is revealed. When a respectable lady, Grace, is shot and presumed dead, Mercy there-fore borrows her identity to start a new life, quickly gaining the love and respect of all who encounter her. Mercy becomes engaged to an upright young man, Horace, but when Grace inconveniently reappears, fully cured and harshly self-righteous in

    [22] W. S. Gilbert, *Charity* (London, 1874—no publisher given), II, 18; IV, 38. First produced Haymarket Theatre, 3 January 1874.
    [23] Mary Hume-Rothery, *A Letter to the Right Hon. W. E. Gladstone, M.P.* (Manchester, 1870), 8, quoted in Susan Kingsley Kent, *Sex and Suffrage in Britain, 1860–1914* (Routledge: London, 1990), 69.
    [24] William Archer, *English Dramatists of To-Day* (Sampson Low: London, 1882), 158.

her denunciation of Mercy, Horace shrinks from his fiancée in horror and disgust. After an initial struggle with her conscience, Mercy finally makes a full and humble confession, for which she is rewarded by an offer of marriage from a broad-minded clergyman, who proclaims her 'the noblest of Heaven's creatures' and suggests they start afresh in the 'new world'.[25] By making Mercy gentle, graceful, and kind, while Grace is harsh, hectoring, and arrogant, Collins was clearly challenging the notion that sexual purity was the exclusive measure of female virtue. But the sensational contortions of the plot confused any such argument, making Mercy guilty not only of streetwalking but also of a readiness to see Grace incarcerated as a lunatic in order to retain her stolen identity.

Even critics who were caught up in the emotional sweep of the play remained resistant to Collins's sexual politics; as the *Athenaeum*'s critic remarked, 'So plenary, indeed, is the indulgence accorded [Mercy], that the mind, under the influence of the story, cannot, without effort, return to its first convictions, or grasp the truth that, after all, it is better never to have sinned than to have sinned and been penitent.'[26] Dutton Cook, writing in the *Pall Mall Gazette*, objected strenuously to Collins's attempt to elicit sympathy for Mercy, declaring Grace and Horace to be entirely correct in their repudiation of the ex-prostitute, and claimed that the audience shared his view, being 'somewhat perplexed by the author's special pleading', while they 'sympathized on the whole rather with the sufferings of Grace than with the sins of Mercy'.[27] Clement Scott's judgement was unambiguously hostile, judging it to be 'one of the most hateful and unjust plays ever written.... opposed to all one's sense of justice and moral right'.[28] The English stage was clearly not yet ready for the sex-problem play, even if mixed with a heavy dose of sensation and sentiment.[29]

Over a decade later, playwrights were still complaining that the drama lagged hopelessly behind the other arts thanks to an anxiety to avoid all possible offence; as Henry Arthur Jones railed in his 1885 essay 'Religion and the Stage', 'all treatment of grave subjects' was banned from the stage, leaving it 'hopelessly cut off from the main current of modern intellectual life'.[30] Jones's particular ire was prompted by the furore which greeted his play *Saints and Sinners* (1884), an attack on religious hypocrisy delivered within an entirely conventional melodrama of seduction and abandonment. Despite the play's sexual politics being indistinguishable from those of *The Lear of Private Life* (1820) or *Clari, the Maid of Milan*

---

[25] Wilkie Collins, *The New Magdalen* (published by the author: London, 1873), II, 58. First performed Olympic Theatre, 19 May 1873.

[26] *Athenaeum*, No.2378 (24 May 1873), 673.

[27] *Pall Mall Gazette* (21 May 1873), 12.

[28] Clement Scott, *Dramatic Table-Talk* in *Thirty Years at the Play* (The Railway and General Automatic Library: London, 1892), 99.

[29] By the 1890s *The New Magdalen* had become an established crowd-pleaser, played in repertoire, for example, by Mrs Kennion alongside her perennial starring role in *Nina*; see *Era* (10 October 1890), 17.

[30] H. A. Jones, 'Religion and the Stage', reprinted from the *Nineteenth Century* (January 1885), in H. A. Jones, *Saints and Sinners: A New and Original Drama of Modern Middle-Class Life* (Macmillan: London, 1891), 120.

(1823), Jones's attack on the hijacking of professed Christian principle to cover the self-serving and unscrupulous interests of commerce provoked widespread censure, convincing Jones that the English theatre was condemned to intellectual irrelevance.

In April 1887 Jones exchanged letters with his fellow playwright Arthur Wing Pinero, agreeing that they envied French playwrights for possessing an audience that 'can listen respect and learn'.[31] Less than two years later, Pinero attempted his first serious theatrical engagement with a difficult subject in *The Profligate* (1889), a play which drew on the familiar tale of seduction and betrayal but relocated as a back-story to the seducer's marriage to a pure young girl fresh out of school. Where Collins and Gilbert had raised critics' hackles by championing sexually fallen women as models of feminine grace, Pinero was more careful and conservative in his approach to the sexual double standard. Dunstan Renshaw is the profligate of the title, who marries pure Leslie Brudenell on the basis that 'Ladies...are like nations—to be happy they should have no histories. But don't you know that Marriage is the tomb of the Past, as far as a man is concerned?'[32] Renshaw laughs at current social purity notions of 'actually putting men on a level with ladies', and ignores warnings from Leslie's lawyer that his wild oats will 'thrust their ears through the very seams of the floor trodden by the wife whose respect you will have learned to covet' (I, 5; I, 38). Sure enough, Janet, whom Renshaw seduced with false promises of marriage and then abandoned, accidentally turns up at their door, and Leslie shrinks from her husband in shock and horror. Rejected by his beloved wife, Renshaw despairs and takes poison. In Pinero's original version, Leslie arrives just too late to save Renshaw with her message of wifely forgiveness, but the actor-manager John Hare advised against unnecessarily distressing the audience, and Pinero re-wrote the ending to allow the husband a last-minute reprieve.

Pinero's willingness to re-write the ending of the play to suit audiences' tastes was not a sign of authorial disdain for his work; he remained proud and protective of the play, stipulating, for example, that while German adapters were welcome to change his sentimental comedy *Sweet Lavender* 'until it is sage and onions for all I care', *The Profligate* should be faithfully translated.[33] As Pinero argued, the revised ending 'in no way distorted my original scheme'.[34] Though the original version had the fallen man die by his own hand, as so many fallen women had done before him, such a bald plot summary suggests a far more radical attack on the sexual double standard than the play really contains. In both versions the play questions a worldly morality which would shrug off a man's sexual past as unimportant, demonstrating instead the painful loss of status and respect such a revelation may prompt. But, though Leslie may be disgusted by her husband's past exploits, she nonetheless forgives them, and, in both versions, bursts into the

[31] Arthur W. Pinero to H. A. Jones, 17 April 1887, *The Collected Letters of Sir Arthur Wing Pinero*, ed. J. P. Wearing (University of Minnesota Press: Minneapolis, MN, 1974), 92.

[32] Arthur W. Pinero, *The Profligate* (Heinemann: London, 1891), I, 5. First performed Garrick Theatre, 24 April 1889.

[33] Letter to H. A. Jones (15 October 1889), *Collected Letters of A.W. Pinero*, 113.

[34] Letter to Clement Scott (7 May 1889), ibid, 106.

room promising to 'be your Wife, not your Judge'.[35] If the pure-minded and virtuous Leslie is the moral touchstone in the play, as her horror at her husband's treachery suggests, then she also validates a different treatment for male and female sinners. Janet may have been a trusting, naive and genuinely loving victim of Renshaw's lies, but there is no question of her being socially reintegrated; Leslie quickly scotches her brother's tender interest in Janet, and packs her off to the colonies. Nor crucially is there any question of Renshaw's past constituting an irreversible 'fall'. After only a few weeks of marriage Renshaw is described as having lost his dissipated look under Leslie's purifying influence, while his newborn moral seriousness and the very agonies of shame which lead him to contemplate suicide are evidence that, as he says, 'the companionship of this pure woman is a revelation to me' (II, 67).

Even with its revised ending of marital reconciliation, *The Profligate* raised objections from some reviewers for the stringency with which it addressed male guilt. The *Athenaeum*'s reviewer, for example, complained not only that Pinero's morality was 'higher than is generally adopted', but that the 'tremendous crop of evils' which follow on Renshaw's misdeed were hard to accept, though it remained ambiguous whether the reviewer was referring to abstract justice or melodramatic convention in declaring that 'When...indiscretion or wickedness have been committed by a man before marriage, Nemesis is not supposed to be implacable.'[36] Reviewers were united in their reading of the play's message as an ultimate validation of the sexual double standard, tempered by a serious critique of male profligacy, but they were divided in their response according to their own personal code of sexual morality. The dependably conservative Clement Scott, writing in the *Daily Telegraph*, praised the high moral tone of the play, which he welcomed as both 'a scheme for discussion' and 'a contribution to earnest dramatic literature', identifying the 'extremely beautiful' idea at its centre as being 'that the influence, and the devotion of a pure and innocent woman can ennoble and sanctify a man, however worldly, however tainted, however debased'. Scott particularly welcomed the dramatization of this idea that the 'mere contact of this pure woman is the bad man's salvation', at a time when such thinking was under fierce attack from feminist writers.[37] William Archer, coming from a different end of the critical and moral spectrum from Scott, was equally enthusiastic about the play's intellectual seriousness on a topic which constituted theatrically 'strong meat', greeting it as 'A Real Play At Last!' But he warned against naively accepting the notion of a good woman's reforming influence, 'which (as the cause of the most poignant suffering on earth) will always afford material for the victim is apt to find that she has lowered herself more than she has elevated the object of her sacrifice'.[38]

Only a few years separate Pinero's first tentative staging of a serious social issue in an age-old theatrical form and the firm establishment of the fashionable sex-problem

[35] *The Profligate*, 123 and ix.
[36] *Athenaeum* (27 April 1889), 546.
[37] *Daily Telegraph* (25 April 1889), 3.
[38] *Pall Mall Gazette* (25 April 1889), 1.

play by the mid-1890s. The catalytic force behind this rapid transformation of the English theatrical landscape was the advent of Henrik Ibsen. Less than three months after *The Profligate* opened at the Garrick Theatre, *A Doll's House* received its first professional production in England at the Novelty Theatre on 7 July 1889, produced by and starring Janet Achurch and her husband Charles Charrington. By 1891 Ibsen had become an established part of the London theatre scene, with productions of *Rosmersholm*, *Ghosts*, *Hedda Gabler*, and *The Lady from the Sea* all opening in a mere ten-week period between the end of February and the beginning of May. Ibsen was not big box office: *Ghosts* was a private and unlicensed Independent Theatre performance; *Rosmersholm* was only given a single matinee performance at the Vaudeville Theatre; and *Hedda Gabler* was produced by the joint management of actresses Elizabeth Robins and Marion Lea, less as a commercial venture than in despair of seeing male actor-managers produce plays with the rich acting opportunities offered by Ibsen's women.[39]

Nora Helmer's assertion in *A Doll's House* of a higher duty to herself above her duties as wife and mother, her determination to re-educate herself, and her vision of a 'miracle of miracles'—a real, adult relationship with her husband—established an indelible association between Ibsen's plays and the campaign for women's rights. As Kirsten Shepherd-Barr has explained: 'The fact that it was this play that gave the English their first taste of Ibsen virtually determined the way he would be received there throughout the nineties: a champion of the New Woman and dramatist of social problems.'[40] The scandal of *Ghosts*, in which a son pays the price of his father's debauchery by developing hereditary syphilis, while his mother watches in agony, blaming herself for having condoned her husband's sins rather than walking out as Nora does, further cemented associations between Ibsen's plays and the unsightly feminists who supposedly constituted the majority of his plays' audiences. So an unnamed reviewer in *Truth* characterized *Ghosts*'s admirers:

> The unwomanly women, the unsexed females, and the whole army of unprepossessing cranks in petticoats who have no opportunities just now to discuss the Contagious Diseases Act in drawing-rooms, sit open-mouthed and without a blush on their faces whilst a Socialist orator reads aloud *Ghosts*, the most loathsome of all Ibsen's plays, that illustrates freely enough the baneful result of the abolition of the Contagious Diseases Act in Norway.[41]

---

[39] For further details see Elizabeth Robins, *Ibsen and the Actress* (L. & Virginia Woolf: London, 1928); Joanne E. Gates, *Elizabeth Robins, 1862–1952: actress, novelist, feminist* (University of Alabama Press: London, 1994); Angela V. John, *Elizabeth Robins: staging a life* (Tempus: Stroud, 2007); Gay Gibson Cima, *Performing Women: Female Characters, Male Playwrights and the Modern Stage* (Cornell University Press: London, 1993), ch. 1.

[40] Kirsten Shepherd-Barr, *Ibsen and Early Modernist Theatre, 1890–1900* (Greenwood Press: Westport, CT, 1997), 22. As she explains, in France, by contrast, where *Ghosts*, *The Wild Duck*, *An Enemy of the People*, and *The Master Builder* had established Ibsen's associations with naturalist and symbolist dramatic techniques, before the first commercial performance of *La Maison de Poupée* in 1894, Nora was received more as a symbol of revolutionary ideas than as a specifically feminist revolt. See chs 1, 2.

[41] Unsigned notice, *Truth* (5 March 1891), in Michael Egan (ed.), *Ibsen: The Critical Heritage* (Routledge: London, 1972), 179–80.

Ibsen requisitioned the stage as the location for socially challenging debates, and in England those debates became inescapably associated with the 'Woman Question'.

For society dramatists such as Jones, Pinero, and Sidney Grundy, Ibsen's plays were never an ideal to be aspired to; instead they acted as a violent purgative or catalyst. Ibsen's naturalism, unresolved and troubling endings, complex characterization and shockingly outspoken subject matter made conventional dramatic styles look painfully outdated, though his dramas lay beyond the pale, out in a territory into which fashionable English dramatists had little desire to venture. Henry Arthur Jones likened Ibsen's effect on English drama to 'an emetic or liver pill', the sincerity of his methods forcibly purging the stage of 'stock dummies...our masterpieces of impossible virtue and impossible vice'; but Jones distanced himself from Ibsen's plays as concerned too exclusively with 'disease and moral deformity,...curious and exceptional depravity'.[42] In 1893 A. B. Walkley summarized the path for an aspiring literary dramatist who sought to combine literary discernment with commercial taste as being to 'attempt a golden mean between the dramatic Quixoticisms and exoticisms of the Independent Theatre, and the outworn conventionalisms of the orthodox houses; that while renouncing Ibsen and all his works as "bad form," he will be careful to satisfy the higher demand upon the drama which Ibsenism has so largely helped to create'.[43]

The 'higher demand' on the theatre was for something beyond mere entertainment, for plays which had a connection to modern life. Ibsen's theatrical methods and his concern with social and moral issues were, of course, strongly indebted to the contemporary French theatre; as William Archer noted, Ibsen's 'constant employment for several years in mounting the plays of Scribe and his school must have had a determining influence on his technique'.[44] Ibsen, however, eschewed the resolution of the *pièce bien faite*; his plays did not comfortably reassert Victorian prejudices, tie up their action in neat solutions, or invite and expect stock responses. Working within and disrupting the well-made play genre, dramas such as *A Doll's House*, *Ghosts*, and *Rosmersholm* were not just shockingly outspoken, they also asked disturbing questions without offering reassuring answers. English audiences and critics had spent decades resisting precisely the theatre beyond which Ibsen now progressed. The shock of Ibsen's challenge to moral orthodoxy and social conformity was sufficient to make his French predecessors look comparatively palatable. As the *Licensed Victualler's Mirror* exclaimed of the Lord Chamberlain's failure to prevent the Independent Theatre's production of *Ghosts*, having kept so many French plays off English boards: 'Verily he straineth at a French gnat and swalloweth a Norwegian camel.'[45] Indeed, *Ghosts*' 'gross, and almost putrid indecorum' was sufficient to prompt comparative nostalgia for Marguerite Gautier: 'Even the *Lady of the*

[42] Report in *Era* (2 May 1891), 10, in ibid, 233–4.
[43] Walkley, *Speaker*, 8 (7 October 1893), 378.
[44] Archer, 'Ibsen and His Letters', *Fortnightly Review* (1 March 1905), in Egan, *Ibsen: Critical Heritage*, 421–2.
[45] Unsigned notice, *Licensed Victuallers' Mirror* (17 March 1891), 128, in ibid, 203.

Camelias—that hectic harlot—coughed her frail soul away with some external propriety.'[46]

In the wake of Ibsen's disturbing impact, direct discussions of illicit sexuality on the French model were no longer taboo; indeed 'French' became a term not of abuse but of praise. When Pinero's *The Second Mrs Tanqueray* opened at the St James's Theatre on 23 May 1893, critics greeted this tale of a kept woman seeking social reintegration and acceptance as a respectably married woman as 'the finest native play that this generation has produced', 'a masterpiece and a glory to the British stage'.[47] William Archer had long railed at the restrictions which kept the *pièce à thèse* off the English stage in anything but a hopelessly bowdlerized and sanitized form, so it was hardly surprising that he should pronounce *The Second Mrs Tanqueray* 'a play which Dumas might sign without a blush'.[48] It was more surprising that the *Era* should similarly declare that the play meant Pinero 'claims kindred with the most successful authors of the French stage', or that *Punch* should comment that, 'When we have two original plays like PINERO's *The Second Mrs Tanqueray* and GRUNDY's *Sowing the Wind*, we may congratulate ourselves that they do *not* "do these things better in France".'[49] Significantly, critics were also careful to mark the distance between Pinero's and Ibsen's works; the *St James's Gazette*, for example, complimented Pinero on vindicating 'the right of the stage to reflect the most serious side of human life and to handle questions which society cannot', but 'without arrogating the licence of a Norwegian'.[50]

One final and more mundane cause for this development of a home-grown theatre of social engagement and debate in England can be found in the 1887 Treaty of Berne, which accorded the same copyright protection to foreign plays as to native ones. Thereafter theatre managers looking to fill their bill with bowdlerized French plays were obliged to pay both the original French author and the English adapter or translator. As the French critic Augustin Filon noted, this greatly reduced the importation of French theatrical goods, for one thinks twice before paying two authors: 'It seems preferable to study our methods, and learn from us, if possible, how to dispense with us. Nothing has contributed so efficaciously, for some years past, to the progress of the English drama.'[51]

The popularity of the fallen woman play for both audiences and playwrights was undoubtedly given a huge boost by the unprecedented critical and commercial success of Pinero's *The Second Mrs Tanqueray*. Opening at the St James's Theatre on 27 May 1893, it achieved a total run of 288 London performances and made actor-manager

[46] Editorial, *Daily Telegraph* (14 March 1891), 5.

[47] *Queen, the Lady's Newspaper* (3 June 1893), 943; *Era* (June 1893), 9.

[48] William Archer, *The Theatrical 'World' for 1893* (Benjamin Blom: New York, 1894, reissued 1969), 128.

[49] *Era* (June 1893), 9; *Punch* (21 October 1893), 105.

[50] *St James's Gazette* (29 May 1893), 4.

[51] Augustin Filon, *The English Stage: Being an Account of the Victorian Drama*, trans. by Frederic Whyte, with an introduction by Henry Arthur Jones (John Milne: London, 1897), 208.

George Alexander a profit of over £10,000. Pinero described it as a play 'for grown-up people' and for many critics from the 1890s onwards it marked English theatre's coming of age.[52] The play dramatizes widower Aubrey Tanqueray's ill-fated attempt to rehabilitate Paula, a woman who has lived as the mistress of a series of rich men. Aubrey marries Paula, thinking he is alone in the world and answerable to no one, only to find that Ellean, his convent-educated daughter by his first marriage, has decided to live with him. Paula seethes with resentment and jealous affection as her husband visibly shrinks from encouraging any intimacy between his daughter and her stepmother. Ellean coldly repulses Paula's advances, until Ellean begins to relent when she falls in love with Hugh Ardale, a heroic young captain whom Paula recognizes with horror as a former lover. Concluding with despair that 'the future is only the past again, entered through another gate', Paula takes her own life.[53]

The Second Mrs Tanqueray portrayed the high-class kept woman with unprecedented frankness and sympathy. Warm, intelligent, articulate and witty, Paula offers an education to those who, in Aubrey Tanqueray's words, 'see in the crowd of the ill-used only one pattern' and 'can't detect the shades of goodness, intelligence, even nobility there.' (I, 155) She is positioned carefully between the opposite poles of Lady Orreyed—a vulgar, affected, brainless doll who has similarly married her way out of prostitution—and Aubrey Tanqueray's frigidly religious first wife, summed up in his friend Drummle's words: 'I believe she kept a thermometer in her stays and always registered ten degrees below zero' (I, 150). Some degree of sexual warmth and knowledge of human passion is valuable in a woman, Drummle suggests, reproving his friend Tanqueray for wishing to keep Ellean in sheltered ignorance.

Critics variously registered shock and admiration for the play's explicitness and its sympathetic depiction of Paula's desire for social reintegration, but they were united in their reading of the play's message: *The Second Mrs Tanqueray* asked whether a kept woman could be reabsorbed into polite society, and delivered the unequivocal answer 'No'.[54] Likened by several reviewers to Augier's *Le Mariage d'Olympe*, it was not, as one critic noted, a play about which people argue as they do about Ibsen's, but one which they discuss 'as they discuss some terrible fatality of life itself, some law to which all must adjust themselves'.[55] A number of modern critics have tried to position the play as a protest at Paula's fate and a critique of the narrow morality of the well-made play and the society it portrayed.[56] But, as its Victorian audiences recognized, the play drew on a range of genres, condemning

[52] Letter to Edmund Gosse (2 May 1893), *Collected Letters of A. W. Pinero*, 144. See e.g. William Archer, *The Old Drama and the New* (Dodd, Mead & Co.: New York, 1929), 292; A. B. Walkley, *Drama and Life* (Methuen: London, 1907), 41; George Rowell, *The Victorian Theatre, 1792–1914* (Cambridge University Press: Cambridge, 1978), 103.

[53] Arthur Wing Pinero, *The Second Mrs Tanqueray*, in A. W. Pinero, *Trelawny of the 'Wells', and other Plays*, ed. J. S. Bratton, (Oxford University Press: Oxford, 1995), IV, 209.

[54] See e.g. *Punch* (10 June 1893), 273; *Era* (June 1893), 9; *Echo* (29 May 1893), 3; *Lady's Pictorial* (8 June 1893); *Stage* (1 June 1893).

[55] *The Queen, the Lady's Newspaper* (10 June 1893), 981. See e.g. *Morning Post* (29 May 1893), 8; *Times* (29 May 1893).

[56] See e.g. Austin E. Quigley, *The Modern Stage and Other Worlds* (Methuen: New York, 1985); Heather Anne Wozniak, 'The Play with a Past: Arthur Wing Pinero's New Drama', *Victorian Literature and Culture* (September 2009), 37:2.

Paula in the language and iconography of them all. *The Second Mrs Tanqueray* is a hybrid, shaped by and rooted in the plethora of theatrical forms which helped shape the *fin-de-siècle* sex-problem play. In order to interpret a play's implications and potential meanings audiences must necessarily draw on their knowledge of generic signifying systems. As Martin Meisel explains, ' "Meaning" for . . . playgoers means being able to accommodate new matter in familiar frames of reference, being able to interpret what is happening and what is said within and with the help of those frames of reference.'[57] A mixture of genres within a play could thus potentially lead to confusion as to how to 'read' or interpret its implications, but Pinero's play avoids such uncertainty by delivering the same judgement upon Paula in the theatrical language of each of the theatrical genres it draws upon.

The Scribean well-made play of coincidence and epistolary revelation is visible in the vital role that letters perform in *The Second Mrs Tanqueray*: repeatedly read just too late or not at all, they form a web of coincidence which manoeuvres Paula to her death. But they can also be seen as both metaphorical and realistic indicators of Paula's character. Paula generously offers Aubrey Tanqueray a letter detailing her past, which he throws unopened on the fire, symbolically attempting to erase a past which is not so easily destroyed. Paula jealously steals letters from Ellean and her companion Mrs Cortelyon announcing Ellean's engagement to Hugh; Paula's inability to control her jealousy and anger thereby ensure that Hugh's dramatic encounter with his past lover cannot be foreseen and avoided.

The play is shot through with the familiar language and iconography of melodrama. Hugh Ardale's heroism, holding out against a native mutiny, wins him Ellean's forgiveness for his chequered history, in the curious moral equation of melodramas like *Youth* and *Human Nature*, whereby military valour redeems a man's sexual past. Melodrama's impetus towards the revelation of ethical imperatives, true character made manifest, is also a structuring force within the play. The question of who Paula really is precedes her first entrance: Drummle repeatedly stumbles over which of her past names to use—Mrs Jarman, Mrs Dartry, Miss Ray—until Aubrey naively insists that her married name will erase all which preceded it. (I, 145, 155) This fluid multiplicity of identity, the mystery of who Paula really is, resolves in melodrama's inescapable revelation of truth. Two moments fix Paula's character: the first is when Aubrey explains to Paula that her former life has irreversibly damaged her mind, morals, and beliefs, rendering her an unfit companion for Ellean—a portrait of herself which Paula at first angrily rejects and then accepts, in a paroxysm of weeping for the pure self she was, 'A few years ago!'; the second is Paula's vision of the future as her beauty finally fades away: 'A worn-out creature . . . my hair bright, my eyes dull, my body too thin or too stout, my cheeks raddled and ruddled—a ghost, a wreck, a caricature, a candle that gutters' (III, 187; IV, 210). This is the familiar language of Parent-Duchâtelet, Tait, Logan, Greg, and all the other writers on prostitution who saw beneath the deceptively pretty surface to the disease, degradation, and filth which marked out the prostitute's future.

[57] Martin Meisel, *How Plays Work: Reading and Performance* (Oxford University Press: Oxford, 2007), 192.

In accordance with melodramatic tradition, Pinero also omits to provide any detail of the economic or social circumstances of Paula's fall, while her conversation with Lady Orreyed suggests a courtesan's life driven by casual greed and an unscrupulous appetite for luxury (III, 180). Paula, the play makes clear, is irreparably corrupted by her past experiences; she is, her husband declares, 'a good woman, as it were, maimed'—a word which suggests mutilation beyond the power of healing (II, 169). Aubrey's repeated refrain is that Paula is 'not mistress any longer of your thoughts or your tongue', that 'her words, her acts even, have almost lost their proper significance for her, and seem beyond her control' (III, 187; II, 169). Significantly, Paula's lack of self-restraint, impulsiveness, and bursts of temper fit precisely with the description of the inherently corrupt character of all prostitutes offered by commentators such as William Tait, who characterized prostitutes as given to 'Irritability of Temper', 'the most violent fits of passion', and being 'so restless and unsettled in their disposition' that 'Like pampered spoiled children, they must have their own way; and any attempt to thwart or contradict them, is sure to rouse their indignation.'[58] Working on the familiar assumption that the primary cause of prostitution was the essential weakness of a woman's character, the *Queen's* theatre critic could thus comfortably declare the play's message to be that men and women 'do what they do because they are what they are', finding the key to Paula's past as well as her future in a temperament that 'could not live without excitement'.[59]

The Second Mrs Tanqueray presents domestic femininity as a role which the upper-middle-class woman is expected to play. But it is not, as Nina Auerbach has argued, the role that is ultimately found wanting; rather it is Paula's ability to play it which proves inadequate—she lacks the necessary discipline and self-control.[60] Mrs Cortelyon, the embodiment of respectable femininity, has to restrain her true feelings and perform courteous friendship in order to secure Ellean's companionship in Paris. Paula cannot similarly contain her anger; she throws Mrs Cortelyon's belated hospitality back at her with spiteful wit. Unable to command the self-restraint needed for polite society, Paula impulsively cuts off a possible avenue to social integration. She may thus be caught in the play's inexorable plotting, but, as the *Evening News and Post* concluded, she 'carries the tragedy of her life in her own nature'.[61]

The surface realism of the play's unprecedentedly frank dialogue similarly demonstrated the impossibility of Paula's rehabilitation. It was the casual realism of the ex-lovers' exchanges which rendered the encounter between Paula and Hugh 'more daring and unconventional than any witnessed upon the English stage in modern times', in the words of the *Morning Post*.[62] While absorbing the shock of their situation,

[58] William Tait, *Magdalenism. An Inquiry into the Extent, Causes and Consequences of Prostitution in Edinburgh* (P. Rickard: Edinburgh, 1840), 85, 50–1.

[59] *Queen, the Lady's Newspaper* (10 June 1893), 981.

[60] Nina Auerbach, 'Before the Curtain', in Kerry Powell (ed.), *The Cambridge Companion to Victorian and Edwardian Theatre* (Cambridge University Press: Cambridge, 2004), 12–13.

[61] *Evening News and Post* (29 May 1893), 2.

[62] *Morning Post* (29 May 1893), 8.

the former lovers discuss what happened to their shared flat and furniture, in dialogue devoid of the heightened moral language which reviewers found it necessary to reintroduce, as in the *Era's* description: 'They recall little incidents of their former companionship without shame and without remorse, showing how completely the life they had led had blunted the finer elements of human nature.'[63] Paula's off-hand nostalgia for 'those jolly times on board Peter Jarman's yacht' provokes a stare of horror from the worldly Drummle, the very casualness of her *nostalgie de la boue* confirming the ingrained damage to her moral sense (II, 168).

Paula dreams of acceptance in Aubrey's 'little parish of St James's', absorbing its values and its valuation of her past life, so that by the time of Hugh's arrival, she simultaneously understands the impossibility of her integration and shrinks in disgust from the 'devil-may-care, café-living' world to which she previously belonged (I, 155; II, 164). Her aspirations and her internalizing of the values of Aubrey's social circle become her punishment. This is simply a more sophisticated version of the classic double-bind of melodrama, whereby the fallen woman's remaining moral sense is manifested as shame, self-hatred, and the urge to self-destruction. Like Marguerite Gautier before her, she accepts a punitive sexual morality and judges herself worthless by its standards. There is no possibility of a happy resolution, and her death invites tears of pity or horror while tidying up the uncomfortable question of what to do with her.[64]

George Bernard Shaw attributed *The Second Mrs Tanqueray's* reputation for cutting-edge modernity to the performance of Mrs Patrick Campbell, whose personal magnetism and unusually low-key acting style introduced a sense of revelation to Pinero's 'conventional wicked woman with a past'.[65] Pinero went to great lengths to cast an actress whose performance and stage history would mark the role out as a new one, and, as critics from Shaw onwards have agreed, her performance made a significant contribution to the impression of depth, subtlety, and nuance in the role.[66] A trained pianist, she transformed a moment in which Paula idly strums on the piano by performing a piece of Bach, surprising *Punch's* reviewer with the courtesan's 'refined taste' in music, and inevitably encouraging the audience at least unconsciously to associate the depth and beauty of the music with the player herself.[67] The degree of restraint and dignity which Mrs Patrick Campbell insisted on bringing to the role, even in conflict with Pinero's explicit instructions, helped further to distance Paula from the archetypal uncontrolled prostitute. Mrs Pat replaced hysterical sobbing by quietly turning her back and blowing her nose—a gesture of emotional repression rather than indulgence—

---

[63] *Era* (June 1893), 9.

[64] Even William Archer can imagine no better future for the Tanquerays than exile and estrangement: see *The Theatrical World for 1893*, 32–5.

[65] Shaw, *Our Theatres in the Nineties*, vol. 1 (Constable: London, 1948), 60, 44–8.

[66] See, for example, Shaw, 'Mr Pinero's New Play', *Saturday Review* (16 March 1895), 346–7; John Dawick, 'The "First" Mrs Tanqueray', *Theatre Quarterly*, 9:35 (1979); Joel Kaplan, 'Pineroticism and the Problem Play: Mrs Tanqueray, Mrs Ebbsmith and "Mrs Pat"', in Richard Foulkes (ed.), *British Theatre in the 1890s: Essays on Drama and the Stage* (Cambridge University Press: Cambridge, 1992), 38–47.

[67] *Punch* (10 June 1893), 273.

and refused to storm across the stage and sweep everything off the top of the grand piano. In rehearsal, according to Ben Webster, she instead picked up a very small ornament: ' "Here", she said in tones of black ice, "I knock something over", and dropped it delicately onto the carpet.'[68] In the face of the actress's insistence that she could not make Paula do anything 'rough and ugly with her hands, however angry she is', Pinero cut the stage business, thus endowing Paula with a greater degree of self-restraint and further distancing her from the degraded Orreyeds, who habitually leave a room 'rather wrecky' after an argument (III, 180).[69] On the other hand, Mrs Pat's extraordinary thinness added a *fin-de-siècle* morbidity to Paula's appearance, an anorexic 'Pineroticism', as Joel Kaplan has noted, which both prefigured her vision of the skull beneath the skin and marked her sexuality as unhealthy and self-consuming, despite its appeal in contrast to the chilling frigidity of the first Mrs Tanqueray.[70]

Despite Aubrey's curse upon those who like Hugh Ardale, Drummle, and himself have led 'a man's life', the play ultimately asserts the necessity and inevitability of sexual orthodoxy. The implications of Paula's social inadmissibility reach beyond moral conformity to encompass wider issues of gender roles and social structure. Sex-problem plays, whether implicitly or explicitly, addressed contemporary concerns about the role of women and patriarchal authority. Paula's wilful temper and unmanageable impulses were outer signs of inner decay, but also vitally, in the *Era*'s words, meant that 'Poor Mr Tanqueray finds her completely beyond his control'.[71] Just as so many earlier seduction melodramas ended with the guilty couple kneeling to beg forgiveness of an offended, white-haired father, simultaneously representing church, state, and family, so *The Second Mrs Tanqueray* ends with all its characters submitting to the terrible justice of conservative social mores.

In the last decades of the nineteenth century private sexual behaviour was viewed increasingly as a matter of public concern. The right of the state to legislate on private sexual acts was repeatedly confirmed: the Contagious Diseases Acts conferred the right to arrest working-class women suspected of sexual promiscuity, regardless of whether their behaviour constituted a breach of the peace or a public nuisance; and the Labouchere Amendment of 1885 outlawed acts of 'gross indecency' between men, whether 'in public or private'. Such legislation, alongside the compulsive categorizing and pathologizing of sexual proclivities and behaviour, as Foucault has influentially argued, demonstrate a late nineteenth-century identification of sexuality as a legitimate and vital arena for the exercise of social power.[72] A perceived connection between sexual behaviour and the health of the state was accepted across a wide spectrum of political viewpoints: from William Morris's vision of a utopian anarchist state, where marital monogamy has been abolished

---

[68] Margaret Webster, *The Same Only Different* (London, 1969), 160, quoted in Dawick, 'The "First" Mrs Tanqueray', 82.

[69] Mrs Patrick Campbell, *My Life and Some Letters* (Hutchinson; London, 1922), 69.

[70] Kaplan, 'Pineroticism', *passim*.

[71] *Era* (June 1893), 9.

[72] See Michel Foucault, *The History of Sexuality*, vol. 1, *The Will to Knowledge* (Penguin: Harmondsworth, 1990).

alongside all other forms of exclusive ownership; to Max Nordau's vision of sterility, inherited idiocy, and social collapse in the wake of blurred gender roles; through
to the Boy Scout movement's emphasis on male continence as a necessary guaran-
tor of healthy bodies to defend nation and empire.[73]

Nordau was typical of commentators both within and outside the theatrical
world in linking any questioning of women's traditional and exclusive role as wife
and mother to the influence of Ibsen. Quite accurately, plays such as *A Doll's House*,
Ghosts, and *The Lady from the Sea* were seen as challenging the imperative of social
conformity and the subordination of individual conscience to inherited notions of
duty. As one horrified reviewer exclaimed in response to *Ghosts*,

> He lays the blame at the door of Society, and would destroy Society root and branch;
> but is it not rather the natural corruption of the human heart and the vile passions it
> engenders that are the cause? And yet he proposes to free those passions from every
> moral and religious restraint, and let them work their will.[74]

In *A Doll's House*, Nora Helmer sets aside her role as wife and mother in order to
establish an independent adult relationship with the world outside because she
realizes that her husband Torvald is inadequate to protect her from the exigencies
and realities of that world. Content to be a mere doll while she leads the protected
existence of a plaything, Nora's disillusion comes when she realizes Torvald is not
about to sacrifice his social standing and take responsibility for her forgery. Once
she understands that Torvald is not the fairytale hero she imagined, ready to forfeit
everything to protect her, she leaves his house to set about becoming an adult; it
only makes sense to be a doll if you can live forever safely in a doll's house. Significantly, Henry Arthur Jones and Henry Herman adapted the play to suit popular
English tastes by restoring Helmer's patriarchal authority and protection; their
Breaking a Butterfly (1884) transformed Helmer into Herbert, the ideal husband of
Nora's deluded imagination.

Herbert nobly takes responsibility for his wife's crime and, once disaster has
been averted, his wife shelters herself lovingly from the dangers of the world against
his manly chest.[75] Retrospectively begging forgiveness for this play as a youthful
transgression, Jones noted that back then 'I knew nothing of Ibsen, but I knew a
great deal of Robertson and H. J. Byron.'[76]

The model for Herman and Jones's re-write of Ibsen and for a slew of sexual
problem plays which followed it could be found in Tom Taylor's perennially
popular sentimental drama, *Still Waters Run Deep* (1855). Mr Mildmay is the
'still waters' of Taylor's title, a self-effacing man who allows his household to be
dominated by his wife and her 'strong-minded' aunt—'strong-minded' being an

---

[73] See William Morris, *News from Nowhere, or, An Epoch of Rest, being some chapters from A Utopian
Romance* (Reeves & Turner: London, 1890); Max Nordau, *Entartung* [*Degeneration*] (1892); and
Robert Baden-Powell, *Scouting for Boys* (Horace Cox: London, 1908).

[74] Unsigned notice, *Licensed Victuallers' Mirror* (17 March 1891), 128, in *Ibsen: The Critical
Heritage*, 204.

[75] First performed Prince's Theatre, 3 March 1884.

[76] Jones, Introduction to Filon, *The English Stage*, 13.

epithet commonly used to denote a feminine delusion of intellectual strength rather than its actual possession. Mrs Mildmay is about to slide into an adulterous affair with a swindling aristocrat, who is simultaneously blackmailing the aunt over her incriminating love-letters to him. Disaster is only averted when Mildmay belatedly asserts his authority; he demands and receives acknowledgement as 'The master of this house!', and wins his wife's grateful promise to correct all the faults he points out, and to 'honour and obey you, as a wife should'.[77] Taylor's play remained a repertory staple throughout the second half of the century. It was revived in 1889, by actor-manager Charles Wyndham, who as Shaw cynically observed, clearly found the role of a dominant and heroic husband far more attractive than Ibsen's self-involved and deluded Torvald Helmer.[78] English audiences did not flock to see Nora Helmer awake from her naive reliance on masculine authority; but they continued to delight in the spectacle of Taylor's nascent feminists brought to a chastened realization of their sexual vulnerability, and sheltering with relief under the restored authority of the male head of the household.

Linking the 'New Woman' in pursuit of greater rights and freedoms to the warning figure of the 'fallen' woman became a standard anti-feminist theatrical tactic. In *The New Woman* (1894), Sidney Grundy parodied feminist social purity criticisms of male profligacy as the flipside of a desire for similar sexual freedoms:

ENID: And *I* say that a man, reeking with infamy, ought not to be allowed to marry
    a pure girl—
VICTORIA: Certainly not! *She* ought to reek with infamy as well.[79]

Sure enough, the supposed New Woman turns out to be 'as old as Eve'; Mrs Sylvester is only interested in writing a book on the ethics of marriage 'viewed from the standpoint of the higher morality' as a cover for initiating an adulterous affair. (III, 51) In Henry Arthur Jones's *The Case of Rebellious Susan* (1894), the eponymous heroine's refusal to accept her husband's adulterous affair as a mundane reality of marriage, a 'respectable average case', stands alongside her cousin Elaine's crusading feminism; both women's attempts at rebellion end in humiliation. Ibsen's influence was indicated in the repeated echo of Nora Helmer's assertion that she has a higher duty than that to husband and children, her duty to herself; Elaine declares her intention to pursue 'the plainest and most sacred duties that lie before

[77] Tom Taylor, *Still Waters Run Deep* (T. H. Lacy: London, ?1857), III,57, 50. First performed Royal Olympic Theatre, 14 May 1855. Major London productions included revivals at the Olympic (November 1856, June 1866), Sadler's Wells (March 1859), Adelphi (February 1866), St James's (June 1862, March 1880), Criterion (October 1890). For further details see Donald C. Mullin, *Victorian Plays: A Record of Signifcant Productions, 1837-1901* (Greenwood Press: New York, 1987), 361.

[78] Shaw, Introduction to William Archer, *The Theatrical 'World' of 1894* (Walter Scott: London, 1895), xxvi.

[79] Grundy, *The New Woman*, in Jean Chothia (ed.), *The New Woman and Other Emancipated Woman Plays* (Oxford University Press: Oxford, 1998), I, 16. First performed Comedy Theatre, 1 September 1894.

us—duties to ourselves'.[80] Similarly, in Dorothy Leighton's *Thyrza Fleming* (1894) a newly married bride deserts her husband's house at the instigation of her crop-haired, divided-skirt wearing cousin, who hires private detectives to investigate the past of all prospective husbands. The young bride asserts that 'a woman's first duty is to respect herself', but her mother, who once deserted husband and child on a similar basis, dismisses this as 'modern claptrap'.[81] Before attempting suicide in shame at her sexual past, the mother corrects her daughter's mistaken belief that 'weak pandering to the man's view of life is the cause of women's enslavement', teaching her instead that a woman's highest aspiration should be to sympathize with her husband's point of view. (III, 56) Male and female playwrights similarly rushed to castigate any challenge to the sexual double standard. In Constance Fletcher's *Mrs Lessingham* (1894) the independently minded Lady Anne instructs her fiancé to marry his former lover. The marriage turns out badly and the wife, like Paula Tanqueray, kills herself in despair, leaving Anne to regret her abrogation of authority and cry out for male guidance: 'I am not strong enough. Will you tell me what to do?'[82] R. C. Carton offered a variation on this theme in *The Tree of Knowledge* (1897) where Nigil cannot bring himself to declare his love for the pure young Monica because years before he was tempted 'to climb the tree of know-ledge' by the play's diabolical temptress, Bella. Monica is having nothing to do with such foolish modern notions, as indicated by her amusement at the sexual excesses of a new woman novel in the opening scene. Having seen the wicked Bella safely out of the neighbourhood, Monica firmly informs Nigil that his sexual past poses no obstacle to their marriage. Women, she avers, should not judge men's weaknesses but understand and sympathize, as suffering's 'chief solace' is the cura-tive love of a woman.[83]

A wonderful exception to this common rule of female submission to male authority in the face of the terrors of sexual sin is offered by Adelene Votieri's *That Charming Mrs Spencer* (1897)—whose radical sexual politics belie a title clearly designed to attract admirers of Pinero's *The Second Mrs Tanqueray* and *The Notori-ous Mrs Ebbsmith*. Votieri's indefatigable heroine, Kitty, has rescued her ancestral Irish home from bankruptcy by dancing and singing at the Variety Theatre, and now determines to restore the fortunes of her spineless aristocratic husband, Cecil. Kitty disguises herself as a merry widow, Mrs Spencer, in order to charm Cecil's father into blessing their marriage and restoring his son to his rightful inheritance. Kitty is equally undaunted by the wicked Lord Kelvin's threat to reveal her sexual past as victim of a false marriage and by her husband's demand that she obey him

[80] Jones, *The Case of Rebellious Susan*, in Russell Jackson (ed.), *Plays by Henry Arthur Jones* (Cambridge University Press: Cambridge, 1982), I, 119. First performed Criterion Theatre, 3 Octo-ber 1894.

[81] Dorothy Leighton, *Thyrza Fleming*, LCP, BL Add MS 53565F, I, 19. First performed Terry's Theatre, 1 January 1895, by the Independent Theatre Society.

[82] Constance Fletcher ['George Fleming'], *Mrs Lessingham*, LCP, BL Add MS 53546A, IV, 71. First performed Garrick Theatre, 7 April 1894.

[83] R. C. Carton, *The Tree of Knowledge*, LCP, BL Add MS 53616K, V, 98. First performed St James's Theatre, 25 October 1897.

and cease acting with 'an utter want of womanly respect'.[84] Kitty laughs at Cecil's attempt to 'play the role of despotic husband', declaring defiantly that, 'I'm a vagabond Bohemian at heart, & have the greatest contempt for the barriers that men erect to restrain endeavours, I must be free, free to work out life my own way' (III, i). Cecil gets a chance to assert his manhood by knocking down Lord Kelvin, but the play's happy ending is entirely due to Kitty's energy and warmth, winning her husband's forgiveness for her sexual past and her father-in-law's acceptance of them both into the family. Mrs Spencer's resourcefulness was well enough received at the premiere in Ipswich, but the play's sexual politics were too novel to achieve more than a brief provincial run.

The melodramatic tradition of female sexual vulnerability and passivity remained a central trope in the vast majority of sex-problem plays. If a woman escaped a sexual fall it was more likely to be due to her would-be lover sparing her than to her own will power or considered choice: in H. A. Jones's *The Masqueraders* (1894) and Pinero's *Letty* (1903), for example, it is the man who pulls back from the brink, claiming the title of chivalrous protector. French playwright Victorien Sardou offered a comic take on the *Still Waters* theme of the mundane but heroic husband seeing off the more dashing lover; in his *Divorçons* a husband falsely announces a change in the divorce laws, and cedes the role of legal spouse to his wife's aspiring lover, deviously claiming for himself the status of forbidden pleasure. Excited by the now supposedly illicit temptation of sex with her husband, the wife, Cyprienne, comes to a clearer appreciation of his attractions. Sardou's presentation of Cyprienne's frankly carnal appetite shocked English reviewers, who quoted with horror the husband's advice to the lover not to satiate his wife's desire in advance of their marriage: 'Ne tuez pas le dîner par le lunch!'[85] The discretion of an English translation which rendered this as 'Do not let the present spoil the future' did not prevent the play becoming a watchword for indecency, demonstrating a critical unease with female desire even when directed at a man the audience knows to be an entirely legal spouse.[86] Shaw deliberately reversed this formula of strong husband and vulnerable wife in *Candida* (1895), in which the wife chooses the husband over the romantically poetic lover on the basis that it is her crusading clergyman husband who would be helplessly lost without her guidance and support. While eschewing the tipsy *déshabille* in which Sardou stages Cyprienne's sexual arousal, Shaw comically represents the sexual aspect of Candida's choice by having her half-listen to her admirer's poetry while holding a light brass poker upright in her hand and 'looking intently at the point of it'.[87] Wilde similarly dis-

---

[84] Adelene Votieri, *That Charming Mrs Spencer*, LCP, BL Add MS 53654E, III, i. First performed Lyceum, Ipswich, December 1897.

[85] Victorien Sardou, *Divorçons*, *Théâtre Complet*, XI (Albin Michel: Paris, 1950), II, 107.

[86] William Archer, for example, declared himself readily 'willing to forgive the refinement' which prompted Eleanora Duse to shrink from playing the role as 'frankly sensual'. Archer, *Theatrical 'World' of 1894*, 152.

[87] Shaw, *Candida, Bernard Shaw, Collected Plays with their Prefaces*, vol. 1 (Bodley Head: London, 1970), III, 572. Copyright reading Theatre Royal, South Shields, 30 March 1895. First performed Her Majesty's Theatre, Aberdeen, 30 July 1897, by the Independent Theatre Company.

placed the husband from the role of manly protector in *Lady Windermere's Fan* (1892), in which Lord Windermere pompously dismisses his fallen mother-in-law, Mrs Erlynne, in the deluded belief that he is thereby protecting his wife's innocence, whereas it is Mrs Erlynne who is the resourceful agent of resolution, bringing her errant daughter back to the domestic hearth with a warning that she has 'neither the wit nor the courage' to survive in the *demi-monde*.[88]

The late-Victorian sex-problem play was thus a clear response to agitation for increased women's rights. Conservative playwrights repeatedly depicted women questioning traditional sexual morality or seeking greater autonomy as being dangerously vulnerable; social strictures were a necessary protection for foolhardy and frail women. The flawed nature of so many men within such plays makes clear how far the authority they validated was not individual but social and universal. Where seduction melodramas demanded reverence for the noble elderly father, there was a notable paucity of such dignified and principled embodiments of the older generation in late-Victorian society plays; the sentimental serial adulterer Admiral Sir Joseph Darby in H. A. Jones's *The Case of Rebellious Susan* was typical of the period's many *louche*, fatuous, and self-serving fathers, uncles, and husbands. The presence of such dubious representatives of male authority was an indication that English playwrights were engaging with wider issues of social order rather than simply producing sentimental dramas of individual experience. Submission to a wise and virtuous husband was one thing; submission to a foolish and flawed husband in recognition of essential social imperatives was another. The originator of the *pièce à thèse*, Alexandre Dumas *fils*, littered his dramas with unfaithful, selfish and weak-willed husbands, in plays such as *L'Étrangère*, *Francillon*, and *La Princesse Georges*, concluding that women's acceptance of such men was rooted in the necessary wisdom of structures designed to protect them from worse fates.[89]

A key scene in Dumas's plays and those of his English followers was the stripping away of delusions and self-deceptions to uncover the woman's true instinctive self. In accordance with the traditional melodramatic structure of revelation and recognition, the woman is brought to acknowledge both her own essential nature and the naturalness and inevitability of social conformity. Social law is natural law, the imperatives of gender and instinct not merely man-made but decreed by Providence. Injustice, if it exists, is a burden of nature which must be born. Pinero's *The Notorious Mrs Ebbsmith* (1895) is a perfect example. Agnes Ebbsmith is a radical political activist, whose unhappy experience of marriage has led her to form a free union with promising young politician Lucas Cleve, who has separated from his unsympathetic wife. Lucas's family pursues him to Venice in hopes of a marital

---

[88] Wilde, *Lady Windermere's Fan*, in *The Importance of Being Earnest and other plays* (ed.), Peter Raby, (Oxford University Press: Oxford, 1995), III, 40. First performed St James's Theatre, 20 February 1892. Subsequent references to Wilde's plays are to this edition and are incorporated in the text.

[89] This point is one that Toril Moi crucially misses when she places Ibsen in conversation with the idealism of George Sand rather than with the pragmatic conservatism of Augier, Dumas, Sardou, and the well-made play of French boulevard theatre, in her fascinating study, *Henrik Ibsen and the Birth of Modernism: Art, Theater, Philosophy* (Oxford University Press: Oxford, 2006).

reconciliation, at least for public show, and Lucas shocks Agnes with his readiness to accede to their plan for a 'marriage "*à la mode*"', with Agnes housed secretly as Lucas's mistress while using the cover of a sham marriage to relaunch his career.[90] Despite her genuine love for Lucas, Agnes spurns such ignominy and entrusts herself to the pious care of a sympathetic curate and his sister.

The play was written as a follow-up to *The Second Mrs Tanqueray* with the lead role specifically designed for Mrs Patrick Campbell. The actress's gaunt figure underpinned Pinero's depiction of Agnes's radicalism as an aberration of nature. The unhealthy thinness of Mrs Pat's body was deployed to mark Agnes out as a hysteric, a woman whose denial of her true instincts and needs is eating away at her bodily and mental health.[91] Despite the atheism of her parents, Agnes grew up 'devout—as any girl in a parsonage'—piety and purity are clearly the natural state of young girls, in Pinero's view. (I, 73) But an unhappy marriage, in which she was treated as a 'woman in a harem' for the first year and a 'beast of burden' for the next seven, puts paid to Agnes's faith and she turns political speaker, earning the soubriquet of 'Mad Agnes' (I, 73; II, 91). The justice of this label is revealed when Agnes turns oratorical on the subject of class exploitation, her radical views framed by Pinero's stage-directions as a hysteric's displaced passion; she speaks, '*With changed manner, flashing eyes, harsh voice, and violent gestures*' (II, 90).

Beneath the hysterical self-distortion of the new woman, Agnes's true character is then revealed, in scenes rooted in the melodramatic dynamics of moral disclosure. Agnes can see her hold over Lucas slipping as his vanity and sensuality are offended by her plain dress and her suggestion that their relationship aspire to a still higher plane of purely spiritual union. Desperate to keep him, Agnes therefore dons the extremely low-cut and luxurious gown which Lucas has bought her, and finding Lucas enthralled by her new allure, she greets this as her 'One supreme hour' (III, 113). Conceding that 'My sex has found me out', Agnes proceeds to tremble, cry, and faint in conventional womanly fashion. (III, 113) Dressed in the traditional finery of the woman who has exchanged virtue for venery, in a relationship which no longer even pretends to be a marriage of true minds, the new woman is revealed to have been a self-deceiving fallen woman all along. Her virtuous friend Gertrude begs her to repent and gives her a bible, which Agnes thrusts into a convenient furnace, but her true nature cannot be suppressed and in horror she burns her hands snatching it from the flames. Agnes's character is thus fixed, and she retires to a vicarage to contemplate her own weakness and the necessity of social constraints: '*I—I* was to lead women! *I* was to show them, in your company, how laws—laws made and laws that are natural—may be set aside or slighted; how men and women may live independent and noble lives without rule, or guidance, or sacrament' (IV, 133).

---

[90] A. W. Pinero, *The Notorious Mrs Ebbsmith*, in Chothia, *The New Woman and Other Emancipated Woman Plays*, III, 114. First performed Garrick Theatre, 13 March 1895.

[91] On Victorian diagnoses of hysteria as the result of women's suppression of natural impulses and emotions, see Elaine Showalter, *The Female Malady: Women, Madness and English Culture, 1830–1980* (Virago: London, 1987), chs 5 and 6.

Though Pinero had written Mrs Pat's body into the heart of his play, her performance was once again in tension with his script; Mrs Pat projected discomfort and resentment not feminine triumph when she donned the famous dress, and expressed frustration at Agnes's passivity in the last act—Mrs Pat imagined Agnes's crusading zeal for her newly recovered values, where Pinero could only envisage female virtue as meek and submissive.[92] Nonetheless, critics had no difficulty in interpreting the play as 'a splendid sermon to the modern restless woman' and 'an unconventional homily upon the value of social conventions'.[93] Clement Scott was delighted with the play's message, reading it as a triumph of 'love and religion', exclaiming of Agnes, 'With what a subtlety of persuasion does Nature defeat her!'[94] Where a number of critics found the bible-burning scene gratuitous and artificial, Scott applauded Pinero's implicit riposte to *Hedda Gabler*, welcoming the sequence as 'the strongest and most natural in the play'.[95] Where Ibsen's plays challenged the constraints laid upon individual conscience and liberty by outdated notions of morality and duty, Pinero's asserted the vital need for such restraints.

Agnes realizes that her notion of an ideal union disguises her true womanly love for Lucas, but without the religious and social sanction of marriage she finally sees her love as degradation not glory. This affirmation of moral orthodoxy and the need for individual submission to social conformity was all the more remarkable for Pinero's clear depiction of the flaws and hypocrisies of his society. Lucas Cleeve is not so much possessed of feet of clay as entirely composed of that element, as is every other man in his society, with the sole exception of the Reverend Amos, whose protection Agnes finally accepts. Patriarchy is a necessity not an ideal: husbands are brutal and sensual, but dispensing with one leaves women even more vulnerable and debased. When Agnes comes face to face with Lucas's wife Sybil, the equation is at its clearest. Agnes has broken off with Lucas, but Sybil asks her to become his mistress to lure him back to London—whether she genuinely wishes to rescue his career, or needs his return to the marital home to restore her own social standing is never made clear. It is when Agnes looks in Sybil's face that her humiliation is complete—despite Sybil's complicity in the plan to set her up as Lucas's secret mistress in order to preserve her own sham marriage, Agnes experiences the conventional shame of the 'fallen' woman encountering the 'good' woman. Struck by the tears in Sybil's eyes, Agnes *totters away* in horror at the wrong she has done by stealing her husband, returning to clutch at Sybil's skirts, begging for forgiveness (IV, 131). Sybil rejects Agnes's sacrifice as unworthy of her own dignity, and sweeps out, having been offered Gertrude's hand in gratitude. Whatever the shifts and evasions of her society, Sybil's wedding ring makes her a good woman wronged, and Agnes belongs at her feet.

---

[92] See Campbell, *My Life*, 98–100; Joel Kaplan and Sheila Stowell, *Theatre and Fashion, Oscar Wilde to the Suffragettes* (Cambridge University Press: Cambridge, 1995), 62–9.
[93] *Lady's Pictorial* (23 March 1895), 382, 392.
[94] *Illustrated London News* (23 March 1895), 348.
[95] Ibid. For an example of a contrary view see *Stage* (21 March 1895), 13.

In the 1880s playwrights and critics had bemoaned the enforced infantilization of the English stage, held back from an adult discussion of serious issues by audience tastes and the Lord Chamberlain's strictures. *The Profligate, The Second Mrs Tanqueray*, and *The Notorious Mrs Ebbsmith* were identified as significant events in the stage's coming of age, drawing large audiences to plays on controversial issues, and winning a licence for performance despite their unusually explicit action and dialogue—a licence which surprised many reviewers and was generally credited to Pinero's established reputation as a fashionable playwright.[96] Frustrated by the limits to such progress, Bernard Shaw's theatre criticism was a self-declared 'siege laid to the theatre of the XIXth century', prompted by a vision of the stage performing as vital a role as the Church in the Middle Ages, and taking itself seriously as 'a factory of thought, a prompter of conscience, an elucidator of social conduct, an armoury against despair and dullness, and a temple of the Ascent of Man'.[97] *Fin-de-siècle* theatre undoubtedly acted as a forum and prompt for discussion, a sounding board for different ideas, and an arena in which various views could be aired. But the theatre, as Shaw himself well knew, was neither a pulpit nor a soapbox, and plays were necessarily engaged with established conventions of representation and interpretation, signifying systems and generic expectations. Market forces, audience tastes, and performance conditions must be negotiated. A play's 'message' was necessarily subject to and in conversation with all of these.

The Second Mrs Tanqueray drew on multiple theatrical genres and delivered its verdict on the impossibility of Paula's rehabilitation via all of them. Mrs Patrick Campbell set herself to 'plead for Paula', and the unusual naturalism of her acting style inspired pity and horror at her fate; as with Marguerite's fate in *La Dame aux Camélias*, a naturalistic enactment of the time-honoured expulsion and death of the 'fallen' woman had the potential to arouse unease at the reality of a commonplace cliché.[98] But the play's construction was sufficiently robust to render its message unambiguous to contemporary audiences despite a performance from Mrs Pat so sympathetic that one critic described her as having 'not only idealised' but 'absolutely etherealised' the character of Paula.[99] Differently nuanced performances did nothing to unsettle the moral politics of the play. Mrs Kendal, an actress renowned for her respectability, pained her admirers by taking on the scandalous role of Paula in 1893. Her interpretation hinged on Paula's refinement in the course of the play, emphasizing at first the seamy side of her character and then slowly transforming Paula's 'mocking bravado' into 'ineffable tenderness'.[100] But this demonstration of moral improvement and the association of the actress's virtuous reputation with the damaged but aspiring courtesan did nothing to mitigate the play's message. Instead the most moving moment in the play became Paula's despairing

---

[96] For the details on the Examiner of Plays's possible excision of ten lines from *The Notorious Mrs Ebbsmith*, see Joel Kaplan, 'Mrs Ebbsmith's Bible Burning: Page versus Stage', *Theatre Notebook*, XLIV, no.3 (1990), 99–101.

[97] Shaw, 'Author's Apology' (1906), *Our Theatres in the Nineties*. Vol. 1, v–vii.

[98] Campbell, *My Life*, 70.

[99] T. Edgar Pemberton, *The Kendals: A Biography*, (Dodd, Mead & Co: New York, 1900), 273.

[100] Ibid, 278.

realization of the irreparable degradation written on her face, as she ends Act III staring the mirror. Madge Kendal held this moment wordlessly for two long minutes, real tears coursing down her face.[101] The double-bind of Paula's moral value being expressed in her recognition of her own corruption meant that the pathos of her death fed back into the logic of its inevitability. While the play's sign-system was clearly legible to contemporary audiences its message was clear.[102]

Oscar Wilde's *Lady Windermere's Fan* (1892) and *A Woman of No Importance* (1893) stand as structural counterpoints to Pinero's problem plays. Where Pinero's plays are structured around the melodramatic revelation of inherent character and the ultimate assertion of inevitable and natural law, Oscar Wilde's operate on an opposite dynamic; though brim-full with melodramatic situations, they eschew revelation and closure, destabilizing moral certainties and leaving their implications deliberately unfixed. In Pinero social performances and self-deceptions are stripped off to reveal the moral imperatives and essential character beneath. In Wilde pretence is never abandoned; instead social morality itself is a performance. Wilde's society women like Lady Plymdale and Mrs Allonby are clearly adept at conducting their sexual affairs with the requisite skill and style to emerge unscathed. As Mrs Allonby insouciantly explains, 'The one advantage of playing with fire, Lady Caroline, is that one never gets even singed. It is the people who don't know how to play with it who get burned up' (I, 102).[103] Society's morality is a question of who gets invited to which parties, and charm, ingenuity, and money are all that are required to play the game: the fallen Mrs Erlynne wins her re-entry easily by flattering the women and fascinating the men; Mrs Arbuthnot, far from having her sexual past written on her face, has a reputation for extraordinary virtue and is sought after to add the weight of moral seriousness to social gatherings. Wilde reverses the conventions of the fallen woman play: there is an extraordinary similarity between the 'fallen' Mrs Erlynne and her 'good' daughter, the one difference being the mother's greater compassion, resourcefulness, and generosity. Mrs Erlynne does not repent or even acknowledge the morality which judges her; instead she remains opaquely unreadable and poised to the final curtain. She rejects the role of mother, '*hiding her feelings with a trivial laugh*', but what those feelings are beyond sympathy with her impulsive daughter is never made clear to the audience, let alone to the other characters. (IV, 54) Lord Windermere scornfully points to Mrs Erlynne's girlish self, as represented by a miniature his wife innocently covets, as the true self which the mature woman's false appearance and fallen sexuality have betrayed: 'It's the miniature of a young innocent-looking girl

---

[101] *Dame Madge Kendal, By Herself* (John Murray: London, 1933), 266–7.

[102] Plays do not exist in only one historical moment, so this is not to fix the play's meaning in perpetuity. Once Paula's rebuff of Mrs Cortelyon and her initial rejection of Tanqueray's judgement can be viewed as feisty self-assertion rather than a lack of moral awareness and self-control, Paula's death can become a tragic testament to the human cost of a rigid or inhuman morality.

[103] *A Woman of No Importance*. First performed Haymarket Theatre, 19 April 1893. For further discussion of the relation between Wilde's plays and the theatrical conventions and traditions of the era, see Kerry Powell, *Oscar Wilde and the Theatre of the 1890s* (Cambridge University Press: Cambridge, 1991), and Sos Eltis, *Revising Wilde: Society and Subversion in the Plays of Oscar Wilde* (Oxford University Press: Oxford, 1996).

with beautiful dark hair.' No Paula-like paroxysms of tears on the ottoman for Mrs Erlynne; instead she deconstructs the miniature as merely another performance for social consumption: 'It was done before I was married. Dark hair and an innocent expression were the fashion then, Windermere!' (IV, 53). Morality is reduced to a series of melodramatic roles, discarded as claustrophobic and lacking in style. So she mocks her son-in-law's expectation that she will 'retire into a convent, or become a hospital nurse, or something of that kind, as people do in silly modern novels', eschewing a role whose costume does not fit her:

> Repentance is quite out of date. And besides, if a woman really repents, she has to go to a bad dressmaker, otherwise no one believes in her. And nothing in the world would induce me to do that.
>
> (IV, 54)

Mrs Erylnne's mask is never removed; indeed, it is impossible to tell what is a mask and what her true self. The play ends on a contradiction, when Lady Windermere corrects her husband's barbed description of Mrs Erlynne as 'a very clever woman', with her own equally inadequate labelling of her as 'a very good woman' (IV, 59). Neither character knows the full truth about Mrs Erlynne's identity or actions, and the complexity of her character evades their easy labelling.

A Woman of No Importance (1893) similarly toys with melodramatic expectations, but eschews revelation for performance; its characters are not fixed and delivered to the audience, but continue to play roles whose relation to their inner thoughts and feelings remains ambiguous and unanswerable. When Mrs Arbuthnot prevents her son striking Lord Illingworth with the cry of 'Stop, Gerald, stop! He is your own father!', falling at her son's feet in shame, the situation, language, and gesture are straight from melodrama (III, 143). As William Archer wryly commented, 'It would be a just punishment if Mr Wilde were presently to be confronted with this tableau, in all the horrors of chromolithography, on every hoarding in London, with the legend...in crinkly letters in the corner.'[104] Mrs Arbuthnot adopts the time-honoured role of seduced maiden, but Lord Illingworth calmly mocks the moral simplicity of such a version of events, answering in a contrary register of calm, if cynical, rationality which leaves her rhetoric sounding hyperbolic and histrionic:

MRS ARBUTHNOT: Are you talking of the child you abandoned? Of the child who, as far as you were concerned, might have died of hunger and want?
LORD ILLINGWORTH: You forget, Rachel, it was you who left me. It was not I who left you.
MRS ARBUTHNOT: I left you because you refused to give the child a name. Before my son was born, I implored you to marry me.

---

[104] Archer, *Theatrical 'World' of 1893*, 108.

LORD ILLINGWORTH: I had no expectations then. And besides, Rachel, I wasn't much older than you were. . . .

MRS ARBUTHNOT: When a man is old enough to do wrong he should be old enough to do right also.

LORD ILLINGWORTH: My dear Rachel, intellectual generalities are always interesting, but generalities in morals mean absolutely nothing. As for saying I left our child to starve, that, of course, is untrue and silly. My mother offered you six hundred a year.

(II, 127)

Mrs Arbuthnot is ultimately as difficult to read or categorize as Mrs Erlynne. Her adoption of the role of repentant magdalen is only skin-deep; as she informs her son, she only visited the poor and tended the sick because she had no other outlet for her unwanted maternal passion, and she has no nostalgic longing for innocence: 'I cannot repent. I do not. You are more to me than innocence' (IV, 150). Nor is this confession a melodramatic revelation of inner character which pins Mrs Arbuthnot down for the audience's judgement, for it is never clear whether her adoption of the roles of seduced innocent and repentant magdalen was conscious or unconscious, whether she is a moral original, a hypocrite, or a female rebel, according to Lord Illingworth's definition, 'in wild revolt against herself' (III, 133).

In Pinero's theatre false ideas and social performances are stripped away to reveal moral imperatives; in Wilde's theatre moral imperatives are revealed to be a performance. In *The Importance of Being Earnest* (1895) this performance is reduced to absurdity.[105] Poetic justice and punitive morality are parodied in the person of Miss Prism, who greets the news that Jack's wicked (and fictional) brother Ernest is dead by exclaiming, 'What a lesson for him! I trust he will profit by it' (II, 277). When Jack mistakenly believes himself to be Miss Prism's illegitimate son, he compresses the emotional journey of an entire melodrama into one accelerated piece of dramatic rhetoric:

Unmarried! I do not deny that is a serious blow. But after all, who has the right to cast a stone against one who has suffered? Cannot repentance wipe out an act of folly? Why should there be one law for men, and another for women? Mother, I forgive you.

(III, 305)

Such performative antics left contemporary critics understandably bewildered, searching in vain for moral certainties or an extractable message. In the case of *A Woman of No Importance*, for example, some attempted to read the play as a sermon on the corruption of *fin-de-siècle* society, some saw it as Ibsenite radicalism, some dismissed it as old-fashioned melodrama, but all were to a degree perplexed by the play's obstinate refusal to flatten out into any consistent theatrical genre or meaning.[106] None of them, however, could see past their search for the

---

[105] First performed St James's Theatre, 14 February 1895.
[106] See e.g. *Black and White* 5 (29 April 1893), 318; *Athenaeum* 3417 (22 April 1893), 515–16; *Illustrated Church News* (27 May 1893), 556; *Saturday Review* 75 (6 May 1893), 482–3; *Bookman* (March 1893), vii–viii; *Theatre* 21 (June 1893), 330.

play's final judgement to its challenge to very concept of sexual judgement itself; as Wilde commented to an interviewer:

> Several plays have been written lately that deal with the monstrous injustice of the social code of morality at the present time. It is indeed a burning shame that there should be one law for men and another law for women. I think that there should be no law for anybody.[107]

Wilde deliberately played with audiences and critics, but even the polemically driven theatre of Shaw could produce a similar interpretative confusion. Plot had so long been the carrier of meaning that many critics were left confused by Shaw's *Candida* which replayed the familiar plot of female adultery averted but with radically different causation. Candida remains with her husband and sends her young admirer packing not because of any concern for her 'goodness and purity', which she declares she would give to her would-be lover 'as willingly as I would give my shawl to a beggar dying of cold', but because she knows her husband is the weaker man who stands in greater need of her love and support—he is the doll in her doll's house, Shaw quipped.[108] While a few critics were able to recognize Candida's rejection of conventional morality, many could not see past the usual resolution of restored marital harmony, in one case concluding that Candida 'so far defers to convention as to remain with her husband'.[109] As one journalist astutely observed, '[Shaw] writes a brilliant play, with a subtle and profound aim; the public pronounce it excellent, while getting out of it a meaning of their own, essentially different from the meaning of the author.'[110]

Shaw's mission to revolutionize nineteenth-century theatre, unsettle its traditions and challenge its underlying assumptions makes it unsurprising that contemporary critics often had difficulty knowing how to approach his plays. Yet the works of fashionable society playwright Henry Arthur Jones could on occasions produce similar interpretative uncertainty, highlighting both the critical assumption that plays must necessarily adopt a moral standpoint or assert a moral conclusion, and the complexity of identifying such meaning within the fluid and often competing theatrical sign systems of plays which could be variously and multiply classed as melodrama, *pièce à thèse*, well-made play, satirical comedy, problem play, or fashionable society drama. Where plays like *The Second Mrs Tanqueray* delivered the same moral conclusion via each of the different sets of theatrical conventions and languages which it deployed, a number of Jones's plays, by contrast, offered different implications according to which genre they were located within. Each theatrical genre carried in-built mechanisms for conveying moral judgements: from poetically just resolution, to the pronouncements of a *raisonneur*, the direction of audience sympathies, or character-based demonstrations of virtue and vice, the range of signifying systems was wide and diverse.

---

[107] Quoted in Hesketh Pearson, *The Life of Oscar Wilde* (Methuen: London, 1946), 251.
[108] *Candida*, II, 565. Shaw, 'Author's Note' in programme for production at the Globe Theatre, London, 10 February 1937, reprinted in *Bernard Shaw, Collected Plays*, vol. 1, 601.
[109] *Era* (7 August 1897), 11.
[110] *Newcastle Weekly Courant* (15 June 1895), 5.

There was thus a potential for generic instability to produce uncertainty of meaning, or for the various signifying systems to offer conflicting and diverse implications. Such instability and uncertainty featured in a number of Jones's drama, producing unsettling currents which variously intrigued and provoked audiences and critics.

Jones's *The Case of Rebellious Susan* (1894), for example, was clearly modelled on the French problem play, but the dark thread running through its comic lightness and the patent lack of romance in its conclusion left critics unsure of the author's standpoint. *The Case of Rebellious Susan* reproduces the problem at the heart of Dumas's *Francillon* (1887) as to whether a wife is entitled to repay her husband's infidelity in kind. In Dumas's *pièce à thèse* a young wife announces she has paid her unfaithful husband tit for tat. Francillon's enraged spouse threatens to throw her off, until, assured by friends that his wife is incapable of such baseness, he eavesdrops on a conversation which confirms her innocence, and the couple are reconciled. Both Pinero and Jones reproduced Dumas's scenario and his conservative morality in *The Benefit of the Doubt* (1895) and *Joseph Entangled* (1904) respectively. But in *The Case of Rebellious Susan* Jones departed radically from moral and theatrical convention by suggesting that the betrayed wife has gone through with her threat of adulterous revenge and that, cowed by her fear of social opprobrium, she reluctantly returns to a husband who remains ignorant of her affair. In the play's first production, however, there was only a faint hint of Susan's possible guilt, the actor-manager, Charles Wyndham, having insisted that Jones remove any evidence of the wife's adultery before he would produce the play. The issue was crucial in Wyndham's view, for if Susan had not consummated her love then 'the woman's mind has strayed, but not her soul'.[111] In Wyndham's opinion, female adultery was not a subject for comedy, and no husband would bring his wife to the theatre to be taught such a 'lesson'.[112] Jones capitulated, but, in a 'Letter to Mrs Grundy' prefacing the published edition, he wrested back his authority, clearly stating that the play's moral was 'that as women cannot retaliate openly, they may retaliate secretly—and *lie*!'[113]

Even in its watered-down form a number of reviewers were uneasy with the play's ending and its uncertain relation to theatrical genre. The *Morning Post* clearly wished to see it as a romantic comedy, but found insufficient reassurance of marital harmony in the play's closing dialogue which was condemned as 'altogether too *banal* for the occasion'.[114] The *Lady*'s critic complained that Jones 'plays shuttlecock and battledore…with one of the most momentous themes of the end-of-the-century', commenting tartly that, 'There are moments when his robust and healthy sentiments lead us to believe that he holds the marriage-tie to be sacred and inviolable. There are others, when we are compelled to think he is laughing in his sleeve.'[115] The *Theatre*'s

---

[111] Doris Arthur Jones, *The Life and Letters of Henry Arthur Jones* (Victor Gollancz: London, 1930), 165–6.

[112] Ibid, 165.

[113] 'To Mrs Grundy', in Jackson (ed.), *Plays by Henry Arthur Jones* (Cambridge University Press: Cambridge, 1982), 107.

[114] *Morning Post* (4 October 1894), 3.

[115] *Lady* (11 October 1894), 463.

critic was even more uncertain as to whether Jones was offering Susan's marital reconciliation as a comic restoration of harmony or a woman's hopeless entrapment in a loveless marriage, wondering if 'Mr Jones, under the guise of a happy ending, has not placed his heroine in a more tragic, a more pitiful plight than if he had allowed her to fall into disgrace.'[116] The lack of satisfactory closure was underlined for many critics by C. P. Little's less than dashing appearance as the adulterous husband, with his 'bald head, eye-glass, and generally vacuous expression', prompting *Vanity Fair* to liken him to 'a garden mole' or a 'Southdown sheep'.[117] Most disturbingly, as Augustin Filon noted, Little's 'hungry glances' as he helped Susan off with her opera cloak, hinted that 'The love that she is offered and the love she wants are not the same love.'[118]

Counterbalancing the play's subversive refusal to confirm Susan's innocence or to inject any romance into the reconciliation of husband and wife, it remains stubbornly anti-feminist courtesy of its plotting and the philosophy of Sir Richard Cato, the play's *raisonneur*. Female rebellion is presented as fruitless and self-damaging: Susan's romance ends in ignominious abandonment—her lover is engaged to another woman within weeks of swearing undying love—and her cousin Elaine's political activities are reduced to farce. Sir Richard Cato is thus supported by the plot in his confident assertion that there is 'no gander sauce' and that gender roles are fixed by nature.[119] Sir Richard was greeted by reviewers as a fount of good sense and wisdom, and numerous papers quoted in full (presumably for the edification of female readers) his grandstanding speech declaring that, 'There is an immense future for women as wives and mothers, and a very limited future for them in any other capacity' (III, 153–4).[120] Critics thus perceived Sir Richard as an authorial mouthpiece, on the model of Dumas's *raisonneurs*, delivering the play's moral. In Jones's next huge hit, *The Liars* (1896), Sir Christopher Decring was similarly positioned as a moral adjudicator and was accepted by reviewers as such. Sir Richard Cato declares marriage to be 'a perfect institution...worked by imperfect creatures', and this mixture of orthodox idealism and cynical pragmatism is even starker in *The Liars*, where Sir Christopher returns an unhappy wife to her brutish husband, complimenting English society on its wisdom because, 'We're not a bit better than our neighbours, but, thank God! we do pretend that we are, and we do make it hot for anybody who disturbs that holy pretence.'[121] Shaw commented astutely on the tension between the play's action and the ideals it upheld:

> The comedic sentiment of *The Liars* is from beginning to end one of affectionate contempt for women and friendly contempt for men, applied to their affairs with shrewd, worldly common sense and much mollifying humour; while its essentially pious theology

---

[116] *Theatre* (1 November 1894), 250.
[117] *Morning Post* (4 October 1894), 3; *Vanity Fair* (25 October 1894), 287.
[118] Filon, *English Stage*, 250.
[119] *The Case of Rebellious Susan*, in Jackson (ed.), *Plays by Henry Arthur Jones*, I, 112. First performed Criterion Theatre, 3 October 1894.
[120] See e.g. *Daily Telegraph* (4 October 1894), 3; *Morning Post* (4 October 1894), 3; *St James's Gazette* (4 Oct 94), 12. This speech echoed some of the most virulent contemporary anti-feminism, as for example, Charles Harper's *Revolted Woman: Past, Present, and to Come* (1894).
[121] *Case of Rebellious Susan*, I, 113; *The Liars*, in *Plays by Henry Arthur Jones*, IV, 215.

and its absolute conceptions of duty belong to a passionate and anti-comedic conception of them as temples of the Holy Ghost.[122]

In performance Charles Wyndham's stage presence and charisma did much to resolve this tension, wresting authority back to the conservative voice of the *raisonneur*. So Irene Vanbrugh described Wyndham's off-stage preparation for the climactic moral speech in *The Liars*:

> Part of his method was to stand in the wings for some minutes before his entrance, concentrating mentally and exercising physically. Then when all his powers were well assembled he entered like a vital spark, illuminating the whole stage and unerringly focussing the attention of the audience.[123]

Charles Wyndham's theatrical charisma and authority implicitly claimed the status of authorial mouthpieces for the characters he portrayed, but even with Wyndham once again in the role of moral guide and adjudicator, Jones's next sex-problem play, *Mrs Dane's Defence* (1900), proved even harder to interpret as delivering one unambiguous moral message. The emotional trajectory of the play was in tension with the *raisonneur*'s positioning as the ultimate voice of truth.

In *Mrs Dane's Defence*, Lionel Carteret is engaged to marry the charming and intelligent widow Mrs Dane, when a local gossipmonger, Mrs Bulsom-Porter, starts the scandalous rumour that Mrs Dane is living under an assumed identity and is in fact Felicia Hindemarsh, quondam lover of a married man whose wife committed suicide when the affair was revealed. Lionel's guardian, Sir Daniel Carteret, sets about clearing Mrs Dane's name, but in a sensational cross-examination scene he instead extracts a confession of guilt. Despite being genuinely in love with Lionel and determined to make him an excellent wife, Mrs Dane is unhesitatingly shown the door, even her besotted fiancé agreeing the match must be broken off.

Mrs Dane's Defence thus seems to rescind the saving grace of uncertainty Jones had previously allowed his rebellious Susan; in the later play, no doubt can be tolerated as to a woman's sexual guilt, and it is the *raisonneur* who roots the transgressive woman out and expels her. But the audience is in little doubt as to Mrs Dane's true identity; it is relayed in the melodramatic language of gesture. The climactic curtain of Act One has her left alone on stage, furtively observing her honest hosts from behind a curtain, '*watching, listening, with drawn, frightened face*'.[124] Her physical gestures and expressions speak her real identity long before she is seen to persuade a hired detective to lie on her behalf. But this does not fix her character as corrupt. Mrs Dane's performance in public remains seamless and convincing, so that the difference between a guilty woman and an innocent one is indecipherable;

---

[122] Shaw, *Our Theatres in the 90s*, vol. III, 212–13.

[123] Irene Vanbrugh, *To Tell My Story* (Hutchinson & Co.: London, 1948), 38. For more on Wyndham's stage presence see, Wendy Trewin, *All on Stage: Charles Wyndham and the Alberys* (Harrap: London, 1980), and George Rowell, 'Criteria for comedy: Charles Wyndham at the Criterion Theatre', in Foulkes, *British Theatre in the 1890s*.

[124] Jones, *Mrs Dane's Defence*, in Michael R. Booth (ed.), *English Plays of the Nineteenth Century*, Vol. II: *Dramas, 1850–1900* (Clarendon Press: London, 1969), I, 366. First performed Wyndham's Theatre, 9 October 1900.

the audience repeatedly witnesses the lightning transformation of her haggard face into a radiant smile, the suppression of a spasm of fright and its replacement with a look of '*the utmost frankness*' (III, 407). Virtue and vice are outwardly indistinguishable; her past, unlike Paula Tanqueray's, has left no impression on her face, manners or conversation. The melodramatic language of truth revealed is thus transformed into a more troubling world in which the difference between a fallen and a chaste woman is indecipherable, distinguishable only with inside knowledge or painstaking investigation. Privy to Mrs Dane's secret, the audience's interest is necessarily focused on whether she will be found out, watching her ruthlessly tracked down, at first winning a private detective's mercy, then cornered by Sir Daniel. As the *Times's* reviewer noted, all along the audience's sympathy 'had been with the hunted, tortured woman. But its sympathy became something fierce and passionate when the poor creature was at last brought to bay.' This was, the reviewer concluded 'the effect, of course, at which the playwright had aimed'.[125]

Apart from fearfully living under an assumed identity, there is no suggestion that Mrs Dane is in any way debased or coarsened by her experiences—she is perfectly assimilated into polite society and wins the affectionate friendship of Lady Eastney, who questions the need to expel her—why the cold-heart or cunning to resist should mark one woman as good and another as untouchable. Though Sir Daniel himself once attempted to persuade Lionel's mother to leave her husband and child, he answers Lady Eastney's challenge with unconscious heat, insisting that, 'A man demands the treasure of a woman's purest love. It's what he buys and pays for with the strength of his arm and the sweat of his brow' (IV, 416). This answer is enough to win Lady Eastney's hand in marriage, but Sir Daniel's appeal to nature's law sits awkwardly alongside the language of economic power and exclusive ownership; the supposedly unshakeable moral law sounds suspiciously like a buyers' market in which men dictate the terms of sale.

Sir Daniel's defence of men's right to dictate sexual morality because they pay the bills is an unsettling mix of pragmatism, morality, and the self-assurance of the powerful. The question of whether this speech should be taken as an authorially validated 'lesson' of the play is further complicated by the fact that a number of Jones's other plays satirize moral hypocrisy in remarkably similar terms. Morality is repeatedly revealed to be the tool of those in power, a set of attitudes and phrases adopted to acquire and consolidate social position and wealth. *Saints and Sinners* satirized the fraudulence of aspiring shopkeepers who dressed their commercial greed in the language of religious piety. In *The Hypocrites* (1906) Jones again combined seduction melodrama with biting social satire, as landowning parents lie, threaten, and manipulate to prevent their son's financially 'profitable' marriage being shipwrecked by the appearance of the pregnant lover he abandoned. The church and the law conspire to dress ruthless ambition in the language of moral superiority, condemning the woman and condoning the man in order to keep hold of valuable mortgages and secure class alliances.

These tensions between the play's emotional structure and the precepts of its *raisonneur*, between idealism and pragmatism, morality and power, are seen most clearly in

---

[125] *Times* (10 October 1900), 3.

The Princess's Nose (1902), Jones's most ruthless staging of the sexual double standard as the morality of those in command. It left audiences and critics unsure whether the play intended to validate or satirize the moral dynamics it anatomized. The Princess of the title is Norah, a young wife who, like Dumas's Francillon, has just emerged from nursing her first child to find that her husband is rumoured to be having an affair. The Prince is French—Jones's one sop to an English audience presented with a husband unashamedly asserting his right to sexual freedom while demanding fidelity from his wife. The object of the Prince's attentions is Mrs Malpas, a former school friend of his wife's. However, despite the rumours, the Prince's desires have not yet been consummated; as he complains, she eggs him on but he is still out in the cold. An extraordinary scene ensues, in which Mrs Malpas carefully negotiates the terms of her acquiescence. There is no question of frailty or impulse here; the would-be adulterous woman is entirely in control, dictating conditions and ensuring the odds are in her favour. She will not become the Prince's lover until she is assured of his financial protection and social support should the affair become public. Her husband enters before the negotiation is complete, and Mrs Malpas lays out her final demands to the Prince via an apparently innocent discussion with her husband over whether he should accept an appointment to work for a brewery in Brussels. Mrs Malpas looks pointedly at the Prince as she questions her husband:

MRS MALPAS: You know, dearest, you brew terribly heavy beer; now this good
Pilsener gentleman brews the merest light lager, yet he is even stouter and heavier than you are. If—?!
MR MALPAS: If what?
MRS MALPAS: Adversity makes some people fat. [*Looking at him.*]
If—?![126]

Mrs Malpas thus discusses the possibility of an illegitimate pregnancy with her lover through the guise of wifely concern for her husband's waistline. This dialogue was unsurprisingly described by the *Manchester Guardian* as 'sometimes crude' despite its wit.[127] Satisfied with her terms, the bargain is sealed.

The mistress is well aware of the vulnerability of her position and takes care to insure herself against mishap. Norah is rudely awakened to the terms of her marital contract when her uncle, Sir John, the closest the play has to a *raisonneur*, advises his niece against making her husband's infidelity public; if she does so the Prince will be forced to stand by the woman whose reputation he has ruined, leaving Norah either to forgive him or to face a judicial separation, limited allowance, and a lonely life. If she seeks companionship herself, she then becomes *déclassée*. While acknowledging the harshness of Norah's situation, Sir John blithely attributes the sexual double-standard to 'Providence' (I, 27). The *raisonneur* does not merely advise submission as Sir Richard Cato does to rebellious Susan, but makes it Norah's responsibility to woo back her husband, not to reproach him or confront him, but to seduce him:

---

[126] Jones, *The Princess's Nose* (Chiswick Press: London, 1902. Privately printed), I, 17. First performed Duke of York's Theatre, 11 March 1902.
[127] *Manchester Guardian* (13 March 1902), 9.

It isn't always the husband's fault when things go wrong. Five times out of ten it's the wife's. She's on the spot! She's in possession! My dear girl, we're the vainest, weakest, silliest creatures. We're always ready to let any of you conquer us—even when you're married to us—much more when you're married to us—if you only know your weapons, and keep them bright, and use them carefully.

(I, 28)

Genuinely in love with her husband, Norah cannot play a silent game and confronts him with his infidelity, for which he coolly refuses to apologize, informing her she is powerless to intervene, and threatening her with ruin should she attempt to enjoy a similar sexual freedom.

A carriage waits at the door to take the Prince abroad for an assignation with Mrs Malpas, and the Princess desperately adopts her uncle's advice. Having ordered brandy and warm clothes to make his carriage ride more comfortable, she asks her husband to delay his departure for a few minutes so he can give his opinion on her new negligée. He reluctantly agrees, and the Princess then pretends a seductive desire which she does not feel:

PRINCESS *opens the curtains, and appears in a very beautiful negligée gown.*
PRINCESS: Keep your eyes shut till I tell you to open them.
[*She comes slowly down the steps to him; stands close to him; makes first an angry gesture at him with her two clenched hands; then makes a pretty little appealing gesture.*
PRINCESS: Now you may open your eyes.

(III, 67)

The wife must play the whore, arousing her husband's sexual passion when she feels none. Nora Helmer's famous tarantella is ambiguously part self-expression, a hysterical release of pent-up energy, part seduction, performing her husband's favourite dance to distract him from reading the incriminating letter. Jones's brutal replay of Ibsen's scenario contains no ambiguity; his Norah's performance is equally desperate and exclusively sexual. The dynamics of power are made ruthlessly clear: having softened her husband's heart, the Princess lets slip that she has already cancelled his carriage and sent a message to his waiting lover; incandescent with rage at having his orders countermanded, the Prince leaves to meet Mrs Malpas. All real power is the husband's; the wife's is only the prostitute's arsenal of seduction, pretence, and persuasion.

Having laid bare the power relations within this marriage, Jones quickly veils them in a comic resolution. Driving to meet the Prince, Mrs Malpas's nose is broken in a carriage accident, rendering her damaged goods to be handed back to her husband; so the Prince responds, 'Her nose in ruins! [*Long pause.*] How extremely unfortunate for poor Malpas' (IV, 85). Though the play ends with a marital embrace, the comic resolution does not attempt to dispel the cynicism which preceded it; the Prince promises fidelity only so long as 'you hold me as close as you do now' (IV, 91). The wife's position is only secure while her attractions surpass her rivals'.

Critics were unsure how to take Jones's play. The *Manchester Guardian* declared it unclear at any point in the play 'whether the author intends his theme to be taken as serious or as comic'; the *Times* described the play as 'Henry Arthur Jones Gallicized' and noted in puzzlement that 'The Prince we in our innocence should have regarded—and, we cannot help thinking, the fundamental True-Born Englishman in Mr Jones would in the old ungallicized days have regarded—as a finished black-guard.'[128] Bernard Shaw wrote to Jones in horror at 'this most turpitudinous play', equally nonplussed at the playwright's apparent validation of Sir John's advice:

> I quite admit that the proposition of your infamous old *raisonneur*, that a man's wife is simply his whore, and must compete with all his other whores if she is to retain her hold of him, is as a matter of fact true of a considerable number of marriages.... But that you of all men should embrace this position and make comedy capital out of it, as if it were an entirely satisfactory and sensible one... is utterly unendurable.[129]

As Shaw pointed out, the cynicism of Sir John's advice in *The Princess's Nose* cast a dark light on the role of Jones's previous *raisonneurs*, retrospectively emphasizing their moral ambiguity: 'The Wyndham plays were immoral (as their climax in *The Princess's Nose* now shows).'[130] Reading the public taste correctly, Shaw predicted pecuniary as well as moral bankruptcy for the play, which closed after only a few weeks. At the opening night, the audience had enthusiastically applauded Irene Vanbrugh as the Princess, H. B. Irving as the Prince, and Gilbert Hare as Sir John, but when one audience member timidly cried 'Author!' a sudden silence fell upon the house. The play's anatomizing of marriage as a contract in which the husband held all the power and was free to pick up or discard mistresses as damaged goods, while the wife had to play the whore to retain her place in society and his affections, was not one which met with public approval.

The personal key to a possible resolution of the apparent tensions between Jones's anti-feminist assertion of traditional gender roles and his anatomizing of morality as the reflection of social and economic power may lie in his reading of Herbert Spencer. In *The Dancing Girl* Spencer's teaching is summed up as 'You must bring yourself into perfect agreement with your environment or get crushed!' Jones's declaration that 'Any clear thinking I've done I owe to Herbert Spencer' may thus suggest that his belief that women should submit to social morality was founded on pragmatic laws of survival rather than a belief that orthodox sexual morality represented an inevitable and natural state of affairs.[131] In his analysis of the relation between economic power and social morality *The Princess's Nose* could thus be aligned with plays such as Shaw's *Widowers' Houses* (1892) and *The Philanderer* (1893) or later feminist plays such as Elizabeth Robins's *Votes for Women!* (1907), but where Shaw and Robins sought to rouse outrage and protest, Jones

---

[128] *Manchester Guardian* (13 March 1902), 9; *Times* (12 March 1902), 10.

[129] Shaw, Letter to Henry Arthur Jones, 22 March 1902, quoted in D. A. Jones, *Life and Letters of Henry Arthur Jones*, 212.

[130] Ibid.

[131] Quoted in Jones, *Life and Letters,* 114. As Kirsten Shepherd-Barr has interestingly pointed out, this line is only present in the licensing copy of *The Dancing Girl* and not in the printed editions of the play. For further discussion of Jones and evolutionary theory, see Kirsten Shepherd-Barr, *Theatre and Evolution* (Princeton University Press: Princeton, NJ, forthcoming 2014).

advocated pragmatic resignation. The difference between a radical protest play and a conservative drama of social integration and adaptation could thus be virtually imperceptible, depending crucially on the playwright's reputation, and on consequent audience expectations and assumptions. Certainly *The Princess's Nose* left audiences uncomfortable in a way which Shaw's dramas were explicitly designed to do. Positioned between dark comedy, satire, and cynical problem play, its *raisonneur* validated by the play's resolution but voicing a brutal logic which left audiences dismayed, *The Princess's Nose* confronted audiences with the equation between morality and power without a let-out of sentiment or disapproval.

This apparently endless wave of plays on sexual guilt and judgement hit the stage at a point when the sexual status of acting as a profession for women was particularly contested. For centuries actresses had been viewed as sexually tainted and easily available, their bodies—like prostitutes'—publicly displayed and financially purchasable for male pleasure.[132] The later decades of the nineteenth century saw an increasing recognition of the professional training, expertise, and hard work demanded of actresses, and the strenuous efforts of women such as Helen Faucit, Fanny Kemble and Madge Kendal to refigure the profession as fully compatible with sexual propriety and domestic conformity had done much to gain a far more respectable image for female stage performers. Indeed, when Clement Scott expressed the view that 'It is nearly impossible for a woman to remain pure who adopts the stage as a profession', in an interview for the periodical *Great Thoughts* in 1897, the storm of outraged protest raised in response forced him to resign as theatre critic of the *Daily Telegraph*.[133] The low wages, long and late hours, often-revealing costumes, and dependency on the whims of generally male theatre managers, together with Victorian pornography's enduring fascination with the figure of the actress, all combined to place the female performer in a position of particular sexual vulnerability. Yet, for those who rose to the top of the profession, the remuneration and employment opportunities offered women quite exceptional independence and autonomy. Leading actresses such as Sarah Bernhardt, Mrs Patrick Campbell, Lillie Langtry, Eleonora Duse, and Helena Modjeska were able to set up their own production companies, eschewing male management if they wished and choosing their roles and repertoires according to their own and audience tastes.

It is noticeable that all these performers included in their repertoires, or indeed filled them almost exclusively with, plays centring on sexually transgressive roles. Sex-problem plays, whether by Dumas, Augier, and Sardou, or by Pinero, Jones, and Wilde, offered rich opportunities for showcasing the celebrity actress and her

[132] See e.g. Kristina Straub, *Sexual Suspects: Eighteenth-Century Players and Sexual Ideology* (Princeton University Press: Princeton, NJ, 1992); Tracy C. Davis, *Actresses as Working Women: their social identity in Victorian Culture* (Routledge: London, 1991); Kirsten Pullen, *Actresses and Whores: on stage and in society* (Cambridge University Press: Cambridge, 2005).

[133] Raymond Blathwayt, *'Does the Theatre make for Good?': An interview with Mr Clement Scott*, reprinted from *Great Thoughts* (A. W. Hall: London, 1898), 4. See also, Mary Jean Corbett, *Representing Femininity: Middle-Class Subjectivity in Victorian and Edwardian Women's Autobiographies* (Oxford University Press: New York, 1992).

sexual appeal—opportunities which were equally exploited by male playwrights and managers and by the actresses who starred in them. So popular were some of these roles that theatre audiences could compare different actresses performing them in London at the same time: Bernhardt's performance of Gilberte in *Frou-frou* coincided with Helena Modjeska's performance of the same role in June 1881, and with Gabrielle Réjane's in 1897; and in 1895 London audiences could compare two Agnes Ebbsmiths, four Fedoras, two Marguerite Gautiers and three Magdas. An apocryphal story makes clear the sexual appeal of these roles, as well as their status as a battleground for competing performers: a salacious tale circulated of a party given by Marie Colombier which climaxed with a competition between illustrious actresses, including Helen Faucit, Bernhardt, and Modjeska, in which each played a scene from *La Dame aux Camélias* naked, the prize being judged by Ellen Terry and awarded to Helena Modjeska.[134] The very existence of such a story speaks volumes.

Plays centring on female desire and transgression, in which the audience's attention was focused on the actress's body and its imagined sexual history, proved a profitable theatrical commodity for theatre managers, and one which the actresses themselves were quick to exploit. So Sarah Bernhardt, for example, structured her lucrative international touring career around a series of sexually sensational roles: her first tour of America, for example, involved 156 performances of which 65 were of *La Dame aux Camélias,* 41 of *Frou-frou*, 17 of *Adrienne Lecouvreur* and 6 of *Phèdre*. To these staples Bernhardt added over the years a further sequence of murderous and erotically-charged roles, such as Sardou's Tosca, Théodora and Fédora, and Hermann Sudermann's Magda. It was a repertoire which showcased Bernhardt's most saleable skill, summed up by the *New York Dramatic Mirror* in 1892 as 'portraying the abandonment of animal passion—the idiosyncrasies, the hysteria, the caprices, and the tragic denouements of illicit love'.[135] Bernhardt fostered a public image which complemented and helped to advertise her sensational repertoire, encouraging rumours, for example, that she travelled with the skeleton of a past lover and slept every night in silk-lined coffin.[136] Lillie Langtry, who moved into acting after first coming to public notice as a society beauty and the Prince of Wales's mistress, similarly cultivated off-stage notoriety as a complement to her sensational repertoire. She first tried to mark out a stage career in sentimental comedy but soon switched course in response to audiences' and critics' resistance to such a re-typing of herself. Langtry instead proceeded to make a fortune producing herself in a repertoire rooted in her sexual celebrity, with plays whose titles

---

[134] Henry Knepler, *The Gilded Stage: The lives and careers of four great actresses, Rachel Félix, Adelaide Ristori, Sarah Bernhardt and Eleonora Duse* (Constable: London, 1968), 203–4.

[135] Quoted in Susan A. Glenn, *Female Spectacle, The Theatrical Roots of Modern Feminism* (Harvard University Press: Cambridge, MA, 2000), 19. See also Elaine Aston, *Sarah Bernhardt: A French Actress on the English Stage* (Berg: Oxford, 1989); Sarah Bernhardt, *My Double Life: The Memoirs of Sarah Bernhardt* (State of New York Press: Albany, NY, 1999).

[136] Bernhardt was notably less happy with the unwanted publicity of an entrepreneur who followed her American tour in 1881 with the carcass of a huge whale, advertised as supplying ribs for Bernhardt's corsets. See Knepler, *The Gilded Stage*, ch. 7, esp. 154.

marketed themselves: Clement Scott's *A Wife's Peril* (1888), Sidney Grundy's *The Degenerates* (1899), Percy Fendall's *Mrs Deering's Divorce*, and Cecil Raleigh and Henry Hamilton's *The Sins of Society* (1911).[137]

But even for the powerful and financially independent celebrity actress there was a careful line to tread between potentially profitable notoriety and outright scandal or social ostracism. Both Sarah Bernhardt and Lillie Langtry were careful to excise any mention of their illegitimate offspring from their autobiographies, and declined to put in print any mention of the numerous affairs about which rumours constantly circulated, adding to their box-office drawing power.[138] Mrs Patrick Campbell in particular attempted a careful balancing act between associating herself closely enough with the roles she played to encourage her audiences' suspension of disbelief and help maintain a personal claim on them, yet retaining enough distance to protect her professional status and aristocratic friendships. Having made her name as Paula Tanqueray, Mrs Pat was successively cast as fallen women in plays by Pinero, Jones, Sardou, and Haddon Chambers, and she remained well aware of their box-office draw; when she set up in production herself, her standard touring roles were Paula Tanqueray, Agnes Ebbsmith, Hedda Gabler, and Magda.[139] Keen to maintain her own personal claim on a role she had first created, she scoffed at the idea of a woman as famously domestic as Madge Kendal playing Paula Tanqueray, telling an interviewer:

> I have never ceased being amused at dear Mrs Kendall attempting Paula Tanqueray. Fancy that domestic soul with six children sobbing over her past misdeeds and social ostracism. The scene was flat when I remembered her own happy domesticity. It's the temperament of the actress, I may add the personality, that gives these stage women their charm.[140]

Yet Mrs Pat was careful to emphasize her own wifely and maternal devotion in her autobiography, pulling a careful veil over her extramarital relationships.

On occasions, an actress's personal reputation for sexual decorum could make audiences reluctant to accept them in a scandalous role, as evidenced by the discomfort of Madge Kendal's fans when she played Paula Tanqueray, and the critical unease which greeted Marion Terry's last-minute casting as Jones's 'lost angel' Audrie Lesden, when Mrs Pat dropped out of the role. In an era when acting theories tended to emphasize the need for imaginative sympathy between performer and character, and naturalistic acting styles encouraged audiences to view performers as 'being' rather than embodying the women they played, actresses were necessarily wary of inviting

---

[137] See Lillie Langtry, *The Days I Knew* (Hutchinson: London, 1925); Laura Beatty, *Lillie Langtry: Manners, Masks and Morals* (Vintage: London, 2000).

[138] See Bernhardt, *My Double Life*; Langtry, *The Days I Knew*.

[139] See Campbell, *My Life*; Margot Peters, *Mrs Pat: The Life of Mrs Patrick Campbell* (Hamish Hamilton: London, 1985).

[140] *The Philharmonic*, p.38, n.d. (but mention of *Beyond Human Power* and *The Joy of Living* places it as *c.*1903), Mrs Patrick Campbell Collection, Harvard Theatre Collection, Houghton Library, Harvard University. Madge Kendal's name was variously spelt as 'Kendall' or 'Kendal', the latter being the spelling she herself preferred.

too intimate an association with immoral roles.[141] So, for example, William Archer sympathized with Duse's evident reluctance to play the tipsy and lecherous Cyprienne of Sardou's *Divorçons* with more than the tips of her fingers, eschewing the frank sensuality and vulgarity of the role.[142] This equation could work both ways: Ellen Terry's public reputation was constructed in response to her repertoire of virtuous and generous heroines, such as Portia, Imogen, and Cordelia, rather than her off-stage life which included three marriages and two illegitimate children.[143]

Yet the very proximity between an actress's off-stage celebrity persona and her on-stage repertoire could serve to disrupt the moral message of the plays themselves. Women like Lillie Langtry and Sarah Bernhardt accumulated and spent large fortunes, ran their own theatre companies, and mixed freely with members of the aristocracy, while taking and discarding lovers as they wished. The heroines they portrayed suffered guilt, social ostracism, and frequently death as the price of similar sexual transgressions. The off-stage lives of the actresses who brought these roles to life could thus highlight the gap between the punitive and strict morality of the drama's created reality and the far greater space for manoeuvre and self-determination allowed in real life. In contrast to mid-century writers' application of melodramatic narratives and tropes to the world around them, theatre critics at the turn of the century therefore increasingly alluded to stage conventions as a hermetically-sealed system; so, for example, the *Times*'s critic commented of Mrs Dane's unmasking and expulsion, 'It was right, no doubt, conventionally right, that the marriage should be broken off; women who have made "mistakes" and lied to conceal them are not allowed on the English stage to have their reputations whitewashed, or their characters redeemed by matrimony.'[144]

In the case of Sarah Bernhardt this contrast between the flourishing, independent artist and the doomed and self-destructive roles she played became more marked as the years passed. Bernhardt built her career on stage spectacles of female desire, played out predominantly in a framework of martyrdom, punishment, and painful death—the combined ecstasies of physical passion and long-drawn extinction producing a particularly potent eroticism. The tension between Bernhardt's financial success, artistic power, and famed agelessness and the theatrical narratives she enacted, tales of the supposedly inevitable divine or social punishment awaiting the trangressive heroine, grew sufficiently stark and unavoidable for Bernhardt's performances to verge on camp spectacle—a knowingly performative, self-mocking, consciously artificial, but skilfully rendered enactment of scenes which conjured up

---

[141] See e.g. Lynn Voskuil, *Acting Naturally: Victorian theatricality and authenticity* (University of Virginia Press: Charlottesville, VA, 2004).

[142] Archer, *Theatrical World of 1894*, 152. Such concerns applied to both sexes; Shaw noted of Herbert Waring's performance in the first English professional production of *A Doll's House*, 'The resultant performance, excellently convincing up to fully nineteen-twentieths, was, as regards the remaining twentieth obviously a piece of acting in which a line was drawn, as a matter of self-respect, between Mr Waring and Mr Helmer.' *Our Theatres in the 90s*, III, 131.

[143] For more on the relation between actresses' repertoires and their celebrity reputations, see Sos Eltis, 'Reputation, Celebrity and the late-Victorian Actress', in Mary Luckhurst and Jane Moody (eds), *Theatre and Celebrity in Britain, 1660–2000* (Palgrave Macmillan: London, 2005), 169–90.

[144] *Times* (10 October 1900), 3.

powerful emotions but did not aspire to moral seriousness or politically-inflected mimetic realism. The uncomfortable juxtaposition of Bernhardt's thriving longevity and the doomed adulteresses she played on stage highlighted the increasingly stark disjunction between stage conventions and real life. This may perhaps help to explain the rising chorus of critical opprobrium which greeted her enduringly popular performances at the *fin de siècle*. So, for example, A. B. Walkley admitted that Bernhardt's genius had created a new theatrical type—what he termed her 'embodiment of Oriental exoticism; the strange, chimaeric, idol-woman: a compound of Baudelaire's Vierge du Mal, Swinburne's Our Lady of Pain, Gustave Moreau's Salome, Leonardo's enigmatic Mona Lisa'—but while Bernhardt distilled and embodied the quintessence of such a remarkable panoply of doomed (and male-authored) visions of *fin-de-siècle* female desire, she simultaneously, in Walkley's view, emptied them of meaning and reality, rendering them 'a sort of nightmarish exaggeration, something not in nature, the supreme of artifice'.[145]

While Sarah Bernhardt's extraordinary artistry had the potential to destabilize the imagined reality of the plays in which she performed, in other cases it was crucially the performer who made a play appear radical and challenging compared to the theatre of past decades. In a letter to the *Era* in June 1895, a self-styled 'Anti-Problemist' mocked *The Second Mrs Tanqueray* for any claim to social significance, commenting that 'all the absurd nonsense written by young critics of the realist school about the terrible moral of this "tragedy of modern life" is ridiculously refuted by the fact that, if one has any really broad acquaintance with modern life, one can point to numbers of instances in all sections of society where good-natured men have married women like Paula who have turned out excellent wives and exemplary mothers'.[146] From all the exuberant praise of *Mrs Tanqueray*, the writer continues, 'one would imagine that such plays as *Camille*, *The New Magdalen*, *Man and Wife*, and *Charity* had never been written'. There was more truth to life, he (or she) concludes in Boucicault's *Formosa* than in Pinero's 'modern' drama. Shaw had passed the same judgement on Pinero, locating the modernity of his *fin-de-siècle* problem plays not in the scripts but in the actresses who performed them. The potential significance of the actress's interpretation of her role was highlighted in an 1895 revival of Collins's *The New Magdalen*, starring Janet Achurch, England's original Nora Helmer, as Mercy Merrick. Shaw described Collins's fallen heroine as an 'old-fashioned man made angel-woman', but argued that Achurch's performance transformed her from a victim of her society to a rebel.[147] Thus, when Achurch's Mercy asks her fiancé whether his love would stand the test of the loss of her social position, she did so with 'a gleam of rage', and when she delivered the famously pathetic line 'I can't get back: I can't get back' (into society) it 'came out almost with suppressed impatience and contempt'—scorning society's judgements, the

---

[145] A. B. Walkley, 'Sarah Bernhardt' (July, 1889), reprinted in Walkley, *Playhouse Impressions* (T. Fisher Unwin: London, 1892), 241. See also e.g. William Archer, *The Theatrical World of 1895* (Walter Scott: London, 1896), 184, 205–6.

[146] *Era* (22 June 1895), 19.

[147] *Our Theatres in the Nineties*, I, 231, 234.

reformed prostitute asserts her right to rehabilitation and integration.[148] Intelligent, self-assured, independent, and commanding actresses like Janet Achurch and Elizabeth Robins, who did not depend on the conventional actress's appeal to 'sex and sympathy', therefore had to be kept out of ordinary fashionable plays or their self-possession and power would knock them to pieces: 'after all', as Shaw put it, 'one does not want a Great Western locomotive to carry one's afternoon tea upstairs'.[149] Ibsen's plays had the power to make the old sentimental dramas look old-fashioned and outdated, and so did the Ibsenite actresses.

The modern intelligent actress needed a vehicle worthy of her, and the play repeatedly chosen by every international celebrity actress, including Bernhardt, Duse, and Campbell (though Shaw was unwilling to accord her such status), was Sudermann's *Heimat*, translated from the German as *Magda*. The title role is an acclaimed opera singer, who returns to her home town and the father who threw her out for refusing to marry the man he chose. Magda was a role, Shaw declared, which depended not on mere physical artistry and charm but on 'the sense of humanity', her long speeches appearing dull unless imbued with 'truth as the utterance of a deeply moved human soul'.[150] Magda encounters the family friend who years before took advantage of her vulnerability and youth, leaving her pregnant and alone, but who now agrees to her father's request for their marriage when her fame and wealth will benefit his own career and social standing. But when this self-satisfied ex-lover demands that Magda send their child abroad and deny her parentage for the sake of social appearances, she laughs at the absurdity, angrily showing him the door and turning back with relief to the joys of motherhood, independence, and her career. Asserting her right to love and happiness where she can find it, and refusing to submit to the morality of a male-dominated home which has neither supported nor protected her, Magda refuses to marry the father of her child. As her father threatens violence if she will not marry her former lover, she offers a final blow to his complacent morality, asking defiantly how he knows 'Whether, according to your ideas, I am still fit for him? I mean— whether he was the only one?'[151] Aghast, the father suffers a fatal stroke as he attempts to shoot her.

Magda is an acclaimed artist, whose international status and economic self-sufficiency enable her to choose her sexual partner. Without shame or rancour she embraces her past and shakes her former lover's hand, explaining that their affair transformed her from 'a foolish ignorant young thing, enjoying my freedom like a runaway monkey' into a woman, and set her on the road to artistic greatness by opening up 'the whole sympathy of the emotions without which woman is an incomplete being'. (III, 21, 22) Her defiant and dignified refrain is 'I am I, and I have no right to abjure myself'—her sexual experience is not a sin to be atoned for,

[148] Ibid, 233, 234.
[149] *Our Theatres in the Nineties*, III, 113; II, 148.
[150] Ibid, II, 145.
[151] Hermann Sudermann, *Magda,* translated by Louis N. Parker, LCP, BL Add MS 53604B, IV, 19. First performed Lyceum, 2 June 1896.

but an inseparable part of her identity; when she reminds her father that she may have had several sexual partners it is a declaration of her autonomous identity, and the idea is the death of him and secures her freedom (II, 16).

Magda asserts her right to sexual self-determination and self-respect on the grounds of her economic independence, claiming, as she puts it, 'no more than any maidservant or sempstress who scrapes up her crumbs of food and of love among strangers' (IV, 18). The popularity of the role among performers (though not with audiences) may have lain not only in the acting opportunities it offered, but also in the play's celebration of the self-supporting professional woman and its validation of the sexual rights which accompany economic independence. As working women, actresses were well aware of the relation between employment opportunities, wages, and sexual choice. When Clement Scott mused that a woman working in the theatre 'who endeavours to keep her purity is almost of necessity foredoomed to failure in her career', it was male actor-managers who signed a letter to the *Daily Telegraph* demanding his resignation; actresses were notable by their absence. Madge Kendal was asked for her signature and refused; years later Elizabeth Robins herself echoed Scott's views on the sexual compliance often required of actresses whose careers relied on the favour of male managers.[152] *Magda* was one of the first plays to voice the crucial connection between income and sexual self-determination, and actresses were to help lead the way in challenging the rhetoric of female frailty, sexual temptation, and the necessary protection of social conformity and the patriarchal family, introducing instead the cold realities of economic survival, starvation wages, and working conditions. As Shaw scathingly commented of the moral furore which greeted Scott's musing on the supposed moral corruption of the acting profession, the comparatively generous wages paid to actresses gave them sexual choices denied to other female workers such as, for example, those 'employed in the manufacture of sacred books on terms which make the prostitution of a certain percentage of them virtually compulsory'.[153]

[152] *Dame Madge Kendal, By Herself*, 52–3; Elizabeth Robins, *Theatre and Friendship: Some Henry James Letters with a commentary* (Jonathan Cape: London, 1932), 29–30.
[153] *Our Theatres in the Nineties*, III, 297.

5

Workers and Wages

'What is any respectable girl brought up to do but to catch some rich man's fancy and get the benefit of his money by marrying him?—as if a marriage ceremony could make any difference in the right or wrong of the thing! Oh! the hypocrisy of the world makes me sick!'[1] So declares the eponymous heroine of George Bernard Shaw's *Mrs Warren's Profession* (1893). When her daughter Vivie demands to know her father's identity, Mrs Warren finds herself unable to narrow the field sufficiently to name a specific man. Abandoning any pretence of conventional shame at the revelation that she worked as a prostitute, Mrs Warren instead challenges her daughter's complacent disgust with '*an overwhelming inspiration of true conviction and scorn*' (II, 309). Eschewing the conventional scene in which the 'fallen' woman repents her lost purity and recalls her innocent youth with tearful nostalgia, Mrs Warren expresses not shame but pride in her ability to provide for herself and her daughter. She responds to Vivie's insistence that character not circumstance is the vital factor in determining an individual's fate by describing the choices available to an unskilled working woman in the 1890s: one of her half-sisters married a government labourer and lived in a state of exhaustion, keeping their family on eighteen shillings a week, until he took to drink; the other half-sister 'worked in a whitelead factory twelve hours a day for nine shillings a week until she died of lead poisoning. She only expected to get her hands a little paralyzed' (II, 310–11). Learning from her sisters' experiences, Kitty Warren abandoned her position as barmaid, in which she worked fourteen hours a day for four shillings a week plus board, and decided instead to make the best money she could from her good looks and talent for pleasing men, rather than leaving her employers to profit by them. Prostitution was the only employment available, she explains, which offered her any possibility of saving money or preserving her 'self-respect' in the face of starvation and slavery (II, 314). The immorality, Vivie concedes, is not her mother's for choosing to become a prostitute but society's for offering her such an invidious choice.

As Shaw declared, *Mrs Warren's Profession* was a dramatic riposte to the long line of plays about 'beautiful, exquisitely dressed, and sumptuously lodged and fed' women, whose luxurious lives of sin are only interrupted when they 'die of consumption to the sympathetic tears of the whole audience, or step into the next room to commit suicide'—a barbed reference to *La Dame aux Camélias* and *The*

---

[1] George Bernard Shaw, *Mrs Warren's Profession*, in *The Bodley Head Bernard Shaw: Collected Plays with their Prefaces*, Vol. 1 (Bodley Head: London, 1979), II, 313.

Second Mrs Tanqueray, both of which were attracting large audiences to the theatre in the months before Shaw began writing *Mrs Warren's Profession*.[2] Shaw wrote the play 'to draw attention to the truth that prostitution is caused, not by female depravity and male licentiousness, but simply by underpaying, undervaluing and overworking women so shamefully that the poorest of them are forced to resort to prostitution to keep body and soul together.'[3] Far from being the glamorous occupation depicted in so many society plays, Shaw's Mrs Warren describes her professional life as anything but easy, sensual, or self-indulgent: 'I've often pitied a poor girl, tired out and in low spirits, having to please some man that she doesn't care two straws for—some half-drunken fool that thinks he's making himself agreeable when he's teasing and worrying and disgusting a woman so that hardly any money could pay her for putting up with it' (II, 313).

While challenging the notion that the sale of sexual services was rooted in women's vanity and moral frailty, Shaw was nonetheless keen to examine the role played by character. Drama, as he explained, 'is no mere setting up of the camera to nature: it is the presentation in parable of the conflict between Man's will and his environment'.[4] It is Mrs Warren's 'high English social virtues', as Shaw calls them—her vitality, thrift, energy, outspokenness, and managing capacity—which give her the courage and determination to choose prostitution over respectability and destitution, and then to make such a success of her career that she is able not only to support her daughter through to her graduation from Newnham College, Cambridge, but to establish a thriving business running a chain of international brothels.[5] Vivie Warren, a self-possessed and determinedly rational young woman, accepts with humility the justice and wisdom of her mother's initial choice. She responds to the revelation of her mother's history with admiration and a newfound affection for the parent she previously barely knew. But when Vivie learns that Mrs Warren is still in the business, managing brothels to make a fortune from other women's financial desperation as others once traded on hers, she turns her back on her mother, rejecting her financial support and severing all future contact. Vivie chooses to live independently on the small income she can earn as an actuary. Mrs Warren's attempt to persuade Vivie to live as a lady of leisure on her mother's earnings slyly mimics her proceuress's patter to a prospective employee:

MRS WARREN: But you don't know what all that means: youre too young. It means a new dress every day; it means theatres and balls every night; it means having the pick of all the gentlemen in Europe at your feet . . . it means everything you like, everything you want, everything you can think of. And what are you here? A mere drudge, toiling and moiling early and late for your bare living and two cheap dresses a year.

[2] 'The Author's Apology', Preface to the 1902 Stage Society edition of *Mrs Warren's Profession*, in Bernard Shaw, *The Complete Prefaces, Vol. 1: 1889–1913*, ed. Dan H. Laurence and Daniel J. Leary (Allen Lane: London, 1993), 115.
[3] Ibid, 111.
[4] Ibid, 124.
[5] Ibid, 127.

Think it over. [*Soothingly*] Youre shocked, I know. I can enter into your feelings; and
I think they do you credit; but trust me, nobody will blame you: you may take my
word for that. I know what young girls are; and I know youll think better of it when
youve turned it over in your mind.

VIVIE: So that's how it's done, is it? You must have said all that to many a woman,
mother, to have it so pat.

                                                                            (IV, 350)

Mrs Warren has become part of the system she despises, trading in other women's
bodies, no longer driven by financial necessity but by the restless energy and
accumulative instincts which mean she must pursue some business—and there's
only one she knows. Energetic, business-minded Vivie is every inch her mother's
daughter, but the same qualities which led Mrs Warren into prostitution lead her
daughter to become an actuary rather than her mother's kept woman, supported
by other women's exploitation—the crucial difference is not character but the education which gives the younger woman access to a decent living wage.

   In his 'Author's Apology' prefacing the first publication of *Mrs Warren's Profession*, Shaw inveighed against the immorality of a stage censorship which licensed
salacious farces and glamorous though doomed courtesans, but refused a licence to
his own highly moral drama. In fact, at the point of composing this preface, Shaw
had not yet submitted the play to the Lord Chamberlain's Office, being sure that a
licence would be refused. He was entirely right. The play's sexual explicitness
alone—both in Vivie's uncertain parentage and Mrs Warren's references to the
distasteful nature of the work—provided sufficient grounds for its rejection, but
Shaw's implicating of everyone from the Duke of Belgravia to the Archbishop of
Canterbury as recipients of wealth earned from women's sexual subjection could
hardly have helped (III, 330–1). George Redford, the Examiner of Plays, refused
permission even for the necessary copyright reading in order to secure performance
rights for the published play, until Shaw had completely excised the second act and
transformed Mrs Warren's profession from prostitute and brothel-keeper to training young women in the lesser art of pickpocketing.[6] Over the next three decades
the play was regularly re-submitted to the censor; Shaw declared himself quite
content to pay the reader's fee annually because, as he informed the Lord Chamberlain, ' "Mrs Warren's Profession" should be read carefully through every year by
your whole staff.'[7] Its first public performance in England did not take place until
27 July 1925 at the Prince of Wales Theatre, Birmingham. By that time the play
had been performed around the globe, from North America to Japan, Austria,
Hungary, Estonia, Latvia, and Lithuania. As Bache Matthews, manager of the
Birmingham Repertory Theatre, wrote in frustration at the Lord Chamberlain's

---

   [6] See L. W. Conolly, '*Mrs Warren's Profession* and the Lord Chamberlain', *SHAW: The Annual of
Bernard Shaw Studies* 24 (2004), 46–95.
   [7] Shaw, letter to Lord Sandhurst, 20 October 1916, quoted in Dominic Shellard and Steve Nicholson, with Miriam Handley, *The Lord Chamberlain Regrets …: A History of British Theatre Censorship*
(British Library: London, 2004), 70.

continued intransigence in 1921, the play had 'undoubtedly taken a permanent place in standard English drama'.[8]

The play did, however, achieve a number of private performances. In January 1902 the Stage Society secured two performances at the New Lyric Club, with comedian Fanny Brough playing Mrs Warren. The casting of Brough, described by the *Times*'s reviewer as 'perhaps the most humorous actress on our stage', helped to win sympathy for Shaw's unconventional heroine, leading the *Times* to embrace Mrs Warren's 'humanity of character', judging her 'a good sort but a bad lot' in contrast to the strictly virtuous Vivie, who was played by Madge McIntosh as 'a thinking machine with no capacity whatever for emotion'.[9] Further private productions included one by Edith Craig's feminist theatre company, the Pioneer Players, in 1912, prompting some members of the society to resign in protest, though the suffrage press greeted the play as 'highly moral'.[10] By the time of its London premiere at the Strand Theatre in September 1925, even the mainstream press agreed; the *Times* noted that the play was received with 'perfect equanimity', musing that perhaps it had simply been written before its time.[11]

In ideological terms, *Mrs Warren's Profession* could be seen as providing the template for all subsequent feminist theatrical engagements with prostitution. Shaw's play covered all the essential points: the driving force of economic necessity; the equivalence between marriage and prostitution where both are premised on women's need to please men in order to secure a living; the irrelevance of female sexual immorality as a supposed causation of prostitution; the unpleasantness of the work for the women concerned; and the self-serving hypocrisy of a society which profits from women's sexual exploitation while condemning the women themselves.

Mrs Warren's Profession was not, however, an ideal artistic model. Most obviously the thirty-year embargo on its public performance emphasized the need for greater tact and circumspection. But more crucially the play's apparent defeatism made it unappealing to feminist campaigners. Shaw described it as 'a play of instincts and temperaments in conflict with each other and with a flinty social problem that never yields an inch to mere sentiment'.[12] Refusing the audience any emotional release or resolution, the play ends with Mrs Warren's continued complicity and Vivie's determined detachment, washing her hands of both her mother and her money, and retreating into self-sufficient isolation. Though critics have habitually identified Vivie as a New Woman, thanks to her firm handshake, preference for cigarettes and whisky, and her mathematics degree from

---

[8] Matthews, letter to Lord Chamberlain, 6 July 1921, quoted in Conolly, '*Mrs Warren's Profession* and the Lord Chamberlain', 23.

[9] *Times* (7 January 1902), 9. For details of Mary Shaw's toning down of the coarse vulgarity of Mrs Warren in an unsuccessful attempt to assuage hostile responses in New Haven and New York in 1905, see Celia Marshik, *British Modernism and Censorship* (Cambridge University Press: Cambridge, 2006), 54–6; Katie N. Johnson, *Sisters in Sin: Brothel Drama in America, 1900–1920* (Cambridge University Press: Cambridge, 2006), 96–102.

[10] *Votes for Women* (7 June 1912), 583.

[11] *Times* (29 September 1925), 12.

[12] 'Author's Apology', 125.

Cambridge, she is no feminist campaigner, but rather a second-generation woman benefiting from the expansion in women's rights and opportunities gained by her predecessors; she eschews wider activism to combat the social injustice newly revealed to her, instead settling for individual comfort.[13] Vivie's emotional withdrawal also raises the more complex and contested issue of how individual women could understand and express their sexuality in a society rooted in female sexual exploitation. Vivie withdraws in reflex disgust not just from her admirer Frank's sentimental approaches—now tainted by the possibility that he is her half-brother—but also from 'beauty and romance', as offered by the aesthete Praed's invitation to tour the culture capitals of Europe, locations now irredeemably associated in Vivie's mind with her mother's international chain of brothels (IV, 340). The commercial trade in women's bodies spreads its taint over love, art, and poetry, raising the question of whether emotional and physical sterility were a thinking woman's inevitable response.

The first private performances of *Mrs Warren's Profession* were given by the Stage Society, one of a number of new private theatre societies founded to provide a platform for plays which had been refused a licence for public performance or which did not suit the demands of a commercially-driven theatrical marketplace. J. T. Grein's Independent Theatre Society was founded in 1891, inaugurated with the first English production of Ibsen's *Ghosts*, and in 1899 the Stage Society was founded, producing new dramas by playwrights such as Shaw, Harley Granville Barker, Gilbert Murray, St John Hankin and a range of European playwrights, including Chekhov, Frank Wedekind, and Gerhart Hauptmann.[14] Their experiences with the Stage Society helped to inspire J. E. Vedrenne and Harley Granville Barker's three seasons at the Court Theatre between 1904 and 1907, producing a range of new plays and translations, and relying on subscriptions and cross-subsidies between plays in order to present a repertoire of plays appealing primarily to a middle-class, educated, and largely socialist audience. The Vedrenne-Barker management of the Court Theatre also saw the birth of 'suffrage theatre', with the premiere of Elizabeth Robins's *Votes for Women!* on 9 April 1907, directed by Harley Granville Barker. The play was a box-office success, raising funds for the suffrage cause and helping to inspire the adoption of plays and performances as a central propagandist tool in the fight for female emancipation.

The majority of the plays produced by this alternative, avant-garde theatre were socially engaged, naturalistic in style, and often concerned with the relation between the individual and their social and economic environment. From George Bernard

---

[13] My thanks to Anna Farkas for this observation: see Anna Farkas, *Between Orthodoxy and Rebellion: Women's drama in England, 1890–1918*, unpublished DPhil thesis, University of Oxford, 2010, ch. 2.

[14] For further details see James Woodfield, *English Theatre in Transition, 1881–1914* (Croom Helm: London, 1984); Jean Chothia, *English Drama of the Early Modern Period* (Longman: London, 1996); Christopher Innes, *Avant-Garde Theatre, 1892–1992* (Routledge: London, 1993); Jan McDonald, *The 'New Drama' 1900–1914* (Macmillan: London, 1986); Incorporated Stage Society, *Ten Years, 1899–1909* (Chiswick Press: London, 1909).

Shaw's 'Plays Unpleasant' to Hauptmann's *The Weavers*, Granville Barker's *The Voysey Inheritance*, and John Galsworthy's *Strife*, *Justice*, and *The Silver Box*, this was a socially combative drama, located in the concrete specifics of incomes and working conditions. Employment opportunities, wage levels, education, and class had traditionally been elided or sidestepped in dramatic treatments of seduction, prostitution, and adultery from the very beginning of the nineteenth century. Whether in melodramas of working-class life or fashionable society dramas set in the parish of St James's, character not economics was the crucial factor in determining the fate of a woman's 'purity'. But Shaw's Mrs Warren was to be the first of a succession of voices raised to challenge over a century of dramatic tradition, relocating women's sexual choices in the particularities of the labour market and the conditions of employment.

Prostitution and the sexual subjection of women became a flagship issue in the burgeoning campaign for the general expansion of women's rights and in particular in the fight for the right to vote. A central tenet in the anti-suffragist argument was that there was no need for women to secure votes on their own behalf when their interests were already fully represented by men; as one MP put it, 'The fundamental error in all of this reasoning is that women constitute a class apart...for all practical purposes women are already represented by their husbands, sons and brothers.'[15] Prostitution provided a perfect riposte to such arguments, and accounts of men's sexual exploitation of women provided invaluable material for propagandists, producing forthright texts from Christabel Pankhurst's *The Great Scourge and How to End It* (1913), calling for 'Votes for Women and Chastity for Men', to Laurence Housman's *Sex-War and Women's Suffrage* (1916).[16] Women's suffrage papers, the *Vote* and *Votes for Women*, ran regular columns entitled respectively 'How Men Protect Women' and 'Man-Made Law', which compared the light sentences delivered for men's assaults on women and children compared to the heavy penalties imposed for crimes against property or crimes committed by women.[17]

Back in the 1880s W. T. Stead's 'Maiden Tribute of Modern Babylon' articles had proved the value of sensational journalism. In a series of articles for the *Pall Mall Gazette* in 1885, Stead had exposed the evils of child prostitution, most controversially by purchasing a 13-year-old virgin for £5—his unlawful investigative techniques were later punished with a three-month prison sentence, despite the fact that the girl in question was passed on unharmed to the Salvation Army. The public outrage stirred up by Stead's blood-curdling tales of debauched male villains and helpless female victims helped to secure the passing of the Criminal Law

[15] E. A. Leatham, *Hansard, HC Deb.*, 3rd Series, CCXXIII, 7 April 1875, *c*.415–16, quoted in Martin Pugh, *The March of the Women: A Revisionist Analysis of the Campaign for Women's Suffrage* (Oxford University Press: Oxford, 2000), 36.

[16] Christabel Pankhurst, *The Great Scourge and How to End It* (E. Pankhurst: London, 1913), vii; Laurence Housman, *Sex-War and Women's Suffrage* (Women's Freedom League: London, 1916), 24–6.

[17] Lucy Bland, *Banishing the Beast: Feminism, Sex and Morality* (Taurus Parke: London, 2002), ch. 7.

Amendment Act later that year, raising the age of sexual consent from 13 to 16.[18] When, two decades later, an alliance of early twentieth-century feminists and purity campaigners agitated to raise further the legal age for sexual consent and to enforce tougher penalties for those who procured and used prostitutes as well as for the prostitutes themselves, a further wave of sensational propaganda took hold of the popular imagination.[19] The press was filled with melodramatic tales of young girls abducted and held prisoner in foreign brothels—a favourite tale being that of an old woman who waylaid unsuspecting maidens with requests for help across the road, only to knock them unconscious with a injection of drugs. Unable to persuade Parliament to tighten the laws governing sexual procurement and prostitution, purity campaigners called upon W. T. Stead to give his support to the fight against the so-called 'White Slave Trade'. Fuel was added to the flames by the Queenie Gerald case in 1913, when a brothel in Piccadilly was raided, and despite the young age of the women working there and a ledger containing the names of rich and influential clients, including allegedly several members of Parliament, the brothel keeper was given only a three-month sentence and no clients were arrested.[20]

The White Slave Trade hysteria peaked in England in 1912, and by 1913 cooler-headed feminists like Teresa Billington-Greig were already de-bunking sensational stories of abduction and imprisonment as myths which unhelpfully obscured the poverty and working conditions which really drove women to prostitution.[21] As Greig and other feminists pointed out, the White Slave panic made for bad politics and bad law—the Criminal Law Amendment Act of 1912, pushed through in the emotional wake of Stead's death on the Titanic, was later recognized as doing little to alleviate the ills of prostitution. As Shaw caustically commented, the Act's provision for flogging procuresses' male bullies and pimps left 'Mrs Warren in complete command of the situation, and [her profession's] true nature more effectually masked than ever'.[22] Enshrining in law the category of the 'common prostitute', whose identifying features and attributes remained undefined, the CLA Act reinforced the notion that women selling sexual services constituted a different category from ordinary respectable citizens, and could therefore be denied equal civil and legal rights.[23] This legal distinction between common prostitutes and all other women also ran counter to a central strain in feminist campaigns for better working

---

[18] For further details see Judith Walkowitz, *City of Dreadful Delight: Narratives of Sexual Danger in Late-Victorian London* (Virago: London, 1992).

[19] See e.g., Edward J. Bristow, *Vice and Vigilance: Purity Movements in Britain since 1700* (Gill and Macmillan: Dublin, 1977); Paula Bartley, *Prostitution: Prevention and Reform in England, 1860–1914* (Routledge: London, 2000).

[20] *The White Slave Traffic: Articles and Letters reprinted from 'The Spectator'* (P. S. King: London, 1912); J. Keir Hardie, M.P., *The Queenie Gerald Case* (National Labour Press: London, 191-).

[21] See Teresa Billington-Greig, 'The Truth about White Slavery', *English Review* (June 1913), 428–46. White Slave hysteria was more widespread and tenacious in the United States, and it was claimed that by 1914 over one billion papers had been written on white slavery in North America. (Bristow, *Vice and Vigilance,* 189) For American dramatic responses to the White Slave scare, see Johnson, *Sisters in Sin.*

[22] 1933 Postscript added to 'Author's Apology' to *Mrs Warren's Profession,* 139.

[23] For details of the Act and critique of its wording, see Committee of Inquiry into Sexual Morality, *The State and Sexual Morality* (Allen & Unwin: London, 1920).

conditions and wider access to the professions. As Cicely Hamilton phrased it in her polemical *Marriage as a Trade* (1909), all women without an independent income were essentially dependent on selling their sexual services in the absence of alternative employment:

> For woman, who has always been far more completely excluded [than man] from direct access to the necessities of life, who has often been barred both by law and custom, from the possession of property, one form of payment was demanded and one only. It was demanded of her that she should enkindle and satisfy the desire of the male, who would thereupon admit her to such share of the property he possessed or earned as should seem good to him. In other words, she exchanged, by the ordinary process of barter, possession of her body for the means of existence.[24]

Where parliamentary legislation deemed prostitutes to be a category apart from other women, feminists increasingly insisted on the essential contract upon which so many women's survival was predicated.

From early protests at public meetings to the mud marches of 1907, suffragists were well aware of the propagandist potential of public performance and spectacle.[25] In 1908 the Women Writers' Suffrage League and the Actresses' Franchise League were founded with the express purpose of supporting the suffrage campaign with written propaganda, plays, sketches, and performances. Other sources of feminist theatre included the Woman's Theatre, formed in 1913 by Inez Bensusan, and Edith Craig's Pioneer Players, a company formed in 1911 whose objectives included producing plays in support of contemporary women's movements.[26] Between them these companies produced over twenty plays that centred on women's sexual 'sin' and judgement, from poverty-driven prostitution to sexual harassment, seduction, and royal adultery.[27] These dramas, like so many Edwardian feminist plays, tended to mimic and undermine established theatrical genres, challenging the assumptions that underlay conventional plot structures. The rhetoric of the White Slave Traffic by contrast harked back to seduction dramas such as Haines's *The Life of a Woman* (1841) and Phillips's *Lost in London* (1867), in which young women fell victims to unscrupulous men once they ventured unprotected into the dangerous metropolis. In contrast, suffrage plays on prostitution attempted

---

[24] Cicely Hamilton, *Marriage as a Trade* (Chapman and Hall: London, 1909), 19.

[25] See in particular, Lisa Tickner, *The Spectacle of Women: Imagery of the Suffrage Campaign, 1907–14* (Chatto & Windus: London, 1987).

[26] For a full account of suffrage drama and productions by the AFL, Woman's Theatre, and Pioneer Players, see Julie Holledge, *Innocent Flowers: Women in the Edwardian Theatre* (Virago: London, 1981); Claire Hirschfield, 'The Suffragist as Playwright in Edwardian England', *Frontiers* IX.2 (1987), 1–6; Sheila Stowell, *A Stage of Their Own: Feminist Playwrights of the Suffrage Era* (University of Michigan Press: Ann Arbor, MI, 1992); Susan Carlson, 'Comic Militancy: The Politics of Suffrage Drama', in Maggie B. Gale and Viv Gardner (eds), *Women, Theatre and Performance: New Histories, New Historiographies* (Manchester University Press: Manchester, 2000); Katharine Cockin, *Women and Theatre in the Age of Suffrage: The Pioneer Players, 1911–1925* (Palgrave: Basingstoke, 2001).

[27] See for example, AFL production of P. R. Bennett, *Mary Edwardes* (1911); Pioneer Players productions of Margaret Nevinson, *In the Workhouse* (1911); Laurence Housman, *Pains and Penalties* (1911); Richard Wright Kauffman, *The Daughters of Ishmael* (1914); Woman's Theatre production of Bjornstjerne Bjornson, *A Gauntlet* (1913).

to negotiate the difficult problem of transforming the story of female frailty and vulnerability into one which recognized the vital role of social and economic factors without thereby reducing women to passive victims of determinist social forces.

Over a century of theatrical precedent rooted a woman's fall from virtue in moral weakness, emotional impulsiveness, vanity, and misplaced notions of sexual equality. The argument that, without decent employment opportunities or training, women were left with no option but to trade their bodies for a living, whether in marriage or on the streets, made for strong polemic, but in dramatic form such socially determinist arguments could produce depressingly defeatist work. In John Galsworthy's *The Fugitive* (1913), Clare leaves the sexual bondage of a loveless marriage, only to find herself unable to earn a decent living, and the play ends with her taking poison rather than face prostituting herself night after night.[28] Thérèse undergoes a similar journey in *La Femme seule* (1912) by Eugène Brieux, chosen by the Woman's Theatre to inaugurate their project of giving 'woman her proper chance in dramatic art, both as professional artist and as a typical specimen of her sex reflected in the drama'.[29] Orphaned and penniless, Thérèse cannot marry her fiancé without his parents' consent and instead attempts to earn her own living, but she loses her job at a feminist newspaper after being sexually harassed, and is driven out of her next job at a workshop by angry male workers after she founds a women's trade union. Left jobless, she heads to the railway station to rejoin her fiancé, accepting defeat and, it is implied, going to live with him as his mistress.[30] Reviews in the suffrage press applauded the feminist sympathies that lay behind these plays' depictions of the job market, but several reviewers were troubled by their pessimism. 'With all M. Brieux's earnestness and high ideals, I cannot look upon such a false and pessimistic presentment of woman in the labour-market as desirable propaganda for the Feminist cause', declared a reviewer in *The Suffragette*.[31] A reviewer in *Votes for Women* similarly castigated the 'fastidious weakness' of Galsworthy's heroine and concluded of *La Femme seule* that 'the whole thing is rather a statement of difficulty than a solution, and, though M. Brieux has attempted to state it honestly, there is over all a sense of hindrance and defeat'.[32] Both reviewers clearly favoured plays that, while depicting the obstacles that confronted women, allowed the possibility of women successfully overcoming them.

In Gertrude Vaughan's *The Woman with a Pack* (1911), a middle-class, university-educated woman, Philippa, takes up the fight on behalf of the sexually oppressed

---

[28] John Galsworthy, *The Fugitive,* produced Royal Court Theatre, 16 September 1913. Galsworthy was centrally concerned with the shaping force of environment, commenting that, '[My characters] are part of the warp and woof of a complicated society in which the individual is as much netted in by encircling fates as ever were the creations of the Greek dramatists.' Quoted in Ian Clarke, *Edwardian Drama* (Faber: London, 1989), 54.

[29] Interview with Inez Bensusan, 'The Woman's Theatre', *Common Cause*, 21 November 1913, 591.

[30] Translated as *Woman on Her Own*, by Mrs Bernard Shaw. First performed Coronet Theatre, December 1913.

[31] 'The Woman's Theatre Week', by A. D. A., *The Suffragette*, 12 December 1913, 209.

[32] *Votes for Women*, 12 December 1913, 163.

Franchette, who is shown slipping inexorably from sexually harassed serving-girl to sweated labourer to casual prostitute, selling her body to her boss to keep a roof over her elderly mother's head.[33] Philippa witnesses Franchette's suffering and thereupon joins the suffrage movement and accepts imprisonment—a heroic and more communally-minded counterpoint to Vivie Warren's retreat.[34] The final tableau triumphantly presents Philippa as Joan of Arc with a chorus of children dancing around her. The active intervention celebrated in the play is entirely Philippa's, while a mystical figure, 'The Woman with a Pack', appears in each scene, symbolically bridging the class divide with her sympathetic and silent presence, and suggesting the universal nature of woman's burden.

Elizabeth Robins's *Votes for Women!* staged a similar story of female sexual victimization leading to political activism. The play's heroine, Vida Levering, is a middle-class woman who (in the play's back-story) left the dubious protection of her father's house and found herself unable to earn a living from her fashionable musical accomplishments. Faced with homelessness and destitution, Vida was 'helped' by a family acquaintance, Geoffrey Stonor, ten years her senior. She entered a relationship with him, and, when she fell pregnant, aborted the child in response to her lover's anxiety to retain his father's approval and financial support. *Votes for Women!* was, as Sheila Stowell has remarked, 'a grab-bag of conventions recycled for feminist ends', structured around a number of clichéd plot turns from dozens of Victorian and Edwardian plays on the woman with a past.[35] Vida enters the play as an immaculately-dressed suffragist, whose sexual history is only revealed when Geoffrey Stonor, MP, puzzles his young fiancée by identifying Vida's dropped handkerchief by the initial 'V' alone—a piece of business so well-worn that critic Max Beerbohm declared he could 'hardly suppress a yawn' when it was wheeled out.[36] But, unlike so many theatrical predecessors, Vida's experiences have only served to politicize her, awaking her to the social and economic vulnerability of women and the need to alter those conditions for future generations. She has almost forgotten her former lover, has no interest in marrying him, and only refers to their former relationship in an attempt to pressure him into supporting the suffrage cause.

The absence of decent work for unskilled female labour and the lack of night shelters for destitute women leave the young Vida in desperate straits. But Robins is careful not to depict Vida as helplessly passive even in retrospect, hinting instead at the subtle combination of controlled desire, calculation, and expediency which

---

[33] Gertrude Vaughan, *The Woman with a Pack* (W. J. Ham-Smith: London, 1912). First produced Portman Rooms, 8 and 9 December 1911, by the AFL during the WSPU Christmas fete.

[34] The choice of the name Philippa for the heroic female graduate may have been inspired by Millicent Fawcett's daughter Philippa's success at Newnham, beating male competition to the position of senior wrangler in mathematics at Cambridge University in 1890. See L. W. Conolly, 'Who was Phillipa Summers? Reflections on Vivie Warren's Cambridge', *SHAW: The Annual of Bernard Shaw Studies*, 25 (2005), 88–95.

[35] Stowell, *A Stage of Their Own*, 2.

[36] 'Miss Robins's "Tract"', *Saturday Review* (13 April 1907), 457.

underlay her relationship with Stonor. When Vida announces that Stonor's support for women's enfranchisement will pay his debt to her by making it harder for his grandsons to exert power over 'penniless and frightened women', her older companion is robustly cynical about assigning all the blame to villainous male seducers:

LADY JOHN: (*impatiently*) What nonsense! You talk as though women hadn't their share of human nature. *We* aren't made of ice any more than men.

MISS LEVERING: No, but all the same we have more self-control.

LADY JOHN: Than men?

MISS LEVERING: You know we have.

LADY JOHN: (*shrewdly*) I know we mustn't admit it.

MISS LEVERING: For fear they'd call us fishes!

LADY JOHN: (*evasively*) They talk of our lack of self-control—but it's the last thing they *want* women to have.

MISS LEVERING: Oh, we know what they want us to have. So we make shift to have it. If we don't, we go without hope—sometimes we go without bread.

LADY JOHN: (*shocked*) Vida—do you mean to say that you –

MISS LEVERING: I mean to say that men's vanity won't let them see it, but the thing's largely a question of economics.

LADY JOHN: (*shocked*) You *never* loved him, then!

MISS LEVERING: Oh, yes, I loved him—*once*. It was my helplessness turned the best thing life can bring, into a curse for both of us.[37]

Though lightly thrown out, the acknowledgement that women have sexual appetites but control them better than men was a radical assertion, as was Vida's hint that her desire for Stonor was at least partially a calculated response to necessity not a helpless succumbing to love. The tangential nature of the dialogue—necessitated by the constraints of theatrical censorship, if not by Robins's own artistic preferences—leaves it uncertain whether Vida's 'curse' refers to the aborting of the child or the reduction of her relationship with Stonor to a form of prostitution, or, perhaps, both.[38]

Robins thus seeks to use Vida as a bridging figure, breaking down dichotomies between passive victimhood and active protest, and asserting a common cause which joins women of all classes. A number of critics have pointed out that only one working-class female voice is heard in *Votes for Women!*, the first speaker at the Trafalgar Square meeting, and she is not granted a name beyond the generic 'Working Woman'.[39] Robins implicitly acknowledges this problem when Vida

[37] Elizabeth Robins, *Votes for Women!*, reprinted in Jean Chothia (ed.), *The New Woman and Other Emancipated Woman Plays* (Oxford University Press: Oxford, 1998), III, 197–8.

[38] In 1907 Harley Granville Barker's *Waste* was refused a licence for public performance on the grounds of references to abortion. The reasons for the relative leniency towards Robins's play are unclear, though the tacit indirection of her dialogue may have been crucial.

[39] See e.g. Stowell, *A Stage of Their Own*, 28.

describes having recently taken a trip into 'the Underworld', putting on an old gown and tawdry hat to experience, as she explains, 'the bold, free look of a man at a woman he believes to be destitute—you must *feel* that look on you before you can understand—a good half of history' (I, 151).[40] Robins here drew directly on the investigative work of Mary Higgs, who wrote about her experiences walking through England disguised as a tramp and advised her middle-class readers (in a line which Vida echoes) that 'The bold, free look of a man at a destitute woman must be felt to be realised.'[41] Higgs's experiences of sexual harassment, vulnerability, and danger, led her to conclude that 'the harlot is the *female tramp*, driven by hard social conditions to primitive freedom of sex relationship', forced when all else is sold to sell herself.[42] Vida's emulation of Mary Higgs, divesting herself of the protection of middle-class respectability and thereby attempting to experience life on the other side of the class divide, was a crucial attempt on Robins's part to replace the patronizing division between working-class subjection and middle-class activism, which mars Vaughan's *The Woman with a Pack*.

Robins's reminder of the social and class divisions which cut across the shared interests of gender was both salutary and necessary. Class and economic divisions remained a problematic factor in the suffrage campaign, most obviously in the question of whether the franchise should be sought for all women, or for a more select and propertied few on behalf of the wider sisterhood—at a time when universal male suffrage had not yet been achieved. The tension between the suffragists' emphasis on the shared interests of all women and the realities of economic and class divisions was perhaps most clearly demonstrated by the support of the leading suffragist Millicent Fawcett for the company of Bryant and May in 1889 in opposition to the 'match girls' striking for higher pay, adequate health safeguards, and better working conditions.[43] As a shareholder, Mrs Fawcett's interests lay with the employer not with the working women—who, like Kitty Warren's half-sister, risked paralysis and lead-poisoning for their meagre wages.

A number of feminist playwrights sought to bridge this class divide by staging dramas of the middle-class woman forced into prostitution to support not only herself but her family, a situation which also drove home the penalties consequent on limiting women's access to practical and professional education and training. In Antonia Williams's *The Street*, for example, produced by the Pioneer Players in November 1913, Margaret Martin is forced to prostitute herself to her landlord in order to keep a roof over her mother's and sister's heads. The play charts Margaret's

[40] *Votes for Women!*, I, 151. An earlier draft of the play, submitted to the Lord Chamberlain for licensing, ended not with Vida identifying herself as particularly suited to political activism because of her childlessness, but rather with a wider identification of herself with all vulnerable women: 'My misfortunes, instead of setting me apart from my kind—it has bound me to all who pass that way.' Deleted line in licensing copy, LCP 1907/6.

[41] Mary Higgs, *Glimpses into the Abyss* (P. S. King & Son: London, 1906), 94.

[42] Ibid, 230, 292.

[43] See Barbara Caine, *English Feminism, 1780–1980* (Oxford University Press: Oxford, 1997), 148.

struggle to protect her sister, Violet, from the landlord's further predations. Margaret is finally rewarded with the love of Castleton, a rich man who has been slumming it as a rent collector in order to observe life at its extremes. Overwhelmed by shame, Margaret at first rejects Castleton's proposal, but he overcomes her scruples, revealing that he is well aware of her sexual status. He insists that Margaret's sale of her body to keep a roof over her family's head does not constitute a loss of virtue but rather a determined triumph over adversity: 'I have learnt that you never yield, never falter, never complain. Because you have fought and won, I know that love will go through every fire inviolable.'[44] Williams deliberately insists upon Margaret's fortitude and determination: her figure is described as '*rigid, strenuous and stoical*' and she repeatedly declares that 'I fear nothing'. (56, 80) But however active her language and posture, Margaret's role at the end of the play is essentially passive, held back by the traditional ideology of sexual dishonour until she is rescued by Castleton. In the play's silent denouement, Margaret covers her face, in the fallen woman's time-honoured posture of shame, until Castleton's view of her sacrifice as heroic finally wins over: '*He compels her to return his glance. As her eyes scan his face, at first anxiously, and then with confidence, and she realises there her truth and happiness, she is drawn very slowly but irresistibly forward to his heart*' (131–2). The stage action thus has Margaret slowly succumbing to Castleton's belief that she is not victim but conqueror. The conventional tableau of shame transforms into the equally familiar spectacle of the faithful lover rescuing the dishonoured woman; the crucial difference lies in Castleton's belief that Margaret's redemption lies not in her marriage to a good man, but in the very act of selling her body to protect her family, described by him as a victory of spirit over flesh. His celebratory rhetoric remains in tension with the physical presence of Margaret's body, her shrinking disgust reminding the audience of the reality of the sexual transactions which she still feels inscribed on her flesh.

H. M. Harwood's *Honour Thy Father* (1912) created a similar portrait of a middle-class woman supporting her family as a prostitute, though its heroine, Claire Morgan, is a more caustically critical protagonist than Williams's stoically suffering Margaret. Claire is visiting her idle expatriate father in Brussels, when one of his friends recognizes her as a prostitute and assumes she is therefore sexually available. Enraged by her summary rejection, he informs her parents how she is earning the income which supports them. Claire responds to her parents' outrage with a cool invitation, reminiscent of Nora Helmer's to her husband, to 'Please sit down' and discuss the matter.[45] Holding the floor, Claire accuses her father of having denied her right to professional training, instead having insisted on keeping her fashionably idle as a badge of his own social status. She details her precise market value—fifteen shillings a week living in as a shop girl, with the expectation that she be 'accommodating' to the men in charge—and the choice she made

[44] Antonia R. Williams, *The Street*, in *Three New Plays* (T. Werner Laurie: London, 1907), 126.
[45] H. M. Harwood, *Honour Thy Father*, in *Three One-Act Plays* (Ernest Benn: London, 1926), 47. Produced by the Pioneer Players, Little Theatre, 15 December 1912.

between casually supplementing her wages and becoming a full-time prostitute. (49) Claire calmly corrects her mother's assumption that her career must have been started by some man betraying her; on the contrary, Claire responds, she propositioned her first client. While outlining the social and economic circumstances that forced her into prostitution, Claire's narrative of pragmatic survival separates her from the sensational and passive victims of White Slave mythology, supposedly trafficked to Brussels—the ironic location of Claire's expatriate family.

Using the language of silent gesture, Harwood also seeks to separate disgust at prostitution from condemnation of the prostitute. When Claire's younger sister, Madge, remarks on the smartness of her hat, Claire is anxiously surprised, having selected it as suitably quiet and innocuous. She snatches it quickly from Madge's head when she innocently tries it on. The hat effectively symbolizes Claire's profession, in which 'smartness' is an essential tool of the trade—a professional necessity rather than telling evidence of the prostitute's fatal vanity. Claire shows none of the conventional self-disgust of the theatrical fallen woman, nor does she shrink from physical contact with her unpolluted sister—unlike, for example, the errant mother in Pierre Leclerc's *Illusion* (1890) who pulls on gloves and a floor-length veil before embracing her innocent daughter.[46] Claire, by contrast, insists on her right to remain close to her sister, finally exiting arm-in-arm with Madge, her hat on and her head up, a physical representation of her defiant defence of her occupation. The final image of the play, however, is of Claire's mother who '*sits looking straight before her and the tears run down her face unnoticed and unchecked*' (57). Mother replaces daughter as helpless victim in the tableau of despair.

These playwrights' depictions of women driven to sell their bodies by poverty and an absence of alternative employment appeared at the same time as a new emphasis on economic causation appeared in a number of early twentieth-century texts on prostitution. However, the force of public opinion and long-held beliefs meant that any emphasis on economic factors had to be carefully balanced with an acknowledgement of the vital role of moral and religious training in helping to prevent women's descent into prostitution. So Beatrice Webb began her paper on 'The Social and Economic Causes of Vice', at the Public Morals Conference in 1910, on a significantly defensive note:

> Those who talk about the social and economic causes of vice are often accused of 'materialism' or of omitting what is called 'the moral factor', or are, at any rate, supposed to undervalue the efficacy of spiritual influences, or to be contemptuous of the work of religious and reformatory agencies. I am anxious, at the outset, to avoid this assumed antagonism.... Nothing that I propose is proposed as an alternative to the spiritual influences that can, by good and loving people, be brought to bear on individual cases. On the contrary, all the religious and reformatory agencies will be greatly helped and encouraged, stimulated and assisted, by everything which removes

---

[46] Pierre Leclerc, *Illusion*, LCP, BL Add MS 53453G, III. First produced Strand Theatre, July 1890.

those dreadful economic and social forces that, in a certain number of cases, at any rate, push women into prostitution, just as they push men into crime.[47]

To point to economic necessity as a primary cause of prostitution was thus clearly still controversial even by the 1910s. Analysts identifying the roots of prostitution in childhood abuse, social deprivation, and poor employment and housing conditions found themselves up against not only the traditional notions of women's sexual weakness and vanity, but also a more recent set of popular myths, derived variously from the theatre and the arguments of social purity and suffrage campaigners. The multiple authors of *Downward Paths: An Inquiry into the Causes which contribute to the Making of the Prostitute* (1916), for example, complained that the vast body of public opinion favoured being 'kind' to the prostitute 'whom it imagines as a picturesque and incredibly wronged Marguerite Gautier: it thinks that the problem will presently be solved by a campaign for purity among men and a recognition of the equality of women: or it persecutes the prostitute whenever it gets hold of her with severities such as the refusal of certain institutions to treat unmarried women suffering from venereal disease'.[48] Character, the traditional determinant of a woman's fate, was no longer to be understood separate from environment. As the writers of *Downward Paths* concluded,

> The net result of our enquiry is to confirm the experience of other writers, that prostitutes in the vast majority of cases come from regions where economic conditions cramp and deform human beings to such a degree that we can only guess what stature 'nature' intended them to attain.[49]

One of the crucial factors in producing this shift in attitudes was the influence of the methodology, made famous by Mayhew's *London Labour and the London Poor* (1861), of actually speaking to the women in question. A more detailed knowledge of poor women's working conditions and the limitations imposed on their lives helped to produce a more nuanced definition of economic deprivation, encompassing quality of life rather than just the ability to live:

> 'Economic pressure' does not begin with starvation: it ends there. There has gone before, the long strain of under-feeding and overwork, of the absence of interest, variety, and colour, and all that makes life worth living to a human being. Poverty often means isolation, and isolation the absence of all those ties which keep us in our place in the social order, and make it worth while to preserve our self-respect.[50]

The perspective had significantly shifted here from the prostitute as social problem to the problems within women's lives which had motivated their move into

---

[47] Mrs Sidney Webb, 'The Social and Economic Causes of Vice', in *The Nation's Morals, Being the Proceedings of the Public Morals Conference held in London on 14th and 15th July 1910* (Cassell & Co: London, 1910), 206. See also, J. Ramsay MacDonald, 'Social and Economic Causes of Vice', in ibid, 212–18.

[48] *Downward Paths: An Inquiry into the Causes which contribute to the Making of the Prostitute,* with a foreword by A. Maude Royden (G. Bell & Sons: London, 1916), 3–4.

[49] Ibid, 187.

[50] Ibid, x–xi.

prostitution, including, crucially, women's desire for fulfilment, pleasure, companionship, and community, seen not as a moral weakness but as a natural impulse and a basic human right.

The authors of *Downward Paths* also included in women's 'natural' impulses that of sexual appetite, arguing that all 'normal' adolescent girls had sexual appetites, noting that in the case of the leisured middle classes these could usefully be sublimated into healthy physical pursuits and pastimes.[51] Women's sexual desires, frustrations, and fulfilments were a central concern of a wealth of stories and novels of the 1890s by so-called 'New Woman' writers such as Olive Schreiner, 'George Egerton' [Mary Chavelita Dunne], and Ménie Muriel Dowie; Edwardian novelists, both male and female, continued and developed their refrain.[52] For all that late-Victorian theatre was dominated by plays about adultery, high-class prostitution, and the uncovering of a woman's sexual past, the censorship system and the conservatism of managers and critics meant that overt female desire was barely visible in their scripts or scenarios. It was in the new realist drama that active female desire was most clearly visible, not located simply as sin and temptation, but as an essential human impulse.

Helen, the heroine of Inez Bensusan's *The Apple* (1909), for example, is a female clerk torn between attraction to her married boss, her desire for the entertainment and luxuries he offers, unaffordable on her narrow salary, and her inescapable sense that an affair with him would mean, for a girl like her, 'losing something that's best in her. Something she can *never get back.*'[53] Helen is trapped by gender inequalities at every turn: underpaid, sexually harassed, denied an equal education or inheritance by her parents. She ends the play with tears streaming down her cheeks, caught by the invidious choice between abandoning her self-respect and submitting to the 'hopeless monotone' of her typist's existence (153). Her tears may signify regret for her about-to-be-lost virtue or for her resignation to a life of drudgery—the choice is painful and unjust but the decision is hers. Aware of Helen's attraction towards him, her boss is no melodramatic villain, but a mundane and unheroic man, content to exploit the power gifted to him: if she denounces him publicly for sexually harassing her, then her father will be honour-bound to resign his job in the firm, and her own reputation will inevitably be tainted by scandal. The power of the male manager over female employees dependent on his favour was a new subject of concern in analyses of the causes of prostitution, but had long been recognized as one of the hazards of women's employment in the theatre—and was doubtless a factor in Bensusan's founding of the Women's Theatre in 1913, with the express project not only of providing a platform for feminist issues

---

[51] Ibid, 30–1.

[52] For an excellent study of Edwardian novelists' treatment of female sexuality, see Jane Eldridge Miller, *Rebel Women: Feminism, Modernism and the Edwardian Novel* (Virago: London, 1994).

[53] Inez Bensusan, *The Apple*. Reprinted in *How the Vote was Won and Other Suffragette Plays*, selected and introduced by Dale Spender and Carole Hayman (Methuen: London, 1985), 153. First performed Court Theatre, 14 March 1909.

but also of employing women as directors, producers, and technical staff within the theatre.[54]

For all the hardships and hazards associated with women's employment, a living wage could signify economic independence, and with that came the freedom for women to step outside familial and male control. Financial self-sufficiency potentially offered women sexual freedom and choice, meaning that the expansion in female employment which accompanied industrialization and commercial development became a significant factor in challenging sexual attitudes. As Mary Higgs observed in her survey of shifting moral attitudes which prefaced her influential reportage account, *Three Nights in Women's Lodging Houses* (1905), 'We are still in a transition period, but largely in the middle and working classes women before marriage, and even after, are escaping to economic independence. This change is so vast and far-reaching, involving an adjustment of all our social institutions, that we can hardly yet appreciate it.'[55] Women's employment opportunities were a disruptive factor in traditional social organization, and playwrights' recognition of them proved the most significantly disturbing factor in the reworking of old plots. J. M. Barrie's *The Twelve-Pound Look* (1910) offered a humorous one-act précis of women's altered position.[56] The complacent Sir Harry Sims encounters his ex-wife, Kate, in the unexpected role of hired typist, but his smug superiority is punctured when he learns that Kate left their marriage not for another man, as he had always assumed, but for financial independence. The 'twelve-pound look' marks out a woman who knows she can earn that sum to support herself, and the play ends with Harry's second wife casting envious glances at Kate's typewriter. Independence not adultery poses a threat to the old order.

Kate's wage-earning power enables her to step outside marriage and her role as an object of display in Harry's social circle. Just as realist playwrights examined the role that social environment and economic factors played in influencing women's sexual choices, so they in turn located women's sexual choices within the wider workings of industry, commerce, social and familial structures and in the context of human evolution. Education, professional opportunities, working conditions, wage levels, and moral attitudes all played a role in constraining, influencing, and directing women's sexual choices; where liberty of choice shaded into constraint took careful and close examination to discern. But the focus also went outwards, locating women's sexuality as a vital element in larger social systems and commercial structures.

While the *fin de siècle* saw a wider recognition and acceptance of intrinsic and spontaneous female desire, it also rapidly saw its co-option in the greater interests of the race. The old ideology of women's self-abnegation and duty to society took

---

[54] Interview with Inez Bensusan, 'The Woman's Theatre', *Common Cause* (21 November 1913), 591. See, e.g. Ramsay MacDonald, 'Social and Economic Causes of Vice', in *Nation's Morals*, 211–16; *Downward Paths*, 175–83. On sexual harassment in the acting profession, see e.g. Hamilton, *Life Errant*, 47, and Elizabeth Robins, *Theatre and Friendship: Some Henry James Letters with a commentary* (Jonathan Cape: London, 1932), 29–30.

[55] Mary Higgs, Preface, *Three Nights in Women's Lodging Houses* (John Heywood: Manchester, 1905).

[56] *The Twelve-Pound Look*. First performed Duke of York's Theatre, London, 1 March 1910.

a new form, as eugenicists emphasized the vital importance of women as mothers of the next generation, not as moral educators but as biological vessels and genetic transmitters. In the Men and Women's Club, founded in 1885 to discuss human sexuality, feminists such as Olive Schreiner, Henrietta Muller, and Emma Brooke found themselves in conflict with the eugenic imperatives propounded by the club's founder, Karl Pearson, demanding that women's individual interests must be subordinated to the all-important cause of breeding a healthy race for the future.[57] Bernard Shaw's *Man and Superman* (1903) was one of the first plays where a respectable young woman's sexual drive was both the crux of the plot and a central topic of debate. The play's heroine, Ann Whitefield, pursues her man across Europe, at first within the carefully veiled limits of public decorum and then with open determination. In an extended dream sequence set in Hell, a debate over evolution and the need to breed a 'superman' to lead humanity forwards takes place, and woman's destiny and duty is agreed to be ensnaring a mate in order to populate the world. Ann Whitefield's overt desire was thus a core part of the play's message, as Shaw commented in his 'Epistle Dedicatory' to the first edition:

> Among the friends to whom I have read this play in manuscript are some of our own sex who are shocked at the 'unscrupulousness', meaning the utter disregard of masculine fastidiousness, with which the woman pursues her purpose. It does not occur to them that if women were as fastidious as men, morally or physically, there would be an end of the race. Is there anything meaner than to throw necessary work upon other people and then disparage it as unworthy and indelicate.[58]

Beatrice Webb, herself a keen eugenicist, embraced the play's discussion of 'the subject of human breeding', announcing enthusiastically, 'I realize that it is the most important of all questions, this breeding of the right sort of man. GBS's audacious genius can reach out to it.'[59]

A few years later Shaw's emphasis on women's sexual drive and their reproductive vocation repelled Webb. In his *Misalliance*, Hypatia Tarleton chases the handsome and reluctant Joey Percival up a hill, only to be rewarded by his pursuing her down it. On Shaw's reading of the play, Webb greeted it as 'amazingly brilliant' but complained that 'the whole "motive" is erotic'.[60] Her qualified enthusiasm turned to marked distaste after attending a performance in 1910 of Harley Granville Barker's *The Madras House*, running in repertory together with *Misalliance*, dismissing their 'rabbit-warren' view of humanity and female sexuality in particular as debasing and limited:

> GBS is brilliant but disgusting; Granville-Barker is intellectual but dull. They both harp on the mere physical attractions of men to women, and women to men, coupled

---

[57] See Walkowitz, *City of Dreadful Delight*, ch. 5; Bland, *Banishing the Beast*, Part One.

[58] 'Epistle Dedicatory' (1903), *Man and Superman*, in *The Bodley Head Bernard Shaw*, vol. II (Bodley Head: London, 1971), 507.

[59] Beatrice Webb, diary entry 16 January 1903, *The Diary of Beatrice Webb*, Vol. II, 1892–1905 (Virago Press: London, 1983), 267.

[60] Diary entry, 27 December 1909, *The Diary of Beatrice Webb*, Vol. III, 1905–1924 (Virago: London, 1984), 133.

with the insignificance of the female for any other purpose but sex attraction, with tiresome iteration. That world is not the world I live in.[61]

The shift in Beatrice Webb's response to the staging of female sexual desire reflected wider developments in the debate over sexuality and the contradictions and dilemmas that these threw up. In 1903 *Man and Superman*'s depiction of an active and spontaneous female appetite was sufficiently uncommon to prompt the critic Max Beerbohm to insist that Shaw had made the mistake of 'confusing the natural sex-instinct with the desire for marriage'; normal women, Beerbohm asserted, felt only the latter because, as all countries and ages attest, 'Man is the dominant animal.'[62] Shaw's championing of female sexual desire appeared, with the theatre's usual belatedness, a decade after 'New Woman' fiction's celebration of women's sexuality in the 1890s. By the later 1900s many feminists had begun to feel that a widespread recognition of female sexuality was not liberating but potentially constricting and reductive.

The feminist playwright Cicely Hamilton, for instance, inveighed against the valuation of women's lives only in their relation to men as implied in the 'the identification of success with marriage, of failure with spinsterhood, the artificial concentration of the hopes of girlhood on sexual attraction and maternity'.[63] In her play *A Pageant of Great Women* (1909), a perennial suffrage favourite, Prejudice claims that women's innate stupidity makes her incapable of mature thought, to which Woman retorts:

> Oh well, indeed, does this come from you
> Who held the body as all the spirit as nought.
> For you who saw us only as a sex![64]

In *The Great Scourge and How to End It*, Christabel Pankhurst similarly characterized the Anti-Suffragist as believing women to be 'of value only because of their sex functions', whether as wives, prostitutes or mothers, with any woman falling outside those categories being classed as 'superfluous'.[65] A writer to *Common Cause* in 1910 summed up this frustration at such limited notions of women's duties, nature and professional prospects which meant that 'men can do anything they *can* do; women are to exist merely for the propagation of the race and for the enjoyment of man'.[66]

The wider acceptance of female sexual desire as natural and intrinsic, especially in the context of woman's vital role in perpetuating the race, was potentially a

---

[61] Diary entry, 13 March 1910, ibid, 137. *Misalliance* and *The Madras House* were produced by Charles Frohman at the Duke of York's Theatre as part of an experimental repertory season of new plays which opened on 10 February 1910. Neither play was a success, *Misalliance* achieving only 11 performances, *The Madras House* just 10 performances.

[62] 'Mr Shaw's New Dialogues', 12 September 1903, reprinted from *Saturday Review*, in Max Beerbohm, *Around Theatres* (Rupert Hart-Davis: London, 1953), 271.

[63] Cicely Hamilton, *Life Errant* (Dent: London, 1935), 65.

[64] Cicely Hamilton, *A Pageant of Great Women* (International Suffrage Shop: London, 1910), 25.

[65] Pankhurst, *The Great Scourge*, 134–6.

[66] *Common Cause* (14 April 1910), 3. Quoted in Susan Kingsley Kent, *Sex and Suffrage in Britain, 1860–1914* (Routledge: London, 1995), 236.

double-edged weapon: it could be deployed to define woman's social role as primarily or exclusively that of child-bearer; or it could be used to challenge the opprobrium attached to women's extramarital desires and the stigma of unmarried motherhood. The language of biological necessity, evolutionary imperatives, and the greater good of the race offered an alternative discourse to that of temptation, sin, and social disgrace. St John Hankin's *The Last of the De Mullins* (1908) perfectly demonstrates the ways in which the eugenic celebration of female sexual desire and fertility could both enhance and restrict notions of women's freedom. Janet De Mullin is the unmarried mother of a fine young boy, the only grandchild of her ageing and domineering father. Janet rejects a half-hearted marriage proposal from her one-time lover, and defies her father's attempts to assert authority over her or her son, glorying in the independence secured by the successful millinery business she runs. When her mother assumes that she was a victim of seduction, Janet tells her she sounds 'like a sentimental novel'; she was twenty-seven, and her lover only twenty when they met, so she's happy to take responsibility.[67] She ends the play celebrating unmarried motherhood as infinitely preferable to spinsterhood, advising her sister to acquire a lover and child, whether inside or outside marriage, as her only defence against premature old age. Defiant of male ownership and conventional morality, Janet locates woman's fulfilment exclusively in her sexuality, recalling her affair as the realization of her true womanhood: 'It was so splendid to find some one at last who really cared for me as women should be cared for! Not to talk to because I was clever or to play tennis with because I was strong, but to kiss me and make love to me!' (III, 262). She refuses her father's desire to absorb her back into his patriarchal family—her son is hers alone, and is not to take his place as 'the last of the De Mullins'.[68] Janet does, however, recognize her place as a valuable perpetuator of the species: 'What on earth were women created for,' she asks, 'if not to have children?' (III, 262). It was Janet's New Womanish bicycle-riding jaunts which gave her the freedom to engage in an affair—an association between female emancipation and sexual irregularity which could have been offered as a dark warning by Sidney Grundy or Henry Arthur Jones. But Janet's business skills transform her 'fall' into a triumph, as she achieves both financial and emotional independence, despite denigrating any female ambition beyond motherhood.[69]

[67] St John Hankin, *The Last of the De Mullins*, in Chothia (ed.), *The New Woman and Other Emancipated Woman Plays*, II, 248–9. First performed Haymarket Theatre, 6 December 1908, by the Stage Society.

[68] Janet's assertion of sole parental rights and her rejection of her son's inheritance aligns her with rebellious unmarried mothers, like Wilde's Mrs Arbuthnot in *A Woman of No Importance*, and in contrast to the long tradition of self-sacrificing mothers leading back to Dumas *fils*'s *Le Fils naturel* (1858) and forwards to F. Tennyson-Jesse and H.M. Harwood's *The Pelican* (1924), whose title affirms that a good mother will ultimately give her life's blood for her child.

[69] The notion that motherhood had the power to divert women from radical causes was familiar among female writers and mainstream feminists too; in the first version of *Votes for Women!*, for example, Vida Levering reassures the MP, Geoffrey Stonor, that his newly politicized fiancée will soon change her mind if she has children, for it was always 'the little, little arms that subdued the fiercest of us'. *Votes for Women*, LCP 1907/6, Act III.

The Last of the De Mullins was produced for two matinees at the Court Theatre by Granville Barker, with his wife Lillah McCarthy, who had previously played Shaw's Ann Whitefield, in the role of Janet. The heroine's radical morality proved too strong even for the Court's exclusive audience, as Shaw noted:

> In the 3rd Act Lillah appealed with extraordinary gusto to every unmarried woman of twenty-eight in the house to go straight out and procure a baby at once without the slightest regard to law or convention. As Lillah regards this as a most obvious and reasonable doctrine, she had no idea of the effect she was producing in the audience. At the end of the Act the majority were simply afraid to applaud: the thing had gone quite beyond mere play-acting for them, and although they were interested, they felt—quite rightly—that to clap such sentiments would be to vote for them.[70]

The audience's reservations were echoed by a number of critics: the *Morning Post* fastidiously described Janet's ideals as 'difficult to record in seemly language', though finding 'ample precedent' for them in 'the drama of the last ten years, and particularly in the works of Mr Bernard Shaw'; while the *Pall Mall Gazette* refused to believe that Hankin could be offering such ideas seriously, proposing instead that the play should be viewed as a satire on Shavian drama.[71] There was a stark division between reviewers: the *Illustrated Sporting and Dramatic News*, for example, remained coldly disapproving of the play's morality, despite McCarthy's picturesque performance, declaring she was 'for ever rubbing up the wrong way an audience with far more tolerance of such moral vagaries than would be shown by any assembly of ordinary average playgoers'; the *World*, by contrast, delighted in the 'full-blooded' energy of McCarthy's performance, seeing in it 'a really charming touch of gay wilfulness which could not hide, however, the strong, straight character that lay beneath'.[72] The modernity of Janet's views and behaviour prompted Max Beerbohm to confess a nostalgic preference for old-style magdalens like Olivia Primrose and Dickens's Little Em'ly; Janet's views, he declared, would not have been held by a woman and certainly not expressed by one—if Hankin had to express them, the critic mused, he should have put them in the mouth of one of the play's minor male characters.[73]

Viewing female sexuality from a eugenic perspective could challenge traditional moral attitudes, but, as Janet De Mullin's rhetoric reveals, the co-option of women's desire for the reproductive good of the race, while being in some ways liberating and empowering, was in other ways potentially limiting and reductive. A number of 'new dramatists' offered critiques of the appropriation of female sexuality to further wider interests, whether commercial, industrial, racial, or familial. By relocating women's sexual choices within concrete realities of income, working

---

[70] Shaw letter to Granville Barker (7 December 1908), in *Bernard Shaw's Letters to Granville Barker*, ed. C. B. Purdom (Phoenix House: London, 1956), 142–3.

[71] *Morning Post* (8 December 1908); *Pall Mall Gazette* (8 December 1908), 10.

[72] *Illustrated Sporting and Dramatic News* (19 December 1908), 650; *World* (8 December 1908), 1097.

[73] *Saturday Review* (12 December 1908), 726–7.

conditions, education, and the commercial marketplace, dramatists challenged conventional divisions between licit and illicit sexuality, marriage and prostitution, romance and pragmatic survival. It was often a subtle balancing act to retain a sense of women's active sexual choices within the subtle network of environmental factors conditioning and constraining their freedom, whilst maintaining a focus on the exploitation of women's bodies in the name of the greater cause of profit, reputation, and the market.

In *Marriage as a Trade*, Cicely Hamilton stripped off notions of romance or sexual destiny to analyse matrimony as women's socially allotted profession, comparing its poor employment rights, wages, and working conditions with other lowly-paid occupations by which women were allowed to earn a living. It was, however, in her unexpected stage-hit *Diana of Dobson's* (1908) that Hamilton's views found their most effective showcase.[74] The play was a Cinderella-tale of a shop girl who escapes the drudgery of working fourteen hours a day for £13 per annum plus board and lodging when she inherits £300 from a distant relative. Instead of investing it to secure marginal relief from her cramped existence, Diana chooses to blow it all on 'one crowded hour', or in her case month, of life.[75] Fashionably dressed and holidaying in the Swiss Alps, Diana receives a marriage proposal from Captain Bretherton, who is in search of a rich wife to enhance the £600 per annum income which he finds insufficient to support his lifestyle. Bretherton is outraged when Diana reveals the truth, accusing her of being an adventuress—her murky secret being a commercial rather than a sexual one.[76] Diana turns his insult back upon him, declaring with dignity that she is an independent wage-earner, and casting doubt upon his ability to be the same. The last act finds both Diana and Bretherton on the embankment, her ill health and his inability to find honest employment having reduced them both to homelessness and starvation. Realizing that his £600 income is sufficient for them both, Bretherton offers Diana a slice of bread and his hand in marriage, and she hungrily accepts both. Hamilton subtitled *Diana of Dobson's* 'A Romantic Comedy in Four Acts' but the question of how romantic or pragmatic its ending is has divided critics from its first performance onwards.[77] Diana reminds Bretherton she is penniless, homeless and hungry, and '*laughing harshly*' she asks, 'don't you think that you are putting too great a strain upon my disinterestedness?' (IV, 76). Diana admits that she would have had no hesitation in accepting when she was in a better financial state and that it is

[74] The play ran for 143 performances at Lena Ashwell's Kingsway Theatre from 12 February 1908. Not foreseeing its considerable success, Hamilton sold Ashwell rights to the play for a single lump-sum rather than a percentage of box-office receipts.

[75] Cicely Hamilton, *Diana of Dobson's*, reprinted in Linda Fitzsimmons and Viv Gardner (eds), *New Woman Plays* (Methuen: London, 1991), I, 42.

[76] Hamilton's original title for the play was *The Adventuress*, under which it was submitted for licence to the Lord Chamberlain's Office.

[77] See, e.g. *Daily Telegraph* (13 February 1908), 191; *Era* (15 February 1908); *Stage* (13 February 1908); Stowell, *A Stage of Their Own*, 90–2; Christine Dymkowski, 'Case Study: Cicely Hamilton's *Diana of Dobson's* 1908', in Baz Kershaw (ed.), *Cambridge History of British Theatre*, Vol. 3, *Since 1895* (Cambridge University Press: Cambridge), 122–6.

pride holding her back, but the presence on the bench of a bedraggled sleeping woman '*of the hopelessly unemployed class*' is a pointed reminder of the fate that could await Diana if she were to refuse—whether Diana is accepting marriage as a more secure profession remains an unsettling possibility. (IV, 70)

The play gathered most notice for its first-act depiction of a women's dormitory in Dobson's drapery establishment, as the women undress for bed. The scene was deliberately choreographed to be asexual and unalluring, as the workers do not remove their clothing to reveal seductive flesh but instead awkwardly and discreetly shuffle off the shapely clothes, adornments and false hair which constitute their professionally attractive uniform.[78] Diana and her workmates strip themselves before the audience of what Peter Bailey has termed their 'parasexuality', the glamour of an 'open yet licit sexuality' associated with those female workers employed behind bars and shop counters, on the interface between public and private, whose attractiveness was deployed as a complement and accompaniment to the goods on sale around her.[79] By 1908 nubile shop girls had taken centre stage for over a decade at the Gaiety Theatre in musical comedies such as *The Shop Girl* (1894), *The Girl from Kays* (1902), and *The Girl Behind the Counter* (1906). Hamilton's play deliberately stripped away the light-hearted glamour on which the shop girl musical depended, revealing the exhausted bodies beneath their professionally attractive apparel, and the dingy dormitories and bullying regulations behind the luxurious shop floors with which audience members were familiar.

Diana of Dobson's was, however, by no means the first play to depict the hardships of life for women moving into the newly expanded work place. A possible influence on Hamilton's play can be found in Netta Syrett's 1902 play, *The Finding of Nancy*, which won a competition run by the Playgoers Club to select and stage the best unperformed play. Syrett's script was submitted anonymously alongside hundreds of others, and won the prize of being produced by George Alexander, who had promised to take a role in the winning drama alongside fellow actor-manager Herbert Beerbohm Tree. *The Finding of Nancy* was duly given a matinee performance at the St James's Theatre on 8 May 1902 to an enthusiastic and packed house and admiring, if condescending, critical reviews. The first act of *The Finding of Nancy* was a detailed naturalistic study of the cramped and joyless life of the low-waged working woman. Nancy describes the drudgery of a typist's existence, denied any company beyond that of the other female employees, working long hours into the night for a salary which forces her to choose between furnishing her room and buying her dinner. It is the emptiness and isolation of this life which persuade her to consent to a sexual relationship with Will Fielding, a married man tied to an alcoholic wife. Fielding offers her companionship, dinners, and theatre trips, but insists their friendship cannot continue platonically. Nancy at first refuses, though

---

[78] For details of the performance and reception of the dormitory scene, see Joel Kaplan and Sheila Stowell, *Theatre and Fashion: Oscar Wilde to the Suffragettes* (Cambridge University Press: Cambridge, 1994), 108–14.

[79] Peter Bailey, *Popular Culture and Performance in the Victorian City* (Cambridge University Press: Cambridge, 1998), 151–2.

not on principle—she concedes that if she loved him 'overwhelmingly' she might feel differently, and that their union harms no one, their existence being too lowly and obscure to attract any notice.[80] But her revulsion at the loneliness of her life forces her into his arms at the end of the first act.

The *Illustrated London News* praised this first act as 'a perfect miniature drama, convincing and complete', and critics were united in acclaiming its verisimilitude and power to throw 'a light on the lives of struggling, hard-working women, such as has rarely been thrown by any earnest essayist, and still more rarely seen on any boards'.[81] But critics were equally in agreement that, as Clement Scott put it, this 'curiously-effective prologue led nowhere; there was an admirable porch, but no house'.[82] The second act of the play moves to the more familiar theatrical setting of a luxury hotel on the Riviera; both Fielding and Nancy have inherited fortunes, and Fielding's wife has died. The hitch in this fairy-tale resolution is that, as Nancy puts it, she's in love with 'the wrong Prince'—she is attracted to the louche Captain Egerton, and so rejects Fielding's proposal of marriage. (II, 23) Fielding steps quietly aside, scrupulously protecting Nancy's reputation, and carelessly engages himself to a woman who cares only for his fortune. Nancy's true feelings for Fielding are revealed to herself—and to the rest of the hotel's residents—when she overhears what she mistakenly believes to be news of his suicide. Her hysterical cries of horror and then relief leave her reputation in tatters. The final act sees Nancy and Fielding happily reunited in the cramped lodgings of the first act, in which they had lived together in unmarried bliss:

FIELDING: There's nothing else for it. We must take up life together again, and go on like the old married couple—
NANCY: (*earnestly*) We have always been.

(IV, 55)

Edwardian critics were left dissatisfied: Syrett had set out 'an interesting conjunction of circumstances' but did not 'work out the case on its merits', and the power of the first act subsequently fell into 'sentimentality and melodrama'.[83]

One clear thesis runs through the play, however: that, in the words of a minor character who defies her mother to marry an impoverished suitor, 'it is less immoral to live with a man she loved than to marry one she didn' t'—a view which her mother disapprovingly attributes to her reading of Ibsen and Hardy. (II, 16) The socially-approved view of marriage is expressed by Fielding's waspish fiancée and her mother:

VIOLET: It isn't my idea of a brilliant match, but it will do.
MRS STUART: He has six hundred a year and with your allowance—
VIOLET: Mr Brackenhurst has a thousand.

---

[80] Netta Syrett, *The Finding of Nancy*, LCP 1902/14, Act I, 11.
[81] *Illustrated London News* (17 May 1902), 708; *Daily Telegraph* (9 May 1902), 10.
[82] *Daily Telegraph* (9 May 1902), 10.
[83] *Manchester Guardian* (9 May 1902); *Illustrated London News* (17 May 1902).

MRS STUART: (*practically*) It would probably never have come off. Men of sixty
prefer girls of eighteen, as a rule.

(III, 41)

Syrett's satire depicts marriage as a buyers' market in which aspiring goods need a
clear sense of their saleability.

Where the play seemed to lose coherence for critics was when Nancy falls in
love with the rakish Captain Egerton. This marked a clear point where critics fell
out of sympathy with the heroine. The *Athenaeum*'s reviewer dismissed Nancy as
making 'not too successful an appeal to masculine sympathies', finding the only
explanation for her attraction to Egerton in a likeness to Cyprienne in Sardou's
Divorçons, a woman aroused only by illicit sex.[84] Syrett's plotting and dramatic
construction do indeed appear to descend into theatrical effect and random
complication—unless one views the play's romantic complications as a means of
asking where do romance and spontaneous female desire find a place in a society
in which the power to compel or secure sexual submission lies so unequally in
the hands of men?

For all the happiness and friendship Fielding and Nancy have shared, and despite
her conviction that she was right to choose his companionship over her former
lonely existence, the initial compulsion which Fielding exercised over Nancy has
never been entirely excised. She has always paid her way and never been a kept
woman, but, as their conversation after she reveals her passion for Egerton shows,
the relationship has not been an equal one. As Fielding bitterly notes, she never
loved him:

NANCY: (*looking at him in a frightened way*) I never knew that until—
FIELDING: Until you loved someone else. No, how should you?
(*a pause*)
NANCY: (*desperately*) Will! I'll marry you if you wish it. It is what I ought to do.
FIELDING: My dear child, I can stand much; more than I thought in fact—but
not a dutiful wife.
NANCY: (*miserably*) Oh, I deserve you to speak so, I know.
FIELDING: (*rising and crossing to her*) No, it's I who deserve to be kicked. I guessed
this was coming, but when it actually comes, it's worse than one—But never
mind that. I only wanted to tell you that I haven't been quite blind these four
years, and if you've had your bad days—well! so have I!
NANCY: (*breathlessly*) Not because you thought our life together wrong?
FIELDING: I? A thousand times no. It was the knowledge that it troubled you.
I knew your loneliness you see, and used it as a weapon against you. I won, but
you have often made me pay for victory.
NANCY: But I never said one word.

---

[84] *Athenaeum* (17 May 1902), 636.

FIELDING: No. It was when you were rather gayer than usual, strange to say, that
I felt a blackguard. At such moments the fact that nine men out of ten would
have taken the same advantage scarcely seemed a justification.

NANCY: No! No! You mustn't blame yourself. After all, if you had left me that
evening what would my life have been? I should feel now perhaps that I had
missed my chance. It is I who am unreasonable. I lost my peace of mind—yes,
But, oh Will! We have had many happy times!

FIELDING: I may at least remember that?

NANCY: (*restlessly*) Oh if only I could get rid of this terrible new feeling, and let
things be as they were. It is a madness, and yet—

FIELDING: (*looking at her*) Impossible. Nancy you love this man. I see it. For four
years I have longed in vain to see you look as you look now. It's like my luck that
it shouldn't be for me...

(II, 28–9)

As this exchange makes clear, Nancy's new-found wealth does not correct the balance or make her choice of marrying Fielding an entirely free one: their past relationship leaves her with a sense of obligation, and an inescapable sense that
according to social morality their relationship has left her as damaged goods. It is
only her passion for Egerton and the subsequent realization that it is Fielding she
really loves that render her choice a free and instinctive one.

More subtly, Syrett also suggests that Fielding's initial use of Nancy's loneliness as a lever to secure her sexual submission has left her out of touch with her
own spontaneous sexual desires. Nancy initially refuses Fielding's request that
they become lovers by confessing that 'I can't love you altogether!'—if she did
love him 'overwhelmingly', she calmly admits, things might be different (I, 13,
11). In contrast to her lack of consuming passion for Fielding, Nancy describes
her feelings for Egerton as 'madness—a possession of the devil', which in retrospect she recognizes as 'an infatuation' that was already passing when the shock
of Fielding's supposed death clarified her feelings for him (II, 24; IV, 45). This
can be read as implying that lust leads Nancy astray, until she gains an understanding of the more important things she shares with Fielding. But, more significantly, Syrett seems to suggest that, constrained by Fielding's desire and her
own reluctant submission as the price extracted for his companionship, Nancy
has remained out of touch with her own spontaneous sexual feelings throughout
their time together. Ironically, it is her attraction to Egerton which brings an
awareness of her own unforced desires—Fielding's punishment being to witness
this awakening. The play's romantic resolution is thus dependent on Nancy's
realization of her own spontaneous sexual desires, free from compulsion, making
possible a true equality with Fielding and her recognition of him as 'my friend,
my child, my lover' (IV, 55).

For all the convolutions and theatrical set-pieces of its plot, *The Finding of Nancy* is
most remarkable as a detailed portrayal of a woman attempting to chart her own way
amidst conflicting pressures, prejudices, and inherited ethics. The play unequivocally

champions her right to happiness, and the justice of her decision to step outside socially approved morality in order to seek it; Nancy is explicitly not a revolutionary, but
simply a woman negotiating between her own needs and a social morality she has
internalized. As she explains to her sympathetic friend Isabel:

NANCY: Theories are all very well, but there are things that women never get used to.
   Foolish unreasonable things, of course, but real to <u>us</u> all the same.... Even now,
   when I hear someone say 'She lived with him for years', or 'she's his mistress'—you
   know the voice! I grow cold with horror. I think, that's what <u>you</u> are, you are living
   with a man like that!
ISABEL: But that is not what you <u>think</u>?
NANCY: (*quickly*) No! only what I <u>feel</u>. And a man never understands that you
   can think one way and feel another, without being fundamentally unreasonable.
ISABEL: Yes. Reason ahead, feeling lagging behind. It's different for men, I
   suppose. For ages they have been free.
NANCY: And so they take such matters easily, naturally. We can't do it, Isabel.
   There's age-long tradition against us;... training... the old Puritan instinct. These
   things hang around us like grave clothes.

(II, 23–4)

The play's particular concentration on such internal struggles led the *Observer*'s
critic to describe Nancy as 'neurotic, self-conscious and morbidly introspective',
and male reviewers were unanimous in dismissing the play as appealing exclusively
to female tastes: as the *Speaker* put it, 'a rather militant pamphlet on the subject of
the social disabilities of women, addressed to the rather limited public which
occupies itself with these questions'.[85] The *Times* even complained that the female
playwright made a 'disproportionate fuss' over the difference between marriage
and 'concubinage'—a somewhat remarkable view given that the contemporary
theatrical repertoire of mainstream playwrights such as Pinero and Henry Arthur
Jones was almost exclusively concerned with precisely that distinction.[86] Certainly
Syrett paid a different price for her authorship. The *Observer* and, most influentially, Clement Scott writing in the *Daily Telegraph* speculated that the verisimilitude and conviction of the play must be traceable to the author's own experience—a
suggestion which Syrett was convinced prompted her dismissal from a school-
teaching post, and perhaps, she hints, George Alexander's failure to give the play a
longer run than its single, well-received, matinee performance.[87]

Where so many plays by Pinero, Grundy, and Jones had asserted the naturalness
and inevitability of orthodox sexual morality, a number of feminist playwrights in
turn emphasized the man-made status of law, examining the complex interplay

---

[85]   *Observer* (11 June 1902); *Speaker* (17 May 1902), 191.
[86]   *Times* (9 May 1902), 8.
[87]   Syrett also notes that she never received any payment from the venture. See Netta Syrett, *The
Sheltering Tree* (Geoffrey Bles: London, 1939), 125–7.

between sexual morality, patriarchal authority, and the law. In *Votes for Women!* Vida Levering tells the gathered crowd in Trafalgar Square of the case of a young girl, sent to prison for the death of her illegitimate child while her seducer and former employer is left untouched by the law, a law framed and enforced by men in their own interests; as Vida notes, the girl was 'arrested by a man, brought before a man judge, tried by a jury of men, condemned by men, taken to prison by a man, and by a man she's hanged! Where in all this were *her* "peers"?'[88]

Margaret Wynne Nevinson's one-act play *In the Workhouse*, produced by the Pioneer Players in 1911, was deliberately written to 'show the parlous condition of twentieth-century womanhood under the unjust Gilbertian muddle of uni-sexual legislation', and to illustrate 'some of the hardships of the law to an unrepresented sex'.[89] Nevinson's robustly naturalistic portrait of a workhouse ward and the laws governing its female inhabitants raised a press furore over its 'unpleasantness', proving far more effective, as Nevinson remarked, than all the pamphlets she had written on the subject which she had seen 'fall to the bottom of the Dead Sea of printed matter'.[90] The strongest voice amongst Nevinson's workhouse inmates is Penelope, the proud mother of five children by different fathers, who has negotiated far better maintenance payments than the courts ever secure, enabling her, together with her cook's salary, to bring them up 'clean and respectable' under her sole parental jurisdiction as an unmarried mother. Brought up on the parish after her father beat her mother to death, Penelope's first experience of joy was when, working as an underhousemaid, 'I found as the young master wanted me, the first time since Mother died as any human soul had taken any interest in me, and Lord! I laughs now when I think what an 'appy time it was' (55). While a hardworking seamstress is held prisoner in the workhouse at her drunken husband's will, Penelope departs with her new baby, after a comfortable lying-in on the parish, commenting happily that the 'law is on the side of us bad 'uns' (65). Hearing from the other inmates about the lack of rights accorded to married women, Lily decides not to marry the father of her baby, but to follow the example of Penelope and retain her legal and financial independence. In the play's cold-eyed depiction of the legal position of women, conventional sentiments become absurd—or darkly ironic: the play's final line is an ecstatic shriek of 'I do love my biby!' from Monica an 'idiot girl' of eighteen, who has just given birth to her third baby—all three of whom are named 'Bill' after the three different fathers who have exploited and abandoned her, presumably under a commonly assumed pseudonym (69). In Nevinson's analysis of the absurdities of man-made law, men's convenience not morality underlies the marriage laws, prompting any woman ruled by common sense to prefer the social stigma of unmarried motherhood to the legal bondage of matrimony.

[88] *Votes for Women!*, II, 184. Josephine Butler recorded similar sentiments expressed by a prostitute: 'It is *men, men, men*, from the first to the last that we have to do with! To please a man I did wrong first, then I was flung from man to man, then men police lay hands on us—by men we are examined, handled, doctored and messed on with. . . . We are had up before Magistrates who are men, and we never get out of the hands of men till we die!' Quoted in Kent, *Sex and Suffrage*, 60.

[89] Margaret Wynne Nevinson, Preface, *In the Workhouse* (International Suffrage Shop: London, 1911), 11, 21.

[90] Nevinson, 'A Bewildered Playwright', *Vote* (3 June 1911), 68.

One of the most intellectually ambitious plays to anatomize women's sexual exploitation and subjugation in the interests of business and to lay bare the ways in which male interests helped to frame laws and attitudes, was Harley Granville Barker's *The Madras House* (1909). Dramatizing a day in the life of the Madras House fashion firm and its employees, Barker's play brought together the various dramatic modes of domestic comedy, Shavian debate and workplace realism, analysing the evils of the living-in system, the plight of the 'superfluous' middle-class spinster, the relation between prostitution and marriage, the commercial exploitation of female sexuality and its marketability, and the familiar plots of a wife's dangerous flirtation and the shop girl who falls pregnant by a rich man. *The Madras House* binds these elements together, its four acts exploring different interlinked aspects of the 'woman question'. As Desmond MacCarthy commented, rather than 'writing six action plays on sex', Barker constructed a conversation play 'presenting the essence of each aspect interlocked and together', thereby offering 'a bird's eye view of a gigantic theme'.[91]

The first act introduces the six unmarried daughters of Henry Huxtable, a partner in the Madras House, who live a life of empty gentility in Denmark Hill, rapidly advancing beyond marriageable age and denied the opportunity of paid employment as their salaries are not needed. Their emotional and sexual development is arrested; one 34-year-old daughter is condemned as 'wanton' by their mother for treasuring the collar of a matinee idol. The living-in system examined in the second act is the flip-side of the same coin: separating husbands and wives, purchasing the private lives of its employees with wages too low to enable them to live independently of its dormitories, Huxtable's firm has appropriated rights over its workers' lives just as he has over his daughters'. Two employees have concealed their marriage and cannot afford to have children on their meagre salary, while Miss Yates, the one worker who is not downtrodden and drained but shines with life, has fallen pregnant by an unnamed man and faces dismissal. In the words of Constantine Madras, another partner in the firm and a converted 'Mahommedan', the firm's living-in workforce constitute an 'industrial seraglio', the firm itself a 'harem of industry'.[92]

In Act Three, the two partners and Constantine's son Philip meet to negotiate the sale of the Madras House to an American businessman, Eustace State—the act being dominated by a fashion show of the latest designs, modelled by French 'mannequins', women who mechanically pout and pose, while being rudely ignored or prodded about, as one reviewer remarked, 'as if they were domestic animals rather than human beings'.[93] While discussing the problem of women, the men admire the alluring fashions, which, as Philip protests, are designed to make it look as though women cannot walk, digest food, or bear children. The clothes reduce their wearers, like the 'mannequins' who model them, to aestheticized sexual objects, a

---

[91] Desmond MacCarthy, *Theatre* (MacGibbon & Kee: London, 1954), 115.
[92] Harley Granville Barker, *The Madras House: A Comedy in Four Acts* (Sidgwick & Jackson: London, 1911), III, 105. First performed Duke of York's Theatre, 9 March 1910.
[93] *Bystander* (23 March 1910), 594.

point underlined by one design inspired by a famous Parisian courtesan—as Philip ironically comments, 'what can be more natural and right than for the professional charmer to set the pace for the amateur!' (III, 79–80). Constantine Madras recommends polygamy as the solution to the parallel problems of Huxtable's six virgin daughters and the exploited workers in the firm: kept more decorously out of sight, their attractions no longer emasculating men and distracting from the serious business of running the country, such women would be restored to their 'perpetual use' of procreation (III, 100).

Constantine's critique of the commercial ownership and exploitation of women's bodies rings true, and his emphasis on women's fulfilment through motherhood seems to find validation in Miss Yates, who successfully determines to be proud and happy about her pregnancy.[94] The fourth act revelation that Constantine is the father of Miss Yates's child, however, highlights the self-serving function of his doctrine: it is ultimately about dignifying the behaviour which taught Philip in his youth that 'every pretty, helpless woman was a man's prey' (IV, 127). With women kept out of public view, Constantine escapes the knowledge of what he is in England, an ageing man with 'a loose lip and a furtive eye' (IV, 127). Miss Yates's refusal to take his money leaves him degraded in his own eyes, her independence denying him what he feels is his right to her body and 'my own child' (IV, 128–9). Barker made Constantine's predatory intentions even clearer in his revised 1925 version of the text, where he inveighs against the 'scandalous laws' which make the child hers, and asks his son to fire Miss Yates 'with sufficient brutality' to persuade her to accept his money.[95] The clarification may have seemed particularly necessary in the light of some critics' reactions to the 1910 production of the play: critics for the *Era* and the *Evening Standard and St James's Gazette*, for example, took Constantine's views as Barker's own, concluding that the play recommended polygamy and argued against the modern woman's entry into the struggle for life.[96] Max Beerbohm, writing in the *Saturday Review*, more intelligently located Barker's views in those of Philip Madras, who looks for a solution in the companionship of the sexes, wishing his daughter to be practically educated in order to take an active role in tackling society's ills, and wishing to abolish the inequalities which mean one woman's cultivated leisure is secured at the cost of others' sexual enslavement. But Philip's revulsion from what he terms 'the farmyard world of sex' struck many critics as 'sterile'; even Max Beerbohm described him as 'always perspicacious, unselfish, and charitable by virtue of being himself so shadowy and cold'.[97] While

---

[94] In the revised 1925 text of the play, Miss Yates explains if she could not at least pretend to be pleased about it, 'I'd be better in the river', *The Madras House* (1925), in *Granville Barker. Plays: Two* (Methuen: London, 1994), II, 149.

[95] Ibid, IV, 221, 224.

[96] *Era* (12 March 1910), 17; *Evening Standard and St James's Gazette* (10 March 1910), 4. These reviewers could, perhaps, be forgiven for their confusion when contemporary commentators such as Walter Heape in *Sex Antagonism* (1913) and Walter Gallichan in *Woman under Polygamy* (1914) were advocating polygamy as a solution to the 'problem' of the spinster. See Sheila Jeffreys, *The Spinster and Her Enemies: Feminism and Sexuality, 1880–1930* (Pandora: London, 1985), ch. 7.

[97] *Saturday Review* (19 March 1910), 363.

many critics were unable to grasp the sweeping analysis of modern commercial society's systematic manipulation and abuse of female sexuality, seeing the four acts of the play as hopelessly fractured and disconnected, many who did appreciate Barker's argument were repelled by what they felt was his fruitless shying away from female sexuality altogether.[98] As the *Graphic* concluded: 'Mr Barker feels as strongly as anybody that the defining line in life is sex . . . But you feel that Mr Barker really disapproves of this enormous force; and while unable to get rid of it, seeks to obscure it by the same sort of idealism that animates a great deal of the feminism of the day. The general result is a strange note of sterile helplessness (in the face of great physical forces) characteristic of the school of thought to which Mr Barker belongs.'[99]

Where Harley Granville Barker's analysis of the economic, legal, and moral constraints placed on women ended in stasis and what so many critics identified as sterility, similar dramatic analyses of the relation between industrial capitalism and the appropriation of women's bodies from the heart of industrialized England drew considerable critical acclaim. Githa Sowerby grew up in Tyneside and was born into the industrial dynasty which owned glassworks in Gateshead. In her first performed play, *Rutherford and Son* (1912), Sowerby depicted the inhumanity of the values upheld and perpetuated by specifically patriarchal commerce, while offering an alternative female perspective which denaturalized and questioned the validity of industrial society's intertwined capitalist and moral norms of male ownership. The powerful centre of Sowerby's *Rutherford and Son*, exercising a godlike power over his household, is John Rutherford, a domineering northern industrialist whose life is devoted to social advancement and the perpetuation of the family firm. The essential conflict is between the patriarchal and commercial framework in which Rutherford operates and the alternative value system of love and desire, put forward by his daughter, Janet, and her sister-in-law, Mary. Sowerby's play thus echoes Dickens's novel *Dombey and Son* (1847–8) in more than title. Dickens's patriarch is obsessed with the family firm and the male line of inheritance, neglecting and abusing his daughter, until her self-sacrificing love redeems him, bringing him to accept a more humane set of values. No such happy resolution is reached between Rutherford and Janet, whose values remain in profound conflict. The father asserts a natural right to dictate his children's lives, as though they were property he had invested in; as his sister puts it, 'Folk like him look for a return from their bairns.'[100] Janet is sullenly and resentfully moving into unfulfilled middle age. Her sterile life is a badge of the family's social status; she is denied employment or marriage, an unpaid domestic servant in an aspirant middle-class home, carefully isolated from the working women whose lives she envies, 'with their bairns wrapped in their shawls and their men to come home to at night' (II, 175).

---

[98] See, e.g. *Vanity Fair* (17 March 1910), 327; *Evening Standard and St James's Gazette* (10 March 1910), 4.

[99] J. M. B., 'The Gamble of First-Nighting: Disappointing Plays', *Graphic* (19 March 1910), 398.

[100] Githa Sowerby, *Rutherford and Son,* reprinted in *New Woman Plays*, I, 144. First performed Court Theatre, London, 31 January 1912.

When Rutherford learns that Janet is having an affair with his foreman, Martin, he accuses her of having 'dragged the man's heart' out of Martin, asserting that his own loss is greater than hers, as she has only herself to lose, whereas he is now 'the laughing-stock—the Master whose daughter does wi' a working man' (II, 173–4). Janet rejects his judgement: 'Confessed?' she exclaims, 'As if I'd stolen something.' Sheila Stowell glosses this 'something' as the theft of Rutherford's social standing and his foreman, but the issue extends beyond this to Janet's rejection of her father's rights of ownership over both his children and his workman, accusing him of stealing their lifeblood and their happiness.[101] Janet views her sexual liaison with Martin not as a loss of virtue but the assertion of her sense of autonomous identity, the reclaiming of rights over her own body and future. She greets exile from the family home as liberation from a prison, commenting wonderingly to Mary that 'I've done what women are shamed for doing—and all the night I've barely slept for the hope in my heart' (III, 177). Far from repenting her loss of virtue or reputation, Janet proudly admits she made the first move in the relationship, and her sexual awakening prompts her to claim control over her own life.

Janet's bright hopes of a shared future with Martin are, however, shattered by the revelation that his values are those of her father; Martin not only views their love as dishonest but also persists in tying Janet's identity to her father's:

MARTIN: He'll be lookin' to me to right ye. He'll be lookin' for that.
JANET: To right me?
MARTIN: Whatever's been, they munna say his daughter wasn't made an honest woman of. He'll be lookin' for that.
There is a silence. She draws back slowly, dropping her hands.
JANET: What's he to do with it?

(III, 180)

Rejecting Martin's money and sending him back to the 'Master' whom he regards as exercising a natural right over both their lives, Janet silently exits the play '*stumbling forward as if she were blind*' (184). Sowerby, however, reframes this familiar image of the tragically stricken fallen woman. Janet's last sighting is by her aunt who complains she saw her 'gone along the road wi' her shawl over her head like a common working lass' (III, 186). Janet thus becomes a figure in exile, but her banishment is simultaneously a release; the shawl over her head serves both as an image of self-concealing shame and a claiming of her true place among the working women whose lives of hardship and fulfilled love she had envied.

Critics admired the force and conviction of Sowerby's portrait of the single-minded industrialist, but were repelled by the obsessive and single-minded doctrine he espoused. Rutherford's obsessive pursuit of respectability and profit, his conviction that all other interests must be sacrificed to feed the 'Moloch' of Rutherford and Son, led critics to embrace Janet's rebellion as a life-affirming contrast. Even the

---

[101] Stowell, *A Stage of their Own*, 143.

usually conservative *Daily Telegraph* described Janet approvingly as 'strong as the strongest', 'passionately rebellious for her right to the joy of life', and praised Edyth Olive's performance as 'commanding': 'The passion and thrill of her voice and gesture have in them something elemental, invincible.'[102] Despite acknowledging Janet's strength and determination, some critics were unable to shake off their old assumptions. The *Morning Post* blithely assumed that Janet 'rushes out of the house apparently to commit suicide' at the end of the play.[103] The *Times*'s critic displayed a similar inability to conceive an alternative dramatic trajectory, concluding that Janet leaves 'either to commit suicide or to bear her child and fend for herself as best she could'—despite neither pregnancy nor suicide being mentioned in the play—in curious juxtaposition to the critic's own description of Janet as 'a brave woman who speaks her mind and chooses her own life'.[104] Old plots died hard.

Janet Rutherford discovers her independent identity through her sexual awakening, claiming a life free of the domestic imprisonment and celibacy which advertise her father's commercial success. In contrast, Fanny Hawthorn, the Lancashire mill worker at the centre of Stanley Houghton's *Hindle Wakes* (1912) has no doubts about her economic or sexual independence, both secured by her earning power as an experienced mill operative. Houghton's comedy was brought to London in 1912 by Annie Horniman's Manchester Gaiety Theatre company, opening in June and playing to large and appreciative audiences at the Aldwych and then the Court Theatre until November. Middle-class commentators like Mary Higgs viewed with consternation the sexual independence and freedom from familial and social control acquired by young female workers, but the resilience and humour of Houghton's Fanny offered an optimistic and life-affirming alternative to such anxieties.

Hindle Wakes begins with Fanny Hawthorn's parents learning that their daughter has spent the bank holiday festivities (the 'wakes') at Llandudno with Alan Jeffcote, the mill owner's son. Mrs Hawthorn scents an opportunity for Fanny to secure an advantageous marriage and is ready to pursue it aggressively. The two fathers agree that Alan must 'do right' by Fanny. Nathaniel Jeffcote is a self-made man, and he and his wife are deeply disappointed at this obstacle to Alan's marriage to the mayor's daughter, Beatrice, which would have consolidated the family's position. Alan tries to protest, but faced with both his and Beatrice's father declaring that he'll inherit none of their money, and Beatrice agreeing that Fanny's right to him now supersedes her own, he gives in. At which point Fanny takes them all aback by announcing she has no intention of marrying Alan—and not, as he assumes, because she is ready to sacrifice her own hopes for the sake of his future happiness. As Fanny explains to Alan—in the much the same terms as Alan had explained their jaunt to his fiancée Beatrice—'Why on earth should I love you? You were just someone to have a bit of fun with. You were an amusement—a lark.'[105] Alan is astonished, having assumed, like Fanny's mother, that Fanny was

[102] *Daily Telegraph* (12 March 1912).
[103] *Morning Post* (1 February 1912).
[104] *Times* (2 February 1912), 9.
[105] Stanley Houghton, *Hindle Wakes*, in George Rowell (ed.), *Late Victorian Plays, 1890–1914* (Oxford University Press: Oxford, 1972), III, 503.

manoeuvring to marry him if she got the chance; but Fanny, like Alan himself, is looking for different qualities in a life-partner than she is in a companion for a weekend of fun:

FANNY: You're not good enough for me. The chap Fanny Hawthorn weds has got to be made of different stuff from you, my lad. My husband, if ever I have one, will be a man, not a fellow who'll throw over his girl at his father's bidding!
  . . . You're a nice lad, and I'm fond of you. But I couldn't ever marry you. We've had a right good time together, I'll never forget that. It *has* been a right good time, and no mistake! We've enjoyed ourselves proper! But all good times have to come to an end, and ours is over now.

(III, 503–4)

Alan is at first shocked by Fanny's challenge to his double standards, but this soon gives way to bewildered admiration and relief. Though her mother throws her out of the house in disgust, Fanny needs neither parents nor a husband to support her; as she declares, she is a Lancashire lass with a trade at her fingers and can earn 25 shillings a week, 'so long as there's weaving sheds in Lancashire' (III, 506).

Despite the different shades of pragmatism, religious faith, and social ambition which mark out individual characters' attitudes, no-one is greatly shocked at Fanny and Alan's behaviour. As Nathaniel Jeffcote comments, 'There's many a couple living happy to-day as first come together in that fashion'—though his wife points out, there are many marriages made that way which haven't lasted five years (I, ii, 464; II, 478). When Alan tries to explain to Beatrice that his feelings for Fanny were 'base', whereas what he feels for her is 'higher—finer', Beatrice muses, 'I wonder which feeling a woman would rather arouse. And I wonder which is most like love?' (II, 489). The prevalence of premarital sex is accepted without moral posturing or outrage, simply as a fact of life. Even the most idealistic and devoutly religious character in the play acknowledges her own desires and those of other women: the difference between men and women, she notes, is simply that 'Men haven't so much self-control.' (II, 490)

The novelty of the plain speaking, pragmatic, down-to-earth behaviour and attitudes of this Lancashire community charmed the London critics, who found the play commanded absolute conviction as a realistic and genuine slice of provincial life.[106] Indeed, *Hindle Wakes* was seen as exposing the artificiality of fashionable drawing-room dramas, which, as the *English Review* commented, would conventionally have made Alan a hero and have had 'true love asserting itself dutifully before the footlights'.[107] But while acknowledging the play as realistic, they were careful to keep its morality at arm's length, the anthropologically interesting customs of a different tribe. The *Athenaeum* described the play as 'flashing a curious light on the unconventionality of working-class notions of morals', and the *Illustrated*

---

[106] See, e.g. *Times* (18 June 1912), 10; *Illustrated London News* (20 July 1912), 88.
[107] *English Review* (July 1912), 655.

London News similarly described it as 'sending a flashlight over the gulf that separates working-class from bourgeois notions of morality'.[108] The suffragists were even more careful to distance themselves from the play's affirmation of a single standard of morality—insisting that the levelling should be up not down. So *Votes for Women* approached the play with humorous curiosity bordering on disdain: 'Miss Evelyn Hope's Beatrice is a gentle modest maiden, no more shocked than Mrs Hawthorn or Mrs Jeffcote that the young man she is about to marry has been spending a weekend with Fanny, and only sad that Fanny and not she has enjoyed the privilege. What a set these Hindle people! Not a suffragette among them!'[109] It was the vigour and incisiveness of Edyth Goodall's performance as Fanny which broke down some critics' defences, commanding their admiration and approval for her independence and forthrightness. Conventional morality was breathlessly set aside by the *English Review's* critic, who ecstatically declared of Fanny's final exit: 'here is a lass whom some good fellow will love right enough; she aint afeerd. She walks out a queen.'[110]

Theatre from the industrial heartlands of England offered an alternative perspective and register both to the fashionable society problem play and to new avant-garde realist drama of the Court Theatre and its admirers. Another alternative was to be found in the popular entertainments of musical comedy and melodrama, both of which played to large and diverse houses in West and East End, in the suburbs of London and across the provinces, drawing audiences of both sexes and all classes. Musical comedy plots centred on the shop girl and the chorus girl; her romantic adventures and their resolution in a happy marriage forming the thread on which to hang songs, dances, and the spectacle of youthful and attractive female bodies. In his analysis of the popular figure of the working girl both on and off stage, Peter Bailey defines the sexual appeal of the musical comedy girl as essentially 'naughty but nice', a manifestation of 'parasexuality', an innocent vaccination of contained licence and flirtation, carefully channelled sexuality which is never fully discharged; it is, as Bailey explains, 'in vulgar terms, "everything but"'.[111] Bailey supports his depiction of the world of musical comedy as essentially 'nice' by quoting Max Beerbohm's characterization of it as an 'innocent libertinism', a 'good time…of a wholly sexual order. And yet everyone from the highest to the lowest is thoroughly good.'[112] But Beerbohm's vision of musical comedy's sexual terrain as ultimately innocent was certainly not universal. W. T. Stead, for example, inveighed against such entertainments as little better than the antechamber to a brothel, dedicated to 'making attractive a multitude of pretty young girls who, to judge from the words placed in their mouths, regarded the Seventh Command-

---

[108] *Athenaeum* (20 July 1912), 72; *Illustrated London News* (20 July 1912), 88.
[109] *Votes for Women* (26 September 1913), 740. See also *Votes for Women* (2 August 1912), 714. A similar acknowledgement but not endorsement of a working-class rejection of the middle-class morality can be found in e.g. *Downward Paths* (152).
[110] *English Review* (July 1912), 656.
[111] Bailey, *Popular Culture and Performance*, 151–1, 183.
[112] Beerbohm, *Saturday Review* (30 October 1901), quoted in ibid, 172.

ment as non-existent and to whom the *summum bonum* of earthly existence was triumphant adultery'.[113] Bernard Shaw similarly characterized Gaiety girl choruses as sung 'with the deliberate intention of conveying to the audience that a Gaiety chorister's profession—their own profession—is only a mask for the sort of life which is represented in Piccadilly Circus and Leicester Square after midnight'.[114]

Bailey offers Pinero's *The 'Mind-the-Paint' Girl* (1912) as an example of the genre's depiction of sexual transactions as an echo and counterpart of the speculative commercial transactions of the business world, but Pinero's depiction of the musical comedy heroine was as much a corrective to as a reproduction of the typical Gaiety girl. Pinero's Lily Paradell is a singer who has risen to fame and fortune with a song whose exhortation to 'Mind the paint!' invites her admirers to look but not touch.[115] Lily's sexual purity is explicitly confirmed, as is her ultimate lack of financial or professional ambition. Where her colleagues negotiate an exchange of cars and holidays for sexual favours—and the precise nature of those favours is left unclear, but the extent of the financial payments accepted imply generous rewards—Lily signs a blank cheque to an admirer in trouble. Lily finally wins an aristocrat's hand in marriage, but only after she has resigned herself to marrying a down-at-heels and hopeless guardsman who has ruined himself tagging after her; her self-abnegation is rewarded when the guardsman nobly hands her on to the aristocrat, like a dainty and unopened parcel. Where the other chorus girls are grasping, unscrupulous, and vulgar, Lily is ultimately passive, for all her professional success. Her significant contribution to the aristocracy is to be a eugenic infusion of new blood to counteract their inbred inclination towards narrow chests and receding chins.

Lily's passivity and purity speak volumes about Pinero's notion of acceptable femininity but very little about the typical musical comedy heroine. Where Pinero is punctilious in clarifying Lily's virgin status, musical comedy joyously avoids asking such difficult questions. While endless sex-problem plays debated and agonized over the precise degree of sexual guilt which precluded a woman's integration in polite society, and realist drama challenged the language of sexual temptation and weakness with the realities of female employment conditions and wage levels, musical comedy simply skipped lightly round such matters as ultimately irrelevant. Bessie Brent the eponymous heroine of *The Shop Girl* (1894) is reproved by the shop manager for coming in at 1am after a night out with her 'cousin', and when the proprietor caustically notes that last week her cousin was in the Coldstream and last night he was in the Grenadiers, Bessie blithely responds 'No, he hasn't changed his regiment, I changed cousins.'[116] In *A Gaiety Girl* (1893), the production which first launched the genre on the London stage, all the 'girls' are in search of fun, and the society debutantes switch costumes with the professional chorus girls in order to evade the constraining watch of their chaperones. Savvy, knowing,

---

[113] Stead, 'The Relation of the Theatre to Public Morals', *The Nation's Morals*, 189–90.

[114] Shaw, *Our Theatres in the Nineties*, III, 353.

[115] Arthur W. Pinero, *The 'Mind-the-Paint' Girl* (Heinemann: London, 1913), I, 52–3. First produced Duke of York's, London, 17 February 1912.

[116] H. J. W. Dam, *The Shop Girl*, Licensed to Gaiety Theatre, 1894. LCP, BL Add MS.53562B, I, 10.

and self-possessed, whether aristocrats, shop girls, or singers, these women are in search of a good time and are able to negotiate their way cannily around the modern urban landscape. Sexual and commercial markets overlap, but the shop girl is far from being a passive object of display in the glamorized spectacle of the department store. *The Shop Girl* opens with a comic hymn to the eclectic and exhaustive list of goods for sale, but the sales women are expert at negotiating the market themselves. As Bessie Brent sings:

> When I came to the shop some years ago
>   I was terribly shy and simple;
> With my skirt too high and my hat too low
>   And an unbecoming dimple.
> But I soon learnt with a customer's aid
> How men make up to a sweet little maid,
> And another lesson I've learnt since then
> How a dear little maid 'makes up' for men!
>   A touch of rouge that is just a touch
>   And back [*sic*] in the eye, but not too much;
>   And a look that makes the Johnnies stop
>   I learnt it all in the shop, shop, shop! (I, 31)

Nor is it only the shop girls who play the game; it is operating at all levels of society. A chorus of professional performers in *The Shop Girl* wear tiny costumes to help raise money at a charity bazaar, while aristocratic young women run stalls in aid of a philanthropic fund from which they cream off 99 per cent expenses. As Erika Rapapport has summed it up, 'Instead of constructing a world divided into virtuous and fallen women, musical comedies put "girls" in charge of their own commodification. They re-reworked the well-trodden image of the sexually knowledgeable shop girl into a new feminine ideal that stressed youth, style and performance.'[117] Both Bailey and Rappaport emphasize the obvious attraction of musical comedy's array of young, attractive, and companionable women for male audiences, but these women were not so easily reduced to a passive spectacle.[118] Actively selecting and pursuing their mates and knowingly negotiating the contemporary marketplace, on stage these women offered a carefree vision of sexual and economic independence, regardless of social judgements or parental control.

The sunny world of musical comedy glossed over the real grievances of shop workers, but another hugely popular theatrical genre brought together the resourcefulness, energy, and determination of the musical comedy 'girl' and some of the real life challenges and hardships she had to face. Walter and Frederick Melville's 'bad-girl' melodramas were such a success with cross-class audiences that their com-

---

[117] Erika Diane Rapapport, *Shopping for Pleasure: Women in the Making of London's West End* (Princeton University Press: Princeton, NJ, 2001), 203.

[118] Ibid, 192; Bailey offers a rather Darwinian version of women's sexual role, judging that by casting women as sexual adventurers musical comedy encouraged 'a greater sexual competitiveness in women's bid for men's favour'—it is thus still ultimately the man who is the active agent who seals the deal, *Popular Culture and Performance*, 192–3.

mercial base extended well beyond their theatrical roots in the East End to encompass central London and reach into the Midlands, the East Midlands, the north west, the south coast, Scotland, and Wales.[119] Following the success of *The Worst Woman in London* in 1899, the brothers produced a string of melodramas with titles such as *That Wretch of a Woman* (1901), *The Ugliest Woman on Earth* (1904), *The Girl Who Took the Wrong Turning* (1906), *The Girl Who Wrecked His Home* (1907), *The Bad Girl of the Family* (1907), and, in glorious contrast to the sunny optimism of musical comedy's titles, *The Shop Soiled Girl* (1910). Central to the genre's appeal was the spectacle of a wicked woman unscrupulously pursuing her desires. Erika Rappaport has dismissed bad-girl melodrama as ultimately upholding that 'stark dichotomy between virtue and vice, common in melodrama' but absent from musical comedy.[120] Certainly Melvillean melodramas made capital out of their wicked women, whose strong bodies and resourceful wit offered a robust contrast to the tragically suffering and emaciated form of Mrs Patrick Campbell's Paula Tanqueray and Agnes Ebbsmith, while their ruthlessness owed a clear debt to the villainesses of Augustus Harris's spectacular Drury Lane melodramas.[121] But the Melville brothers' female protagonists do not so much reproduce the old melodrama types of seduced maiden, vengeful villainess, and resourceful maid, as merge them, producing an innovative amalgam of vulnerable and knowing, fallible but quick-witted and determined women. In *The Girl Who Wrecked His Home*, for example, Walter Melville produced an updated version of Watts Phillips's *Lost in London*, but Melville's Bertha combines the gullibility and regrets of Phillips's seduced wife with the strong arm and quick action of his Lancashire maid: seduced and abandoned to make her way alone in London, she seizes a gun and fires at the first man to proposition her, prompting him to make a rapid exit, declaring there is 'Too much of the tigress about her for me.'[122] Significantly, Bertha is finally forgiven by her offended husband and is taken back into the family home.[123]

The hardships of working life are a standard ingredient in the Melvilles' plays. Whereas musical comedy took a predominantly outsiders' view of working-class lives, its shop girl heroines often being revealed as long-lost heiresses and marrying out of the business, bad-girl melodramas tended towards the traditional working-class perspective of early Victorian melodrama, focusing on the shop floor and casting shop managers and aristocratic male customers as greedy sexual predators.

[119] David Mayer, 'Why Girls Leave Home: Victorian and Edwardian "Bad-Girl" Melodrama Parodied in Early Film', *Theatre Journal* 58:4 (December 2006), 584.

[120] Rappaport, *Shopping for Pleasure*, 202.

[121] On the strong body images associated with bad-girl heroines, see Elaine Aston and Ian Clarke, 'The Dangerous Woman of Melvillean Melodrama', *New Theatre Quarterly* 12, issue 45 (1996), 32–4.

[122] Walter Melville, *The Girl Who Wrecked His Home*. First performed Standard, Shoreditch, 30 September 1907. LCP 1907/21 H, II, i, 42.

[123] Notably, this ending is missing from the copy of the play submitted for licence to the Lord Chamberlain's Office, which tails off inconclusively, but the full ending is to be found in a prompt copy in the Theatre Collection, V.&A. Museum. A similarly incomplete ending is to be found on a number of Lord Chamberlain's Plays Collection Melville scripts, suggesting a regular practice, whether caused by the desire to procure a licence at speed before the play script was fully completed, or in order to slip past the censor endings which did not conform to standard practice of punishing sexually errant heroines.

Melvillean heroines are united in their proud ability to support themselves by earning an independent living, however long their hours or low their salary. In Frederick Melville's *Between Two Women* (1902), Violet spurns her husband when he believes the villain's lie that she is adulterous; taking up work in a drapery store, she proudly rejects her husband's forgiveness: 'Do you think I am so mean spirited as to accept my bread from you, to be dependant [*sic*] on you, to have a bargain in exchange for myself', refusing to be 'your slave, your property', and only accepting reconciliation when her husband realizes her innocence.[124] In *The Shop Soiled Girl*, the eponymous heroine has been seduced and abandoned by an upper-class customer but she soon learns to fight off the unwanted attentions of a floor manager thanks to her colleague's advice that 'He picks out the weak-minded ones not the strong fisted ones'.[125] Working-class characters share knowing jokes with the audience at the expense of their employers' values: a shop girl's boyfriend pretends to be a member of the Board of Directors and warns off a lecherous manager by exclaiming, 'How dare you sir, how dare you maul the goods about?'[126] There is a similar humorous cynicism at the expense of the traditional formula of female shame and self-destruction: when the pregnant and despairing Jessie announces, 'I will throw myself in the river', her unrepentant seducer comments in aside, 'What a splendid idea!'[127]

The Bad Girl of the Family offers the best example of a bad-girl melodrama which melded the seduced maiden and the resourceful maid of early Victorian melodrama to produce a modern heroine, financially self-supporting, quick-witted and strong-armed. Frederick Melville's play appealed to both West End and East End audiences, opening at the Elephant and Castle in 1909, and later achieving a hugely successful run at the Adelphi Theatre. The eponymous bad girl, Bess Moore, is a shop girl in a drapery store who, as she later explains, finally gave in to the blandishments of the manager, Harry Gordon, after being worn down by poor food, long hours, and sexual harassment. But when her sexually pure and sneeringly jealous sister Honour betrays her secret to her parents, Bess gives her a good slap and angrily insists that Harry Gordon may have tricked out of her virginity with false promises of marriage, but she's always relied on her own honest earnings. Bess bemoans her lost purity, but wastes no time on self-destructive shame; when Harry Gordon's money-lending father suggests she console herself as his mistress, she shoots him and goes on the run. Men are heartless persecutors of women, ready to exploit their power within commerce or the family, while women's final defence is their ability to earn their own living. Harry sets his eye on Gladys, an earl's daughter, and the earl is happy to pay off his debts to Harry's father by forcing his daughter into a loveless marriage; but Gladys repulses both of them: 'I am not for sale', she declares, while offering to

---

[124] Frederick Melville, *Between Two Women*. First performed Terriss Theatre, Rotherhithe, 27 October 1902. LCP, BL Add MS 65632F, III, ii, 78; III, iii, 85.
[125] Walter Melville, *The Shop Soiled Girl*. First performed Elephant and Castle Theatre, 3 October 1910. LCP 1910/22, I, ii, 17.
[126] Ibid, 22.   [127] Ibid, 26.

support herself and her father through any honest employment.[128] Bess comes to the rescue, exploiting her professional skills to produce an identical wedding dress and substitute herself for Gladys at the altar, marrying Harry not to secure her happiness but as 'my idea of revenge' (II, iv, 55).

Only for one fleeting moment does the play pay lip-service to the conventional contrast between Bess's sexual 'fall' and Gladys's sexual purity: Gladys praises Bess as 'the good angel sent from Heaven to me', at which the newly-married Bess calls herself 'a bad 'un', whereupon she is taught to pray by Gladys (III, iii, 5). Her repentance quickly done with, she drinks a refreshing cup of tea and returns to the important business of battling the villainous Harry—planting a powerful right hook on his jaw and locking an accomplice in a cupboard to scotch another attempted abduction of Gladys. Marriage makes remarkably little difference to any of the characters' actions: Harry continues to pursue Gladys relentlessly even when they are both married to someone else. But Melville is careful not to end the play with Bess legally bound to the villainous Harry: he is taken off to be hanged for murdering her childhood sweetheart, a jewel thief who willingly accepts his own death as the price of relieving Bess of her husband.[129]

Betrayed and abandoned by Harry, Bess occupies the time-honoured position of the seduced maiden, but she responds to her situation with determination and ingenuity, finally securing the respectability of marriage without the inconvenience of a husband. She is also sexually knowing, sharing a humorous wink with the audience at the expense of her own lost virginity. So she calmly baits her newly acquired husband:

GORDON: Don't drive me too far, or I won't be answerable for any injury I might do you.

BESS: (*Laughs*) All the injury you could do me has been done some time ago. Oh don't look so annoyed. (*Laughs*) Aren't you going to kiss your wife?

GORDON: No, I'm not. Leave this place—go immediately.

BESS: Have you forgotten the marriage service so soon. A wife's place is by her husband's side, especially on her wedding night, so I will remain.

(III, i, 66)

She then orders the servants to show her to his rooms, while informing him he can stay away with his friends. As Frederick Melville made clear in a note for future productions, Bess is not the 'down trodden heroine in the usual case of melodrama' but should secure laughs through her 'bright, snappy up-to-date intonations on serious subjects'; and Melville gives the 'All the injury you could do me' line as an example of such sassy innuendo.[130]

---

[128] Frederick Melville, *The Bad Girl of the Family*, LCP 1909/19. II, iv, 29.

[129] Again, the script submitted for licence tails off before the end, leaving it unclear if Bess stays married to Harry, but the typescript in the V.&A. Museum ends with his arrest and impending execution for murder.

[130] Frederick Melville, typed and signed note appended to V.& A. typescript.

The Bad Girl of the Family was directly marketed on such sexual knowingness, advertised as a self-styled 'Bedroom Drama' with not one but two bedroom scenes.[131] Bess and Gladys kneeling to say their prayers in their nightgowns constituted one such scene, but the most famous bedroom scene was a set piece of twelve shop-girls preparing for bed in what critics recognized immediately as a rewrite of the dormitory scene from *Diana of Dobson's*.[132] Where *Diana's* dormitory scene was deliberately asexual, *The Bad Girl of the Family's* was sensationally titillating. The shop girls were marketed as part of the play's appeal, and the invasive voyeurism of the audience was emphasized by the added male presence in the dormitory of Snozzle, a sweetheart of one of the girls who has been smuggled in in drag. Critics have argued that Melville restored the sexualized objectification which Cicely Hamilton's feminist play challenged and critiqued.[133] But such an argument seems excessively binary and simple, marking the women's sexuality as necessarily passive and objectifying. At least in the words of the text, Snozzle is terrified at the prospect of being bundled into a dormitory with a dozen shop girls; and well he might be, for when the police come to arrest Bess for shooting the moneylender, the women lay about the officers with pillows and bedclothes, enabling Bess to make her escape. The police then seize the disguised Snozzle, who protests in outrage, 'I'm not Bess Moore, I'm a perfect lady' (II, iii, 52). Decorous femininity is thus enacted by a man in drag, reducing ladylike propriety to an absurd performance, while the real women are more than capable of standing up for themselves.

As the *Times* reported, the play was 'rapturously received' and ran for over 250 performances at the Aldwych, confirming the wisdom of the management's experiment in offering traditionally working-class entertainment to West End audiences.[134] A number of critics were taken aback by the novelty of Melville's heroine—as the *Observer* put it, 'It is not the degree, but the manner, of the girl's badness that is startling.'[135] But Violet Englefield's 'broad and downright methods' as Bess won universal admiration, more than one critic styling the heroine not a bad girl but a 'rough diamond'.[136] As the critic for the *Playgoer and Society Illustrated* concluded, there was precious little virtue and innocence in the play, but Bess was 'quite a nice sort of person' and preferable to 'many of the best girls' in families of his acquaintance.[137] The 'bad girl' of Melvillean melodrama, combining wit, resourcefulness, a strong arm, and a knowing wink, could thus charm critics out of their conventional moral judgements. While 'bedroom scenes' had obvious and well advertised attractions for male viewers, the self-assurance, knowingness, ingenuity and resilience of its heroine could offer an equal but different satisfaction to female viewers.

---

[131] See e.g. *Playgoer and Society Illustrated* (January 1910), 136.
[132] See e.g. *Times* (28 December 1909), 3; *Observer* (2 January 1910), 4; *World* (4 January 1910), 21.
[133] Aston and Clarke, 'Dangerous Woman', 137–8.
[134] *Times* (28 December 1909), 3.
[135] *Observer* (2 January 1910), 4.
[136] *Observer* (2 January 1910), 4; *Illustrated London News* (8 January 1910), 38.
[137] *Playgoer and Society Illustrated* (January 1910), 136.

6

Rewriting the Past

When *The Second Mrs Tanqueray* was revived in 1922, its sexual values appeared patently out of date. 'I love those demoded ethics', remarked James Agate, dismissing as pure fiction the notion that one false step leads to ruin: 'Fallen creatures contract, in real life, the habit of falling on their feet and not requiring to be picked up.'[1] W. A. Darlington similarly observed that the play appeared ludicrous in 1920s costumes. The innocent and puritanical Ellean became a particular anachronism; as played by Molly Kerr, expert at playing modern, hard-as-nails 'Bright Young People', one constantly expected her to bracingly reject Aubrey's paternal protection, and announce she was perfectly aware that Hugh was one of Paula's 'cast-offs' and she entirely approved of Paula's taste.[2] In the new world of the 1920s, Pinero's drama could only be played as a period piece.

Concluding his chapter on science and sex in *The Edwardian Turn of Mind*, Samuel Hynes declared that 'No aspect of human life changed more in the transition from Victorian England to modern England than the way Englishmen thought about sex.'[3] The 1923 Matrimonial Causes Act, which equalized the grounds of divorce for husbands and wives, could be taken to mark a watershed in sexual attitudes, unseating the sexual double standard which had been enshrined in divorce laws since 1857. The 1920s, the era of flappers and Bright Young Things, are popularly mythologized as the death-knell of repressive Victorian morality, a post-war reaction of youthful defiance and sexual licence. Marriage remained, however, an impressively stable and consistent social norm. There was a temporary dip in marriage rates in the early 1920s, but by 1930 they began to rise again sharply, and even in the 1920s a higher proportion of women in their teens and twenties were getting married than was the case before 1914. The proportion of women married by the age of 49 in England and Wales stood at 81 per cent in 1900, and continued to increase gradually in the 1920s and '30s.[4] Nor was there a marked rise in divorce rates, even after the 1923 Matrimonial Causes Act: in the early

---

[1] James Agate, *At Half Past Eight: Essays of the Theatre, 1921–1922* (Jonathan Cape: London, 1923), 118, 119.

[2] W. A. Darlington, *Six Thousand and One Nights: Forty Years a Critic* (Harrap: London, 1960), 102.

[3] Samuel Hynes, *The Edwardian Turn of Mind* (Pimlico: London, 1968), 171. Though, perhaps, the author's concentration on what English*men* thought about sex indicates how little as well as how much had changed by 1968.

[4] See Martin Pugh, *We Danced All Night: A Social History of Britain between the Wars* (Vintage: London, 2009), 127.

1920s the total ran at 2,800 per annum for England and Wales, rising modestly to over 4,000 in the later 1920s and 1930s. A mere 2 per cent of marriages contracted in 1926 had ended in divorce after twenty years.[5]

The really marked shift in the early decades of the twentieth century was in pre- and extramarital sexual behaviour and attitudes. According to census data, only 19 per cent of women who married before 1904 had experienced premarital sex, whereas 39 per cent of those who married during 1915–25 had done so, and 43 per cent of those who married during 1924–34.[6] The upheavals of the First World War, drawing women into a wider range of traditionally male occupations and giving them greater economic and social freedom, inevitably played a role in bringing about this change in the pattern of sexual behaviour, as did the loosening of social taboos on extramarital sex under the hovering threat of death for both soldiers and civilians.

Alongside these changes in sexual behaviour, there was a newly established perception of sexuality as a crucial element in the nature of the individual. The work of pioneering sexologists such as Richard von Krafft-Ebing, Havelock Ellis, and Edward Carpenter in the 1890s had paved the way for the study of sexuality as a serious subject in itself. The first volume of Ellis's *Studies in the Psychology of Sex* was deemed 'lewd and obscene' in a court of law in 1897, but by the 1920s his work had become widely acknowledged and accepted, alongside that of Sigmund Freud, whose theories and practice gained recognition and authority in the context of post-war shell-shock and its treatment.[7] One of the most perceptible shifts in sexual attitudes was the more widespread view of female sexual desire as natural, intrinsic, and spontaneous. In her controversial 1918 book *Married Love*, Marie Stopes deplored the prejudice which meant that 'most women would rather die than own that they *do* at times feel a physical yearning indescribable, but as profound as hunger for food'.[8] Arguing that 'normal' women experienced a natural ebb and flow of desire, which men should observe and respect in order to ensure their partner's pleasure, Stopes's book struggled to find a publisher, but went through six printings within a fortnight of its release. By 1923, in twenty-two reprints, *Married Love* had sold over 400,000 copies.

It was not only controversial authors such as Stopes who regarded sexual desire as a natural and necessary part of any woman's development. Professors Patrick Geddes and J. A. Thomson's *Problems of Sex* appeared in 1912 as part of the morally conservative series, 'Tracts for the Times', commissioned by The National Council of Public Morals. The 'love of the sexes', Thomson and Geddes declared in their popular pamphlet, 'saturates social life', and 'the denial one occasionally hears of any interest in the primary attraction of one sex for the other makes one

---

  [5] Ibid, 145.   [6] Ibid, 160.
  [7] Jeffrey Weeks, *Sex, Politics and Society: The Regulation of Sexuality since 1800* (Longman: London, 1981), 142, and ch. 8 *passim*; Susan Kingsley Kent, *Making Peace: The Reconstruction of Gender in Interwar Britain* (Princeton University Press: Princeton, NJ, 1993), ch. 5.
  [8] Marie Stopes, *Married Love*, ed. Ross McKibbin (Oxford World's Classics: Oxford 2004), 37.

doubt the health or the sanity, the sincerity or the memory, of such an ultra-stoic.'[9] In order to keep both genders' sex-life 'in the right channels' and avoid the consequences of uncontrolled sexuality—which included homosexuality, masturbation, and 'perversion'—the authors recommended an education which recognized adolescence as a period of the 'fuller expression of sex' for both boys and girls, teaching them to control their sexuality, while helping them to understand that 'these are normal and necessary growth-stirrings of life' and freeing them from any damaging belief that 'their young sex-wonderings, sex-hopes and dreams and attractions are dark and evil temptations merely'.[10] The key to 'healthy' and 'pure' sexuality for women as well as men lay not in ignorance but in the active exercise of self-control.

This model of female sexuality as spontaneous and natural, governed by the individual's will and self-restraint, marked a significant departure from popular nineteenth-century conceptions of female sexual desire. If women's sexual appetites were subject to their conscious and rational control, just like men's, this put paid to the common Victorian notion of 'modesty' as a woman's vital defence against illicit sexual experience, that a woman properly brought up in innocence and ignorance would shrink in disgust from any improper advance. This essentially passive quality of 'modesty' once lost, a woman was left defenceless, and the first 'fall' from purity marked the beginning of an inevitable downward trajectory. Hence the notion that a woman's sexual 'virtue' was the crucial factor on which the preservation of her other virtues depended, and hence too the need for male protection and social constraint. These were the assumptions with which a century of dramas concerned with illicit female sexuality had engaged and which so many had reinforced and confirmed; new conceptions of women's sexuality rendered the 'fallen woman' play outmoded.

The most respectable face of female sexuality remained motherhood, a role which could still be presented as the right-minded alternative to feminist discontent. So, for example, in fashionable playwright Haddon Chambers's *Passers-By* (1911), an unmarried mother describes her conversion from 'a revolutionary—a shrieking sister' the moment she holds her baby in her arms, upon which joy enters her heart and she laughs 'To think that I had ever dreamed of any ambition but simply to be a mother.'[11] She only has to meet the father of her child once more, however, to abandon all her former independence and kneel at his feet, viewing him, as an observer admiringly comments, as 'her God on earth'. (IV, 134)

Chambers's attitude and language were old-fashioned ('shrieking sisterhood' was a term most commonly used in the 1880s), but the issue of how motherhood related to feminism was to become increasingly contested. Previously brought together by a concentration on achieving the franchise, once the vote

---

[9] J. A. Thomson and Patrick Geddes, *Problems of Sex* (New Tracts for the Times, Cassell; London, 1912), 11–12.

[10] Ibid, 40, 48–9.

[11] Haddon Chambers, *Passers-By* (Duckworth: London, 1913), IV, 121. First produced Wyndham's Theatre, London, 29 March 1911.

had been at least partially granted in 1918 the women's movement divided over whether to campaign for equal rights or whether the focus should be on pressing for better provision for women's particular and different needs. 'New' feminists supported a campaign for the state endowment of maternity, viewing it as the best means to grant economic independence and status for mothers. Those whose feminism was rooted in the Edwardian campaigns for equal political, legal, and professional rights saw a dangerous return to the Victorian language of separate spheres in such a focus on motherhood as woman's particular sexual 'destiny'. While acknowledging the value of increased respect for motherhood, feminists like Vera Brittain were wary of, in her words, 'the tendency of fertility-worship to degenerate into the belief that women have no social value apart from their reproductive functions—a belief which immediately removes them from the category of human being'.[12] The question of whether sexual equality means legislating for sexual difference remains a complex and contested one to this day, but many feminists saw in the new psychological theories on women as human beings with sexual identities not a liberating impulse, but one which could once again co-opt women's bodies to suit male sexual appetites. Birth control and child allowances could be seen as means by which women were to be returned to the home.[13]

There were no simple answers to such questions, and the complexity of the debate and the ways in which it re-wrote old theatrical types and assumptions can be clearly seen in H. M. Harwood's *The Interlopers* (1913). The play's central character is Jack, a husband who feels neglected by his child-centred wife, Margaret, and leaves her for another woman, Iris. Jack eventually returns to the family home, drawn back by his enduring love for Margaret and his frustration at the need to keep his relationship with Iris clandestine if he is to pursue a political career. The 'interlopers' of the play's title are never explicitly identified, yet the clear implication is that it is not the 'other' woman who has intervened between husband and wife, but rather their offspring, who have absorbed all their mother's care and attention. Beatrice, a committee-running spinster, believes '*with all the certitude of the barren woman*' that motherhood is women's 'highest function' and 'their destiny'; while Jack turns in disgust from the notion that the cultivation of women's senses and the fullness and variety of life should be to no better end than 'the performance of a duty that is done better by any savage than by the finest flower of English womanhood'.[14] Female sexual appetite is accepted by the younger generation as healthy and natural; Jack's desire for a genuine erotic response from his wife, not just a fulfilment of conjugal duty, elicits sympathy from Margaret and her sister but leaves their parents bewildered. Similarly Iris is no seductress, but a

---

[12] Vera Brittain, 'Men on Women', *Time and Tide* (22 June 1928), quoted in Kent, *Making Peace*, 124.

[13] See Sheila Jeffreys, *The Spinster and Her Enemies: Feminism and Sexuality, 1880–1930* (Pandora: London, 1985); Kent, *Making Peace*, chs 4–6; Pugh, *We Danced All Night*, ch. 9.

[14] H. M. Harwood, *The Supplanters* (Ernest Benn: London, 1926), III, 84–5. First performed Royalty Theatre, London, 15 September 1913 under title *The Interlopers*.

woman who offers Jack the intellectual and emotional companionship he craves; as Margaret's sister tells their mother, 'she isn't a bit what you think. She's just an independent person—and rich and pretty and clever—and—and she does just what she likes' (III, 71). But there is also a recognition that the modern acceptance of women's sexual desires is not necessarily liberating for women like Margaret, called upon to be a mother, wife, and lover. As Margaret and Iris ruefully agree, 'A woman can't be everything' (IV, 112).

As sexual attitudes shifted, so too did the theatrical landscape. A more wide-spread acceptance of women's sexuality and premarital sexual experience helped to erode the status of the prostitute as a symbol of social and sexual malaise. The mor-ally frail woman tempted into prostitution by vanity and frivolity was a figure of the past, and in plays such as Charles McEvoy's *The Likes of Her* (1923) and Sewell Collins's *G.H.Q. Love* (1920), adapted from a French original by Pierre Rehm, the causes of prostitution are clearly depicted as social deprivation and economic ne-cessity. Collins's prostitutes are world-weary women looking to pay the rent in a post-war slump, while McEvoy offers a sympathetic portrait of a neglected and physically abused teenager instinctively learning to use her sexuality as the only way of acquiring male attention.[15] These women are individuals, presented neither as symbolic representations of social or moral disease, nor as symbols of women's sexual and economic exploitation. They are pragmatic survivors, like their neigh-bours, clients, and colleagues.

The familiar nineteenth-century figure of the vain, frivolous, weak-willed woman, tempted into sin and unable to prevent her subsequent downward trajec-tory was recognizable, however, well into the twentieth century. Pinero and Jones remained productive, if increasingly less popular, right into the 1920s, and their underlying assumptions of female frailty and the need for male protection and social constraint were essentially unchanged. In Pinero's *Mid-Channel* (1909), for example, Zoë Blundell and her husband Theo quarrel and separate, leaving Zoë to fall into a sexual relationship with Leonard, an immature and selfish admirer. Humiliated and frightened by her sexual lapse, Zoë seeks reconciliation with Theo, who has been consoling himself by bankrolling Mrs Annersley, a serially divorced woman of easy morals. Having paid Mrs Annersley off with a large cheque, Theo complacently expects Zoë's forgiveness, but rejects her with anger and contempt when he learns of her own indiscretion. Turning back in desperation to Leonard, Zoë is further humiliated by the news that he has just proposed to a suitably vir-ginal young woman. Left isolated, Zoë throws herself to her death from the bal-cony of her expensive apartment. Zoë's passivity and weakness of will provoked irritation in some reviewers, who had begun to look for something more deter-mined in their heroines, even if her suicide was still accepted as the inevitable response to her situation.[16] Critics were, however, more resistant to the play's

---

[15] Charles McEvoy, *The Likes of Her*, LCP 1923/2. First performed Town Hall, Battersea, 30 January 1923; Sewell Collins, *G. H. Q. Love*, LCP 1920/21. First performed Little Theatre, 1 August 1920.

[16] See e.g. *Athenaeum* (11 September 1909), 307; *Times* (3 September 1909), 8; *English Illustrated Magazine* (October 1909), 89–90.

fashionable implication that Zoë's moral decay and the collapse of her marriage were due to her childlessness, the result of the couple's deliberate decision not to be held back by parenthood in their pursuit of social advancement.[17]

The mercenary Mrs Annersley is instantly recognizable as a modern version of an old type. She is an up-to-date reincarnation of Augier's Olympe Taverny or the self-interested and venal prostitutes who surround Marguerite Gautier, a manipulative and unscrupulous woman, happy to exchange sexual favours for financial support, whether in cash or in kind. Importantly such a woman is no longer presented as a professional prostitute but as an amateur, *au fait* with the ways of the divorce court and quick to grasp any opportunity to trade up from one husband to another. Elsie Fraser in St John Ervine's *The First Mrs Fraser* (1929) is a similar *habituée* of the divorce courts, viewing marriage as a potentially lucrative contract and interested only in the bottom line. Divorce, in these plays and numerous others, is not portrayed as a welcome release from unhappy marriage, nor are the divorce courts purveyors of justice. Rather it is a labyrinthine and absurd system, which can be manipulated by the cynical and clever—as a serially adulterous husband points out to his wife in Somerset Maugham's *The Tenth Man* (1910), it's not a question of truth but of who can spin the most convincing story. Far from being a much-needed means of release from unhappy marriage, divorce is framed as a dangerous temptation to give up too soon. In *The First Mrs Fraser,* James is no sooner released from his mercenary second wife Elsie than he determines to woo and win the love and forgiveness of his still-beloved first wife, who assures him that she would easily enough have forgiven his infidelity had he merely indulged in an affair with Elsie rather than determining to marry her. As in H. A. Jones's *The Case of Rebellious Susan*, wives were advised to be indulgent of their husbands' occasional lapses; in the 1930s, under titles such as 'I wish I hadn't divorced my husband', *Woman's Own* magazine offered the familiar advice that 'Men get these attacks like kiddies get the measles.... Let him have his fling and he'll come back a thousand times more in love with you than ever.'[18] Had Jones been alive, he would doubtless have nodded sagely in agreement.

The Lord Chamberlain's Office remained wary of theatrical treatments of female sexuality, especially when any explicit reference to biological or medical facts was involved. Edward Garnett's *The Breaking Point* was refused a licence in 1907, despite a plot which, as the author protested, offered no encouragement to immorality, centring as it did on the suicide of a fragile woman caught in a fight for possession between her married lover and her fiercely moral father. Apart from the play's implicit criticism of male egotism, the clearest explanation for the censor's intransigence lay in the uncertainty over whether the woman was truly pregnant, the very possibility of doubt raising the question of proof and with it unspoken references to menstruation. It was therefore entirely predictable that Marie Stopes's play *Vectia* should be refused a licence in 1926, containing as it did a pivotal scene in which a lawyer questions a wife accused of adultery about her marital sex life, asking her to draw diagrams to explain what she cannot bring herself to speak, as a result of which he realizes she is still *virgo intacta*. Such explicitness was never likely to pass the censor, though Stopes published the play complete with a preface in which she expressed vociferous outrage at the hypocrisy of a system which licensed depictions of adultery and male debauchery, but banned a play centring on a young wife's desire to conceive a child.[19]

Even when free of such biological detail, the staging of overt female desire remained a problematic issue so far as the censorship was concerned, as the controversial banning of Eden Phillpotts's *The Secret Woman* in 1912 demonstrated. The play's central theme is a clandestine affair between a Dartmoor farmer, Redvers, and a local girl, Salome. The farmer's wife, Ann, witnesses the lovers' meeting from afar, and when she later confronts her husband over his infidelity she loses her temper and accidentally pushes him to his death down a ravine. Not known to be the secret lover, Salome is left to mourn Redvers in silence. A licence was refused purportedly on the grounds of the explicitness of the dialogue, in particular Ann describing her glimpse of the lovers coming together in the mist as seeing two shadows 'thicken into one'.[20] Phillpotts refused to cut the offending lines, and the play was produced privately by Harley Granville Barker at the Kingsway Theatre on 20 February 1912 to great critical acclaim. Ten years later G. S. Street, a Reader of Plays, recommended to the Duke of Atholl, then Lord Chamberlain, that the play be licensed as it was 'one of the finest of modern tragedies' and its dialogue was 'never prurient or suggestive'; the offending line, he urged, 'surely need not be taken in any extreme sense'.[21]

While the dialogue of *The Secret Woman* was not, as Street observed, salacious, the play was unusual in depicting Salome's overt and deep-seated joy in her hidden lover and the impoverishment of her life on losing him. When Ann finally discovers that her husband's lover was the young, quiet, intense, and otherwise unremarkable Salome, she exclaims at the unfathomable nature of her husband's taste, having imagined him seduced by some 'shameless wretch' or 'scarlet female'.[22] The ironically named Salome is nothing like the wanton harlot of the community's fevered and clichéd imagination, but a slight and self-contained woman who remains fiercely proud of her love for Redvers; so she tells a wondering Ann: 'He was my sun, and air, and food. I only nursed my flesh to keep it plump and sweet for him. His very, very own I was—a part of himself; and all my light and joy you killed when you killed him—all—all. I am his widow—not you' (IV, 72–3). The play

[19] Marie Stopes, *A Banned Play and a Preface on the Censorship* (John Bale: London, 1926), 7; II, 112–15. Further grounds for refusing a licence were the husband's impotence which prevented him consummating their marriage, and the implied causes of this in some unspecified experiences, possibly homosexual.

[20] G. S. Street, Reader of Plays, report on *The Secret Woman*, 24 August 1922. Lord Chamberlain's Correspondence (hereafter LC Corr), *The Secret Woman* 1922/4401. Street is referring back to correspondence of 1912 which is not included in the file.

[21] Ibid.

[22] Eden Phillpotts, *The Secret Woman* (Duckworth: London, 1912), 70–3.

ends with Salome wistfully singing the folk song 'Widecombe Fair', with which Redvers had always serenaded her; Salome's tender singing hints at the depth of a love which leaves her community confounded. The play does not frame Redvers's death and Salome's bereavement as a poetically just punishment; rather, the intensity of their love, the physical joy and the fulfilment it brings them are the centre of the play, a demonstration of the mysteries and wonders of the human heart. As the Duke of Atholl observed, when he finally granted it a licence in 1922, *The Secret Woman* 'is not a moral play, and it does not point a moral, but it is a pretty strong play'.[23]

Even when free of any suggestion of illicit sexual activity, the depiction of a woman's active longing remained a sensitive issue, as the reader's report on Dorothy Brandon's *Wild Heather* (1917) reveals. Brandon's Heather believes herself to be legally barred from marrying the man she's in love with, but assures him '*with a little sob of glory and gladness*' that she'd have come to him if he'd asked, and laughs at her mother's scandalized response to this confession of desire '*as one who knows greater glory*'.[24] The open intensity of Heather and her lover's yearning for each other is such that her father protests, 'I feel as though Adam and Eve, in their original costume, were camping out in the middle of my study carpet', but it is only once the legal bar to their marriage is removed that they kiss '*hungrily and openly*' (III, 114, 117). Street's reader's report for the Lord Chamberlain commented admiringly that 'Once more Miss Horniman has got a play with far more merit than a dozen of the rubbish produced in London', but he clearly anticipated complaints about the play's propriety; he recommended it for licence with the coded warning that 'There is nothing to offend anything but false delicacy'—a phrase used both to signal possible future complaints and to strengthen the Lord Chamberlain's resolve in the face of them.[25]

Street's careful wording was also a sign that the censor's office was coming under increased pressure to defend its role and the grounds and consistency of its judgements. In response to the refusal of a licence to Harley Granville Barker's *Waste* in 1907, because of its explicit references to abortion, seventy-one playwrights addressed a petition to the editor of the *Times*, outlining their objections to theatre censorship as an arbitrary power which undermined their artistic status and craft and against which they had no legal right of appeal. Continuing agitation finally resulted in the establishment in 1909 of a Joint Parliamentary Select Committee on theatre censorship, which took evidence from a broad range of dramatists, managers, and critics. Managers were almost unanimously in support of the current system as giving them convenient establishment guidance and protection in the difficult business of selecting which plays were to be deemed suitable for public performance. Playwrights were almost unanimously opposed to the constraints of a system which, they complained, licensed indecency while banning intelligent discussion

---

[23] Letter, from Atholl, 30 August 1922, LC Corr. *The Secret Woman* 1922/4401.
[24] Dorothy Brandon, *Wild Heather*. LCP 1917/17, III, 87; III, 117. Produced Gaiety Theatre, Manchester, August 1917 and later transferred to Strand Theatre, London.
[25] Street's report, 4 August 1917, LCP 1917/17.

and serious engagement with moral issues—precisely the same criticism that had so often been made of the censorship system throughout the preceding century.[26] The inability of the Examiner of Plays, George Redford, to provide a coherent rationale for his decisions prompted the Committee to include amongst their recommendations that plays should be permitted a licence unless they could reasonably held

a) To be indecent;
b) To contain offensive personalities;
c) To represent on the stage in an invidious manner a living person, or any person recently dead;
d) To do violence to the sentiment of religious reverence;
e) To be calculated to conduce to crime or vice;
f) To be calculated to impair friendly relations with any Foreign Power; or
g) To be calculated to cause a breach of the peace.[27]

The emphasis in these conditions is predominantly upon putative effect upon an audience rather than the basic subject matter per se, an emphasis which complemented the stance adopted by the incumbent Lord Chamberlain, Viscount Althorp.[28] The committee's recommendations were never put into law, but Althorp acted upon some of them in order to shore up the position of his office, securing Redford's resignation and instituting an Advisory Board of readers to offer their opinions to the Lord Chamberlain and defend him from the accusation of arbitrary and subjective judgements. The support of an Advisory Board was to prove particularly useful at a time when the censor's office was caught between continued pressure from playwrights and critics frustrated at the limiting of the theatre's artistic freedom and the contrary pressure for stricter control emanating from conservative bodies such as the London Public Morality Council, which in 1913 instituted a specific Stage Plays Committee to enable more efficient checks on what it judged to be improper stage productions.

One result of laying the emphasis in licensing decisions upon the putative effect of a play on its audience was that judgements could more easily be reversed in the light of changed circumstances. Thus Eugène Brieux's 1901 play *Les Avariés* [Damaged Goods], depicting the ravages inflicted by syphilis upon a middle-class family and the medical profession's reluctant complicity in concealing the dangerous infection, was finally licensed for public performance in 1917, on the basis that it could provide a valuable warning at a time when 55,000 British soldiers were hospitalized with venereal disease.[29] A year later Brieux's *Maternité* [Maternity] (1904)

---

[26] See e.g. Steve Nicholson, *The Censorship of British Drama, 1900–1968*, vol. 1: *1900–1932* (University of Exeter Press: Exeter, 2003); David Thomas, David Carlton and Anne Etienne, *Theatre Censorship: From Walpole to Wilson* (Oxford University Press: Oxford, 2007).

[27] Draft report of the 1909 Select Committee, quoted in Thomas et al, *Theatre Censorship*, 96.

[28] See Nicholson, *Censorship of British Drama*, vol. 1, 24.

[29] Dominic Shellard and Steve Nicholson, with Miriam Handley, *The Lord Chamberlain Regrets . . . : A History of British Theatre Censorship* (British Library: London, 2004), 74; Weeks, *Sex, Politics and Society*, 188.

was refused a licence after the Archbishop of Canterbury advised that the play's "'lesson", such as it is, that the production of many children is cruel to the wife, selfish on the husband's part and, in present economic conditions incapable of working well except among rich people' was not, in a time of war, one which 'wise people will say England needs to learn just now'.[30] Theatre was thus positioned as a valuable tool in the deployment of women's bodies in the greater interests of the state.

It was a sign of the changing culture that it was not simply the sexual explicitness of August Strindberg's *Miss Julie* (1888) but its class politics which continued to prevent it securing a licence in the early twentieth century. In the aftermath of the Russian revolution, the Lord Chamberlain's Office were particularly wary of anything they saw as stirring up class antagonisms or destabilizing established social hierarchies. The question of whether a play promoted 'public disorder' became grounds, crucial and usefully indeterminate, for refusing a licence. Thus, when *Miss Julie* was re-submitted for licence in 1925, the incumbent Lord Chamberlain, the Earl of Cromer, expressed his extreme distaste for the play's 'sordid and disgusting atmosphere', and further commented that the liaison between Julie and the valet, John, was a 'very questionable theme in these days of the relations between masters + servants, which this play tends to undermine'.[31] Back in 1912, as a member of the Advisory Board, Oxford professor Walter Raleigh had fought hard for *Miss Julie* as a significant work of art, despite what others perceived as its 'socialistic tendencies', but finally admitted defeat, acknowledging that 'it might be terribly mishandled on the stage . . . I have bought it, and put it on my shelf; which closes this chapter.'[32] The potentially incendiary combination of class antagonisms and female sexual desire were best kept off the stage and in the more controllable medium of print, where the threatening and unstable dynamics of performance and reception need not be reckoned with.

The extent to which class antagonism—meaning the lower classes' hostility towards their social betters, rather than its comparatively harmless opposite—was regarded as more dangerously inflammatory than depictions of illicit sexual desire is perhaps best exemplified by looking at the licensing history of John Van Druten's *Young Woodley* (1928) and M. C. Underwood's *The Girl from Crawley's* (1933). Van Druten's play is a drama of teenage sexual awakening, in which Woodley, a seventeen year-old schoolboy, falls in love with the young wife of his desiccated and cold-blooded schoolmaster. The master finds them kissing, and when Woodley is crudely mocked by a fellow pupil, he attacks him in furious rage and is expelled from the school. The play was at first refused a licence on the grounds of indecency,

[30] Quoted in *Lord Chamberlain Regrets*, 76.
[31] Quoted in *Lord Chamberlain Regrets*, 91. *Miss Julie* was finally licensed in 1935, when Street's reader's report sardonically commented, 'The play may disgust some, but it can corrupt nobody. No footman nor chauffeur need fear the more for his virtue for its passing, nor society disintegrate in one glorious orgie [*sic*] in the servants hall.' Ibid, 92–3.
[32] LCO Theatre Files, not catalogued, quoted in Nicholson, *Censorship of British Drama*, 79–80.

but after a private Stage Society production was greeted by the press as 'beautiful and true', 'gentle', and of a 'delicate and honourable kind', the Lord Chamberlain's Office reversed its decision and granted a public licence.[33] Reviewers accepted with approval the play's attack on a school system which sought to suppress and deny the burgeoning sexual impulses of youth, and the *Times* reviewer was typical in admiring Kathleen O'Regan's performance as the master's wife, describing her reciprocated passion for the schoolboy as played 'with an enchanting grace, [which] gives to this love, which is like sunlight moving on water, her share of its loveliness'.[34]

Five years later, inspired by off-stage characters and minor details in *Young Woodley*, M. C. Underwood wrote *The Girl from Crawley's*. In Van Druten's play, Woodley admits to having worked off his frustrated desires for the master's wife by having sex with a shop girl from Crawley's, an experience which he describes as 'horrible—beastly. I feel dirty all over'.[35] He speaks with the same revulsion and nausea of the anonymous shop girl as he does of the ageing Tottenham Court Road prostitutes whom he found too repulsive to have sex with. Underwood declared he was inspired by Van Druten's 'beautiful little play' to do justice to the unseen shop girl, whom he brings to the stage as Evvie, a warm-hearted, impulsive teenager, who has had to look after herself since childhood.[36] Evvie copes with casual sexual harassment from the schoolboys who visit Crawley's, and is delighted when Woodley's distant contempt for her changes to tender interest. Not understanding that the poetry he recites to her was written for another woman, Evvie has sex with him in the woods, only to realize the truth with anger and disgust: 'You loved *her*—and you used *me* like an animal! Oh! Oh! That was VILE!' (III, 179). Woodley's assurance of class superiority is at first unshaken, telling her to pull herself together because 'You ought to be damn glad, Evvie, you had the chance to go out with me', and even as he realizes the depth of her feeling for him and the genuine anguish she is suffering, he can offer no more than the assurance that he has plenty of money and can therefore take care of her: 'on my *honour*—if any trouble comes to you through me' (III, 180). Woodley's view of Evvie as nothing but a physical convenience is ironically complemented by his housemaster's concern that his pupils be kept safe from social climbing shop girls and 'the predatory powers of female sensuality' (III, 186). In his reader's report for the play, H. C. Game noted the tenderness and sympathy of the scenes between Evvie and a fellow assistant, and tentatively suggested the play might be passed for licence if sexual references were muted and it was no longer made clear that Evvie and Woodley had sex. Another reader, G. S. Street, however, judged that 'Schoolboys messing about with shop girls as the central theme of the play is altogether impossible', and the Lord Chamberlain,

---

[33] *Times* (14 February 1928), 12; *Saturday Review* (25 February 1928), 218; *Manchester Guardian* (14 February 1928), 5.

[34] *Times* (14 February 1928), 12.

[35] John Van Druten, *Young Woodley* (Samuel French: London, 1930), III, i, 47.

[36] M. C. Underwood, *The Girl from Crawley's. A Comedy of Character in Action* (Phipps-Walker & Fuller: London, 1935), viii.

Lord Cromer, agreed that 'The theme and viciousness of the play is impossible', declaring a licence 'unconditionally Refused', a decision which was upheld in sub-sequent years despite Underwood's heated protests.[37] Van Druten's romance be-tween a married woman and schoolboy of the same class could be viewed as delicate and tender, but the same schoolboy's contemptuous exploitation of a girl he viewed as inescapably beneath him (a view the censors clearly shared) remained dangerously inflammatory and too repugnant to stage.

The Lord Chamberlain's Office could, however, be impressively liberal on occa-sions. In 1926 a licence was granted to *The Fanatics* by Miles Malleson, a play in which there is little explicit sexual action but much extended discussion of sexual morality, with the majority of its characters condemning pre-war sexual orthodox-ies on premarital chastity, the evils of birth control, and the merits of sexual igno-rance. The decision to licence *The Fanatics* may have owed much to the fact that it is primarily a discussion play, strikingly similar in many ways to Bernard Shaw's *Getting Married* (1908) in which a young couple hesitate on the brink of matri-mony, horrified by the illogicality and inhumanity of the marriage laws. Devoting an entire act to an extended discussion of sexual manners and morality, Malleson's drama offered an unusual example of a Shavian-style play of ideas. The plot, in so far as such a term is appropriate, concerns John, a young veteran of World War One, who is engaged to Frankie, a girl who shrinks away from so much as a pas-sionate kiss. While loving Frankie, John is also having a friendly sexual relationship with Toby, a chorus girl in whose open passion and joyful sensuality John finds great relief from the combination of puritanical asceticism and sordid lubricious-ness which he feels characterizes society's hypocritical attitudes to sex. When John's relationship with Toby is revealed, Frankie breaks off their engagement and a long discussion ensues between them, John's younger sister, and two older friends over the idiocies and inadequacies of society's inherited sexual morality. John condemns the current 'unclean, intolerant, silly system', which produces loveless marriages, sexual disease, millions living without love, and girls brought up in a 'prison of asceticism'.[38] Having listened with rapt attention to the experiences of a poised and thoughtful woman who has had a number of short-term and longer-term sexual relationships and is at ease with what she has gained and learnt from each of them, John's younger sister refuses to marry her fiancé until they have taken a trip together and discovered if they have the sexual compatibility which she is now convinced is essential to a happy marriage.

The play has no resolution and little action beyond the interchange of various views on sexual morality, the ending of one engagement and the testing out of another. The one traditionally dramatic moment in the play is when John's father surprises his son in a passionate embrace with Toby, who is wearing only 'the scant-iest and daintiest of undergarments' (II, 47). Moments before, John expressed his

[37] H. C. Game, Reader's Report, 4 December 1933, on application for licence to Fortune Theatre, 15 January 1934; Street note, 5 December 1933; Cromer addition, 7 December 1933; all in LC Corr. *The Girl from Crawley's* LR 1933/6.

[38] Miles Malleson, *The Fanatics* (Ernest Benn: London, 1924), II, 73. First performed Ambassadors Theatre, 15 March 1927.

eternal gratitude to Toby for her joyful and unembarrassed physicality, which have given him a sense of the beauty of human sexuality. When his father enters and turns on the light, the stage direction announces '*Tableau!*'—an ironic anachronism in the casual naturalism of the play, indicating not a change in dramatic method but a description of the scene as the father sees it (II, 50). To the puritanical father it is a tableau of guilty discovery; to John and Toby there is no guilt involved. Lord Cromer licensed the play in 1926, despite warnings from his adviser, and even refused to intervene when Cardiff police later complained that the play was 'a menace to public morality'.[39] Critics were predictably divided between those who condemned the play as 'poisonous rubbish' which would give encouragement to 'male libertines', and those who applauded it as a great play, whose scorching sincerity emitted a 'lustral vigour to impel the spirit upwards'.[40] Cromer's decision was vindicated by the play's impressively long run of 313 performances. There was clearly a public appetite for such radical fare, though some audience members may have been attracted by posters which advertised the play with a large picture of Toby in her scant underwear—Malleson's point was apparently lost on the theatre's publicity department.

The discussion play format of *The Fanatics* prompted some critics to see it as a throwback to the Edwardian era, the *Manchester Guardian*'s critic even labelling its characters 'Ibsenite'.[41] In this respect Malleson's play was entirely characteristic of a widespread and striking tendency in drama of the 1910s and 20s to draw upon theatrical structures and forms from decades or even centuries before. In the years before the First World War, for example, a remarkable number of plays took on the popular melodramatic plot of the woman seduced and abandoned by her former lover, rewriting the standard ending of reconciliation and marriage in order to challenge the assumptions about class, gender, and sexuality which underlay so many Victorian plays. In suffragist Jess Dorynne's *The Surprise of his Life* (1912) Emily Jenkins falls pregnant, and her father sets about negotiating the best price he can get to purchase her lover Alfred as a son-in-law and thereby protect the respectable reputation on which the family's grocery business depends. When Alfred deigns to accept the easy berth offered him, he is taken aback by Emily's declaration that she prefers to retain her economic independence, having been inspired with renewed self-respect thanks to listening to the suffragist speeches of an unseen

---

[39] Quoted in Nicholson, *Censorship of British Drama,* 228. Cromer's decision is all the more notable given the heated debates current in 1926 over the potential educative function of the theatre and how it should be harnessed. Nicholson argues convincingly that Cromer would occasionally tactically refuse a licence to a relatively inoffensive play in order to dissuade the future submission of more radical fare. The licensing of *The Fanatics* may have been a case of Cromer deploying a similar tactic in respect of the conservative forces demanding tighter moral controls over theatrical performances. By licensing Malleson's play, Cromer may have sought to dissuade future objections to less controversial dramas. See Steve Nicholson, 'A critical year in perspective: 1926', in Baz Kershaw (ed.), *The Cambridge History of British Theatre*, Vol. 3: *Since 1895* (Cambridge University Press: Cambridge, 2004), 127–42; Nicholson, *Censorship of British Drama*, Introduction.

[40] *Play Pictorial* (March 1927), 12–13; *English Review* (June 1927), 758; *Manchester Guardian* (30 August 1927), 11.

[41] *Manchester Guardian* (16 March 1927), 14.

Mrs Wilson and her Association of Self-Supporters.[42] Where so many melodramatic seduced maidens were rescued from despair and self-destruction by the penitent love of their seducer, the fate of Emily's Aunt Eliza shines a cynically realistic light on such happy endings: Eliza married in similar circumstances to Emily's and suffered a lifetime of daily humiliation and taunts from a husband who regarded his marriage as an act of extraordinary generosity and condescension.

The essential assumptions underpinning Victorian seduction dramas—that the woman's sexual experience constitutes a 'fall' which only marriage can redeem, that the man's superior status more than atoned for his previous treachery, and that marriage to such a man constituted a happy ending—were repeatedly revealed as misogyny, snobbery, and naivety. In *The Magnanimous Lover* (1912), St John Ervine focused on the role of religion in shoring up the sexual double standard. Inspired by his recent conversion, Henry offers marriage and respectability to Maggie and their ten year-old son, eager to 'wipe out the debt I owe to God', and no more concerned with Maggie's feelings now than he was when he rejected her pleas ten years before, declaring he wasn't going to marry 'a whore'.[43] Far from inspiring an apology for his past behaviour, the misogynist creed of his newly acquired religion only feeds his sense of moral superiority; Maggie, he declares, is the greater sinner because 'it's women that keeps sin in the world with their shameful, lustful bodies.... Every soul that writhes in hell was sent there by a woman' (26). Like Dorynne's Emily, Maggie rejects him together with the notion that marriage to such a selfish hypocrite can confer respectability upon her—her own self-supporting hard work and courage have already done that in the face of public opprobrium.

Alan Monkhouse's *Mary Broome* (1911) was another wryly comic riposte to the traditional plot and its supposedly happy ending. Leonard is given a choice by his morally self-righteous, middle-class father between penury and marriage to Mary, the maid who is expecting his child. Leonard may wince when his family patronize Mary, but the same selfishness, irresponsibility, and weakness of will which first led Leonard to abandon Mary remain unchanged by their marriage. With extraordinary patience and generosity Mary endures Leonard's failure to earn a living, to call a doctor for his ailing son, or even to attend the funeral when the child dies—he sends a prettily-worded letter instead. Wishing only to be a 'proper wife', Mary realizes that it is impossible to remain married to such a weak-willed and self-indulgent man, and she announces that she is leaving for Canada with her former sweetheart, George Truefit, the milkman.[44] A legally unsanctioned union with George will be a truer marriage than the ill-judged match with Leonard, imposed on them by his father in the conventional belief that it would somehow 'make a man' of the son he himself describes as a 'useless dilettante' (II, 29; I, 21). The

    [42] Jess Dorynne, *The Surprise of His Life*. First performed by Pioneer Players, King's Hall, 5 May 1912. Unpublished manuscript, Smallhythe Museum.
    [43] St John Ervine, *The Magnanimous Lover* (Allen & Unwin: London, 1928), 24, 20.
    [44] Alan Monkhouse, *Mary Broome* (Sidgwick & Jackson: London, 1912), IV, 81. First produced Gaiety Theatre, Manchester, 9 October 1911.

father's social snobbery and moral conventionalism is finally unsettled, leaving him bewildered and uncharacteristically unsure of himself, in what Leonard diagnoses as a 'middle stage' through which all those his generation must pass between right-eous prejudice and a more humane set of values (I, 19).

In John Galsworthy's *The Eldest Son* (1912) the target was class snobbery, as manifested in the conflict between an upper-class family's moral principles and their social dismay at the prospect of their son marrying the maid who is carrying his child. It is the maid's gamekeeper father who proves himself a better man than his 'master', rejecting the grudging proposal with dignity as a 'charity marriage' of which they have no need.[45] A number of reviewers linked Galsworthy's play with Stanley Houghton's *Hindle Wakes*, which transferred to the Court Theatre in November 1912, when *The Eldest Son* opened at the Kingsway Theatre. Grouped together, their attack on the 'old convention' and its 'unwritten law' became clearer; though reviewers acknowledged that the similarity ended there, Galsworthy being primarily interested in the aristocratic family's humiliation at the hands of their own snobbery, while Houghton's sexually independent heroine struck a comic and convincingly modern note.

This return to the plots of the previous century was a marked feature in the work of the two playwrights who dominated the post-war London stage, Somerset Maugham and Noël Coward. Treating the sexual mores and manners of the rich and leisured classes, Maugham and Coward drew on the plots and situations of their Victorian predecessors, using them as Galsworthy, Ervine, and Dorynne used the seduction plot in order variously to engage with and challenge the values and assumptions of previous decades. Dramas by Maugham and Coward posed the Lord Chamberlain's Office many of its most difficult and controversial decisions in relation to questions of sexual morality. Their plays, both for critics and audiences at the time and for theatre historians looking back on the period, characterized the theatre of the 1920s. They spoke for the mood of the moment, and yet they did so repeatedly within the forms and structures of the *fin de siècle*, responding directly to the morality and conventions of decades past.

The post-war period saw a shift in theatre ownership from actor-managers to commercial investors, financial middlemen or companies who would then lease the theatres to producing companies. This arrangement, in which the London theatre became a capitalist ground for investment and profit-making, had the inevitable effect of forcing up producers' costs. In the interwar period production costs rose by some 600 per cent, and rents by as much as 1000 per cent, while admission prices rarely increased by more than 50 per cent—an equation which meant that plays had to gain large audiences and secure long runs in order to break even.[46] Alongside the large commercial theatres, independent theatre subscription

---

[45] John Galsworthy, *The Eldest Son*, in *The Plays of John Galsworthy* (Duckworth: London, 1929), III, 198.

[46] Richard Findlater, *The Unholy Trade* (Victor Gollancz: London, 1952), quoted in Maggie B. Gale, 'The London Stage, 1918–1945' in Kershaw (ed), *Cambridge History of British Theatre*, vol. 3, 148.

clubs and independent production companies, such as the Stage Society and the Pioneer Players, together with a crop of new small independent theatres, continued to offer a lower-budget theatrical scene through which plays could be performed without a public licence and where work by unknown or less mainstream writers could be presented. As Maggie Gale has rightly observed, it is too simple to set the commercial West End and the 'other theatres' in opposition to each other, since commercial hits often began life as alternative 'private' productions, just as playwrights could learn their craft by seeing their plays produced at smaller venue theatres.[47] Nor were theatre audiences divided along class lines; despite the rise in ticket prices and theatre's enduring fascination with the lives of the rich and privileged, gallery prices remained low enough to draw working-class audiences. W. A. Darlington recalled his early years of theatre-going alongside a devoted first-night audience of cockney women, who for decades had not only secured seats for every opening night but who had an encyclopaedic knowledge of the 'notables' in the stalls and their affairs.[48] Such compulsive theatre-going provided a cross-class audience, within which not just theatre critics and well-heeled 'notables' could pick up intertheatrical references to past decades, but so could equally well informed galleryites with a bird's-eye view of those on show on stage and in the stalls.

William Somerset Maugham was himself a compulsive London playgoer in the 1890s, when he was training to become a doctor. Thoroughly versed in the sex-problem plays of Wilde, Pinero, Grundy, and Jones, his first performed play was *A Man of Honour* (1903), a pessimistic vision of a doomed cross-class marriage between a decorated officer and a barmaid, who has fallen pregnant as a result of their casual affair. Written a decade before other such challenges to the convention of the repentant seducer making reparation through marriage, the class politics of Maugham's play are characteristically uncertain. Where Galsworthy and Monkhouse were to challenge the snobbery inherent in the conventional 'happy' resolution, Maugham's play roots the marriage's failure in the barmaid's inherent vulgarity and lack of intellect and education. The decorated officer marries her according to his code of 'honour' but is not honourable enough to hide his impatience and distaste, finally declaring his love for a woman of his own class, at which the barmaid commits suicide. The play secured two matinee performances from the Stage Society, though Maugham was not interested in the financially unrewarding admiration of a 'small band of intellectuals' but the more remunerative admiration of 'the great public'.[49] Maugham's subsequent theatrical career was established on predominantly comic rather than tragic versions of the dramatic forms of the previous century.

---

[47] Gale, 'The London Stage', 146–51. See also Clive Barker and Maggie Gale, *British Theatre between the Wars, 1918–1939* (Cambridge University Press: Cambridge, 2000); Jean Chothia, *English Drama of the Early Modern Period, 1890–1940* (Longman: London, 1996).

[48] Darlington, *Six Thousand and One Nights*, 62.

[49] W. Somerset Maugham, *The Summing Up* (Vintage: London, 2001), 112. First published 1938.

Lady Frederick (1907) was his first commercial success, a retread of the old vehicle of the respectable young man enamoured of a woman with a dubious past. In the style of nineteenth-century English playwrights adapting racy French dramas, Maugham takes the sexual sting out of the situation by revealing that the notorious Lady Frederick is unjustly maligned and has been selflessly carrying the blame for another's indiscretion. In the play's central scene, the merry widow deliberately discourages her young admirer by revealing the secrets of her dressing table, transforming herself before his and the audience's eyes from a frowsy ageing woman into a carefully-painted picture of elegance and youth. The young man turns tail but his uncle proposes marriage to the bewitching Lady Frederick; it takes a mature eye, Maugham suggests, to appreciate the illusions and tastes of a former age—both in women and plays.

Maugham specialized in such comic revisions, extracting the potentially troubling sex problems from the original form and replacing them with cynically humorous resolutions. *Penelope* (1909) echoed Jones's *The Princess's Nose*, but with the difference that the betrayed wife takes the cynical *raisonneur*'s advice and happily wins back her errant husband, having learnt to play hard to get rather than stifling him with wifely affection. Where the barbed cynicism of *The Princess's Nose* brought Jones's play to a close after only two weeks, Maugham's *Penelope* ran for 246 performances. His transformation of the Victorian bigamy play into a satirical comedy was similarly successful. In *Home and Beauty* (1919)—known in the U.S. as *Too Many Husbands*—an officer returns from his assumed death in the First World War to find his wife married to his best friend. A covert battle ensues in which each man tries to offload their pretty but phenomenally selfish wife onto the other. The play ends with her decision to divorce them both for good measure, and upgrade to a third and far wealthier spouse—to both her husbands' considerable relief.

Maugham was well aware that changing sexual attitudes could render long-established plots outmoded; as he noted in the 1931 preface to the first collected volume of his plays, old dramas risk becoming 'quaint' as not only manners and technology change, but even sentiments 'profoundly rooted in human nature'. So, he averred, 'We no longer look upon a woman's chastity as her essential virtue. I submit to the dramatists of today that the faithfulness of a wife is no longer a subject for drama, but only for comedy.'[50] But, as many of Maugham's plays demonstrate, familiar Victorian plot-lines could be rendered serviceable with only minor adjustments. *Caesar's Wife* (1919), for example, hinges on the time-honoured situation of an older and wiser husband fighting to keep his young wife, despite her growing passion for another man. The wife finally conquers her desires, remaining with her elderly spouse despite the acknowledgement of all her sympathetic onlookers that she and her lover were ideally suited. In order to render her marital fidelity as morally important as it had been in the 1890s, Maugham makes

---

[50] Maugham, Preface, in *The Collected Plays of W. Somerset Maugham*, 3 vols (William Heinemann: London, 1931, reprinted 1952), vol. 1, xix–xx. Seven years later in *The Summing Up* Maugham reiterated this opinion, while noting that its expression had provoked 'so much indignation' that he would refrain from enlarging upon it further. (128)

her wife of the British Consul to Egypt so that any sexual irregularity on her part risks endangering the reputation of the ruling British elite, thereby threatening her imperial power. As the *Times* reviewer commented: 'Even the oldest of themes Mr Maugham can furbish up for you and re-lacquer and make it look as good as new.'[51]

In *East of Suez* (1922), Maugham similarly updated the Victorian fallen woman play by relocating it to China. By the 1920s the idea that extramarital sex rendered a woman irredeemably degraded and morally depraved could no longer serve as the central assumption on which a play hinged. Make the woman mixed-race, however, and by mixing misogyny with racism the old prejudices could be reinstated. As in Dumas *fils*'s *Le Demi-Monde*, Augier's *Le Mariage d'Olympe*, and Pinero's *The Second Mrs Tanqueray*, Maugham's *East of Suez* opens with an honourable man about to marry a woman who has previously been kept by a series of men. Daisy, Maugham's half-Chinese *femme fatale*, persuades her former lover George to overcome his scruples and allow her to begin a new life as supposedly virtuous wife to his friend Harry. Overcome by native *nostalgie de la boue*, Daisy seduces George into renewing their affair, and when his self-disgust drives him to suicide, she returns to the control of a manipulative Chinese lover, declaring that 'The jungle takes back its own.'[52] George Street approved the play for licence as 'a wholesome warning' which, despite being 'a painful story', offered 'a practical moral against such connections'.[53]

As such plays demonstrate, Maugham was hardly a libertarian or an advocate for women's sexual rights; in *The Land of Promise* (1914), for example, marital rape lays the foundations for a happy marriage. His plays repeatedly question, probe, and satirize sexual mores, but they do not issue an outright challenge or cohere to form any consistent viewpoint or set of values: in *East of Suez* and *The Letter* (1927) adulterous female desire is depicted as murderous, unscrupulous, and deceitful; in *The Land of Promise* and *Smith* (1909), women only want a virile and dominant male to rediscover their true role as compliant wives; in *The Sacred Flame* (1928) and *For Services Rendered* (1932), sexual fulfilment is acknowledged as central to a woman's right to happiness. Maugham was scornfully dismissive of the 'play of ideas'; the need to please socially and intellectually diverse audiences meant that plays could never be at the forefront of debate.[54] But he was alert to shifting sexual attitudes, the changes in mores which rendered the drama of past eras 'quaint', and by reaching back to drama of the 1890s, he brought its morality up to date, not challenging its underlying assumptions but taking them forward another logical step—a

---

[51] *Times* (28 March 1919), 15.

[52] *East of Suez*, *Collected Plays of W. S. Maugham*, vol. 3, VII, 218. First performed His Majesty's Theatre, London, 2 September 1922.

[53] LC Corr. *East of Suez* 1922/4209, quoted in Nicholson, *Censorship of British Drama*, 285. *East of Suez* was one of a slew of plays licensed by the Lord Chamberlain's Office on the grounds that they offered a useful warning against interracial marriage or relationships, thus justifying their sensational and breathtakingly racist depiction of Chinese, African, and Egyptian women combining unscrupulous wiles and bestial appetites. See Nicholson, *Censorship of British Drama*, 280–91.

[54] See *Summing Up*, 128–36.

process which could often prove more disturbing to audiences than an outright and open assault.

In *The Circle* (1921), for example, Maugham took on the familiar *fin-de-siècle* plot of the wife tempted to leave her marriage, and the friends and relatives who rally round to prevent such a dangerous move. Maugham's Elizabeth is unhappily married to a priggish and self-satisfied MP, Arnold Champion-Cheney, but has fallen in love with a young Malaysian planter, Teddie Luton. As in Henry Arthur Jones's *The Liars*, the older generation steps in to keep the marriage together; *The Circle*'s self-appointed *raisonneur* is Arnold's father Clive, who advises his son to control his anger and be as magnanimous and generous as possible towards Elizabeth so that guilt and gratitude will force her to stay with him. In *The Liars*, Jones's *raisonneur* lectured the would-be adulterers on the need for social structures to maintain human virtue and value, warning against the moral degradation and collapse which would inevitably result if they should choose love over polite society, as others have done before them: 'flitting shabbily about the Continent at cheap *tables d'hôtes* and gambling dens, rubbing shoulders with all the blackguards and demi-mondaines of Europe. . . . cut by the county, with no single occupation except to nag and rag each other to pieces from morning to night'.[55] *The Circle* seems at first to confirm the wisdom of such teachings; Arnold's mother Kitty left her marriage to Clive twenty years earlier with Lord Porteous, and their physical and temperamental decay—complete with ill-fitting false teeth, thickly plastered make-up, and constant bickering—offer a salutary corrective to Elizabeth's romantic dreams. But Maugham sets up audience expectations only to overturn them. Teddie overcomes Elizabeth's qualms with his honesty and passionate conviction: 'I don't offer you peace and quietness. I offer you unrest and anxiety. I don't offer you happiness. I offer you love.'[56] The young couple make their escape in Porteous's car, while the ageing lovers muse on the vital importance of character: 'If we made rather a hash of things perhaps it was because we were rather trivial people. You can do anything in this world if you're prepared to take the consequences, and consequences depend on character' (III, 89). Social and sexual conformity are not the absolute rules that Clive Champion-Cheney tries to make them: love does not necessarily depend on legal sanction and society's approval for its survival; adulterous relationships are not necessarily doomed; it's a question of character and circumstance.

The boldness of *The Circle*'s ending drew boos from the gallery at its first performance, and J. T. Grein, one-time founder of the Independent Theatre now turned theatre critic, sounded like a ghostly echo of the 1890s. Just as Clement Scott had once protested that Wilde's good woman, Lady Windermere, could never have contemplated leaving her husband and child, so Grein confidently declared that a 'young, impressionable, womanly woman' like Elizabeth would

---

[55] *The Liars*, Russell Jackson (ed.), *Plays by Henry Arthur Jones* (Cambridge University Press: Cambridge, 1982), IV, 215. First performed Criterion Theatre, London, 6 October 1897. As St John Ervine noted, Maugham also audaciously borrowed from Jones the line, 'I may be a fool, but I'm not a damned fool.' *Observer* (6 March 1921), 11.

[56] *The Circle*, *Collected Plays of W. Somerset Maugham*, vol. 2, III, 87.

never have left her husband for a man who promises her 'nothing better than physical pleasure, a life of adventure and ... a kind of purgatory existence that must end in unhappiness'.[57] But the majority of the house, as the *Times* reported, 'approved the solution as the right one', their judgement influenced, the critic surmised, by Maugham's tactical structuring and humour: 'Approve ethically, or not, you must approve aesthetically.'[58] Notably critics were universally admiring of the power and poignancy of Elizabeth and Teddy's declarations of love, describing them variously as of 'natural and moving intensity', 'very modern and very true', and 'two of the most striking love-scenes written for the contemporary theatre'.[59] Significantly a number of critics also expressed a degree of admiration and warmth towards Porteous and Kitty, whom the *Times* felt could not quite be regarded 'as an awful warning to intending "bolters"'; the *Daily Telegraph* actually judged them the most sympathetic characters in the play, having 'still manage[d] to be fond of each other after a thirty-year illicit union'.[60]

The play's comic climax further encouraged the tilting of sympathies towards the two adulterous couples; the curtain descends on Clive Champion-Cheney smugly congratulating himself on the success of his ruse, oblivious to Elizabeth's departure. As a representative of the establishment, he advocates conformity but is more markedly flawed than any of Jones's *raisonneurs*. Luxuriating in the image of the abandoned husband, Clive has comforted himself with a constantly refreshed supply of mistresses; as he puts it, 'I have allowed myself the luxury of assisting financially a succession of dear little things, in a somewhat humble sphere, between the ages of twenty and twenty-five', who are discharged on their twenty-fifth birthday with a diamond ring and 'a most affecting scene', to be rapidly replaced by a younger model (II, 54). As an advocate of social conformity, Clive smugly demonstrates how moral orthodoxy still allows men to have their cake and eat it; but, unlike Jones's *raisonneurs*, the play's outcome fails to validate his predictions. *The Circle* does not refute the vision offered by so many *fin-de-siècle* plays of the degradation of life in the *demi-monde*, but it does qualify it; conformity is not the only way, though it may be the safest one for many.[61]

In *The Constant Wife* (1926) Maugham drew directly on a late-Victorian plot, producing a play which simultaneously shocked audiences and critics while reminding them of the sexual politics of previous decades—that the play could simultaneously appear so old-fashioned and yet so disturbing speaks volumes about how little attitudes had fundamentally changed. *The Constant Wife* was based on a scenario sketched out by Oscar Wilde in 1894, in which a simple sweet

[57] Clement Scott, reviewing *Lady Windermere's Fan*, *Illustrated London News* (27 February 1892), 278; Grein, *Illustrated London News* (26 March 1921), 418.

[58] *Times* (4 March 1921), 10.

[59] *Manchester Guardian* (4 March 1921), 14; *Observer* (6 March 1921), 11; *Saturday Review* (12 March 1921), 214.

[60] *Times* (4 March 1921), 10; *Daily Telegraph* (4 March 1921), 7.

[61] For other examples of Victorian plays teaching the horrors of life in the *demi-monde* see e.g. Constance Fletcher ['George Fleming'], *Mrs Lessingham* (1894); A. W. Pinero, *The Notorious Mrs Ebbsmith* (1895); Clement Scott, *Odette* (1894), adapted from the French play by Victorien Sardou.

country girl is unhappily married to an adulterous man of fashion. The wife falls asleep in her boudoir, only to be woken when her husband enters the room and makes love to his mistress, unaware that his wife is in the same room. When the mistress's husband hammers angrily on the door, the good wife opens it and calmly provides the guilty lovers with an alibi. The wife then leaves her husband for a man who truly loves her, and when her husband later begs her to return, she coolly rejects his pleas and reproaches her lover for even contemplating sacrificing their love to a misplaced sense of duty. Learning that his wife is pregnant by her lover, the husband shoots himself. Wilde designed his scenario as a riposte to Meilhac and Halévy's popular 1869 play *Frou-Frou*, in which a wife commits adultery, sees her lover shot by her outraged husband, and then dies in heartbroken repentance. In his play, by contrast, Wilde wanted the '*sheer passion of love to dominate everything*', with no 'morbid self-sacrifice' or renunciation.[62] Though Wilde never wrote up the play himself, he sold rights to the scenario to several writers and producers, including Frank Harris, who composed a version under the title *Mr and Mrs Daventry*.[63] The play opened at the Royalty Theatre in 1900, starring Mrs Patrick Campbell as Mrs Daventry, and provoked cries of moral outrage from several critics, despite the fact that Harris ended his play on a more muted note, as guilt at the husband's death hangs over the lovers' future.[64]

Maugham's heroine, named Constance in tribute to Wilde's intended title for his play, similarly covers for the adulterous relationship between her husband, John, and her best friend, Marie-Louise—though instead of a screen-scene, Maugham makes a cigarette case the revealing piece of evidence, left under Marie-Louise's pillow by John and claimed by Constance as her own when it is found by Marie-Louise's outraged husband.[65] Constance then coolly explains the logic of her actions: while she is financially supported by her husband, she has no more right to protest at his preferring another woman's love to her own than does a prostitute whose client does not wish to take advantage of the sexual services he has purchased. A year later, however, having gone into business as an interior decorator, Constance pays £1,000 into her husband's account for her board and lodging, and announces that she is leaving for a romantic holiday with an old admirer to once again experience the romantic excitement which her husband similarly sought with Marie-Louise. Outmanoeuvred and nonplussed, her husband reluctantly

---

[62] Letter to George Alexander, August 1894, *The Complete Letters of Oscar Wilde*, ed. Merlin Holland and Rupert Hart-Davis (Fourth Estate: London, 2000), 599–600.

[63] Wilde also sold the scenario to a number of other potential writers and producers in order to raise much-needed funds, for further details see Sos Eltis, *Revising Wilde: Society and Subversion in the Plays of Oscar Wilde* (Oxford University Press: Oxford, 1996), 201–5.

[64] See e.g. *Athenaeum* 3810 (3 November 1900), 587; *Daily Telegraph* (6 October 1900), 8.

[65] *The Constant Wife*, *Collected Plays of W. S. Maugham*, vol. 2, II, 139–41. See introduction by H. Montgomery Hyde to Frank Harris, *Mr and Mrs Daventry. A Play in four acts... based on a scenario by Oscar Wilde* (Richards Press: London, 1956), ii. Constance was, of course, the name of Wilde's wife. Maugham's choice of a cigarette case as evidence of sexual guilt may have been inspired by the prominent role of cigarette cases as evidence in the trials of Oscar Wilde. See Merlin Holland, *Irish Peacock and Scarlet Marquess: the Real Trial of Oscar Wilde* (Fourth Estate: London, 2004), 147, 173, 199, 203.

declares her 'the most maddening, wilful, capricious, wrong-headed, delightful and enchanting woman man was ever cursed with having for a wife', but concedes his readiness to take her back on her return (III, 198).

Constance's argument is the logical extension of Sir Daniel's justification for the sexual double standard in Jones's *Mrs Dane's Defence*: if a wife's purity is what a man purchases by the sweat of his brow, then with financial independence a wife can buy it back. A number of reviewers recognized Maugham's play as a reference back to earlier sexual debates and arguments of feminists like Cecily Hamilton: as the *Saturday Review* commented, Constance's intellectual position is one 'that might have been established by a formidable young Fabian round about 1890. Marriage, she thought, is my trade.'[66] The response of H. M. Walbrook, writing in *Play Pictorial*, to Constance's argument was characteristic of many: 'There is, of course, a sort of logic in such a demand; but *au fond* what a disgusting arrangement it is, and what a degradation of marriage!'[67] The sexual double standard was still sufficiently embedded for Constance's adulterous husband to be spared any expressions of critical opprobrium, while the heroine's cool logic repelled reviewers who shrank from what they perceived as Maugham's cynicism. In New York the play achieved an impressive run of 295 performances, thanks perhaps to the distance allowed by viewing it as an essentially 'English' play and also perhaps to the production's deliberate eschewal of emotional depth.[68] The London production only achieved a 70-performance run, despite apparently responding to its initial reception by shifting to a performance style similarly designed to take the sting out its sardonic tail; as the *Observer*'s critic noted a month after it opened, 'I found on a second visit to the production that the concluding scenes were lightly, almost farcically acted, whereas on the first night they were acted in a realistic manner which made them intolerable.'[69] Interestingly, the *New York Times* described *The Constant Wife* as based 'on an old model', whereas English critics did not see it as a *fin-de-siècle*-style problem play, despite the heroine's 'Fabian' politics.[70] The play was greeted instead as recognizably modern in the harder-edged more realistic mode of its opening London performances. Maugham had effectively updated the problem play by eschewing a *raisonneur*, leaving critics to view the play not as a feminist attack on the sexual double standard but rather as a sardonic and detached portrait of modern marriage in a mode which achieved novelty by dating back not to the nineteenth but to the seventeenth century; so the *Manchester Guardian* commented on Maugham's unfailing cynicism, 'which pulls back the curtain on a scene which finds its prototypes among the rakes and cuckolds of Restoration drama. In this

---

[66] *Saturday Review* (16 April 1927), 598. See also *Manchester Guardian* (7 April 1927), 7. The American production attracted similar comparisons, heightened by the casting of Ethel Barrymore in the lead role, drawing parallels to her previous performance as Kate, the wife who escapes marriage to support herself as a typist, in Barrie's *The Twelve-Pound Look*. See *Washington Post* (23 November 1926), 11.

[67] *Play Pictorial* (March 1927), 13.

[68] See e.g. *Washington Post* (23 November 1926), 11; *New York Times* (30 November 1926), 26.

[69] *Observer* (8 May 1927), 15.

[70] *New York Times* (30 November 1926), 26; *Saturday Review* (16 April 1927), 598.

case the aridity and abstract ruthlessness of the argument about love provides a further reminiscence of Congreve's world, where the profitable conduct of unseemly affairs was discussed with such poise of phrase and such nicely balanced reckoning.'[71] But such a sardonic portrait was not to be accepted as reality; like the majority of his colleagues, the critic was careful to express his incredulity that any real woman of 'quality' could act upon such theories.

The comparison to Restoration drama was significant, for plays like William Wycherley's *The Country Wife* (1675) and George Etherege's *The Man of Mode* (1676) offered a radically different moral structure from the sex-problem plays of the 1890s. Undermining expectations of poetic justice, such plays hovered ambiguously between satirizing and celebrating the ingenuity and desires of their male and female rakes; they did not offer moral precepts but merely observed the game, noting who was most skilled at preserving their public reputation while satisfying their private passions. This was the mode in which Maugham consciously composed his comedies of sexual manners, and it was this which marked his break with his late-Victorian predecessors. Where Henry Arthur Jones, for example, had sought to combine his cynical analyses of sexual morality with an orthodox assertion of moral norms, Maugham opted more unapologetically for a Restoration mode which, as he put it, 'treats with indulgent cynicism the humours, follies and vices of the world' and if it draws a moral it does so 'with a shrug of the shoulders'.[72]

Our Betters was Maugham's most clearly Restoration-style play, and it raised a public furore, setting new standards for the theatrical treatment of sexuality. Written in 1915, it was first staged in the United States in 1917 but did not reach the London stage until 1923. *Our Betters* follows the manoeuvrings of Pearl, one of a group of rich American women who have each traded their wealth for marriage to an impoverished European aristocrat. Pearl is beautiful, stylish, clever, and unscrupulous. Married to Sir George Grayston, she is bankrolled by her lover, Arthur Fenwick, an elderly American roué. Pearl's manoeuvrings to secure an English lord for her younger sister Bessie are thwarted when she is caught *in flagrante* in the summer house with a friend's lover, Tony. Bessie leaves in disgust for America, but Pearl calmly sets about preserving her reputation, tempting her guests to remain for the rest of the weekend and so defuse the scandal by bribing them with lessons from an effete and highly fashionable dancing master. Pearl ends the play triumphantly in command. Most scandalously, when Pearl makes her post-coital entry with Tony and realizes they have been discovered, she coolly comments, 'You damned fool, I told you it was too risky.'—no shame, remorse or tears, and a clear acknowledgement of shared agency and of a deliberate gamble.[73] Pearl is a world away from the repentant fallen woman of the previous century, and the Lord Chamberlain's demand that the line be altered to 'What did I tell you?', thereby reducing the element of knowing calculation, did little to assuage the shock.[74]

---

[71] *Manchester Guardian* (7 April 1927), 7.
[72] Maugham, *Summing Up*, 119.
[73] *Our Betters, Collected Plays of W. S. Maugham*, vol. 2, II, 78.
[74] Shellard and Nicholson with Handley, *Lord Chamberlain Regrets*, 95–6.

There is no sexual double standard apparent in the play; Pearl's financial backing
from her lover Fenwick is paralleled with Tony's position as the Duchesse de
Surennes's kept man. Maugham anatomizes the shifting balance of power between
keeper and kept, between those who hold the purse-strings and those whose sexual
favours are so desperately desired. The Duchesse promises Tony a motor car in
order to secure a kiss, and not only forgives his infidelity but abjectly surrenders
her financial power over him by agreeing to his demand for marriage and an annual
allowance of £1,000 a year. As the *Daily Telegraph* commented, a 'kind of trade-
union feeling of fellowship' draws Tony and Pearl together, both pandering to
others' sexual self-delusions to secure generous financial returns.[75] Gender roles
and the conventional language of women's moral weakness and their need for male
protection are satirized in Pearl's ability to win Fenwick's forgiveness by bolstering
his absurd self-image as a tower of moral strength. She is well aware that he feels no
real affection for her: 'He loves his love for me.... He sees himself as the man of
iron. I'm going to play the dear little thing racket' (III, 101). With consummate
skill, Pearl acts the frail reed, longing for the support of a good man:

PEARL: You see, strength is easy to you. I'm weak. That's why I put myself in your
    hands. I felt your power instinctively.
FENWICK: I know, I know, and it was because I felt you needed me that I loved you.
    I wanted to shelter you from the storms and buffets of the world.
PEARL: Why didn't you save me from myself, Arthur?
FENWICK: When I look at your poor, pale little face I wonder what you'll do
    without me, girlie.

                                                                    (III, 104)

Pearl's husband is an off-stage irrelevance; she is unconcerned whether he knows
about her infidelities, but she bitterly reproaches the Duchesse for not 'playing the
game' when she informs Fenwick. Maugham here offered a cynically humorous
version of reversed priorities reminiscent of Henri Becque's *La Parisienne* (1885), a
play which opens with a man jealously confronting a woman over her suspected
infidelity; he threatens to search her bureau and angrily reminds her that only by
staying faithful to him can she be called virtuous and respectable—in response to
which, she only warns him urgently that her husband is approaching. Three decades later, the English stage could only stomach such a sardonic version of marriage
when isolated within a small community of rich expatriate Americans.

   Unsurprisingly *Our Betters* caused some anxiety and debate in the Lord Chamberlain's Office, though Maugham's skilful location of his satire in a section of
society which could be distanced as uncharacteristic of both American and English
norms helped to secure his play a licence.[76] Street's reader's report on the play

---

[75] *Daily Telegraph* (14 September 1923), 4.
[76] The Lord Chamberlain nonetheless received an anxious inquiry from King George V about
possible offence to Americans, which was assuaged by the assurance that the play had already been
performed in the USA. See *Lord Chamberlain Regrets*, 93–6.

recommended it for licence despite its 'general viciousness, immorality and sordidness', because 'I think the important point is that the effect is not sympathy with vice but intense scorn of it, not the less because it is made ridiculous as well as odious. If I am right in this it is the reverse of an immoral play.'[77] The widespread critical reception of *Our Betters* as reminiscent of the Restoration stage made Street's assessment look naïve.[78] More convincing was Desmond MacCarthy's verdict in the *New Statesman* that

> It is only a 'satire' for those who attribute to the author their own moral reactions to what he shows them. Each character is allowed rope, and if, at the end of the performance, in your estimation the whole set is left dangling from the gibbet, either it was *you* who strung them up or they hanged themselves; it was not Mr Maugham who put on the black cap.[79]

When Noël Coward first came to prominence as a playwright in 1924 with his scandalous hit *The Vortex*, he was quickly aligned with Somerset Maugham as a daring depicter of upper-class sexual immorality; *The Vortex*, Ivor Brown commented in the *Saturday Review*, could have been subtitled 'Our Best'.[80] The play centres on Nicky Lancaster's shocked realization that his mother, Florence, has had a string of lovers, her current admirer being no older than he is. Nicky blames his own drug-taking and his father's aimless life on Florence's marital infidelities, and the play ends with Florence tearfully promising to be a more dutiful wife and mother. Coward's depiction not only of Florence's affairs, but of her social circle's matter-of-fact acceptance of them, provoked a heated debate between members of the Advisory Board in the Lord Chamberlain's Office. The Lord Chamberlain, Lord Cromer, and one Advisory Board member, Sir Douglas Dawson, viewed the play as an 'inevitable sequence' to *Our Betters,* and favoured refusing a licence on the basis that it was dangerously 'socialist propaganda', whose depiction of 'a frivolous and degenerate set of people gives a wholly false impression of Society life'.[81] Two other readers, H. H. Higgins and Lord Buckmaster, expressed unease at what seemed like different standards of censorship according to class, pointing out that similar sexual activity had been licensed in a lower-class setting in, for example, McEvoy's *The Likes of Her*, and questioning whether it was right for the 'idle and rich' to be protected from criticism.[82] Dawson angrily responded by denying any class bias, and asserting rather his concern that the play was calculated to 'promote public disorder', being 'liable to foster class hatred'.[83] The nineteenth-century per-

---

[77] Ibid, Fig. 5.
[78] See e.g. *Daily Telegraph* (14 September 1923), 4; *Observer* (16 September 1923), 11; *Illustrated London News* (22 September 1923), 550; *Saturday Review* (22 September 1923), 326.
[79] Desmond MacCarthy, *Theatre* (MacGibbon & Kee: London, 1954), 121.
[80] *Saturday Review* (6 December 1924), 568. *The Vortex, Coward, Plays: One* (Eyre Methuen: London, 1979), III, 169; *Saturday Review* (6 December 1924), 568. First performed Everyman, Hampstead, 25 November 1924.
[81] Letter from Cromer, 12 November 1924, LC Corr. *The Vortex:* 1924/5762.
[82] Reports from Higgins and Buckmaster, 19 November 1924, ibid.
[83] Letter from Douglas Dawson, 23 November 1924, ibid.

ception of female sexual virtue as a vital social cohesive clearly retained its potency. Where Victorian commentators had predicted social collapse as the inevitable result of female sexual incontinence, Dawson and Cromer took a less literal view of the importance of women's chastity. Upper-class women must at least be *believed* to be chaste or class respect could be lost and social hierarchies threatened.

Cromer finally and reluctantly granted a licence, persuaded, Coward himself believed, by the playwright's argument that 'the play was little more than a moral tract'—a viewed supported by reader G. S. Street's report that 'The motive of the play is a good one and there are certainly people like Florence Lancaster whom it would be good to see how they look to an observer.'[84] The play was a commercial success, transferring from the small independent Everyman Theatre in Hampstead to the West End. The critics' verdict that the play's social circle was indeed 'a vortex of beastliness', as Nicky described it, had clearly done its box-office no harm. Critics and audiences seemed happy to treat Coward's play as a sensational but morally neutral portrait of a particular slice of society; certainly critics viewed with scepticism Nicky's claim that his mother's promiscuity was to blame for his own failings, and raised a cynical eyebrow at both Nicky and Florence's chances of changing their ways.

In a number of his 1920s plays, Coward mocked and destabilized this language of moral judgement and self-righteousness. A life-long opponent of punitive laws on sexuality, Coward was nevertheless uneasy with overt campaigning for increased sexual rights and freedoms, whether heterosexual or homosexual. Yet he was no admirer of the idle rich class in which his plays were set—as his letters, diaries, and autobiographies attest, he often loathed and despised the socialites who gathered like flies around him once his hard work had secured him success. But while no love was lost on this milieu, Coward was even more sceptical about moral imperatives and traditions invoked as their antidote. Glamour, style, wit, and self-possession remained watchwords, and his plays deployed these as a means of undermining and unsettling moral orthodoxies and socially imposed norms. Like Maugham, he was steeped in the theatrical traditions of the past and reached back to *fin-de-siècle* plots and situations in a number of his plays on sexual morality. But unlike Maugham, he moved from an intertheatrical dialogue with old forms to creating new ones which unsettled moral judgements and eroded sexual norms.

In '*This Was a Man*' (1926) Coward restaged and then sardonically undercut the sensational situation from Wilde's scenario and *Mr and Mrs Daventry*. Carol embraces her lover and leads him through to her bedroom, warning him not to wake her husband, Edward, as they pass his bedroom door; once they have gone, Edward rises from behind the screen where he has been an inadvertent and unseen witness to their affair, helps himself to a sandwich, and retires to bed with weary amusement. Edward reproaches himself later for his failure to respond in a more traditionally masculine manner:

> Men of my sort are the products of over-civilisation. All the red-blooded honest-to-God emotions have been squeezed out of us. We're incapable of hating enough

---

[84] Noël Coward, *Present Indicative*, in *Autobiography*, introduced by Sheridan Morley (Methuen: London, 1986), 134; Street report, November 1924, LC Corr *The Vortex* 1924/5762.

or loving enough. When any big moment comes along, good or bad, we hedge round it, arguing, weighing it in the balance of reason and psychology, trying to readjust the values until there's nothing left and nothing achieved. I wish I were primitive enough to thrash Carol and drive her out of my life for ever—or strong enough to hold her—but I'm not; I'm just an ass—an intelligent spineless ass! [85]

Edward's friend Evelyn, a '*soldierly, and essentially masculine*' man, then assumes the traditional role of corrective male, showing Carol the error of her ways, as Edward has so signally failed to perform such duties. Evelyn's moral outrage is, however, soon revealed to be little more than sexual pique and hypocrisy: though he is unaware of it, he disapproves of Carol seducing other men primarily because he himself has never been the object of her attentions. Evelyn sets about seducing Carol, and when she shows herself eager to succumb, he berates her for sexual looseness. She is, however, far cleverer than he is, and she calmly outmanoeuvres him by pretending to be a heartbroken, betrayed spouse and thereby easily lures Evelyn into her bed. Faced with Evelyn's guilty confession and suicidal heroics the next morning, Edward responds with sardonic amusement and a determination to divorce Carol. The curtain falls on Carol sweetly pointing out to Evelyn that 'There's still time for you to shoot yourself!' (III, 219). The target of Coward's satire thus turns out not to be Edward's ironic detachment—which is ideally suited to modern conditions—but rather the self-satisfied and self-deceiving moral heroics of the traditionally masculine man. The play was refused a licence in 1926, Cromer agreeing with Dawson that the play was ideal 'Soviet' propaganda, and moreover devoid of 'serious purpose'.[86] As Coward mockingly observed, 'facetious adultery' was not to be allowed.[87]

Coward's most overt response to the sex-problem play which had dominated the West End theatre for decades was to write his own version in deliberate imitation of the drawing-room dramas of Pinero, Jones, Maugham, and Haddon Chambers. *Easy Virtue* (1925) was inspired by nostalgia for such old-fashioned fare and the 'vanished moral attitudes' which underpinned them, as Coward explained:

> Women with pasts to-day receive far more enthusiastic social recognition than women without pasts. The narrow-mindedness, the moral righteousness and the over-rigid social codes have disappeared but with them has gone much that was graceful, well-behaved and endearing. It was in a mood of nostalgic regret at the decline of such conventions that I wrote *Easy Virtue*.[88]

The play draws most obviously on the plots of *The Second Mrs Tanqueray* and *Mrs Dane's Defence*, dealing as it does with the marriage between John Whittaker, the son of an upper-middle-class country family, and Larita, a rich divorcée, who is

[85] 'This Was a Man', Coward, *Collected Plays: Eight* (Methuen: London, 2000), I, 159–60. Performed in New York and Paris, but never licensed for performance in England.

[86] LC Corr. '*This Was a Man*' LR (1926), quoted in Nicholson, *Censorship of British Drama* Vol. 1, 260.

[87] Quoted in Sheridan Morley, Introduction, *Coward: Collected Plays: Eight*, xi.

[88] Noël Coward, Preface, *Play Parade*, vol. II (Heinemann: London, 1950), ix.

revealed to have been involved in a notorious scandal when one of her past lovers committed suicide. John's mother and sister treat Larita with disdain from the start, their prejudices only confirmed when details of the scandal are brought to light. Larita, however, calmly rejects their judgements: her past sexual experiences are entirely her own private business and no cause for moral outrage, as she comments with wry amusement,

> You seem to be floundering under the delusion that I'm a professional *cocotte*. You're quite, quite wrong—I've never had an affair with a man I wasn't fond of. The only time I sold myself was in the eyes of God to my first husband—my mother arranged it. I was really too young to know what I was doing. You approve of that sort of bargaining, don't you—it's within the law.[89]

Independently wealthy and entirely at home in a smart and cultured Continental set, Larita married John purely for love, not, as her in-laws assume, from any desire to reform or rehabilitate herself: 'On the contrary', Larita explains, 'it's been probably the most demoralising experience that's ever happened to me' (II, 328). The Whittaker women's disapproval is diagnosed, both in Coward's stage directions and in an exasperated diatribe from Larita, as religious hysteria and inhibitions resulting from a life-time of grinding down 'perfectly natural sex impulses'—a diagnosis clearly indebted to Freud. (II, 330) Larita rejects her in-laws' moral values, but she eventually agrees with them that her marriage has been a mistake; John is steeped in his society's narrow values and philistine pursuits, and is too spineless to defend Larita from his family's attacks. Theatrical history repeats itself, as Larita departs—not to shoot herself, but to rejoin her more broad-minded and cultured kind in Paris. For all its modernity *Easy Virtue* reproduced the structure and conclusion of its predecessors: the past resurfaces and the sexually experienced woman exits under a cloud.

The play's critical reception similarly marked both how much and how little the sexual landscape had changed. Critics were quick to note the resemblance between Larita and Paula Tanqueray and the play's debt to the drama of the previous century; as the *Saturday Review* concluded, it was 'a flamboyant, old-fashioned evening, in which the ghosts of the theatrical 'nineties were walking with their lurid pasts in their hands'.[90] While the charm of American actress Jane Cowl's performance as Larita was recognized, as were her character's intelligence and dignity, a number of reviewers reproved Coward for a naive and excessive respect for his heroine. St John Ervine, writing in the *Observer* spoke for many when he opined that 'a woman who has either been an expensive harlot or very nearly been one' is not the sort of woman one welcomes into one's family, and Coward is talking 'in a very jejune fashion when he asserts that people can divide their lives into compartments'.[91] J. T Grein, writing in the *Illustrated London News*, viewed the play entirely through

---

[89] Coward, *Easy Virtue*, in *Plays: One* (Methuen: London, 1979), II, 329–30. First English performance Duke of York's Theatre, 9 June 1926; previously played in New York, December 1925.

[90] Ivor Brown, 'Easy Virtuosity', *Saturday Review* (19 June 1926), 744. See also, *New York Times* (8 December 1925), 28; *Illustrated London News* (15 June 1926), 1112; *English Review* (July 1926), 127.

[91] *Observer* (13 June 1926), 13; see also *Nation and Athenaeum* (26 June 1926), 353.

the lens of the 1890s, describing Larita as 'a woman with a past who hopes to find sanctuary in marriage', and condemning the Whittakers for failing to give Larita a chance of redemption.[92] Paula's maxim that 'The future is only the past entered through another gate' clearly held true both morally and theatrically.

As *Easy Virtue* demonstrated, the deployment of inherited theatrical structures was potentially a double-edged weapon; challenging their values could also mean speaking on their terms. By framing his play as a *fin-de-siècle* sex-problem play, Coward invited judgement of his heroine's sexual past; though Larita might claim her sexual history was her own business and irrelevant to her marriage, the basic structure of the play implied otherwise. The problem play was all about debating and judging sexual morality, and even Coward's challenge to the Whittakers' traditional values risked reiterating and reinforcing their belief that individual sexual behaviour was a matter for social strictures and control. The essential problem, therefore, was how to devise new theatrical structures to suit the playwright's belief in sexuality as a matter of individual choice and self-determination. The answer came with Coward's development of a new theatrical minimalism, plays which were virtually plotless, which did not hinge on moral judgements but deployed wit, style, and frivolity to anaesthetize the audience's moral sense, making previously portentous issues a matter for laughter not debate.

In *Fallen Angels* (1923) Coward first deployed his comic minimalism as a means of destabilizing sexual judgments. The angels of the title are Jane and Julia, two married women who each receive a postcard announcing the imminent arrival of Maurice, a handsome Frenchman with whom they each had an affair before they married. Their husbands are away on a golfing weekend, and Jane and Julia ruefully agree that they will 'go down like ninepins' if Maurice is as attractive and glamorous as ever.[93] Both women hope to be chosen by Maurice 'to have violent and illicit love made to me and be frenziedly happy and supremely miserable', and dread being the one left 'shrouded for ever in unrewarded virtue' (I, 195). They have just determined to preserve their virtue by running away, when the doorbell rings: 'Anyhow, it will be good for our French!' declares Julia, as they plonk their bags down. The second act opens that evening—the earlier doorbell having merely been the plumber—and they are now glamorously dressed to greet Maurice, who fails to turn up, leaving them to get progressively drunker on the champagne and cocktails they had prepared for his entertainment. Jane having stormed out after a fierce argument, each woman believes the other to have run off with the handsome Frenchman, and informs the respective husband accordingly. Maurice's arrival brings affairs to a crisis, which he expertly defuses: picking up with astonishing speed on the situation, he announces that it was all an elaborate pretence to provoke the two husbands out of their complacent neglect of their wives. The husbands are reassured, until they hear Maurice, who has leased the apartment above, serenading Jane and Julia with his signature love-song. The curtain falls on the husbands' stricken faces.

[92] *Illustrated London News* (26 June 1926), 1120.
[93] Coward, *Fallen Angels*, in *Plays: One*, I, 188. First performed Globe Theatre, 21 April 1925.

Coward's minimalist comedy plays nonchalantly with the causal plot structure and weighty moral debate which had characterized dramatic treatments of female adultery for over a century. Jane and Julia are not passive victims of a predatory male, but sensual epicures, anticipating the many delights of Maurice and well aware that passion is 'almost his profession':

JULIA: He's sure to have got fat, or bald, or something.
JANE: No, he'll be the same as ever; he wouldn't come at all if he weren't—he's much too conceited.
JULIA: Not conceited, a little vain perhaps, naturally.
JANE: With those eyes one can't blame him.
JULIA: And those hands—
JANE: And teeth—
JULIA: And legs! Oh, Jane!
JANE: Oh, Julia!

(I, 189; II, 205)

The women's language acknowledges and carelessly skips over notions of virtue, purity, and fidelity, weighing them lightly in the balance compared to the intensely present joys of physical passion: 'Our love for our husbands has been on an entirely different plane all along—much nicer and worthier and everything, but not half so soul-shattering' (I, 189). Jane and Julia's self-knowing and self-delighting acknowledgement of 'the unworthy beastly thing' in both of them and their light-footed dance through social and moral values are disorienting, putting adultery and social etiquette on the same moral plane:

JULIA: Let's do your plan, and fly.
JANE: Together?
JULIA: (*impatiently*) Yes, oh yes, together.
JANE: He'll think it so rude.
JULIA: Jane, don't be so weak.
JANE: Frenchmen are so particular about that sort of thing.
JULIA: It can't be helped, one can carry good manners too far.
JANE: We ought to be hospitable.
JULIA: Well, as we can neither of us be hospitable without giving him the run of the house, we'd better leave him to freeze on the doorstep!

(I, 196)

The offhand language of their exchanges is both euphemism and honest confession, hovering between flippancy and sexual directness:

JANE: We stand or fall together.
JULIA: I don't mind standing together, but I won't fall together, it would be most embarrassing.

(I, 193)

After two acts of such poised banter, their husbands' outraged talk of depravity, shame, and humility sounds pompous, flat-footed, and laughably hypocritical. Jane greets her husband's indignation at her premarital affair by calmly pointing out that 'We couldn't be faithful to you before we met you, could we?'—casually disarming a century's worth of dramatic agonizing (III, 237).

As critic Ivor Brown noted in the *Saturday Review*, Coward's 'clipped, staccato, but explicit dialogue is an excellent instrument of his intentions', offering the knowingness of the music hall but with a directness alien to its winks, nods, and leers.[94] It was the play's 'light and unreal and humorous' atmosphere that convinced Lord Cromer it was safe to grant it a licence, its flippant airiness avoiding the dangerous seriousness and realism of 'some of those horrible sex problem plays', among which he numbered *The Vortex*.[95] The play's humour won it large and appreciative audiences, while many critics were disconcerted by its transgressive combination of traditionally serious situation, brilliant dialogue, music-hall comedians' back-chat, and undisguised flippancy.[96] Where dramatic critics shrugged their shoulders at the impossibility of reading a moral into Coward's witty confection, the Public Morality Council berated the Lord Chamberlain for licensing 'a revolting sex-play' which 'shows vice triumphant, virtue non-existent' and therefore 'must have a demoralising tendency upon the minds particularly of young people who witness it'.[97] Only Ivor Brown managed rather tortuously to read a moral into Coward's play, seeing Jane and Julia as 'marvels of unhappiness': he judged them

> Bad lots, if you will, but also bored, 'nervy', irritable, listless lots. If their *malaise* be the wages of vice, it seems that lechery is a stiff bargainer. Compared with these restless, agonizing creatures in their comfortable homes any derelict recruit of the Salvation Army is living in a paradise of bliss.[98]

Where other critics saw only an abruptly inconsequential end to the play, Brown heard the purgatorial groans of Jane and Julia's souls, not quite drowned out by Maurice's serenade.

Ivor Brown's rather perverse diagnosis of Jane and Julia's inner agonies suggested an enduring belief in the *fin-de-siècle* prescription that the wages of women's sexual sin must be death—in this case if not a literal one, then at least a spiritual one. The critic Horace Shipp was prompted by *Fallen Angels* to hark back explicitly to the 1890s. In an article entitled 'Cocktails and Courtesans', Shipp described current theatrical fashions as the crest of a wave which began with works such as *The Woman Who Did*, *Tess of the d'Urbevilles*, *The Second Mrs Tanqueray*, and *Mrs Warren's Profession*, and complained that the movement had carried the London stage

---

[94] 'Much Ado about Noel', *Saturday Review* (9 May 1925), 486.
[95] Cromer letter, in LC Corr, *Fallen Angels* 1925/6100.
[96] See e.g. *Times* (22 April 1925), 12; *Daily Telegraph* (22 April 1925), 15; *Manchester Guardian* (23 April 1925), 12.
[97] Letter from Public Morality Council (May 1925) LC Corr, *Fallen Angels* 1925/6100.
[98] 'Much Ado about Noel', *Saturday Review* (9 May 1925), 487.

to the point where it 'threatens to become exclusively populated by ladies with Pasts or in the process of manufacturing them; every heroine, wed or unwed, is given to lovers and cocktails, and a cynicism which echoes the Reformation is rapidly becoming the keynote of British drama'.[99] Shipp declared himself merely wearied *ad nauseam* with this theme, unwilling to condemn Coward's plays beyond noting the 'nasty taste' they left behind. The insouciance of Coward's and Maugham's treatment of *fin-de-siècle* themes and their challenge to orthodox sexual values did, however, drive other commentators into a moral frenzy reminiscent of the worst of Victorian hysteria. In the summer of 1925, the Reverend J. Stuart Holden preached a much-publicized sermon on the corruption of the drama which extraordinarily revivified a language similar to that provoked by the first English performance of Ibsen's *Ghosts* back in 1891. Sounding like Clement Scott at his most incandescent, Holden pronounced that

> If these plays bear any relation to English life today we are hastening toward some inevitable catastrophe, for they are dramas of the open drain.
> ...We should not think of tolerating an open sewer in our city, belching out its deadly bacteria of typhoid and typhus.
> Why should they be permitted to fasten on the rising generation of our young men and women with all the clever sententiousness of smart worldly wisdom the moral standards of the jungle and the gutter.
> If these dramatists are right: if there is any considerable section of society which actually lives as these stridently vulgar and unclean-minded people on the stage do, pursuing sexual satisfaction without regard to the laws of God or the rights of men, then society is going to have a rude awakening.[100]

Back in 1891 Clement Scott and his peers confidently spoke out for the moral majority against what was viewed as a dangerous coterie of extremists, but only a few years later they found themselves retrospectively embarrassed by their use of such inflated rhetoric as the panic over the Ibsen 'revolution' receded. But while Ibsen's plays were eventually viewed as acceptable literary works rather than manifestos for social and sexual degeneration, they never displaced traditionalists like Pinero and Grundy in mainstream theatrical tastes. By the 1920s moralists like Holden and the London Council for Public Morals sounded a different note of urgency. The plays of Maugham and Coward dominated the West End, drawing huge and appreciative audiences and setting theatrical fashions. Social and religious conservatives felt their world under threat, and their protests sought to wake audiences out of laughter and back into moral seriousness.

Having received a 'strange pathological avalanche' of insulting letters from around the country in response to *Fallen Angels*, all of them 'crammed with abuse and frequently embellished with pornographic drawings', Coward was well aware

---

[99] 'Cocktails and Courtesans', *English Review* (June 1925), 816. Shipp presumably meant the Restoration rather than the Reformation.

[100] LCO Theatre files, not catalogued (June 1925), quoted in Nicholson, *Censorship of British Drama*, 159–60.

of the viciousness underlying such moral panic. The playwright's response was simply to intensify his assault on theatrical and sexual orthodoxy, perfecting his use of insouciance, wit, and humour as a means of disabling and eroding moral norms. In *Private Lives* (1930) Coward combined the plotless frivolity of *Fallen Angels* and the sardonic humour of '*This Was a Man*' to produce a minimalist drama, anaesthetizing moral seriousness in laughter and airily dissolving the structures and debates of over a century of theatrical tradition.

The plot of *Private Lives* goes nowhere. Elyot and Amanda realize they still love each other, despite having divorced and being on honeymoon with their new spouses, Sibyl and Victor respectively. They run away together, make love, quarrel, make up, and then escape from Sibyl and Victor all over again. The play does not pretend to closure, and it deliberately and explicitly rejects moral seriousness. Marriage is simply an irrelevance, an arbitrary set of rules—or indeed sets of rules, as Elyot points out:

AMANDA: Do you realise we're living in sin?

ELYOT: Not according to the Catholics, Catholics don't recognise divorce. We're married as much as ever we were.

AMANDA: Yes, dear, but we're not Catholics.

ELYOT: Never mind, it's nice to think they'd sort of back us up. We were married in the eyes of heaven, and we still are.

AMANDA: We may be alright in the eyes of Heaven, but we look like being in a hell of a mess socially.[101]

Elyot and Amanda do not challenge orthodox morality, they simply disregard it. They pay notice to social etiquette but with a self-performing archness which mocks the very rituals they enact. Like Wilde's dandies, they empty moral strictures of meaning with their knowing performance. Where Sibyl and Victor subscribe unquestioningly to gender roles and reach automatically for terms of moral opprobrium, Elyot and Amanda dance lightly past them with insouciance. The unrestrained viciousness of Elyot and Amanda's physical fight shocks their spouses, but as Sibyl and Victor lose their tempers at the end of the play, theirs is revealed as the uglier anger and violence, full of self-righteousness, lacking in self-awareness and ultimately manipulative. As Amanda observes thoughtfully as she rejects Victor's approving description of her as 'normal', 'I think very few people are completely normal really, deep down in their private lives' (I, 16). She and Elyot have no interest in fitting themselves or others to a template, and Sibyl and Victor's eagerness to do so is driven by individual agendas as ruthless as their spouses' sparring techniques.

Elyot and Amanda are supreme stylists, camp performers who self-consciously critique their own antics, simultaneously actors and audience. When Elyot jealously bristles at how many affairs Amanda had after their divorce, and tries to

---

[101] Coward, *Private Lives*, in *Plays: Two* (Methuen: London, 1982), II, 42–3. First performed Phoenix Theatre, London, 24 September 1930.

assert a sexual double standard, she easily deflates him: 'Excuse me a moment while I get a caraway biscuit and change my crinoline' (II, 45). As played by Gertrude Lawrence, Amanda was drenched in chic sexuality; so Cecil Beaton commented:

> The long, loose-fitting dresses she wore suggested more than an indication of the vital, well-shaped figure beneath them; she could look remarkably provocative in a dress that covered her body almost completely. She smoked cigarettes with a nuance that implied having just come out of bed and wanting to get back into it.[102]

Coward wrote the part specifically for Lawrence, and their second act is luxuriously post- and pre-coital, with Amanda both sensual and self-contained in her refusal to take a passive role in their love-making; she enrages Elyot by preferring not to have sex on a full stomach, and then mockingly makes up in front of him, declaring ironically that 'The woman's job is to allure the man' (II, 60). They can infuriate each other, but they are ultimately playing the same game, disrupting others' rules and certainties to stake out their own freedom.

Frivolity is both the play's method and its philosophy. As Elyot explains:

ELYOT (*seriously*):   You mustn't be serious, my dear, it's just what they want.
AMANDA: Who's they?
ELYOT: All the futile moralists who try to make life unbearable. Laugh at them. Be flippant. Laugh at everything, all their sacred shibboleths. Flippancy brings out the acid in their damned sweetness and light.

(II, 56)

Admitting defeat at the impossibility of drawing a serious moral or message from the play, critics conceded a perfect marriage of content and form. As Ivor Brown wrote, 'Mr Coward has the courage of his cunning. He concedes nothing to the old rules of play-making, of character, of construction. He trusts to his wits and wins.'[103] Coward's drama was a 'soufflé', its lightness the result of intense labour, its structure apparently a 'ramshackle shed' compared to the 'carefully planned mansion' of a Pinero play, but its resulting effect was to set a new fashion which ensured that 'The well-made play was never less wanted than at present.'[104] As critics recognized, *Private Lives* perfectly married subject matter and form in a minimalist drama whose mode and philosophy were deliberately superficial and flippant, not as a means of avoiding central issues of sexual judgement but as the ultimate rebuttal of the values of the well-made play and its history. Sexuality was not a matter for judgement, debate, or legislation: the wit and airy flimsiness of *Private Lives* renders any such attempt pompous and self-defeating. As the critic Horace Shipp observed,

---

[102] Cecil Beaton, *The Glass of Fashion* (Cassell: London, 1954), 153–4, quoted in Sean O'Connor, *Straight Acting: Popular Gay Drama from Wilde to Rattigan* (Cassell: London, 1998), 115.
[103] *Observer* (28 September 1930), 15.
[104] Ivor Brown, 'The Spirit of the Age in Drama', *Fortnightly Review* (October 1930), 596.

Private Lives is fundamentally witty. Cynical, negative, everything which the moralist will urge against the scintillation of the bright and young, it belongs to our time. So much is this true that, when one has said all the obvious things about its lightness and utter unreality there remains in it a residue of serious defence of that very attitude of mind. Flippancy has found its apologist. Laughter is exalted to a weapon against the cruelty of men and fate. Once at least the trifle drops its mask and reveals the fact of truth as Noel Coward and his kind see it.[105]

In the same year Laurence Housman argued that the ultimate taboo on stage was to 'advocate that men and women shall be allowed to live their own sex life in their own way'.[106] *Private Lives* carved out a theatrical space for Elyot and Amanda to do just that.

---

[105] Horace Shipp, 'Mirth and Magic', *English Review* (November 1930), 650–1.
[106] Laurence Housman, 'Sex and the Censorship', *World League for Sexual Reform: Proceedings of the Third Congress*, ed. Norman Haine (Kegan Paul, Trench, Trubener & Co; London, 1930), quoted in Nicholson, *Censorship of British Drama*, 210.

Afterwords

In 1940 the Earl of Clarendon, then Lord Chamberlain, fending off yet another assault from the Public Morality Council, insisted on the theatre's right and need to reflect the world around it: 'if the Theatre is to remain a living art it must be allowed to draw its inspiration from contemporary life outside. Standards change from decade to decade, and this fact must inevitably be reflected on the stage.'[1] The Public Morality Council's reply asserted in contrast the duty of the stage to improve rather than reflect modern morals. Dismissing any standards but its own, the Council confidently asserted that 'opinions that are universally recognised as evil, such as the upholding of unrestrained sexual intercourse, cannot be expressed, however decorously, without much harmful effect on many individuals and on the good life of the country.'[2]

William Archer, George Bernard Shaw, and Henry Arthur Jones would have been pleasantly surprised to hear the Lord Chamberlain himself voicing their views some forty years after their impassioned campaigns for the drama's right to reflect contemporary life and take a role in social and moral debates. They would undoubtedly have been even more taken aback to hear Examiner of Plays Henry Game declare in 1942 that 'Sex is one of the great natural facts of life and not one which we could, or should, try to suppress in the Theatre', though Game did insist on the censorship's duty to prevent sex being used in a 'blatant manner, merely for the commercial purpose of filling the producer's pocket'.[3] Changing standards in this case mean that the Lord Chamberlain's Office was no longer concerned with measuring the length of ballet girls' skirts, as in Victorian days, but rather with the adequate size of nipple tassels and G-strings, and the particular angle from which nudes would be viewed; moreover, to the censor's credit, the concern in these cases was not only the potentially disturbing arousal of audiences but the pressures placed on young female performers.[4] Throughout the centuries, the Lord Chamberlain's Office consistently saw its role as to reflect and enforce the standards of respectable orthodoxy. It was therefore significant that in 1933 the Office not only

---

[1] 'Minutes of the Proceedings of the Lord Chamberlain's Stage Conference held at St James's Palace on Tuesday, 16th April, 1940', quoted in Steve Nicholson, *The Censorship of British Drama, 1900–1968*, vol. 2: *1933–52* (University of Exeter Press: Exeter, 2005), 201.

[2] Ibid.

[3] LC Corr: 1942/4597: *Revuedeville No. 159*, quoted in ibid, 220.

[4] For details of Victorian ballet dancers' costumes and debates surrounding them, see Tracy C. Davis, *Actresses as Working Women: Their Social Identity in Victorian Culture* (Routledge: London, 1991).

licensed *The Greeks Had a Word for It*, described in G. S. Street's reader's report as concerned with 'the quarrels and intrigues of vulgar and illiterate harlots and their men', but that the Office subsequently defended that decision on the grounds that the play was 'no more shocking or subversive of morals than any other play which shows the wages of sin to be something much more like expensive clothes and a good time than Death'.[5] The punitive morality which had so long insisted that theatrical depictions of non-marital female desire must be accompanied by shame, self-destruction, decay, and death had finally lost its hold not only on the stage but on the conservative institution of stage censorship.

Yet the plots and tropes examined in this book did not disappear, but continued to be adapted, revised, and reinvented. Indeed, the intertheatrical dialogue continues to the present day, as writers reference, engage with or unknowingly recreate the theatrical structures and types from the nineteenth century. Some playwrights deliberately drew on long familiar theatrical traditions. J. B. Priestley's *An Inspector Calls* (1946), for example, combines the various plots of the seduced and abandoned maiden, the underpaid and desperate worker forced to turn to prostitution, the unmarried pregnant woman desperate for help, and the despairing suicide. The woman who passes through these stages before dying in agony is never seen— indeed, may never have existed—instead the focus is on the family whose thoughtless exploitation, cruelty, condemnation, and neglect of those at their economic and social mercy is revealed by the mysterious Inspector Goole. Set in an upper-middle-class drawing room in 1912, Priestley deliberately references the drama of his Victorian and Edwardian predecessors in order to relocate the blame with a financially and sexually exploitative society. Others' appropriation of old Victorian plots was less conscious or deliberate, but rather testament to the solutions they offered to enduring problems of representation and implication. Unintentional bigamy had served as a vehicle for the sympathetic portrayal of female adultery through several decades of the nineteenth century. In 1944 a wife's emotional ambivalence over her husband's safe return from war was a similarly difficult topic with which to enlist audience sympathies. In Daphne du Maurier's *The Years Between* (1944), a war widow has been elected to parliament to take up her dead husband's seat, and is about to embark on a happy second marriage, when her husband returns from secret undercover work to reclaim his place at the head and the centre of the household. Du Maurier's strategy was successful; the play opened in Manchester in November 1944, then transferred to Wyndham's Theatre, London, where it ran for 617 performances.

The enduring afterlife of the plot structures and tropes of the Victorian and Edwardian sex-problem play includes a strong presence in the film industry. The theatre provided a natural and obvious source for early cinema, resulting in film versions of a whole host of sex-problem plays, including Wilde's *Lady Windermere's*

---

[5] LC Corr: 1933: 12340: *The Greeks Had a Word for It*, quoted in Nicholson, *Censorship of British Drama*, vol. 2, 63.

Fan (1916 and 1925), Jones's *The Dancing Girl* (1915), *The Masqueraders* (1915), and *Mrs Dane's Defence* (1918), the Melville brothers' *The Girl Who Took the Wrong Turning* (1915), *The Shop Soiled Girl* (1915), and *A World of Sin* (1915), and Pinero's *The Second Mrs Tanqueray* (1914) and *Iris* (1915). 'Fallen woman' novels, which had already provided a rich source for dramatic adaptation, also proved similarly lucrative for the film industry; there were, for example, a remarkable ten film adaptations of *East Lynne* produced between 1902 and 1915.[6] Film often proved a more conservative medium than the stage, film versions not only being necessarily shorter than the original stage plays, but also bowdlerized and sanitized. In Fred Paul's 1916 silent film of *Lady Windermere's Fan*, for example, Mrs Erlynne displays all the conventional shame and maternal longings that Wilde's original stylishly eschews. Similarly, Maurice Elvey's technically innovative 1927 film of *Hindle Wakes* crucially includes a yearning but unseen gesture from Fanny towards Alan, signalling her genuine love for him, so that her rejection of their proposed marriage becomes a conventional self-sacrifice rather than the scornful self-sufficiency of the original. Such influences stretch from early cinema right through to the twenty-first century. Dumas's *La Dame aux Camélias* had spawned no fewer than six film versions by 1915, and its screen legacy includes the famous 1936 film *Camille*, starring Greta Garbo, and Baz Luhrmann's *Moulin Rouge!* (2001), an exuberant extravaganza that attempts to excise the punitive morality while retaining the pathos of Dumas's mythic tale. Marguerite Gautier remains the supreme 'tart with a heart' to whom her successors pay homage; in *Pretty Woman* (1996), Julia Roberts's prostitute Vivian is taken to *La Traviata* (its off-screen identity revealed only by a few bars of the overture), and her tearful and ecstatic response bears witness to her sensitivity—just as Mrs Patrick Campbell's virtuoso piano playing as Paula Tanqueray had suggested the kept woman's emotional depth over a century earlier.

Consonances and resonances between film genres and their dramatic forebears proliferate—whether deliberate or coincidental. The genre of the Hollywood screwball romances of bigamy and remarriage, including such films as *My Favourite Wife* (1940) and *The Awful Truth* (1937), is clearly allied to earlier dramatic deployments of unintentional bigamy; as Katharina Glitre observes in *Hollywood Romantic Comedy* (2006), the bigamy plot enabled women to pursue their men actively, serving as an acceptable vehicle for female desire in a cinematic era controlled by the conservative strictures of the Hays Code.[7] Shifts in sexual morality and circumstances could rehabilitate old plots or spawn remarkably similar dramatic structures; just as the rhetoric surrounding the Contagious Diseases Acts in the 1870s and 1880s helped create an audience for sensational melodramas of discarded mistresses persecuting errant but repentant husbands and their inno-

---

[6] For further details see Denis Gifford, *Books and Plays in Films, 1896–1915: Literary, Theatrical and Artistic Sources of the First Twenty Years of Motion Pictures* (Mansell: London, 1991) and Alvin H. Marill, *More Theatre: Stage to Screen to Television*, 3 vols (Scarecrow Press: London, 1993, 2008).

[7] Katharina Glitre, *Hollywood Romantic Comedy: States of the Union, 1934–1965* (Manchester University Press: Manchester, 2006), ch. 2. See also, Stanley Cavell, *Pursuits of Happiness: The Hollywood Comedy of Remarriage* (Harvard University Press: Cambridge, MA, 1981).

cently virtuous families, so the fears surrounding the spreading epidemic of AIDS in the 1980s threw up a modern mirror image in *Fatal Attraction* (1987), sexual infection once again being embodied as the hysterically vengeful woman.

While off-shoots, imitations, reincarnations, and adaptations of 'fallen woman' plays are to be found throughout twentieth- and twenty-first-century theatre and film, the clearest legacy of the genre is to be found in dramatic treatments of homosexuality. The essential formula and driving force behind the 'fallen woman' play was the identification and punishment of errant female sexuality: in its starkest form the wages of sin were death. The tears of abandoned maidens, the shame of repentant courtesans, and the ostracizing of women with a past all served to enforce the norm of monogamous marriage. Hardly surprising then, that so many dramatists whose works led the way in challenging and destabilizing the conventions of the genre were writers whose own sexuality placed them in conflict with this socially enforced heterosexual norm. Wilde, Coward, and to a lesser extent Maugham, played a vital role in rendering outmoded the punitive structures of the sex-problem play. The challenge to orthodox sexual morality contained in plays such as *Lady Windermere's Fan*, *A Woman of No Importance*, *Easy Virtue*, *Fallen Angels*, *The Constant Wife*, and *The Circle* can be read as encompassing, by implication, the outlawed homosexual desires of their authors. So Wilde commented of *A Woman of No Importance*'s anatomizing of the damage caused by oppressive sexual morality, 'It is indeed a burning shame that there should be one law for men and another law for women. I think that there should be no law for anybody.'[8] As Sean O'Connor writes in *Straight Acting: Popular Gay Drama from Wilde to Rattigan* (1998), his study of such theatrical subtexts and implications, in a culture of repression and concealment there evolved 'a stage language of discretion, an ability to discuss and explore that which is unspeakable'.[9] Noël Coward's *Design for Living*, which was first performed in New York in 1933 and had to wait until 1939 for a licence for performance on the London stage, charted the complicated three-way relationship of Otto, Leo, and Gilda: Gilda lives with Otto, sleeps with Leo, leaves Otto for Leo, sleeps with Otto, marries Ernest, then leaves Ernest for Leo and Otto. The play deploys all the destabilizing flippancy, theatrical self-consciousness, mockery of gender norms, and lightning switches of verbal register, which Coward had developed in *Fallen Angels* and *Private Lives*, to anaesthetize moral judgements of a trio who finally embrace a *ménage à trois* as the only possible solution to their entwined lives and desires. Whether the triangle is sexually three-sided is left to the audience to determine or elide. As Leo comments to Gilda: 'I love you. You love me. You love Otto. I love Otto. Otto loves you. Otto loves me.'[10] The particular nature of the 'love' between Otto and Leo is unspecified, but the play's symmetry again hints at

---

[8] Wilde quoted in Hesketh Pearson, *The Life of Oscar Wilde* (Methuen: London, 1946), 251.

[9] Sean O'Connor, *Straight Acting: Popular Gay Drama from Wilde to Rattigan* (Cassell: London, 1998), 11.

[10] Noël Coward, *Design for Living* in Coward, *Plays: Three* (Methuen: London, 1994), I, 21.

its parallel to that between the two men and Gilda; each of the first two acts open with the post-coital pairings of Gilda and Leo, then Gilda and Otto, the last act opens with Otto and Leo emerging together in pyjamas from the bedroom.[11]

If the censors' office no longer saw extramarital female sexuality as necessarily to be framed by punishment and shame, the punitive plot structures which had so long been deployed to condemn illicit female sexuality could easily be refurbished to pass judgement on other forms of transgressive desire. *The Green Bay Tree* (1933) by Mordaunt Shairp is generally recognized as one of the first plays to deal with the threat and punishment of same-sex desire, and its similarity to classic fallen woman plays such as Dumas's *La Femme de Claude* and Pinero's *Iris* is striking. The wicked power which spreads its influence like the titular 'green bay tree' is Mr Dulcimer, a rich man who has adopted a young Welsh singer, having bought him for £500 from his drunken father, Owen, and raised him in the lap of luxury. When Julien announces that he intends to marry Leonora, a beautiful and businesslike veterinary surgeon, Dulcie (as Julien calls him) dismays his adopted son by announcing that his allowance will cease with his wedding: Julien will have to earn his own living if he proposes to abandon his post by Dulcie's side. Repelled by the sparse living conditions of his now sober but not wealthy birth-father and by the rigours of attempting to gain professional qualifications, Julien is easily tempted back to the deluxe idleness that Dulcie's protection offers. Belatedly attempting to salvage his son for a healthily productive and reproductive life, Owen shoots Dulcie. But too late; Julien will not give up Dulcie's legacy in order to marry Leonora, and the curtain falls on the young man donning gloves to arrange flowers, in a mirror image of his guardian at the play's opening. Shairp's play follows Dumas *fils*'s exhortation 'Tue-la!' [Kill her!], a call to exterminate the adulterous woman. But, though the sexually corrupting individual has been duly murdered, his influence endures. A final stage direction describes the light glinting off Dulcie's finely made and triumphantly smiling death-mask.

Like so many seduced maidens, from Clari, the frail 'Maid of Milan', onwards, Julien is brought to ruin by his vanity, frivolity, and idleness; hard work, social responsibility, family duty, and marriage are juxtaposed with luxury, indolence, and individualism, as they were from the earliest melodramas through to the problem plays of the *fin de siècle*. Julien's test and his failure precisely parallel those of Pinero's Iris, who cannot overcome her taste for luxury and ease in order to prove worthy of the poor but hardworking man she loves, and so is ensnared into becoming the kept mistress of a rich man, finally rejected and thrown out onto the streets when she proves faithful to neither of them.[12] Homosexuality is figured

---

[11] For further analysis see Sos Eltis, 'Bringing out the Acid: Noël Coward, Harold Pinter, Ivy Compton-Burnett and the Uses of Camp', *Modern Drama*, 51.2 (2008), 211–33. For a contrary reading of the sexual dynamics of the lovers as allowed to be charming in their heterosexuality, while Ernest is a humourless 'queen', see Alan Sinfield, 'Private Lives/Public Theater: Noel Coward and the Politics of Homosexual Representation', *Representations*, 36 (1991), 58.

[12] A. W. Pinero, *Iris*. First performed Garrick Theatre, London, 21 September 1901.

in the same terms as female sexual weakness, and the predicted endpoint is the same: as Leonora exclaims in fear of her fiancé's epicurean tastes, 'I hope I shan't meet you one day in Piccadilly with a painted face, just because you must have linen sheets!'[13] Such comments and the play's reproduction of the fallen woman play's structure and tropes helped to signal its coded concern with sexual transgression; in an era when any theatrical treatment of so-called 'sexual deviancy' lay under an outright ban, only indirection and coded references could sneak past the censor. The play was licensed specifically because G. S. Street, a reader for the Lord Chamberlain's Office, found no trace of homosexuality in the play, and, when later accused of naivety, Street insisted that the critics who found such meanings in the play as performed 'were, I think, influenced by a desire to appear knowing or by the unfortunate fact that homosexuality is in the air very much at present'.[14] Like forbidden female desire in the nineteenth century, same-sex desire could exist only as an implication, or just as a blank, a logical disconnection which required the audience to insert the missing pieces of the puzzle. So Jed Harris, director of the Broadway production in 1933, cut Julien's final flower arranging and the reference to him selling his wares in Piccadilly, and instructed his cast:

As you know, in London the entire production was dominated by homosexuality. There was even swishing on stage. I'll have none of that. [...] When the audience watches it here, I want them to say to themselves, 'It's homosexual. Nothing is said about it, but it's there. It must be there. That's the only explanation for these characters and their story.' So that's what I want. I want to create something without stating it.[15]

Where same-sex love was too scandalous to contemplate even by implication and deduction, a play's structure might still be retained by replacing it with the old fallback of female promiscuity; in 1950 Peter Cotes sought a performance licence for Lillian Hellman's *The Children's Hour*, a play which had been repeatedly refused a licence since 1934 despite the fact that the character accused of lesbianism has not only never acted on the desire she belatedly realizes she has long felt, but also kills herself in shame and self-disgust. Norman Gwatkin, Assistant Comptroller to the Lord Chamberlain, advised Cotes that, 'I am afraid the only alteration you could make in this play would be to substitute for the lesbianism some more normal vice—such as dope or men.'[16]

As with illicit heterosexual female desire, alternative theatrical structures had to be invented to break the grip of the sex-problem play as the dominant mode for

[13] Mordaunt Shairp, *The Green Bay Tree*, in *Sixteen Famous British Plays*, compiled by Bennett A. Cerf and Van H. Cartmell (The Modern Library, Random House: New York, 1942), III, i, 856. First performed St Martin's, London, 25 January 1933.

[14] Quoted in Nicholas De Jongh, *Politics, Prudery and Perversions: The Censoring of the English Stage 1901–1968* (Methuen: London, 2000), 102.

[15] Martin Gottfried, *Jed Harris: The Curse of Genius* (Little Brown: Boston, MA, 1984), 142, quoted in John M. Clum, *Still Acting Gay: Male Homosexuality in Modern Drama* (St Martin's: New York, 2000), 83.

[16] LC Corr: 1964/4458: *The Children's Hour*, quoted in Nicholson, *Censorship of British Drama*, vol. 2, 346.

depicting and condemning same-sex love. So, in Mart Crowley's *The Boys in the Band* (1968), described by Clive Barnes in the *New York Times* as being revolutionarily 'a play that takes the homosexual milieu and the homosexual way of life totally for granted and uses this as a valid basis of human experience', Michael reproves his hypochondriac friend: 'It's not always like it happens in plays, not all faggots bump themselves off at the end of the story.'[17] But the ravages of AIDS and its catastrophic impact on the gay community were to return death to the final act of the play. Barely two decades after the ban on theatrical depictions of same-sex love was lifted, the theatre was called upon to negotiate the inevitable pitfalls of a theatrical heritage which located death as the poetically just, predestined, or pathetic end of those who transgress against orthodox sexual morality. AIDS reincarnated the 'woman with a past', its threat undermining the hard-won claim to self-determination and self-definition; as Susan Sontag observed,

> The fear of AIDS imposes on an act whose ideal is an experience of pure presentness (and a creation of the future) a relation to the past to be ignored at one's peril. Sex no longer withdraws its partners, if only for a moment, from the social. It cannot be considered just a coupling: it is a chain, a chain of transmission, from the past.[18]

As John Clum has observed, 'In mainstream popular drama, particularly television drama, the gay Person With AIDS is heir to the fate of the nineteenth-century "fallen woman", doomed to the punishment of fatal disease', and Marguerite Gautier is 'the ancestor of the gay character with AIDS'.[19] The danger is that, as with the nineteenth-century prostitute, those infected with the disease become conflated with the disease itself, not victims of an illness but themselves embodiments of disease and bodily corruption. Marguerite's pathetic death did not challenge her society's sexual codes but validated them, her sacrifice an acknowledgement of their justice and her own unworthiness. The tears which greeted her death could thus mourn her loss and accept its rightness, as she found her apotheosis in extinction. This formulation haunts and complicates theatrical depictions of AIDS-related deaths; thus even in Larry Kramer's *The Normal Heart* (1985), a play inspired and driven by burning anger at the government's inaction in the face of innumerable fatalities, Felix's death-bed marriage to Ned and his final expiration produces, as Clum sardonically comments, 'a death scene that Dumas or Giuseppe Verdi would have admired'.[20] The emotional impact of Felix's death risks implying an operatic completeness, an orgasmic song of life and death, whose artistic rightness undermines the framing anger at the ignorance, indifference, prejudice, and sheer arbitrary accident which allowed it to happen. It is no coincidence that in Terence McNally's *The Lisbon Traviata* (1985) it is Callas's performance as the ex-

---

[17]   Mart Crowley, *The Boys in the Band* (1968), in Ben Hodges (ed.), *Out Plays: Landmark Gay and Lesbian Plays of the Twentieth Century* (Alyson Books: New York, 2008), II, 55.
[18]   Susan Sontag, *AIDS and its Metaphors* (Straus & Giroux: New York, 1989), 72–3, quoted in Clum, *Still Acting Gay*, 41.
[19]   Clum, *Still Acting Gay*, 41, 42.
[20]   Ibid, 63.

piring courtesan that obsesses the opera-loving Stephen, his absorption in melancholic and ecstatic arias replacing the real physical joys of sex, companionship, and human interaction; the aestheticizing of death, McNally's play implies, is no replacement for the urgent and messy business of living.

The legacy of Marguerite Gautier and her sisters in sin is one which continues to haunt the theatre—and, indeed, the wider cultural landscape. There is no escaping it, but playwrights have employed a plethora of different methods in order to disable, challenge, and subvert its conventions and their underlying assumptions. Theatrical history may repeat itself, but playing it the second time as camp offers one means of denaturalizing and disarming its moral imperatives. So in his *Camille* (1973), for example, the cross-dressed actor Charles Ludlam played Marguerite Gautier in a copy of Greta Garbo's delicately lace-fringed costumes, complete with gloves, fan, and low-cut bodice displaying his abundant chest hair. Paying homage to the whole sequence of actresses who had embodied Marguerite Gautier, from Mme Doche through Bernhardt and Duse to Garbo, Ludlam's version of Dumas's drama lovingly preserved the pathos of the play, while disabling it of any claim to verisimilitude; pathos and humour intertwine in a script which preserves the original's most famous lines alongside knowing quips and asides. In the last act for example, Nanine informs a shivering Marguerite that there are no more faggots in the house; 'No faggots in the house?' exclaims Marguerite plaintively, looking out at the audience.[21] The courtesan's death remained tearfully touching but its emotional indulgence was no acknowledgement of moral or social truths. Theatrically knowing and self-consciously performative, camp simultaneously revels in and lovingly mocks the rituals of erotic martyrdom; it is no accident that Sarah Bernhardt lives on as a camp icon. Absurdity, balanced disturbingly between comedy and tragedy, offers another means of subverting the past's hold on the present: in Edward Albee's *The Goat; or, Who is Sylvia?(Notes toward a definition of tragedy)* (2002) the other woman is a goat, who duly falls to the theatrical imperative of 'Tue la!' when the humiliated and furious wife kills her rival. Verbatim drama has broken with centuries of tradition by building plays from the words of prostitutes themselves, from Alecky Blythe's *The Girlfriend Experience* (2008) to Liverpool Everyman Theatre's *Unprotected* (2006).[22] Constructed from interviews with sex workers, their families and clients, city councillors, drugs and outreach workers, and politicians, *Unprotected* gives urgent voice to those working on the street in the aftermath of the horrific murder of two Liverpool prostitutes—their death presented not as the inevitable conclusion in an inherently dangerous profession, but

---

[21] Charles Ludlam, *Camille (A Tearjerker): A Travesty*, in *The Mystery of Irma Vep and other plays* (Theatre Communications Group: New York, 2001), III, 219. First performed 1973. For further details see Laurence Senelick, *The Changing Room: Sex, Drag and Theatre* (Routledge: London, 2000), and Rick Roemer, *Charles Ludlam and the Ridiculous Theatrical Company* (McFarland & Co.: Jefferson, NC, 1998).

[22] *Unprotected*, by Esther Wilson, John Fay, Tony Green and Lizzie Nunnery. My thanks to director Nina Raine for access to the original script. First performed Liverpool Everyman, March 2006.

as the result of social attitudes, legislation, and policing which exacerbate sex workers' vulnerability to violence and abuse.

Theatrical history cannot be ignored, but the future is not the past again, entered by another gate. The past does not dictate the present, but offers a trove of plots, tropes, conventions, and expectations for playwrights to mine, rewrite, challenge, celebrate, and subvert. The web stretches endlessly outwards, conversations reaching across centuries, and the time-honoured Victorian plots and tropes remain deeply embedded in contemporary culture, a heritage whose influence is still being reckoned with.

Bibliography

Articles and reviews from nineteenth-century periodicals are documented fully in the footnotes, and are not listed here.

Lord Chamberlain's Correspondence Files (LC Corr), Public Records, National Archives, Kew

Lord Chamberlain's Correspondence Files (LC Corr), British Library, London

Lord Chamberlain's Daybook (LCD), British Library Add MSS 53703 (1852–65). 53705 (1873–6)

Anon., *Downward Paths: An Inquiry into the Causes which contribute to the Making of the Prostitute,* with a foreword by A. Maude Royden (G. Bell & Sons: London, 1916)

Anon., 'The Literature of the Social Evil', *Saturday Review* (6 October 1860), 417–18

Anon., *Maria Martin; or, The Murder in the Red Barn* (Marylebone Theatre, April 1840) reprinted in *The Golden Age of Melodrama, Twelve 19th Century Melodramas*, abridged and introduced by Michael Kilgarriff (Wolfe: London, 1974)

Anon. ['The Old Stager'], *The Actor's Hand-Book, and Guide to the Stage for Amateurs* (John Dicks: London, 1884)

The White Slave Traffic: Articles and Letters reprinted from 'The Spectator' (P. S. King: London, 1912)

The Nation's Morals, Being the Proceedings of the Public Morals Conference held in London on 14th and 15th July, 1910 (Cassell & Co: London, 1910)

Acton, William, *Prostitution, Considered in its Moral, Social and Sanitary Aspects in London and other Large Cities and Garrison Towns. With Proposals for the Control and Prevention of Attendant Evils.* (2nd edition. John Churchill and Sons: London, 1870)

James Agate, *At Half Past Eight: Essays of the Theatre, 1921–1922* (Jonathan Cape: London, 1923)

—— *Red Letter Nights* (Benjamin Blom: New York, 1944, reissued 1969)

Albee, Edward, *The Goat, or Who is Sylvia? (Notes toward a definition of tragedy)* (Methuen, London, 2004)

Albery, James, *The Crisis*, in *The Dramatic Works of James Albery, Together with a Sketch of his Career, Correspondence bearing thereon, Press Notices, Casts, etc.*, ed. Wyndham Albery, 2 vols (Peter Davies: London, 1939), vol. 1

—— *Pink Dominoes*, in *The Dramatic Works of James Albery, Together with a Sketch of his Career, Correspondence bearing thereon, Press Notices, Casts, etc.*, ed. Wyndham Albery, 2 vols (Peter Davies: London, 1939), vol. 2

Allen, Grant, 'Plain Words on the Woman Question', *Fortnightly Review*, 52 (October 1889), 448–58

—— *The Woman Who Did* (John Lane: London, 1895)

Andersen, Amanda, *Tainted Souls and Painted Faces: The Rhetoric of Fallenness in Victorian Culture* (Cornell University Press: Ithaca, NY, 1993)

Archer, William, *English Dramatists of To-Day* (Sampson Low: London, 1882)

—— 'The Censorship of the Stage', *About the Theatre: Essays and Studies* (T. Fisher Unwin: London, 1886)

Archer, William, *The Old Drama and the New: An Essay in Re-valuation* (Dodd, Mead and Co.: New York, 1929)

—— *The Theatrical 'World' for 1893* (Benjamin Blom: New York, 1894, reissued 1969)

—— *The Theatrical 'World' of 1894* (Walter Scott: London, 1895)

—— *The Theatrical 'World' of 1895* (Walter Scott: London, 1896)

Aston, Elaine, *Sarah Bernhardt: A French Actress on the English Stage* (Berg: Oxford, 1989)

—— and Ian Clarke, 'The Dangerous Woman of Melvillean Melodrama', *New Theatre Quarterly*, 12, issue 45 (1996), 30–42

Attwood, Nina, *The Prostitute's Body: Rewriting Prostitution in Victorian Britain* (Pickering & Chatto: London, 2011)

Auerbach, Nina, *Woman and the Demon: The Life of a Victorian Myth* (Harvard University Press: Cambridge, MA, 1982)

—— 'Before the Curtain', in Kerry Powell (ed.), *The Cambridge Companion to Victorian and Edwardian Theatre* (Cambridge University Press: Cambridge, 2004)

Augier, Émile, *L'Aventurière, Théâtre Complet*, I (Calmann Lévy: Paris, 1897)

—— *Le Mariage d'Olympe, Théâtre Complet*, III (Calmann Lévy: Paris, 1897)

—— *Les Fourchambault, Théâtre Complet*, VII (Calmann Lévy: Paris, 1897)

Baden-Powell, Robert, *Scouting for Boys* (Horace Cox: London, 1908)

Bailey, Peter, *Popular Culture and Performance in the Victorian City* (Cambridge University Press: Cambridge, 1998)

Barker, Clive, and Maggie Gale (eds), *British Theatre between the Wars, 1918–1939* (Cambridge University Press: Cambridge, 2000)

Barker, Harley Granville, *The Madras House: A Comedy in Four Acts* (Sidgwick & Jackson: London, 1911)

—— *The Madras House* (1925), in Granville Barker. *Plays: Two* (Methuen: London, 1994)

Barrie, James. M., *Alice Sit-by-the-Fire, The Twelve-Pound Look*, in *The Plays of J. M. Barrie* (Hodder and Stoughton: London, 1930)

Barrière, Théodore, and Lambert Thiboust, *Les Filles de Marbre* (Michel Lévy: Paris, 1853)

Bartley, Paula, *Prostitution: Prevention and Reform in England, 1860–1914* (Routledge: London, 2000)

Beatty, Laura, *Lillie Langtry: Manners, Masks and Morals* (Vintage: London, 2000)

Becque, Henri, *La Parisienne* (Calmann Lévy: Paris, 1885)

Beerbohm, Max, *Around Theatres* (Rupert Hart-Davis: London, 1953)

Bensusan, Inez, *The Apple*, reprinted in *How the Vote was Won and Other Suffragette Plays*, selected and introduced by Dale Spender and Carole Hayman (Methuen: London, 1985)

Bernard, William Bayle, *The Farmer's Story*, Dicks' No. 434

Bernheimer, Charles, *Figures of Ill Repute: Representing Prostitution in Nineteenth-Century France* (Harvard University Press: Cambridge, MA, 1989)

Bernhardt, Sarah, *My Double Life: The Memoirs of Sarah Bernhardt* (State of New York Press: Albany, NY, 1999)

Billington-Greig, Teresa, 'The Truth about White Slavery', *English Review* (June 1913)

Binhammer, Katherine, *The Seduction Narrative in Britain, 1747–1800* (Cambridge University Press: Cambridge, 2009)

Bishop, John, ' "They manage things better in France": French Plays and English Critics, 1850–1855', *Nineteenth Century Theatre*, 22:1 (Summer 1994), 5–29

Bjornson, Bjornstjerne, *A Gauntlet*, in *Three Comedies* (Dent: London, 1914)

Bland, Lucy, *Banishing the Beast: Feminism, Sex and Morality* (Tauris Parke: London, 2002)

Blathwayt, Raymond, *'Does the Theatre make for Good?': An interview with Mr. Clement Scott*, reprinted from *Great Thoughts* (A. W. Hall: London, 1898)

Blyth, Henry, *Skittles: The Last Victorian Courtesan. The Life and Times of Catherine Walters* (Rupert Hart-Davis: London, 1970)

Blythe, Alecky, *The Girlfriend Experience* (Nick Hern Books: London, 2008)

Booth, Michael R., *English Melodrama* (Herbert Jenkins: London, 1965)

—— *Theatre in the Victorian Age* (Cambridge University Press: Cambridge, 1991)

Boucicault, Dion, *The Poor of New York* (Wallack's Theatre, New York, 1857), Dicks' No. 381

—— *Forbidden Fruit, and Other Plays* (Princeton University Press: Princeton, NJ, 1940)

—— 'The Decline of the Drama', *North American Review*, 125:2 (September 1877), 235–45

—— 'Leaves from a Dramatist's Diary', *North American Review*, 149 (July/December 1889), 228–36

—— *Jessie Brown; or, the Relief of Lucknow*, Dicks' No. 473

—— *The Octoroon, The Colleen Bawn, The Shaughraun*, in *Selected Plays of Dion Boucicault*, chosen and introduced by Andrew Parkin, Irish Drama Selections 4 (Colin Smythe: Gerrards Cross, 1987)

—— *Arrah-na-Pogue; or, the Wicklow Wedding* in *The Dolmen Boucicault*, ed. David Krause (Dolmen Press: Dublin, 1964)

—— *Formosa; or, The Railroad to Ruin*, LCP, BL Add MS 53078Q

—— *The Two Lives of Mary Leigh*, LCP, BL Add MS 53052H

Braddon, Mary Elizabeth, *Hostages to Fortune*, 3 vols (John Maxwell: London, 1875)

—— *Lady Audley's Secret* (Oxford University Press: Oxford, 1987)

—— *Aurora Floyd* (Oxford University Press: Oxford, 1996)

—— *The Doctor's Wife* (Oxford University Press: Oxford, 1998)

Brandon, Dorothy, *Wild Heather*, LCP 1917/17

Bratton, Jacky, 'The Contending Discourses of Melodrama', in Jacky Bratton, Jim Cook and Christine Gledhill (eds), *Melodrama: Stage, Picture, Screen* (BFI Publishing: London, 1994)

——, Richard Allen Cave et al (eds), *Acts of Supremacy: the British Empire and the Stage, 1790–1930* (Manchester University Press: Manchester, 1991)

—— *New Readings in Theatre History* (Cambridge University Press: Cambridge, 2003)

Braun, Sidney D., *The 'Courtisane' in the French Theatre from Hugo to Becque (1831–1885)* (Johns Hopkins Press: Baltimore, MD, 1947)

Brieux, Eugène, *La Femme seule* (Stock: Paris, 1913)

—— *Maternity, Damaged Goods,* in *Three Plays by Brieux* (Brentano's: New York, 1912)

Bristow, Edward J., *Vice and Vigilance: Purity Movements in Britain since 1700* (Gill and Macmillan: Dublin, 1977)

Brooks, Peter, *The Melodramatic Imagination: Balzac, Henry James, Melodrama, and the Mode of Excess* (Columbia University Press: New York, 1985)

Buckstone, J. B., *Luke the Labourer,* Dicks' No. 830

—— *Victorine; or, 'I'll sleep on it'*, Dicks' No. 856

—— *Henriette the Forsaken,* Dicks' No. 821

—— *The Duchess de la Vaubaliere*, Dicks' No. 815

—— *Agnes de Vere: or, The Wife's Revenge*, Dicks' No. 805

—— *The Green Bushes*, Dicks' No. 827

—— *Ellen Wareham*, Dicks' No. 837

Budden, Julian, *The Operas of Verdi*, vol. 2, *From Il Trovatore to La Forza del Destino* (Oxford University Press: New York, 1984)

Burton, William Evans, *Ellen Wareham; The Wife of Two Husbands* (T. H. Lacy: London, 1833)

Butler, Josephine E., *On the Moral Reclaimability of Prostitutes* (London: 1870)

—— *Social Purity* (Morgan and Scott: London, 1879)

—— *Personal Reminiscences of a Great Crusade* (Horace Marshall & Son: London, 1896)

Caine, Barbara, *English Feminism, 1780–1980* (Oxford University Press: Oxford, 1997)

Caird, Mona, 'Marriage', *Westminster Review*, 130:2 (July 1888), 186–201

Campbell, A. C., *The London Banker; or, The Profligate*, Dicks' No.723

Campbell, Hugh, and Harry Neville, *Voice, Speech and Gesture: A Practical Handbook for the Elocutionary Art* (Charles William Deacon & Co; London, 1895)

Campbell, Mrs Patrick, *My Life and Some Letters* (Hutchinson and Co: London, 1922)

Carlson, Marvin, *The French Stage in the Nineteenth Century* (Scarecrow Press: Metuchen, NJ, 1972)

Carlson, Susan, 'Comic Militancy: The Politics of Suffrage Drama', in Maggie B. Gale and Viv Gardner (eds), *Women, Theatre and Performance: New Histories, New Historiographies* (Manchester University Press: Manchester, 2000)

Carnell, Jennifer, *The Literary Lives of Mary Elizabeth Braddon: A Study of her Life and Work* (Sensation Press: Hastings, 2000)

Carton, R. C., *The Tree of Knowledge*, LCP, BL Add MS 53616K

Cavell, Stanley, *Pursuits of Happiness: The Hollywood Comedy of Remarriage* (Harvard University Press: Cambridge, MA, 1981)

Chambers, Haddon, *Passers-By* (Duckworth: London, 1913)

Chothia, Jean (ed.), in *The New Woman and Other Emancipated Woman Plays* (Oxford University Press: Oxford, 1998)

—— *English Drama of the Early Modern Period, 1890–1940* (Longman: London, 1996)

Cima, Gay Gibson, *Performing Women: Female Characters, Male Playwrights and the Modern Stage* (Cornell University Press: London, 1993)

Clarke, Ian, *Edwardian Drama* (Faber: London, 1989)

Clément, Catherine, *Opera, or the Undoing of Women*, translated by Betsy Wing (Virago: London, 1989)

Clum, John M., *Still Acting Gay: Male Homosexuality in Modern Drama* (St Martin's: New York, 2000)

Cockin, Katharine, *Women and Theatre in the Age of Suffrage: The Pioneer Players, 1911–1925* (Palgrave Macmillan: Basingstoke, 2001)

Cocks, H. G., and Matt Houlbrook (eds), *Palgrave Advances in the Modern History of Sexuality* (Palgrave Macmillan: Basingstoke, 2006)

Collins, Mabel, *The Story of Helena Modjeska* (W. H. Allen: London, 1883)

Collins, Sewell, *G.H.Q. Love*, LCP 1920/21

Collins, Wilkie, *The New Magdalen* (published by the author: London, 1873)

Cominos, Peter T., 'Innocent Femina Sensualis in Unconscious Conflict', in Martha Vicinus (ed.), *Suffer and Be Still: Women in the Victorian Age* (Methuen: London, 1980), 155–72

Committee of Inquiry into Sexual Morality, *The State and Sexual Morality* (Allen & Unwin: London, 1920)

Conolly, L. W., '*Mrs Warren's Profession* and the Lord Chamberlain', *SHAW: The Annual of Bernard Shaw Studies*, 24 (2004), 46–95

—— 'Who was Phillipa Summers? Reflections on Vivie Warren's Cambridge', *SHAW: The Annual of Bernard Shaw Studies*, 25 (2005), 88–95

Cook, Dutton, *Nights at the Play: A View of the English Stage*, II (Chatto and Windus: London, 1883)

Corbett, Mary Jean, *Representing Femininity: Middle-Class Subjectivity in Victorian and Edwardian Women's Autobiographies* (Oxford University Press: New York, 1992)

Corelli, Marie, *The Sorrows of Satan* (Methuen: London, 1895)

Coward, Noël, *The Vortex, Easy Virtue, Fallen Angels*, in Coward, *Plays: One* (Eyre Methuen: London, 1979)

—— *Play Parade*, vol. II (Heinemann: London, 1950)

—— *Private Lives*, in *Plays: Two* (Methuen: London, 1982)

—— *Design for Living*, in Coward, *Plays: Three* (Methuen: London, 1994)

—— '*This Was a Man*', in Coward, *Collected Plays: Eight* (Methuen: London, 2000)

—— *Present Indicative*, in *Autobiography* (Methuen: London, 1986)

Crowley, Mart, *The Boys in the Band* (1968), in Ben Hodges (ed.), *Out Plays: Landmark Gay and Lesbian Plays of the Twentieth Century* (Alyson Books: New York, 2008)

Cruikshank, George, *The Drunkard's Children* (London, 1848)

Cullingford, Elizabeth, *Ireland's Others: Ethnicity and Gender in Irish Literature and Popular Culture* (Cork University Press in association with Field Day: Cork, 2001)

Cvetovich, Ann, *Mixed Feelings: Feminism, Mass Culture, and Victorian Sensationalism* (Rutgers University Press: New Brunswick, NJ, 1992)

Dam, H. J. W., *The Shop Girl*, LCP, BL Add MS.53562B

Darlington, W. A., *Six Thousand and One Nights: Forty Years a Critic* (Harrap: London, 1960)

Davis, Jim, and Victor Emeljanow, *Reflecting the Audience: London Theatregoing, 1840–1880* (University of Iowa Press: Iowa City, IA, 2001)

Davis, Tracy C., *Actresses as Working Women: Their Social Identity in Victorian Culture* (Routledge: London, 1991)

—— 'Nineteenth-Century Repertoire', *Nineteenth Century Theatre and Film*, 36: 2 (December 2009), 6–28

Dawick, John, 'The "First" Mrs Tanqueray', *Theatre Quarterly*, 9:35 (1979), 77–93

De Jongh, Nicholas, *Politics, Prudery and Perversions: The Censoring of the English Stage 1901–1968* (Methuen: London, 2000)

della Seta, Fabrizio, 'New Currents in the Libretto', in Scott L. Balthazar (ed.), *The Cambridge Companion to Verdi* (Cambridge University Press: Cambridge, 2004)

Dillon, Charles, *The Mysteries of Paris. A Romance of the Rich and Poor*, Dicks' No. 980

Donohue, Joseph (ed.), *The Cambridge History of British Theatre*, vol. 2: *1660–1895* (Cambridge University Press: Cambridge, 2004)

Dorynne, Jess, *The Surprise of His Life*. Unpublished manuscript, Smallhythe Museum

Du Maurier, Daphne, *The Years Between*, in Fidelis Morgan (ed.), *The Years Between: Plays by Women on the London Stage, 1900–1950* (Virago: London, 1994)

Dumas fils, Alexandre 'A Propos de *La Dame aux Camélias*' (1867), *Théâtre Complet*, I (Calmann Lévy : Paris, 1896)

—— *Le Demi-Monde*, *Théâtre Complet*, II (Calmann Lévy: Paris, 1890)

—— *Francillon*, *Théâtre Complet*, VII (Calmann Lévy: Paris, 1890)

—— *La Dame aux Camélias*, preface d'André Maurois, édition établie et annotée par Bernard Raffali (Gallimard: Paris, 1974)

—— *La Dame aux Camélias*, edited and introduced by Roger Clark (Bristol Classical Press: London, 1994)

—— *La Femme de Claude*, *Théâtre Complet*, V (Calmann Lévy: Paris, 1890)

—— *Le Dossier 'Tue-La!', constitué, étudié et plaidé par André Lebris* (Édouard Aubanel: Avignon)

Duncan, Dawn, *Postcolonial Theory in Irish Drama from 1800–2000* (Mellen: New York, 2004)

Dymkowski, Christine, 'Case Study: Cicely Hamilton's *Diana of Dobson's*, 1908', in Baz Kershaw (ed.), *Cambridge History of British Theatre*, vol. 3: *Since 1895* (Cambridge University Press: Cambridge, 2004), 110–26

Edelstein, T. J., 'Augustus Egg's triptych: a narrative of Victorian adultery', *Burlington Magazine*, vol. 125, No. 961 (April 1983), 202–12.

Egan, Michael (ed.), *Ibsen: The Critical Heritage*, (Routledge: London, 1972)

Eltis, Sos, *Revising Wilde: Society and Subversion in the Plays of Oscar Wilde* (Oxford University Press: Oxford, 1996)

—— 'Reputation, Celebrity and the late-Victorian Actress', in *Theatre and Celebrity in Britain, 1660–2000*, ed. Mary Luckhurst and Jane Moody (Palgrave Macmillan: London, 2005)

—— 'Bringing out the Acid: Noël Coward, Harold Pinter, Ivy Compton- Burnett and the Uses of Camp', *Modern Drama* 51.2 (2008), 211–33

Ervine, St John, *The Magnanimous Lover* (Allen & Unwin: London, 1928)

—— *The First Mrs Fraser* (Chatto & Windus: London, 1929)

Etherege, George, *The Man of Mode* in *Four Restoration libertine plays*, ed. Deborah Payne Fisk (Oxford University Press: Oxford, 2009)

Evans, Edmund, *The Floral Birthday Book: Flowers and Their Emblems* (Routledge: London, 1878)

Fahnestock, Jeanne, 'Bigamy: The Rise and Fall of a Convention', *Nineteenth-Century Fiction*, 36 (June 1981), 47–71

Farkas, Anna, *Between Orthodoxy and Rebellion: Women's drama in England, 1890–1918*, unpublished DPhil thesis, University of Oxford, 2010

Fawcett, Millicent G., '*The Woman Who Did*', *Contemporary Review*, 67 (January–June 1895), 625–31

—— and E. M. Turner, *Josephine Butler: Her Work and Principles, and their Meaning for the Twentieth Century* (Association for Moral and Social Hygiene: London, 1927)

Fawkes, Richard, *Dion Boucicault: A Biography* (Quartet Books: London, 1979)

Fietz, Lothar, 'On the Origins of the English Melodrama in the Tradition of Bourgeois Tragedy and Sentimental Drama: Lillo, Schröder, Kotzebue, Sheridan, Thomson, Jerrold', in Michael Hays and Anastasia Nikolopoulou (eds), *Melodrama: The Cultural Emergence of a Genre* (St Martin's Press: New York, 1996)

Filon, Augustin, *The English Stage: Being an Account of the Victorian Drama*, trans by Frederic Whyte, with an introduction by Henry Arthur Jones (John Milne: London, 1897)

Findlater, Richard, *Banned! A Review of Theatrical Censorship in Britain* (MacGibbon & Kee: London, 1967)

Fisher, Trevor, *Prostitution and the Victorians* (Sutton: Stroud, 1997)

Fitzball, Edward, *The Earthquake; or, the Spectre of the Nile* (John Cumberland: London, 1829)

—— *A Libertine's Lesson*, Dicks' No. 598

—— *Mary Melvyn; or, A Marriage of Interest,* Dicks' No. 622

Fitzsimmons, Linda, and Viv Gardner (eds), *New Woman Plays*, (Methuen: London, 1991)

Fletcher, Constance ['George Fleming'], *Mrs Lessingham*, LCP, BL Add MS 53546A

Flint, Kate, *The Victorians and the Visual Imagination* (Cambridge University Press: Cambridge, 2000)

Foucault, Michel, *The History of Sexuality*, vol. 1: *The Will to Knowledge* (Penguin: Harmondsworth, 1990)

Foulkes, Richard (ed.), *British Theatre in the 1890s: Essays on Drama and the Stage* (Cambridge University Press: Cambridge, 1992)

Gale, Maggie B., *West End Women: Women and the London stage, 1918–1962* (Routledge: London, 1996)

—— 'The London Stage, 1918–1945' in Baz Kershaw (ed.), *The Cambridge History of British Theatre*, vol. 3: *Since 1895* (Cambridge University Press: Cambridge, 2004), 143–66

—— and John Stokes (eds), *The Cambridge Companion to the Actress* (Cambridge University Press: Cambridge, 2007)

Galsworthy, John, *The Fugitive, The Eldest Son* in *The Plays of John Galsworthy* (Duckworth: London, 1929)

Garnett, Edward, *A Censured Play: The Breaking Point* (Duckworth: London, 1907)

Gates, Joanne E., *Elizabeth Robins, 1862–1952: actress, novelist, feminist* (University of Alabama Press: London, 1994)

Gielgud, Kate Terry, *A Victorian Playgoer*, ed. Muriel St Clare Byrne (Heinemann: London, 1980)

Gifford, Denis, *Books and Plays in Films, 1896–1915: Literary, Theatrical and Artistic Sources of the First Twenty Years of Motion Pictures* (Mansell: London, 1991)

Gilbert, W. S., *Charity* (London, 1874—no publisher given)

Glenn, Susan A., *Female Spectacle: The Theatrical Roots of Modern Feminism* (Harvard University Press: Cambridge, MA, 2000)

Glitre, Katharina, *Hollywood Romantic Comedy: States of the Union, 1934–1965* (Manchester University Press: Manchester, 2006)

Graham, R., *The Tainted Woman* LCP 1917/17

Grand, Sarah, *The Heavenly Twins* (Heinemann and Cassell: London, 1893)

Graves, Joseph, *The Tempter; or, the Old Mill of St Denis*, Dicks' No. 712

Greg, W. R., 'Prostitution', *Westminster and Foreign Quarterly Review*, 53 (April–July 1850), 448–506.

Grene, Nicholas, *The Politics of Irish Drama: Plays in Context from Boucicault to Brecht* (Cambridge University Press: Cambridge, 1999)

Grundy, Sydney, *Sowing the Wind* (Samuel French: London, 1901)

—— *The New Woman*, in Jean Chothia (ed.), *The New Woman and Other Emancipated Women Plays* (Oxford University Press: Oxford, 1998)

Hadley, Elaine, *Melodramatic Tactics: Theatricalized Dissent in the English Marketplace, 1800–1885* (Stanford University Press: Stanford, CA, 1995).

Haines, John Thomas, *The Life of a Woman; or, The Curate's Daughter*, Dicks' No. 468

—— *My Poll and My Partner Joe* (Lacy's Acting Edition No.1058: London, 1866)

Hall, Owen, and Harry Greenbank, *A Gaiety Girl*, LCP, BL Add MS 53535I.

Hamilton, Cicely, *Marriage as a Trade* (Chapman and Hall: London, 1909)

—— *A Pageant of Great Women* (International Suffrage Shop: London, 1910)

—— *Life Errant* (Dent: London, 1935)

—— *Diana of Dobson's*, reprinted in Linda Fitzsimmons and Viv Gardner (eds), *New Woman Plays* (Methuen: London, 1991)

Hankin, St John, *The Last of the De Mullins*, in Jean Chothia (ed.), *The New Woman and Other Emancipated Woman Plays* (Oxford University Press: Oxford, 1998)

Hardie, J. Keir, *The Queenie Gerald Case* (National Labour Press: London, 191–)

Harper, Charles, *Revolted Woman: Past, Present, and to Come* (Elkin Mathews: London, 1894)

Harris, Augustus, and Henry Pettitt, *Human Nature*, LCP, BL Add MS 53342 H

—— —— *A Life of Pleasure*, LCP, BL Add MS 53533H

—— and Paul Merrit, *Youth*, LCP, BL Add MS 53256K

Harris, Frank, *Mr and Mrs Daventry. A Play in four acts... based on a scenario by Oscar Wilde* (Richards Press: London, 1956)

Harwood, H. M., *Honour Thy Father*, in H. M. Harwood, *Three One-Act Plays* (Ernest Benn: London, 1926)

—— *The Supplanters* (Ernest Benn: London, 1926)

—— and F. Tennyson-Jesse *The Pelican* (Ernest Benn: London, 1924)

Hays, Michael, and Anastasia Nikolopoulou (eds), *Melodrama: The Cultural Emergence of a Genre* (St Martin's Press: New York, 1996)

Hazlewood, C. H., *Jessy Vere; or, the Return of the Wanderer* (T. H. Lacy: London, 1856)

Heinrich, Anselm, Katherine Newey, and Jeffrey Richards (eds), *Ruskin, the Theatre, and Victorian Visual Culture* (Palgrave Macmillan: Basingstoke, 2009)

Heron, Matilda, *Camille; or, the Fate of a Coquette*, Dicks' No.614

Higgs, Mary, *Three Nights in Women's Lodging Houses* (John Heywood: Manchester, 1905)

—— *Glimpses into the Abyss* (P. S. King & Son: London, 1906)

Hirschfield, Claire, 'The Suffragist as Playwright in Edwardian England', *Frontiers* IX.2 (1987), 1–6

Holland, Merlin, *Irish Peacock and Scarlet Marquess: the Real Trial of Oscar Wilde* (Fourth Estate: London, 2004)

Holledge, Julie, *Innocent Flowers: Women in the Edwardian Theatre* (Virago: London, 1981)

Houghton, Stanley, *Hindle Wakes*, in *Late Victorian Plays, 1890–1914*, ed. George Rowell (Oxford University Press: Oxford, 1972)

Housman, Laurence, *Sex-War and Women's Suffrage* (Women's Freedom League: London, 1916)

—— *Pains and Penalties* (Sidgwick and Jackson: London, 1911)

Hughes, Winifred, *The Maniac in the Cellar: Sensation Novels of the 1860s* (Princeton University Press: Princeton, NJ, 1980)

Hutcheon Linda, and Michael Hutcheon, *Opera: Desire, Disease, Death* (University of Nebraska Press: Lincoln, NE, 1996)

Hynes, Samuel, *The Edwardian Turn of Mind* (Pimlico: London, 1968)

Ibsen, Henrik, *A Doll's House, Ghosts, Hedda Gabler* in *Four Major Plays*, trans. James McFarlane (Oxford University Press: Oxford, 1981)

Incorporated Stage Society, *Ten Years, 1899–1909* (Chiswick Press: London, 1909)

Innes, Christopher, *Avant-Garde Theatre, 1892–1992* (Routledge: London, 1993)

Jackson, Russell, (ed.), *Plays by Henry Arthur Jones* (Cambridge University Press: Cambridge, 1982)

Jeffreys, Sheila, *The Spinster and Her Enemies: Feminism and Sexuality, 1880–1930* (Pandora: London, 1985)

Jerrold, Douglas, *Black-Ey'd Susan, or 'All in the Downs'* in George Rowell (ed), *Nineteenth Century Plays* (Oxford University Press: Oxford, 1972)

—— *Nell Gwynne* (Theatre Royal, Haymarket, 1833). Dicks' No. 274

John, Angela V., *Elisabeth Robins: staging a life* (Tempus: Stroud, 2007)

John, Juliet, *Dickens and Mass Culture* (Oxford University Press: Oxford, 2010)

Johnson, Catherine B. (ed.), *William Bodham Donne and his Friends* (Methuen: London, 1905)

Johnson, Katie N., *Sisters in Sin: Brothel Drama in America, 1900–1920* (Cambridge University Press: Cambridge, 2006)

Jones, Doris Arthur, *The Life and Letters of Henry Arthur Jones* (Victor Gollancz: London, 1930)

Jones, Henry Arthur, *Saints and Sinners: A New and Original Drama of Modern Middle-Class Life* (Macmillan: London, 1891)

—— *The Dancing Girl* (Samuel French: London, 1907)

—— *The Case of Rebellious Susan, The Liars,* in *Plays by Henry Arthur Jones,* ed. Russell Jackson (Cambridge University Press: Cambridge, 1982)

—— *Mrs Dane's Defence,* in *English Plays of the Nineteenth Century,* vol. II: *Dramas, 1850–1900,* ed. Michael R. Booth (Clarendon Press: London, 1969)

—— *Michael and His Lost Angel* (Macmillan: London, 1896)

—— *The Masqueraders* (Macmillan: London, 1899)

—— *The Princess's Nose* (Chiswick Press: London, 1902. Privately printed)

—— *Joseph Entangled* (Chiswick Press: London, 1904. Privately printed)

—— *The Hypocrites* (Chiswick Press: London, 1906. Privately printed)

—— and Henry Herman, *Breaking a Butterfly* (London: Privately printed, 1884)

Kaplan, Joel, 'Pineroticism and the Problem Play: Mrs Tanqueray, Mrs Ebbsmith and "Mrs Pat"', in *British Theatre in the 1890s: Essays on Drama and the Stage,* ed. Richard Foulkes (Cambridge University Press: Cambridge, 1992)

—— 'Mrs Ebbsmith's Bible Burning: Page versus Stage', *Theatre Notebook,* XLIV, no. 3 (1990), 99–101

—— and Sheila Stowell, *Theatre and Fashion: Oscar Wilde to the Suffragettes* (Cambridge University Press: Cambridge, 1995)

Kendal, Madge, *Dame Madge Kendal, By Herself* (John Murray: London, 1933)

Kennion, Emily, *Nina; or, the Story of a Heart,* LCP, BL Add MS 53336L

Kent, Susan Kingsley, *Sex and Suffrage in Britain, 1860–1914* (Routledge: London, 1990)

—— *Making Peace: The Reconstruction of Gender in Interwar Britain* (Princeton University Press: Princeton, NJ, 1993)

Kershaw, Baz (ed.), *Cambridge History of British Theatre,* vol. 3: *Since 1895,* (Cambridge University Press: Cambridge, 2004)

Kilgarriff, Michael (ed.), *The Golden Age of Melodrama, Twelve 19th-Century Melodramas* (Wolfe: London, 1974)

Knepler, Henry, *The Gilded Stage: The lives and careers of four great actresses, Rachel Félix, Adelaide Ristori, Sarah Bernhardt and Eleonora Duse* (Constable: London, 1968)

Knight, Joseph, *Theatrical Notes* (Lawrence & Bullen: London, 1893)

Kotzebue, August Von, *The Stranger,* as performed at the Theatre Royal, Drury Lane. Translated from the German of Kotzebue by Benjamin Thomson. Printed, under the authority of the Managers, from the Prompt Book. With remarks by Mrs. Inchbald (Longman, Hurst, Rees and Orme: London, 1806)

Langtry, Lillie, *The Days I Knew* (Hutchinson: London, 1925)

Lawlor, Clark, *Consumption and Literature: The Making of the Romantic Disease* (Palgrave Macmillan: Basingstoke, 2006)

Leckie, Barbara, *Culture and Adultery: the Novel, the Newspaper, and the Law, 1857–1914* (University of Pennsylvania Press: Philadelphia, PA, 1999)

Leclerq, Pierre, *Illusion,* LCP, BL Add MS 53453G

Leighton, Dorothy, *Thyrza Fleming,* LCP, BL Add MS 53565F

Lewes, George Henry, 'The Theatres', *Dramatic Essays by John Forster and George Henry Lewes. Reprinted from the 'Examiner' and the 'Leader',* with notes and introduction by William Archer and Robert W. Lowe (Walter Scott: London, 1896)

Lewis, Jane, *Women in England, 1870–1950: Sexual Divisions and Social Change* (Indiana University Press: Bloomington, IN, 1984)

Logan, Deborah Anna, *Fallenness in Victorian Women's Writing: Marry, Stitch, Die or Do Worse* (University of Missouri Press: Columbia, MO, 1998)

Logan, William, *The Great Social Evil. Its Causes, Extent, Results, and Remedies* (Hodder and Stoughton: London, 1871)

Ludlam, Charles, *Camille (A Tearjerker): A Travesty*, in *The Mystery of Irma Vep and other plays* (Theatre Communications Group: New York, 2001)

Lytton, Lord, *The Duchess de la Valliere*, Dicks' No. 847

MacCarthy, Desmond, *Theatre* (MacGibbon & Kee: London, 1954)

McClary, Susan, 'Foreword. The Undoing of Opera: Toward a Feminist Criticism of Music', Catherine Clément, *Opera, or the Undoing of Women*, translated by Betsy Wing (Virago: London, 1989)

McCord, Norman, *British History, 1815–1906* (Oxford University Press: Oxford, 1991)

McDonald, Jan, *The 'New Drama' 1900–1914* (Macmillan: London, 1986)

MacDonald, J. Ramsay, 'Social and Economic Causes of Vice', in *The Nation's Morals, Being the Proceedings of the Public Morals Conference held in London on 14th and 15th July, 1910* (Cassell & Co: London, 1910)

McEvoy, Charles, *The Likes of Her*, LCP 1923/2

Macqueen-Pope, W., *St James's: Theatre of Distinction* (W. H. Allen: London, 1958)

McWilliam, Rohan, 'Melodrama', and Heidi J. Holder, 'Sensation Theatre', *A Companion to Sensation Fiction*, ed. Pamela K. Gilbert (Wiley-Blackwell: Oxford, 2011)

Mainardi, Patricia, *Husbands, Wives, and Lovers: Marriage and its Discontents in Nineteenth-Century France* (Yale University Press: New Haven, CT, 2003)

Malleson, Miles, *The Fanatics* (Ernest Benn: London, 1924)

Mansell, D. H., 'Sensation Novels', *Quarterly Review* 113: 226 (April 1863), 481–514

Marill, Alvin H., *More Theatre: Stage to Screen to Television*, 3 vols (Scarecrow Press: London, 1993, 2008)

Marshik, Celia, *British Modernism and Censorship* (Cambridge University Press: Cambridge, 2006)

Marvin, Roberta Montemorra, 'The Censorship of Verdi's Operas in Victorian London', *Music and Letters*, 82:4 (November 2011), 582–610

Mason, Michael, *The Making of Victorian Sexual Attitudes* (Oxford University Press: Oxford, 1994)

—— *The Making of Victorian Sexuality* (Oxford University Press: Oxford, 1994)

Maugham, William Somerset, *A Man of Honour* (Chapman and Hall: London, 1903)

—— *Lady Frederick, Penelope, Smith, The Land of Promise*, in *The Collected Plays of W. Somerset Maugham*, vol. I (Heinemann: London, 1952)

—— *Our Betters, Home and Beauty, The Circle, The Constant Wife*, in *The Collected Plays of W. Somerset Maugham*, vol. II (Heinemann: London, 1952)

—— *Caesar's Wife, East of Suez*, in *The Collected Plays of W. Somerset Maugham*, vol. III (Heinemann: London, 1952)

—— *The Tenth Man* (Heinemann: London, 1913)

—— *Lady Frederick, For Services Rendered, The Letter* in *Plays: Two* (Methuen: London, 1992)

—— *The Summing Up* (Vintage: London, 2001)

Mayer, David, 'Why Girls Leave Home: Victorian and Edwardian "Bad-Girl" Melodrama Parodied in Early Film', *Theatre Journal*, 58:4 (December 2006), 575–93

Mayhew, Henry, *London Labour and the London Poor*, 4 vols (Dover: London, 1861–2)

Meilhac, Henri, and Ludovic Halévy, *Frou-Frou, Théâtre de Meilhac et Halévy Complet*, I (Calmann Lévy: Paris, 1899)

Meisel, Martin, *Realizations: Narrative, Pictorial and Theatrical Arts in Nineteenth-Century England* (Princeton University Press: Princeton, NJ, 1983)

—— *How Plays Work: Reading and Performance* (Oxford University Press: Oxford, 2007)

Melville, Frederick, *Between Two Women*, LCP, BL Add MS 65632F

—— *Her Road to Ruin* LCP 1907/12

—— *The Bad Girl of the Family*, LCP 1909/19

Melville, Walter, *The Girl Who Wrecked His Home*, LCP 1907/21H

—— *The Shop Soiled Girl*, LCP 1910/22

Middleton-Myles, A., *The White Slave Traffic*, LCP 1913/10

Miller, Jane Eldridge, *Rebel Women: Feminism, Modernism and the Edwardian Novel* (Virago: London, 1994)

Milner, H. M., *Victorine: The Maid of Paris*, Dicks' No.352

Moi, Toril, *Henrik Ibsen and the Birth of Modernism: Art, Theater, Philosophy* (Oxford University Press: Oxford, 2006)

Moncrieff, W. T., *The Lear of Private Life! or, Father and Daughter. A Domestic Melo-Drama* (London: T. Richardson, *c.*1825)

—— *The Lear of Private Life*, Dicks' No. 924

—— *Scamps of London; or, the Cross Roads of Life* (Dramatic Repository: London, 1851)

Monkhouse, Alan, *Mary Broome* (Sidgwick & Jackson: London, 1912)

Morley, Henry, *The Journal of a London Playgoer from 1851 to 1866* (Routledge: London, 1866)

Morris, William, *News from Nowhere, or, An Epoch of Rest, being some chapters from A Utopian Romance* (Reeves & Turner: London, 1890)

Mortimer, James, *Heartsease*, LCP, BL Add MS 53149A

Mullin, Donald C., *Victorian Plays: A Record of Signifcant Productions, 1837-1901* (Greenwood Press: New York, 1987)

Nead, Linda, *Myths of Sexuality: Representations of Women in Victorian Britain* (Blackwell: Oxford, 1990)

Nevinson, Margaret Wynne, *In the Workhouse* (International Suffrage Shop: London, 1911)

—— 'A Bewildered Playwright', *Vote* (3 June 1911), 68

Newey, Katherine, 'Attic Windows and Street Scenes: Victorian Images of the City on the Stage', *Victorian Literature and Culture*, 25:2 (1997), 253–62

—— *Women's Theatre Writing in Victorian Britain* (Palgrave Macmillan: Basingstoke, 2005)

Nicholson, Steve, *The Censorship of British Drama, 1900–1968*, 4 vols (University of Exeter Press: Exeter 2003–13)

—— 'A critical year in perspective: 1926', in Baz Kershaw (ed.), *The Cambridge History of British Theatre*, vol. 3: *Since 1895* (Cambridge University Press: Cambridge, 2004), 127–42

Nicoletti, L. J., 'Downward Mobility: Victorian Women, Suicide, and London's "Bridge of Sighs"', *Literary London*, 2:1 (published online March 2004), <http://www.literarylondon.org/london-journal/march2004/nicoletti.html>

Nord, Deborah Epstein, *Walking the Victorian Streets: Women, Representation, and the City* (Cornell University Press: Ithaca NY, 1995)

Nordau, Max, *Degeneration*, translated from the second edition of *Entartung* (Heinemann: London, 1895)

Norwood, Janice, 'The Britannia Theatre: Visual Culture and the Repertoire of a Popular Theatre', in Anselm Heinrich, Katherine Newey and Jeffrey Richards (eds), *Ruskin, the Theatre and Victorian Visual Culture* (Palgrave Macmillan: Basingstoke, 2009), 135–53

O'Connor, Sean, *Straight Acting: Popular Gay Drama from Wilde to Rattigan* (Cassell: London, 1998)

Oliphant, Margaret, 'Novels', *Blackwood's Edinburgh Magazine*, 102 (September 1867), 257–80

Oxenford, John, *East Lynne*, in Michael Kilgariff (ed.), *The Golden Age of Melodrama: Twelve 19th Century Melodramas* (Wolfe Publishing: London, 1974)

Palmer, T. A., *East Lynne*. in Adrienne Scullion (ed.), *Female Playwrights of the Nineteenth Century* (Dent: London, 1996)

Pankhurst, Christabel, *The Great Scourge and How to End It* (E. Pankhurst: London, 1913)

Paulson, Ronald, *Hogarth*, 3 vols (1991–3), vol. 1: *The 'Modern Moral Subject', 1697–1732* (Lutterworth Press: Cambridge, 1992)

Payne, John Howard, *Clari, the Maid of Milan,* Dicks' No.406

Pearson, Hesketh, *The Life of Oscar Wilde* (Methuen: London, 1946)

Pemberton, T. Edgar, *The Kendals: A Biography* (Dodd, Mead & Co: New York, 1900)

Perkin, Joan, *Women and Marriage in Nineteenth-Century England* (Routledge: London, 1989)

Peters, Margot, *Mrs Pat: The Life of Mrs Patrick Campbell* (Hamish Hamilton: London, 1985)

Phillips, Watts, *Lost in London*, LCP, BL Add MS 53057G

Phillpotts, Eden, *The Secret Woman* (Duckworth: London, 1912)

Pinero, Arthur W., *The Profligate* (Heinemann: London, 1891)

—— *Sweet Lavender* (Heinemann: London, 1893)

—— *The Second Mrs Tanqueray*, in Arthur Wing Pinero, *Trelawny of the 'Wells', and other Plays,* ed. J. S. Bratton (Oxford University Press: Oxford, 1995)

—— *Iris*, in *The Social Plays of Arthur Wing Pinero*, ed. Clayton Hamilton, vol. 2 (AMS Press: New York, 1967)

—— *Letty, His House in Order*, in *The Social Plays of Arthur Wing Pinero*, ed. Clayton Hamilton, vol. 3 (AMS Press: New York, 1967)

—— *Mid-Channel* in *The Social Plays of Arthur Wing Pinero*, ed. Clayton Hamilton, vol. 3 (AMS Press: New York, 1967)

—— *The Notorious Mrs Ebbsmith*, in Jean Chothia (ed.), *The New Woman and Other Emancipated Woman Plays* (Oxford University Press: Oxford, 1998)

—— *The 'Mind-the-Paint' Girl* (Heinemann: London, 1913)

—— *The Collected Letters of Sir Arthur Wing Pinero*, ed. J. P. Wearing (University of Minnesota Press: Minneapolis, MN, 1974)

Pixérécourt, René Charles Guilbert de, *La Femme à deux maris* (Paris, 1802)

—— *A Wife with Two Husbands*, translated from the French by Miss Gunning (H.D. Symonds: London, 1803)

Pocock, Isaac, *The Miller and His Men*, Dicks' No. 28

Poovey, Mary, *Uneven Developments: The Ideological Work of Gender in Mid-Victorian England* (University of Chicago Press: Chicago, IL, 1988)

Powell, Kerry (ed.), *The Cambridge Companion to Victorian and Edwardian Theatre* (Cambridge University Press: Cambridge, 2004)

—— *Oscar Wilde and the Theatre of the 1890s* (Cambridge University Press: Cambridge, 1991)

Priestley, J. B., *An Inspector Calls: and Other Plays* (Penguin: London, 2000)

Pugh, Martin, *The March of the Women: A Revisionist Analysis of the Campaign for Women's Suffrage* (Oxford University Press: Oxford, 2000)

—— *We Danced All Night: A Social History of Britain between the Wars* (Vintage: London, 2009)

Pullen, Kirsten, *Actresses and Whores: On Stage and in Society* (Cambridge University Press: Cambridge, 2005)

Pykett, Lyn, *The Improper Feminine: The Women's Sensation Novel and the New Woman Writing* (Routledge: London, 1992)

Quigley, Austin E., *The Modern Stage and Other Worlds* (Methuen: New York, 1985)

Quilter, Harry (ed.), *Is Marriage a Failure?* (Swan Sonnenschein: London, 1888)

Radcliffe, Caroline, 'Remediation and Immediacy in the Theatre of Sensation', *Nineteenth Century Theatre and Film*, 36:2 (2009), 38–53

Rahill, Frank, *The World of Melodrama* (Pennsylvania State University Press: University Park, PA, 1967)

Rapapport, Erika Diane, *Shopping for Pleasure: Women in the Making of London's West End* (Princeton University Press: Princeton, NJ, 2001)

Reade, Charles, *Peg Woffington* (Richard Bentley: London, 1853)

——, and Tom Taylor, *Masks and Faces*, in George Rowell (ed.), *Nineteenth Century Plays* (Oxford University Press: Oxford, 1972)

Rehm, Pierre, *G.H.Q. Love*, adapted from the French by Sewell Collins, LCP 1920/21J

Reynoldson, T. H., *The Drunkard's Children* (Published for the artist by David Brogue: London, 1848)

Robb, George, 'Marriage and Reproduction', in H. G. Cocks and Matt Houlbrook (eds), *Palgrave Advances in the Modern History of Sexuality* (Palgrave Macmillan: Basingstoke, 2006)

Robertson, Thomas William, *Home* (Samuel French: London, 1869)

Robins, Elizabeth, *Ibsen and the Actress* (L. & Virginia Woolf: London, 1928)

—— *Theatre and Friendship: Some Henry James Letters with a Commentary* (Jonathan Cape: London, 1932)

—— *Votes for Women!*, in Jean Chothia (ed.), *The New Woman and Other Emancipated Woman Plays* (Oxford University Press: Oxford, 1998)

—— *Votes for Women!* LCP 1907/6

Roemer, Rick, *Charles Ludlam and the Ridiculous Theatrical Company* (McFarland & Co.: Jefferson, NC, 1998)

Rounding, Virginia, *Grandes Horizontales: The Lives and Legends of Marie Duplessis, Cora Pearl, La Païva and La Présidente* (Bloomsbury: London, 2003)

Rowell, George, *The Victorian Theatre, 1792–1914* (Cambridge University Press: Cambridge, 1978)

—— 'Criteria for comedy: Charles Wyndham at the Criterion Theatre', in Richard Foulkes (ed.), *British Theatre in the 1890s* (Cambridge University Press: Cambridge, 1992)

Ruskin, John, *The Complete Works of John Ruskin*, ed. E. T. Cook and Alexander Wedderburn, 39 vols (George Allen: London, 1903–12), vol. XII

Sardou, Victorien, *Fernande* (Michel Lévy: Paris, 1870)

—— *Divorçons, Théâtre Complet*, XI (Albin Michel: Paris, 1950)

Scott, Clement, *Dramatic Table-Talk* in *Thirty Years at the Play* (Railway and General Automatic Library: London, 1892)

—— *Odette* (1894), adapted from the French play by Victorien Sardou

Scribe, Eugène, *Le Mariage de raison* (Pollet: Paris, 1826)

Selby, Charles, *London by Night*, in James L. Smith (ed.), *Victorian Melodramas: Seven English, French and American Melodramas* (Dent: London, 1976)

Senelick, Laurence, *The Changing Room: Sex, Drag and Theatre* (Routledge: London, 2000)

Shairp, Mordaunt, *The Green Bay Tree* in *Sixteen Famous British Plays*, compiled by Bennett A. Cerf and Van H. Cartmell (The Modern Library, Random House: New York, 1942)

Shaw, George Bernard, *Our Theatres in the Nineties*, 3 vols (Constable and Co: London, 1948)

Shaw, George Bernard, *Candida, Widowers' Houses, Mrs Warren's Profession*, and *The Philanderer*, in *The Bodley Head Bernard Shaw: Collected Plays with their Prefaces*, ed. Dan H. Lawrence, vol. 1 (Bodley Head: London, 1970)

—— *Man and Superman*, in *The Bodley Head Bernard Shaw: Collected Plays with their Prefaces*, ed. Dan H. Lawrence, vol. II (Bodley Head: London, 1971)

—— *Getting Married*, in *The Bodley Head Bernard Shaw: Collected Plays with their Prefaces*, ed. Dan H. Lawrence, vol. III (Bodley Head: London, 1971)

—— *Bernard Shaw's Letters to Granville Barker*, ed. C. B. Purdom (Phoenix House: London, 1956)

—— *The Complete Prefaces*, vol. I: *1889–1913*, ed. Dan H. Laurence and Daniel J. Leary (Allen Lane: London, 1993)

Shellard, Dominic, and Steve Nicholson with Miriam Handley, *The Lord Chamberlain Regrets …: A History of British Theatre Censorship* (British Library: London, 2004)

Shepherd-Barr, Kirsten, *Ibsen and Early Modernist Theatre, 1890–1900* (Greenwood Press: Westport, CT, 1997)

—— *Theatre and Evolution* (Princeton University Press: Princeton, NJ, forthcoming 2014)

Showalter, Elaine, *The Female Malady: Women, Madness and English Culture, 1830–1980* (Virago: London, 1987)

Sinfield, Alan, 'Private Lives/Public Theater: Noel Coward and the Politics of Homosexual Representation', *Representations*, 36 (1991), 43–63

Smith, James L. (ed.), *Victorian Melodramas: Seven English, French and American Melodramas* (Dent: London, 1976)

Smith, W. H., and 'A Gentleman', *The Drunkard* (T. H. Lacy: London, 1844)

Southerne, Thomas, *The Fatal Marriage; or, the Innocent Adultery* (1694), in *The Works of Thomas Southerne*, vol. II, ed. Robert Jordan and Harold Love (Clarendon Press: Oxford, 1988)

—— *Isabella; or, the Fatal Marriage. A Tragedy*. Altered from Southerne by D. Garrick. Marked with the variations in the Manager's Book at the Theatre Royal in Drury Lane. (London: C. Bathurst, T. and W. Lowndes; W. Nicoll, and T. Wheildon, 1784)

Sowerby, Githa, *Rutherford and Son*, in Linda Fitzsimmons and Viv Gardner (eds), *New Woman Plays* (Methuen: London, 1991)

Staves, Susan, 'British Seduced Maidens', *Eighteenth-Century Studies*, 14:2 (Winter 1980–1981), 109–34.

Stead, W. T., 'Maiden Tribute of Modern Babylon', *Pall Mall Gazette* (6–10 July 1885)

Stephens, John Russell, *The Censorship of English Drama, 1824–1901* (Cambridge University Press: Cambridge, 1980)

—— *The Profession of the Playwright: British Theatre, 1800–1900* (Cambridge University Press: Cambridge, 1992)

Stirling, Edward, *The Bohemians: or, The Rogues of Paris*, Dicks' No. 82

Stokes, John, *The French Actress and Her English Audience* (Cambridge University Press: Cambridge, 2005)

Stopes, Marie, *A Banned Play and a Preface on the Censorship* (John Bale: London, 1926)

—— *Married Love*, ed. Ross McKibbin (Oxford University Press: Oxford, 2004)

Stottlar, James F., 'A Victorian Stage Censor: The Theory and Practice of William Bodham Donne', *Victorian Studies*, 13:3 (March 1970), 253–82

Stowell, Sheila, *A Stage of Their Own: Feminist Playwrights of the Suffrage Era* (University of Michigan Press: Ann Arbor, MI, 1992)

Straub, Kristina, *Sexual Suspects: Eighteenth-Century Players and Sexual Ideology* (Princeton University Press: Princeton, NJ, 1992)

Sudermann, Hermann, *Magda,* translated by Louis N. Parker, LCP, BL Add MS 53604B

Sullivan, Arabella Jane, *Ellen Wareham,* in *Recollections of a Chaperone,* Volume III, edited by Lady Dacre (Richard Bentley: London, 1833)

Syrett, Netta, *The Finding of Nancy,* LCP 1902/14

—— *The Sheltering Tree* (Geoffrey Bles: London, 1939)

Tait, William, *Magdalenism: An Inquiry into the Extent, Causes and Consequences of Prostitution in Edinburgh* (P. Rickard: Edinburgh, 1840)

Taylor, F. A., *The Theatre of Alexandre Dumas Fils* (Clarendon Press: Oxford, 1937)

Taylor, George, *Players and Performances in the Victorian Theatre* (Manchester University Press: Manchester, 1989)

Taylor, Tom, *Still Waters Run Deep* (T. H. Lacy: London, ?1857)

Thacker, Alan, 'The Making of a Local Saint' in Alan Thacker and Richard Sharpe (eds), *Local Saints and Local Churches in the Early Medieval West* (Oxford University Press: Oxford, 2002)

Thomas, David, David Carlton and Anne Etienne, *Theatre Censorship: From Walpole to Wilson* (Oxford University Press: Oxford, 2007).

Thomson, J. A., and Patrick Geddes, *Problems of Sex* (New Tracts for the Times, Cassell: London, 1912)

Thomson, Peter (ed.), *Plays by Dion Boucicault* (Cambridge University Press: Cambridge, 1984)

Tickner, Lisa, *The Spectacle of Women: Imagery of the Suffrage Campaign, 1907–14* (Chatto & Windus: London, 1987)

Travers, W., *A Poor Girl's Temptations: or, A Voice from the Streets,* LCP, BL Add MS 52972H

Trewin, Wendy, *All on Stage: Charles Wyndham and the Alberys* (Harrap: London, 1980)

Trudgill, Eric, *Madonnas and Magdalens: The Origins and Development of Victorian Sexual Attitudes* (Heinemann: London, 1976)

Underwood, M. C., *The Girl from Crawley's. A Comedy of Character in Action* (Phipps-Walker & Fuller: London, 1935)

Valverde, Mariana, 'The Love of Finery: Fashion and the Fallen Woman in Nineteenth-Century Social Discourse', *Victorian Studies,* 32: 2 (Winter, 1989), 168–88

Vanbrugh, Irene, *To Tell My Story* (Hutchinson & Co.: London, 1948)

Van Druten, John, *Young Woodley* (Samuel French: London, 1930)

Vaughan, Gertrude, *The Woman with a Pack* (W. J. Ham-Smith: London, 1912)

Vicinus, Martha (ed.), *Suffer and Be Still: Women in the Victorian Age* (Methuen: London, 1980)

Voskuil, Lynn, *Acting Naturally: Victorian theatricality and authenticity* (University of Virginia Press: Charlottesville, VA, 2004)

Votieri, Adelene, *That Charming Mrs Spencer,* LCP, BL Add MS 53654E

Walkley, A. B., *Playhouse Impressions* (T. Fisher Unwin: London, 1892)

—— *Drama and Life* (Methuen: London, 1907)

Walkowitz, Judith, *City of Dreadful Delight: Narratives of Sexual Danger in Late-Victorian London* (Virago: London, 1992)

—— *Prostitution and Victorian Society: Women, Class and the State* (Cambridge University Press: Cambridge, 1980)

Watt, George, *The Fallen Woman in the Nineteenth-Century English Novel* (Croom Helm: London, 1984)

Wearing, J. P. (ed.), *The Collected Letters of Sir Arthur Wing Pinero* (University of Minnesota Press: Minneapolis, MN, 1974)

Webb, Beatrice, 'The Social and Economic Causes of Vice', in *The Nation's Morals, Being the Proceedings of the Public Morals Conference held in London on 14th and 15th July, 1910* (Cassell & Co: London, 1910)

—— *The Diary of Beatrice Webb, 1873–1943,* 3 vols (Virago Press: London, 1982–85)

Webster, Margaret, *The Same Only Different: Five Generations of a Great Theatre Family* (Gollancz: London, 1969)

Weeks, Jeffrey, *Sex, Politics and Society: The Regulation of Sexuality since 1800* (Longman: London, 1981)

Wilde, Oscar, *Lady Windermere's Fan, A Woman of No Importance, An Ideal Husband,* and *The Importance of Being Earnest,* in *The Importance of Being Earnest and Other Plays,* ed. Peter Raby (Oxford University Press: Oxford, 1995)

—— *The Complete Letters of Oscar Wilde,* ed. Merlin Holland and Rupert Hart-Davis (Fourth Estate: London, 2000)

Wilks, Thomas Egerton, *Woman's Love; or, Kate Wynsley, the Cottage Girl,* Dicks' No. 414

—— *Halvei the Unknown; or, The Bride of Two Husbands,* Dicks' No. 690

Williams, Antonia R., *The Street,* in *Three New Plays* (T. Werner Laurie: London, 1907)

Wills, W. G., *Olivia,* LCP, BL Add MS 53200K

Wilson, Esther, John Fay, Tony Green and Lizzie Nunnery, *Unprotected* (2006), unpublished play script

Winnifrith, Tom, *Fallen Women in the Nineteenth-Century Novel* (St Martin's Press: Basingstoke, 1994)

Wolff, Robert Lee, *Sensational Victorian: the Life and Fiction of Mary Elizabeth Braddon* (Garland Publishing: New York, 1979)

Wood, Ellen, *East Lynne* (Oxford University Press: Oxford, 2005)

James Woodfield, *English Theatre in Transition, 1881–1914* (Croom Helm: London, 1984)

Wozniak, Heather Anne, 'The Play with a Past: Arthur Wing Pinero's New Drama', *Victorian Literature and Culture* (September 2009), 391–409

Wycherley, William, *The Country Wife and Other Plays,* ed. Peter Dixon (Oxford University Press: Oxford, 1996)

Zola, Émile, *Nana* (Gallimard: Paris, 2002)

Index